The Doctrine of God in
African Christian Thought

Studies in Reformed Theology

VOLUME 14

The Doctrine of God in African Christian Thought

The Holy Trinity, Theological Hermeneutics and the African Intellectual Culture

By

James Henry Owino Kombo

BRILL

LEIDEN · BOSTON
2007

This series was previously published by Uitgeverij Meinema, on imprint of Boekencentrum Uitgevers.

This book is printed on acid-free paper.

BT
109
.K65
2007

ISSN: 1571-4799
ISBN: 978 90 04 15804 7

CONTENTS

I. THE DOCTRINE OF THE TRINITY:
THE BIBLE AND THE CHURCH FATHERS

II. WESTERN THEOLOGIES' RESPONSES
TO THE DOCTRINE OF THE TRINITY

III. THE DOCTRINE OF GOD IN
AFRICAN INCULTURATION THEOLOGY

IV. FROM THE AFRICAN CONCEPTS OF
GOD TO THE DOCTRINE OF THE TRINITY.

ACKNOWLEDGEMENTS

Above all my gratitude goes to *Nyasaye*. *Nyasaye*! I cannot think of you

> ... without immediately being surrounded by the radiance of the Three;
> nor can I discern the Three without at once being carried back to the
> One. When I think of any one of the Three, I think of him as a whole
> ... I cannot grasp the greatness of that One so as to attribute a greater
> greatness to the rest. When I contemplate the Three together, I see but
> one luminary, and cannot divide or measure out our individual light
> (Gregory Nazienzen, Oration 40.31).

FOREWORD

James Kombo is a theologian from Kenya, who is presently teaching at the Daystar University in Nairobi. Some years ago he lived in a house that straddled the equator. Walking from one room to another, he was moving from one hemisphere to the other. In a sense, it is symbolic of this work in which the author commutes with consummate ease between the symbolic universe of the church of the northern Western world and its southern African counterpart.

James Kombo is convinced that since the Gospel of Christ crucified is critical of every culture, it is for that very reason that it must be translated into every context. Consequently, theology has the arduous task of trying to transform a specific intellectual culture by making use of the available concepts within that culture. Obviously, this is a demanding mission that is fraught with danger. Like ourselves, our concepts must be 'born again' to be fruitful in the kingdom of God. James Kombo strongly feels that African inculturation theology has too easily identified African notions of God with the God of the Bible who has revealed himself in Jesus Christ through the Holy Spirit. As a result, the doctrine of the Trinity is of critical importance.

Kombo argues that African Christian theologians should take their cue from the early church that interpreted their belief in the Triune God and made use of the prevalent philosophical concepts of Greek metaphysics. An attempt to facilitate inculturation of the Christian doctrine of God within an African context should, therefore, draw on African metaphysics. At the same time, it is imperative that the Christian faith should take root in African soil without compromising the catholicity of the church. Accordingly, the ecumenical significance of this doctrine should be grasped and the historical confessions of the church taken seriously in order to elucidate the doctrine of the Trinity within an African conceptual framework.

Having grappled with the biblical roots of this doctrine and the way the early church dealt with it, the author scrutinizes the different responses by Western theologies within different historical contexts. He identifies three replies that accord with different philosophical presuppositions and their concomitant notions of God, i.e., *God as essence, God as absolute subject,* and *God as community in unity.* All three deal with issues that are vital for any discussion of the Trinity; namely, the *Incarnation,* the concept of *homoousios,* as well as the *identity* of the God we encounter in scripture. Kombo himself prefers the model of *God as community in unity* as according better with the biblical testimony and the early church fathers. However, the three models all utilize Western patterns of thought to articulate their belief in God, and as such make it difficult for people from another 'hemisphere' to fathom their meaning.

In Part Three he discusses the notion of 'God' among the African peoples by making use of the insights of leading African theologians. In contrast to the pluralists that do not accept the unity of the African people, Kombo agrees with those who detect—amidst a great variety of languages and cultures—something that can be called 'the African conceptual framework' that offers a unique way of making sense of the world. He argues that becoming Christian does not entail that the African inheritance be destroyed, but that it be redirected to Christ and, thus, transformed. It is Kombo's clear intention to avoid the danger of equating African concepts of God with the God we encounter in scripture. He wants to clear the ground in order to move beyond these African concepts by taking God's self-revelation in his Son through the Holy Spirit seriously. After all, as Mbiti once said, some Africans "suffered, some have been tortured and others killed, not because of their belief in God, but for the sake of Jesus Christ and his message of Love, Salvation, Justice, Hope and Peace." If Christ is that important for African Christians, that should also be reflected in their formal theological understanding of God. Part Four offers a fascinating, constructive attempt when he moves "from the African Concepts of God to the Doctrine of the Trinity."

Did Kombo succeed? To be sure, there are dangers involved in using philosophical categories for explaining the Christian understanding of God that are patently clear in Western theology as noted by himself. Did he take adequate cognizance of these dangers? Are these hazards inherent in, and, therefore, part and parcel of every theological project? Is Luther's unconventional pastoral advice, *pecca fortiter sed fortius fide,* especially pertinent to the theological enterprise? The reader has to decide. The fact remains that Kombo demonstrates remarkable sophistication, and has provided the African church and theology with an example of rigorous research.

This work is the result of many years of intensive study at the University of Stellenbosch where it was submitted as a doctoral dissertation and then slightly reworked for the present publication. Thinking back over the years to our first meeting, I can still see the young man from Kenya embarking on a new adventure many miles from home, entering the reception hall of Cape Town International Airport—somewhat hesitantly but with dignity. Later his wife, Pamela (a theologian in her own right) and their children—Leonida, Philip, and Samuel—would join him. What a joy it has been to make the acquaintance of these gentle, courageous people who are the epitome of the Bantu expression *umuntu ngumuntu ngabantu*, "a person is a person through the people." I pray that this prime example of fundamental theological discourse may be an inspiration to many African theologians, and a blessing to the people of this wonderful, albeit at the same time, sad and strife-torn continent of ours.

P.F. Theron
Professor emeritus of systematic theology
Stellenbosch University
South Africa

PROLOGUE

Preliminary Considerations: Africa, African Peoples and Theology

It is important, at this early stage, that we place the terms *Africa*, *African peoples* and *African theology* into proper perspective. Understanding these representations is particularly important since this book is about an aspect of Christian theology that is formulated using African philosophical symbols. But even as we enter into these discourses, it is important to note that some African philosophers are of the opinion that the term *Africa* is enigmatic.

V.Y. Mudimbe, in his study on Latin nomenclature, notes that in sixteenth century dictionaries the term *Africa* is treated in texts as "the equivalent of *Afer*, as substantive as well as adjective, and simply designates any person from the continent regardless of his or her color. It literally translates as *Africanus*."[1] Whereas the Latins understood Africa as *Afer* and the persons from the continent as *Africanus*, the Greeks called the African continent *Ethiopia* (*Aithiops*) because the people living near the sun must have been affected by the heat (*calore*), thus the 'burnt' pigment (*colore*).

Decline of the use of the name Ethiopia for the African continent only began at the time of the inception of European exploration. The Europeans favored *Nigritia* (from the Latin *Niger*) as the name for the continent and called the inhabitants *Nigriti*.[2] In the thought of V.Y. Mudimbe, the European *Nigritia* and *Nigriti* are simply used as the equivalents of the Greek *Aithiops*—face burned by the sun. P.D. Curtin has a different opinion. As far as he is concerned, the Europeans favored *Nigritia* because at the time of the European exploration there was a general xenophobia and widespread doctrine of racial differ-

---

[1] V.Y. Mudimbe, *The Idea of Africa* (Bloomington / Indianapolis: Indiana University Press, 1994), 26.

[2] Mudimbe, *The Idea of Africa*, 27.

ences.[3] Therefore it was important that the Europeans find a term that could distinguish Africa and the Africans from Europe and the Europeans as precisely as possible. In order to bring about this distinction, Curtin is of the opinion that the Europeans had settled on *Nigritia* and *Nigriti* by the eighteenth century because the terms had the concepts of primitiveness and savagery as additional nuances.[4] Although this thinking was current then, it is unfortunate that it has refused to go away. Consequently, for many people the distinction between Africa and Europe is the same that exists between the jungle and irrational customs, on the one hand, and the values of the most purified crust of modernity, on the other hand.[5]

Although the European explorers favored *Nigritia*, it must be emphasized that the term *Africa* had been in use since Roman times, but, of course, not in the sense of *Nigritia*. The Romans knew *Africa* as one of their provinces. For the Romans the term *Africa* was an effective replacement of the Greek term *Aithiops* (Ethiopia) or the Egyptian word *Libya* (the land of *Lebu* or *Lubius* in Genesis). The term *Africa*, however, was not applied to the whole of the African continent until the end of the first century before our era.[6]

And so the use of the term *Africa* or *African* in their various nuances is not strange. This book uses the term *Africa* to mean the conventionally recognized land mass and near shore islands and *African peoples* to refer to the varieties of Negroid people that are indigenous to the African

---

[3] P.D. Curtin, *The Image of Africa: British Ideas and Action, 1780–1850* (Madison: The University of Wisconsin Press, 1964), 28–57. Note that the xenophobia that the Europeans experienced in their encounter with the Africans and which resulted in the Europeans naming the Africans *Nigritia* was felt by the Africans also. The eastern Bantu peoples and the Waswahili at the coast of Kenya and Tanzania called Europe *Uzungu*, and the Europeans *Wazungu*. According to C.W. Rechenbach, Swahili-English Dictionary (Washington, D.C.: Catholic University of America Press 1967), 608; the word *uzungu* literally means "strangeness, unusualness, novelty, peculiarity." However the term *mzungu*, as D.C. Scott in his 1929 *Dictionary of the Nyanja Language* has been able to demonstrate, also came to have the nuance of spirit, since spirits are strange and they often perplex. Today, when the Eastern Bantus talk of *mzungu* this later meaning is lost and attention is focused on the Europeans or the white people. Africans no longer treat *mzungus* as strangers.

[4] See Curtin, *The Image of Africa*, 28–57 and Mudimbe, *The Idea of Africa*, 27–28.

[5] See Ali A. Mazrui, *The Africans* (London: BBC Publications, 1986). Cf. H.O. Oruka, *Sage Philosophy: Indigenous Thinkers and Modern Debate on African Philosophy* (Leiden: Brill, 1990), 84. See also his article, "Sagacity in African Philosophy" in *African Philosophy*, edited by Serequeberhan (New York: Paragon House, 1991).

[6] J. Ki-Zerbo, *General History of Africa Volume I: Methodology and African Prehistory* (California: UNESCO, 1981), 1.

land mass. This understanding of Africa assumes a fundamental unity of the African peoples.[7] The unity envisioned here cannot merely be reduced to the slavery and colonialism that Africa experienced in its encounter with the West. Rather, it encompasses the genetics of the African Negroes, the African religions, the African languages, and the African intellectual culture or conceptual framework.[8] In the words of J. Ki-Zerbo:

> ... ever since prehistory, despite natural obstacles and the low level of techniques, there has been a degree of historical solidarity on a continental scale, between the Nile valley and the Sudan on the one hand and the Guinea forest on the other; between the Nile valley and East Africa, including among other things the dispersion of the Luo, between the Sudan and the Central Africa, through the diaspora of the Bantu;

---

[7] Not all scholars agree with the idea of the unity of Africa. The pluralists are of the opinion that the African "cultures differ and each has its own coherence and distinctive truth-functional way in which it conceives of and expresses its world" (R.H. Bell, "Narrative in African Philosophy" in *Philosophy*, 64, 1989:363–379). In frustration, the pluralists at the extreme end of the continuum posit the view that the term *Africa* does not, as a matter of fact, make much sense beyond a reductionist use. Anthony Appiah, Mudimbe and Sam Maluleke seem to be of the opinion that 'Africa' does not exist as such and that what people call Africa is a form and shape for the Africa they desire (T.S. Maluleke, "Half a Century of African Christian Theology" in Journal of Theology for Southern Africa, 99, 1997: 4–23). E.E. Evans-Pritchard's work among the Azande and the Nuer, and Marcel Griaule's work among the Dogon of Mali and Upper Volta (now Burkina Faso) are important contributions to the issue of the diversity of the African peoples and their cultures. Other important contributions to the pluralistic-universalistic debate are Peter Winch's article, "Understanding a Primitive Society" in *Rationality* (Oxford: Basil Blackwell, 1970) and a joint publication by M. Hollis and S. Lukes, *Rationality and Relativism* (Oxford: Basil Blackwell, 1982).

[8] This research rejects the stereotypical image of Africa according to which the term *Africa* means poverty, hunger, backwardness, bad governance, disease, racial-tribal-national tensions, fear, evil, and death. This long held dogma of African exceptionalism must be rejected as Africa cannot just be defined in terms of multifaceted pauperization. And neither can we simply define *African* in terms of shared slavery and colonialism as Appiah seems to suggest (see Maluleke, "Half a Century of African Christian Theology," 1997, 6). There is more to Africa than pauperization and the Western domination of Africa. As Ki-Zerbo has explained, we do not reject the stereotypical images of Africa merely to settle scores. Our purpose of understanding Africa in terms suggested in this research is "... to change perspective or revive images which have been forgotten or lost. We must turn once more to science in order to create genuine cultural awareness. We must reconstruct the real course of events. And we must find another mode of discourse" (Ki-Zerbo, *General History of Africa*, 2). Scholars such as Tempels, Jahn, Kagame, Mbiti, Diop, Idowu, Setiloane, Griaule, and Dieterlen (see chapter 7 of this book) believe that because of the shared cosmology, Africa is not as diverse and divided as we have been made to believe. On the basis of a shared intellectual culture, we may confidently speak about 'African Christianity,' 'African theology,' 'African philosophy,' 'African literature,' or simply 'African.'

and between the Atlantic and east coasts, through transcontinental trade across the Sahara. Migration, which took place on a large scale in both space and time, is not to be seen as a vast human tide attracted by emptiness in its wake. Even the torrential saga of Shaka, the Mfecane, cannot be interpreted only in such terms.[9]

The question of the indigenousness of the African peoples was previously raised in the context of the Hamitic theory, according to which the African peoples are supposed to have originated from Asia.[10] Today the Hamitic theory has eroded to the extent that it cannot be used without express qualification, and, moreover, modern studies on Africa indicate that the peoples of Africa are for the most part indigenous and of a common genetic stock.

> According to Boyd, the author of the genetic classification of human races, there exists only one Negroid group, which spreads over the whole of the sub-Saharan part of the continent, … and it differs significantly from all the other major groupings. Research by Hiernaux has yielded remarkably convincing evidence to support this proposition. Without denying that variations are apparent at local levels, he has produced the findings of an analysis of 5050 distances between 101 populations to show the uniformity of the peoples of the sub-Saharan hyperspace which embraces the 'Sudanese' as well as the 'Bantu', the inhabitants of the coastal regions and those of the Sahel, the 'Khoisan', Pygmies, Nilotic, Fulani, and various minor groups such as those akin to the 'Ethiopians'. On the other hand, he also shows the great genetic distance that separates 'Asian blacks' from African blacks.[11]

Whereas the African blacks people sub-Saharan Africa, the Arab-Berber group (Libyans, Semites, Phoenicians, Assyrians, Greeks, Romans, Turks, etc) occupy the Saharan Africa.[12]

---

[9] Ki-Zerbo, *General History of Africa*, 21.

[10] Commenting on the words 'Hamite' and 'Hamitic,' P. Diagne says "… the words have been used to excess in learned language and everyday speech in the Western world for centuries. This usage originated in a garbled and tendentious reading of the Bible and was responsible for the myth of the curse on the black descendants of Ham. Although the term took on a seemingly less pejorative meaning and at least lost its religious connotation as a result of the researches of the nineteenth-century linguists and ethnologists, it has still continued to be used for discriminating between certain black peoples who are regarded as being superior, and the rest. In any event, the International Scientific Committee is giving encouragement to the critical studies being conducted into the historical uses of the term, which can only be used with express qualification" (P. Diagne, "History and Linguistics" in *General History of Africa Volume I: Methodology and Prehistory*. Ki-Zerbo, ed., (California: UNESCO, 1981), n. 37).

[11] Ki-Zerbo, *General History of Africa*, 268.

[12] E.W. Smith in *The Christian Mission in Africa* (London: The International Mis-

Semantic anthropology or the science of ethnolinguistics divides the African blacks, or Negroes, into four distinct linguistic groups: Khoisan, Nilo-Saharan, Afro-Asiatic, and Niger-Congo. This study further indicates that the Nilo-Saharan and the Niger-Congo phyla in fact belong to a single language family called Congo-Saharan or Zindj group.[13] The Afro-Asiatic phylum is clearly a mixture of the Arab-Berber northerners, the Nilo-Saharan, and the Niger-Congo; the Khoisan phylum,[14] on the other hand, reveals interesting interactions with the Niger Congo.

The Negroes of the Niger-Congo phylum and those of the Nilo-Saharan phylum, who together constitute the Zindj group, occupy the largest landmass. This group is also the majority in terms of numbers. The Zindj group has, over the years, expanded its geographic and cultural ranges at the expense of the Khoisan. The Afro-Asiatic phylum,

---

sionary Council, 1926) indicates that the Le Zoute Conference identified two indigenous race types on the continent of Africa: The Libyan peoples and the Negroes (E.W. Smith, *The Christian Mission in Africa* (London: Edinburgh Press, 1926), 7). The Roman Secretariatus Pro Non-Christians expressed a similar view in 1968 (see "Secretariatus Pro Non-Christians," *Meeting the African Religions*, Rome: np, 1968), 7). The African historiographers working for the UNESCO project are emphatic that the indigenous African peoples cannot be divided into more than two race types. The two African race types they have identified are the Arab-Berber group and the Negro group (see Ki-Zerbo, *General History of Africa*, 267).

[13] Between 1949 and 1950, J.H. Greenberg, using the method of mass comparison while taking into consideration the basic features of grammatical structure and especially vocabulary, distinguished sixteen linguistic families (Niger-Congo, Songay, Central Sudanic, Central Saharan, Eastern Sudanic, Afroasiatic (Hamito-Semitic), Click, Maba, Mimi of Nachtigal, Fur, Tmainian, Kordofanian, Koman, Berta, Kunama, and Nyangiya). In 1954 he narrowed these to twelve (Niger-Kongo, Songay, Macro-Sudanic (Eastern Sudanic, Central Sudanic, Berta, Kunama), Central Saharan, Afroasiatic, Click, Maban, (Maban, Mimi of Nachtigal), Fur, Temainian, Kordofanian, Koman, Nyangiya). By 1963 this number was again reduced to only four (1. Niger-Kordofanian—Niger-Congo, Kordofanian; 2. Afroasiatic; 3. Khoisan–Click; and the rest were grouped under 4. Nilo-Saharan) (See J.H. Greenberg, "African Linguistic Classification" in *General History of Africa Volume I: Methodology and Prehistory*, 292–308). As far as Edgar Gregersen and D. Olderogge are concerned, this number can be reduced to three basic families: 1. The Afro-Asiatic (Semito-Hamitic), 2. Zindj or Congo-Saharan (these are the groups formerly classified by Greenberg as Niger-Kordofanian and Nilo-Saharan), and 3. the Khoisan. According to Olderogge, the Zindj or the Congo-Saharan family display the same type of coherence we see in the Indo-European family (see D. Olderogge, "Migration and Ethnic and Linguistic Differentiations" in *General History of Africa Volume I: Methodology and Prehistory*, 271–286).

[14] See D. Olderogge's interesting study on the difference between the Khoi-Khoi and the San (Olderogge, "Migration and Ethnic and Linguistic Differentiations," 279–282) as well as the interactions of these peoples with the other African Negroes.

on the other hand, is fewer in numbers but spread over a substantial area that mostly consists of desert.

If the geographical and the numerical superiority of the Zindj group as a common language family is of statistical significance, and if we agree with the notion that in the historical process of divergence among the African peoples that there was also convergence and reconvergence, then it is possible to argue that the ontology of the majority of the African Negroes can be deciphered, interpreted, and systematized in one common way. The 'common language family' used by the majority of the African Negroes[15] means that we have a common, crystallizing point for the intellectual and material tools of the majority of the African peoples. This conclusion is important for this research since at a later stage we will speak of a common African conceptual framework that will, in turn, make it possible for us to speak about Africa and African theology. Not in terms of the ethnic divisions—such as Luo theology, Kamba theology, Xhosa theology, and so on—but as a theology of the African Negroes that is decipherable from a common grand cultural milieu.

Moreover, talking about African theology means that we have to apply ourselves to a particular definition of theology. Within the African scene there are at least six theological paradigms. Justin Ukpong has identified African inculturation theology (focusing on theology and the problem of cultural identity), black theology (dealing with the problem of race and color), and liberation theology (addressing the problem of poverty and injustices).[16] To these three we could add African women theology (handling the problem of gender), evangelical theology (seeking to refocus the African Christian thought on the biblical faith), and reconstruction theology (attempting to engage theology in a serious dialogue with democracy, human rights, law-making, and nation-building).

---

[15] It is important to note that the term *Negro-African* is used here in the same way as *Zindj*. D. Olderogge, in proposing the term *Zindj* as a replacement of *Negro Africa*, notes that the term *Negro Africa* is not appropriate because the so-called Negroes of the Americas and parts of Africa speak different languages and the term *Africa* includes all inhabitants of Africa, including the Berbers to the North and the Afrikaners in the South. Moreover, the Negro-African languages cannot be divided into two (Sudanic or Nilotic and Bantu) because the Nilotic and the Bantu have differences, but they also have common fundamental features (see Olderogge, "Migration and Ethnic and Linguistic Differentiations," 282,283).

[16] J.S. Ukpong, *African Theologies Now: A Profile* (Eldoret: Gaba Publications, 1984).

This research applies the term *African theology* to what appears in
Justin Ukpong's classification as African inculturation theology. In this
paradigm of theological reflection, theology penetrates the traditional
philosophical thought that is common to the African Negroes or peoples. It is, therefore, a theology that understands and appropriates the
historical divergence of the African peoples while considering the full
implication of the convergence and reconvergence processes in the
history of the African peoples which must have resulted in a common, intellectual, crystallizing point for all the African peoples. For
theology to be African, it must penetrate and—in the process of its
construction—employ this intellectual, crystallizing point. As Ukpong
explains, this takes place when the theologian is involved in:

> ... re-thinking and re-expressing the original Christian message in an
> African cultural milieu. It is the task of confronting the Christian faith
> and African culture. In the process there is inter-penetration of both.
> Christian faith enlightens African culture and the basic data of revelation
> as contained in the Scripture and tradition are critically re-examined for
> the integration of faith and culture, and from it is born a new theolog-
> ical reflection that is African and Christian. In this approach, therefore,
> African theology means Christian faith attaining African cultural expres-
> sion.[17]

Notable theologians who identify with this paradigm and call it African
theology are J.S. Mbiti, Bolaji Idowu, G.M. Setiloane, Lamin Sanneh,
and Kwame Bediako.

DEFINING THE PROBLEM

The problem of this book is how to deliver the doctrine of the Trinity
to the roots of the African cultural milieu and utilize the African
intellectual tools or symbols to express the same. The Trinity concept is
not new, nor is it strange to the Christian faith. Christian theologies
that are rooted in the scriptural testimony and passed on through
generations to our own time generally view the God that they relate
to within the perplexity of unity and plurality. Christian orthodoxy
presents the Father as God, the Son as God, and the Holy Spirit as
God—yet not three gods, but one God worshipped in the Trinity. How
do we translate this truth into the African thought forms? Is it possible

---

[17] Ukpong, *African Theologies Now*, 30.

to utilize the African conceptual framework in translating the doctrine
of the Trinity instead of utilizing 'the being' of Neo-Platonism or 'the
self-consciousness' of Hegelianism?

In the development of the Christian doctrine of God as we know
it today, the theological questions that dominated the Christian scene
from the very early stages are: "Is the divine that has appeared on earth
and reunited man with God identical with the supreme divine, which
rules heaven and earth, or is it a demigod?"[18] How does this divine
relate to the Holy Spirit?[19] These questions led the church to the belief
that there are three persons in the Divinity. If we were to represent
this concept in terms of a mathematical formula, Henry believes that
that formula would be 3x in 1y and not 3x = 1x as has been done
traditionally.[20]

Of course, the need to bring the doctrine of the Trinity to the roots
of the African cultural milieu and to articulate it using the African
intellectual resources does not only arise because of the difficulty that
was created by the traditional formula of the doctrine of the Trinity.
Even if we adopted Henry's formula (3x in 1y), the problem of the
religious language[21] will still persist. Because of the problem of the
language of the formula, some notable critics of the doctrine of the
Trinity have advanced the view that the latter is "the most enigmatic

---

[18] J. Pelikan, *The Christian Tradition*, vol. I (Chicago: The University of Chicago Press,
1971), 172–175.

[19] Pelikan, *The Christian Tradition*, 213–215.

[20] C.F.H. Henry, *God, Revelation and Authority vol V: God who Stands and Stays part one*
(Waco: World Book Publishing House, 1982), 165.

[21] What is highlighted here is the problem of religious language. S. McFague believes
that Western society has this problem because it is unsure about God, and then it is
unsure of its language about God. The problem of the religious language, therefore,
originates at the experiential level and soon spreads to the expressive level (S. McFague,
Metaphorical Theology, (London: SCM Press, 1983), 1–4). The Christian faith has responded in different ways to this problem. Thomas McPherson has identified at least
four responses to this problem. The first position believes that the Christian doctrines
have absurdities or paradoxes that cannot simply be expressed by language. The second position argues that what is really important is Christian life. Christians and theologians are exhorted to be as children and to stop worrying about the absurdities and
paradoxes. The third response understands that the Christian doctrine has difficulties,
but sense can be made of the difficulties if we allow for the analogical language, that
is—words whose meanings are derived from their application to finite things in everyday speech. The last response is that posited by Positivism—there is no point in trying
to express the inexpressible (Thomas McPherson, "Positivism and Religion" in *Religious
Language and the Problem of Religious Knowledge*, 1986). The third response is the most popular one. The basic argument of this position is that speakers of all languages have
different ways of speaking that is dependent on what may be obligatory or appropriate.

Christian doctrine."[22] Others think it is "a mathematical monstrosity,"[23] while still others are of the conviction that it is "the most brutal and inexcusable error in counting."[24] For such critics, explains Hall:

> ... the Trinity is the great unknown. The Trinity, to use a familiar equation, is viewed as a riddle wrapped up inside a puzzle and buried in an enigma. A riddle for how can any entity be at the same time multiple (three) yet singular (one)? A puzzle for the Trinity is so clearly contrary to any rational thought as not to warrant a second thought from sensible people. An enigma, for even if the Trinity could be understood, of what practical value, even what religious value, would it have for ordinary people?[25]

African theology needs to entrench the doctrine of the Trinity in its own cultural milieu and use the philosophical symbols of the culture to capture the same because the doctrine of the Trinity has practical value and intellectual coherence that must benefit the majority world of Africa also. In making this proposal, we are careful to note that the criticisms leveled above are based on a wrong point of departure; namely, that the starting point of the doctrine of the Trinity is the theological formula 'one God, three Persons.'[26] The beginning point of the doctrine of the Trinity is the fact that God has revealed himself as one, and yet we in the Christian faith have experienced him as the Father, the Son, and the Holy Spirit.

Various African peoples know God by such names as *Modimo*, *Nyame*, *Nyasaye*, *Ngai*, *Mulungu*, and so on.[27] A name like *Mulungu*, for example, simply means God. According to D.C. Scott, *Mulungu* does not mean "

---

[22] C. Hall, "Adding up the Trinity" in *Christianity Today*, 1997 April 28, 26–28.

[23] Henry, *God, Revelation and Authority*, 165.

[24] K.E. Yandell, "The Most Brutal and Inexcusable Error in Counting: Trinity and Consistency" in *Religious Studies*, 30, 1994, 2001–217.

[25] Hall, "Adding up the Trinity," 26.

[26] Traditionally the theological formula, 'one God, three Persons,' has been represented by $3x = 1x$. A formulation that is worked according to this mathematical procedure could easily be interpreted as saying that the Trinity is about 'three gods are one' or 'three isolated persons are one God.' To think along such lines is to be indifferent to the voice of Christian orthodoxy. Just what this plurality in unity and unity in plurality entails for spirituality, thought, and religious language is what is included in the historical-theological concept that has become known to us as the doctrine of the Trinity.

[27] Christoph Barth argues that the name *Yahweh* did not drop from heaven, "... it was God himself who came down. Revealing himself to Israel he adopted Israel's language. His name is rooted in this language. It is taken from words and names in the daily speech of the Hebrews" (C. Barth, *God with Us: A Theological Introduction to the Old Testament*. G.W. Bromiley, ed. (Grand Rapids: Eerdmans, 1991), 71). Moreover, the

... different forces of nature, not spirits, not fetish, but God, the Creator, Spirit, Almighty, Personal God. ... you can't put the plural with God because God is one. There are not idols called gods, and spirits are spirits of people who have died, not gods."[28] The African Christian thought has Christianized[29] the traditional concepts of God so that *Mulungu*, for example, is not just God as the traditional Nyanja community knew him. On the contrary, *Mulungu* now means the God of the Christian worship as the Nyanja people know him.[30] The problem, however, is that African Christian thought has only merged halfway with the Christianization process. A fully Christianized concept of *Mulungu*, for example, should indicate how *Mulungu* (God) has made himself known in the Son and in the Holy Spirit.[31] And, moreover,

---

fathers of Israel had no problem whatsoever in invoking *Yahweh* by divine names that originated in the religious life of the neighboring Gentiles.

[28] D.C. Scott, *Dictionary of the Nyanja Language*. Heatherwick, ed. (London: Religious Tract Society, 1929), 348.

[29] By 'Christianized,' we mean the translatability of biblical ideas of God into the African vernacular languages. It is important to note, however, that the African vernaculars use the personal names for God that the African peoples know in a way that is neither wholly different from nor wholly the same as the idea of God in the Bible. Aristotle believed that in the realm of conversation one word may sometimes carry the same meaning when applied to two things, but sometimes it might bear completely different meanings. In the former case the word would be said to have been used univocally, while in the latter situation the word is used purely equivocally. But in addition to these two uses, Aristotle also distinguished a third use where a word is applied to two objects in senses that are neither wholly different nor wholly the same. When such a use occurs the word is said to have been used analogically. (see Eric L. Mascall, "The Doctrine of Analogy" in *Religious Language and the Problem of Religious Knowledge*, R.E. Santoni, ed. (London: Indiana University Press, 1968).

[30] The African concepts of God, as Dickson has observed, are not borrowed from outside (Dickson, 1984). Mbiti did his research among more than 270 African ethnic groups and came up with the conclusion that African concepts of God "sprung independently out of African reflection on God" (Mbiti, *Concepts of God*, xiii). This is also the point of E.W. Smith, *African Ideas of God*, 1950.

[31] For instance, in order to emphasize the new nuance *Mulungu* has attained due to the process of Christianization, it is important that *Mulungu* be explained in Trinitarian terms. Karl Rahner believes that a Christian view of God first, "[confirms]... that knowledge of the unique, transcendent, personal God which is always stirring into life whether naturally or supernaturally.... Second, the Christian conception will always express God's passionate protest against every kind of polytheistic or pantheistic deification of the world.... Third, it alone will be able to say unambiguously and definitively just how the personal, transcendent desires *in actual fact* to stand to the world in his sovereign freedom: namely, as the God who actually discloses his inmost self to man out of grace.... as the God who gives his definitive sanction to the world in the incarnation of his Son and summons it to share in his Triune life" (Rahner, TI I, 85, 86).

such a view of *Mulungu* should be articulated within the infrastructure of metaphysics that the Nyanja as a people can decipher.[32] According to David Bosch, this step would be important because it is an effort to incarnate the gospel in the African cultural milieu and incarnating the gospel in any cultural milieu is an indelible mark of Christianity. In fact, as Bosch has observed, it comes:

> ... as no surprise that in the Pauline churches Jews, Greeks, barbarians, Thracians, Egyptians, and Romans were able to feel at home.... The same was true of the post-apostolic church. The faith was inculturated in a great variety of liturgies and contexts—Syriac, Greek, Roman, Coptic, Armenian, Ethiopian, Maronite, and so forth. Moreover, during this early period the emphasis was on the local church rather than the church universal in its monarchial form.[33]

The rooting of the doctrine into the African cultural milieu and the utilization of the instruments of the culture in its conceptualization has to do with translation. We have already noticed that, so far, African inculturation theology has been able to indicate the lines of similarity between the African concepts of God and the God of the Christian worship. African inculturation theology, however, has yet to articulate the areas of divergences between the African concepts of God and the Christian view.[34] This, however, is problematic since the average African Christian still understands God in the African sense.[35] What

---

[32] Hendrikus Berkhof (1985) has noted that German theology, Anglo-Saxon theology, French language theology, German language Swiss theology, and American theology are, in fact, distinct European theologies that parallel African theology. They developed by using the infrastructure of the European languages, cultures, and metaphysics. It is, therefore, not strange that we should call for the infrastructure of the African cultures and metaphysics to be used to formulate theology for the African context.

[33] D.J. Bosch, *Transforming Mission: Paradigm Shift in Theology of Mission* (Maryknoll: Orbis Books, 1991), 448.

[34] Of the three African theologians studied in this research, Mbiti is the most prolific and, yet, he has no existing writings on the Holy Spirit, only two known articles on Christ as he is experienced in the life of the African Church—and, of course, several works on the African concepts of God. Idowu's approach is basically the same as Mbiti's. His project is primarily God as he is understood by the traditional Africa. He only has, as Bediako has ably observed, "... scanty speculation on Christ [and] the Holy Spirit ... as items of doctrine in themselves," K. Bediako, *Theology and Identity* (Oxford: Regnum Books, 1992). Setiloane has keen admiration for Idowu, thus his works on the doctrine of God are unavoidably in a similar constellation as Idowu's. In fact, he is even reluctant to study the Holy Spirit (G.M. Setiloane, "Where are we in African Theology?" in *African Theology en Route*. K. Appiah-Kubi and S. Torres, eds. (Maryknoll: Orbis Books, 1979), 65).

[35] There is a large bibliography on the persistence of the African traditional religiosity. Some important readings in this respect are J.S. Mbiti, *African Religions and Philos-*

African Christians need is not African concepts of God; what African
Christians need is a clear picture of the Christian view of God. For-
tunately, it is possible to transpose the Christian idea of God into the
conceptual framework of every culture (African cultures included) without it losing its original flavor.[36]

Kwame Bediako has demonstrated that the Church Fathers trans-
posed the Christian message from its original Jewish matrix into Hellenistic categories of understanding without viewing the latter as a hindrance to the gospel. Bediako, specifically proposing a method of con-
textualizing theology for the contemporary African situation, argues
that an analogous reconceptualization is required if the gospel is to
be understood by African audiences.[37] Might it be true that what Africa
needs today is not just an African contribution to discourses on the
doctrine of God (valuable as such an undertaking may be), but a theological contribution that explains how Africa understands God as
expressed in Trinitarian terms, both for the 370 million Christians in
Africa today[38] and for the global theological situation?

---

ophy (London: Heinemann, 1969), xi; J.U. Young, "Out of Africa: African Traditional
Religion and African Theology" in World Religions and Human Liberation, ed. D. Cohn-
Sherbok (New York: Orbis, 1992), 96; A. Shorter, "African Traditional Religion: Its
Relevance in the Contemporary World," Cross Currents, XXVIII: 4 Winter 1978–1979,
421–431; A. Shorter, "Problems and Possibilities for the Church's Dialogue with African
Traditional Religions" in Dialogue with African Traditional Religions, A. Shorter, ed. 1975, 7;
C. Kibicho, "The Continuity of the African conception of God into and through Chris-
tianity: A Kikuyu case study" in Christianity in Independent Africa, eds. E. Fashole-Luke,
et al (Bloomington: Indiana University Press, 1978), 370–388; J.M. Waliggo, "Ganda
Traditional Religion and Catholicism in Baganda, 1948–1975," Christianity in Indepen-
dent Africa; E. Ikenga Metuh, "The Gods in Retreat" in Continuity and Change in the
African Religions—The Nigerian Experience, (Nigeria: Fourth Dimension Pub. Co., 1985),
and L. Magesa, African Religion (Maryknoll: Orbis Books, 1997), 4–14.
    [36] L. Sanneh, Translating the Message: Missionary Impact on Culture (Maryknoll: Orbis
Books, 1989).
    [37] See K. Bediako, Theology and Identity, 1992 and see also his Christianity in Africa:
The Renewal of a non-Western Religion (Edinburgh: Edinburgh University Press, 1995).
A similar line of argument is observed in the works of Charles Kraft. According to
Kraft, "… it is less Scriptural to preserve western Christianity in Africa than to adapt
it (like Paul did).… Use African culture for Christ. Don't abandon it … there are
riches in African life and culture that can make Christianity so much more alive, so
much more Biblical, than it has ever been before. It could be so much more attractive
to the remaining three-fourths of African peoples than made in 'Europe' Christianity"
(C. Kraft, Christianity in Culture (Maryknoll: Orbis Books, 1979), 290,291). As for Bediako,
the fact that the gospel is translatable means that Christianity is not foreign to Africa
(see Bediako, 1992 and 1995).
    [38] See David B. Barrett's prediction, "AD 2000:350 Million Christians in Africa" in
International Review of Mission, 59 (1970), 39–54. Barrett revised the figure of 350 million

The African Christians must be given a chance to intellectually understand and appropriate the significance of the Christian understanding of God in its full array, and to then tell their own story about how they understand the Trinitarian view of God. After all, the Trinity is at the heart of the Christian faith, and if we are going to give an account of our faith, we will have to grapple with what to make of the Trinity. Moreover, today's reflections on the doctrine of God within Christian thought seem to be gravitating towards the Trinitarian concept of God throughout the world. Moltmann began this trend in 1981 when he bemoaned "… the fact that the doctrine of the Trinity has been neglected by various models of contemporary theological discourse."[39] In the past ten years alone, Christopher Hall has noted that:

> Catherine LaCugna, Thomas F. Torrance, Thomas Marsh, Colin Gunton, Christoph Schwobel, Peter Toon, Millard Erickson, Jung Young Lee, Ted Peters, Alan J. Torrance, Thomas G. Weinandy, and Roderick T. Leupp have authored or edited significant works devoted specifically to the Trinity. Other writers such as Clark Pinnock, Donald Bloesch, Alan F. Kimel, Charles J. Scalise, and Philip Walker Butin have explored Trinitarian connections to broader theological, historical, cultural, and hermeneutical issues and figures.[40]

Even though Trinitarian discourses have been occurring for about two decades, African theology has not been involved in them. Perhaps the question that should pique our interest is: If God has acted to save humanity in Christ in the manner that we see in the New Testament, what are the implications? As far as Marsh is concerned, the answer to this question is simple: the Son saves people in a way that only God does. He must be God.[41] This was also the starting point for Athanasius

---

in his *World Christian Encyclopedia* (WCE), (Nairobi: Oxford University Press, 1982). He further revised his WCE statistics and published them in the *International Bulletin of Missionary Research* in January 1997 and January 1998. The figure of 370 million is a calculation by J.S. Mbiti (see his article "Is the Bible in African Religion and African Religion in the Bible?" Paper delivered at EFSA and University of Stellenbosch, department of Old and New Testaments International Workshop, 14–15 May, 1999, 1) that is based on Barrett's 1998, 1997 and earlier statistics.

[39] J. Moltmann, *The Trinity and the Kingdom*. M. Kohl, trans. (London, SCM Press, 1991).

[40] Hall, "Adding up Trinity," 26.

[41] T. Marsh, *The Triune God: A Biblical, Historical, and Theological Study* (Connecticut: Twenty Third Publications, 1994).

in the fourth century[42] and John Calvin in the sixteenth century.[43] Along with the rest of the Christian community, the African Church must stop being indifferent to the implication of the great salvation of Jesus Christ on the Christian view of God. Our question as African Christians should be: "How can we most effectively, truthfully, and reverently speak of the wondrous God we worship as Father, Son and the Holy Spirit on the basis of the biblical testimony itself?"[44]

WORKING HYPOTHESIS

The Christian view of God must not only penetrate the cultural matrix of Africa by utilizing the infrastructure of the African conceptual framework in its articulation, but it must also seek to promote such a formulation of the doctrine of the Trinity. Such a model for theological reflection is not new. Sanneh and Bediako have proposed the model for African theology and have given it the necessary academic grounding.[45]

The theological basis of the proposed theological model is the Christian view of the revelation of God. On the basis of the fact that God is a communicating God, Sanneh and Bediako agree with older African theologians such as Bolaji Idowu, John Mbiti, and Gabriel Setiloane, who had earlier advanced the view that, such as all men everywhere, traditional Africa also received and perceived God's revelation. This is a basic truth that cannot be denied. To deny that Africa received and perceived God's revelation does not only amount to doubting the humanity of the African peoples, but it also casts aspersions on the authority of the scripture, which comes from the position that God is proclaimed to all men everywhere in nature (Ps. 19:1–6, Rom. 1:20, Acts 14:15–17) and through conscience (Rom. 2:14, Acts 17:21, Ecc. 3:11).

The traditional Africa, however, did not know that God has ultimately revealed himself in the Son and in the Holy Spirit. This is a universal story of the church, and it is a truth that is of tremendous significance to the Christian faith—as is evident in the confessions of the church. A theology that has not recognized that God became man

---

[42] Athanasius, *Contra Arianos*, 1. 4–19, 25–34, 2. 57 f.; 3. 1–6; 4. 1–10.

[43] J. Calvin, *Institutes of Christian Religion*. Translated and annotated by F.L. Battles (London: Collins, 1986), translation of the original 1559 edition. See I. 13.12 f.

[44] Hall, "Adding up the Trinity," 27.

[45] Bediako, *Theology and Identity*, cf. Sanneh, *Translating the Message*.

and is worshipped in the Spirit stands suspect as far as the Christian faith is concerned. Therefore, the African Christians must view God not just as *Nyame, Leza, Nyambe, Modimo, Nyasaye*, and so on. They must begin there, but allow the facts of the Incarnation and the Pentecost to radically modify their prior concepts of God. So, for instance, instead of the Sotho-Tswana's concept of *Modimo*, the Sotho-Tswana can speak of the same *Modimo* having revealed himself in the Son and in the Holy Spirit.

But the willingness, for instance, to proclaim that *Modimo* has revealed himself in the Son and in the Holy Spirit comes with a challenge. The challenge is that we must adequately understand African metaphysics and use it in telling the story of the Trinity. How do the African peoples speak about God? How do they speak of 'being'? How do they speak of 'person'? How we answer these questions is important since the search for the answers force us to return to the basics of African metaphysics. Understanding the basic structure of African metaphysics and its dynamics allows us to effectively describe how the African understands God, and it also facilitates the articulation of the relevant and appropriate meaning of personhood for an African reader.

Christianizing African concepts of God and expressing the new meaning to African audiences by using the infrastructure of the African metaphysics does not mean that we are challenging modernism and, in particular, the appropriateness of Western theologies. To admit to the African philosophical symbols is to say that traditionalism involves longevity of experience and history that recent innovations must be keen to observe. The Western formulations of the doctrine of the Trinity are directly applicable and, therefore, are relevant to the Western context. There must therefore be an African formulation. Such a formulation, explains Dick France, will of necessity require "… more … direction from within, not from without. It needs theology, its own African Christian theology. Until this is achieved, … it will not grow in influence on the new Africa, and it will be increasingly dismissed as a legacy from colonial past."[46] Professor Mbiti, expressing similar sentiments, has stated that:

---

[46] Dick France, quoted in T. Adeyemo, *Reflections on the State of Christianity in Africa* (Potchefstroom: Instituut vir Refomatoriese Studie, Potchefstroom Universiteit CHO, 1995), 5.

Until we can cultivate a genuine Christianity which is truly MADE IN
AFRICA, we will be building on a shallow foundation and living on borrowed time. Let it be said once and for all, as loudly as technology can
make it, that IMPORTED CHRISTIANITY WILL NEVER, NEVER
QUENCH THE THIRST OF AFRICAN PEOPLES. The wisdom of
our forefathers speaks clearly about this in a proverb: "That which comes
from charity is never sufficient to fill the granary". Africa wants and
needs the Gospel. But Africa does not require imported Christianity,
because too much of it will only castrate us spiritually or turn us into
spiritual cripples.[47]

Western theologies have a long history. They have been through the
Neo-Platonic scholastic metaphysics that reached its peak in Aquinas.
During the 17th and the 18th centuries they went through German
Idealism—a philosophical paradigm that seems to have won the admiration of contemporary Western theologians. Today most of the Western theologians clearly understand God in the 'self-consciousness'
terms of philosophical Idealism.[48] Theological formulations worked
within the infrastructures of the philosophies of Plato, Aristotle, and
Hegel cannot be expected to be adequate for the African context,
whose intellectual culture functions under entirely different philosophical presuppositions.[49] Professor Walls explains this very point in the
following words:

---

[47] J.S. Mbiti, "Christianity and African Culture" in *Facing the New Challenges—The
Message of PACLA*, 9–19 December 1976. M. Cassidy and L. Verlinden, eds. (Kisumu:
Evangel Publishing House, 1978), 276.

[48] We can learn the significance of native metaphysics in the formulation of theology
from the time of the church fathers through the period of the Middle Ages to the
present from the history of Western theologies. Western theology has constantly used
the infrastructure of native European philosophies to express theological truth. The
way that Western theologies use the European philosophies helps us to put two things
into perspective. First, it confirms Robertson Smith's opinion that no religion starts
with *tabula rasa* (R.W. Smith, *Lectures on the Religion of the Semite* (London: A & C Black
Ltd, 1923), 2). Second, and perhaps the most important point, is that it encourages us
to use our own native metaphysics in the formulation of theology aimed at our context.
   Perhaps we can also include the conceptions of traditionalism and modernism here.
As Professor Odera Oruka has argued, the essential meaning of tradition is not that
which is outdated or outgoing; rather, it is "... perennial or a part of what has endured
in life or culture of a people... thus the distinction between tradition and modernity
in any given culture is not a distinction between the outdated and the novel. It is a
distinction between what is part of the long history of the people and what is recent
or innovative to that history. And the question as to which of the two (tradition and
modernity) is good or desirable must be left open" (Oruka, *Sage Philosophy*, 80).

[49] Placide Tempels once stated that the Africans live more by *being* than by following
their own idea (P. Tempels, *Bantu Philosophy*, (Paris: Presence Africaine, 1959), 23).
Professor Mbiti has declared that the African is incurably religious. Religion, Professor

It is possible that from now on Western theology will be of little help to Africa. For one thing, Western theology has been for so long insufferably parochial; Western theologians defined Modern Man in terms of an assumed product of affluence, and it is a little late for them now to realize that for millions of modern men the demons, for instance, far from being irrelevant, are the very stuff of life. And Western theology has gone off in directions that are of doubtful relevance elsewhere. The separation of the Gospel from religion may be intelligible in the post-Christian West which provides perhaps the first known example of a religion passing away without being succeeded by another; but it does not readily find an echo in a continent saturated in religion.[50]

The African church is an offshoot of Western Christianity. This, and the historical connection between the West and Africa, has meant that the way that the Western church interprets the Christian story continues to heavily influence developments within the African church up to this day. African theologians seem to agree that the theology that we presently experience in Africa is, to say the least, of Western origin. We are not blaming the Western church for having done her theology. We are saying that the African church has not done her theology. Mbiti says that African Christians "have a faith but not a theology."[51] Tite Tienou believes that African Christians might as well be said to "have a theology of no theology!"[52] Kinoti has observed that "the denominations we belong to, the liturgies we use, the hymns we sing, the theologies which govern our beliefs and conduct, be they liberal or evangelical, are all made in the West."[53] While affirming the fact that the African church is a child of the Western church, it

Mbiti explains, "permeates into all the departments of life so fully that it is not easy or possible always to isolate it" (Mbiti, *African Religions and Philosophy* (London: Heinemann, 1969), 1, 262). The other African theological thinkers who believe that in African traditional societies nothing can be explained outside the Supreme Being are J.B. Danquah and Bolaji Idowu (J.B. Danquah, *The Akan Doctrine of God* (London: Frank Cass, 1968), 2,3,16; cf. B. Idowu, *Olodumare: God in Yoruba Belief* (London: Longman, 1963), 145,146). These scholars might have overstated themselves. However, they have made an important point; namely, that the part played by God and religion as an important phenomenon in the existence of the African is significant.

[50] A.F. Walls, "Towards understanding Africa's Place in Christian History" in Religion in a Pluralistic Society: Essays Presented to Professor C.G. Baëta (Leiden: Brill, 1976), 183.

[51] Statement made by Prof. J.S. Mbiti over the Canadian Broadcasting Corporation on 25 May 1985.

[52] T. Tienou, *The Theological Task of the Church in Africa* (Achimota: Africa Christian Press, 1982), 46, 47.

[53] G. Kinoti, *Hope for Africa* (Nairobi: AISRED, 1994), 74, 75.

is important to indicate that the African church must mature. Growth means cultivating theological thoughts that have taken due cognizance of the thought forms of the African peoples. After all, as Mbiti believes:

> The only tools needed to evolve a viable form of Christianity are: the Gospel, Faith and Culture. Thank God, we have these three fundamental tools now in plenty in our continent. ... What more then do we need? Why then do we need to continue living on borrowed Christianity when all the necessary tools are present with us? Thanks to God for His universal Gospel, thanks to the missionaries who brought it to our forefathers, thanks to the riches of our cultural heritage by means of which this Gospel can be understood, articulated and propagated. ... God has a thousand tongues in this continent by which to speak to us about the mystery of His will and plan for the world. If God did not speak through African languages, there would not be today the 350 million Christians on this continent. Let us therefore not put to silence any of these tongues by which he speaks.[54]

What this means is that African Christian orthodoxy does not have to remain in the terms of Neo-Platonism and German Idealism in order for it to express the Christian truth that it is meant to convey. On the contrary, God has put within the African intellectual culture enough resources to allow for a full translation of the most complex of the biblical concepts into African frames of references. Kraft, using his expertise in cross-cultural communication, writes that:

> Communication is most effective when C[ommunicator], M[essage] and R[eceptor] participate in the same context(s), settings and frame(s) of reference. ... The sharing of cultural, subcultural, linguistic, and frames of reference maximises the possibility that the cultural forms / symbols employed to transmit messages will mean the same thing to both C and R. Differences in the frames of reference of C and R assure that at least some of the symbols employed in M will be understood differently by the participants. If C's frame of reference is adopted as that in terms of which the communication is to take place, R must be extracted from his or her own frame of reference and indoctrinated into that of C. If R's frame of reference is chosen, C must learn whatever is necessary to function properly in that frame of reference.[55]

Besides Christianizing the doctrine of the Trinity and using the African conceptual framework to articulate the Christian doctrine of God for the African context, we also have the conviction that the African theological situation must foster the doctrine of the Trinity developed within

---

[54] Mbiti, "Christianity and African Culture," 276, 277.
[55] Kraft, *Christianity in Culture*, 149–150.

the infrastructure of African metaphysics. Fostering this view of the doctrine of the Trinity involves a deliberate effort as well as leading the audience to have the right attitude towards the doctrine of the Trinity as a whole, and towards the doctrine as it is formulated from the point of view of the African pattern of thought as well. Somehow theology has to discover how this may be made possible. Perhaps the best way of fostering Trinitarianism is by having a fluent understanding of the doctrine of the Trinity, recognizing the problems that African metaphysics raises for the doctrine of the Trinity, clarifying and representing the elements of the problem, proposing solutions to the problem, as well as revising, restating, and re-evaluating.

METHODOLOGY

Foundational Principles

Theology as fides quarens intellectum

We proceed from the position of commitment to the Christian faith. Therefore our starting point is faith itself. It has been argued that the African is incurably religious. This means that, for our situation, theological methodologies that thrive on rationalism, experientialism, evidentialism, and pragmatism may not be very popular. If fideism would be the natural beginning point for theology in Africa, then we have to qualify the faith. What we seek to engage here is not the faith in faith such as we seem to see in the system of Blaise Pascal, not faith that is anti-rationalism such as Søren Kierkegaard posits, not the natural faith in the sense of natural knowledge of God as we see in Brunner, but faith in God who reveals himself. This faith is, therefore, not based on reason, experience, or evidence, but is related to the God who calls us.

Africa knows God, but this knowledge is repressed within the confines of *Modimo, Nyasaye, Mulungu, Leza,* and *Nyame*. Africa needs to not only experience, but also to seek to understand *Modimo, Nyasaye, Mulungu, Leza,* and *Nyame* as revealed in Christ. This cannot happen without the aid of the Holy Spirit. If we are to experience *Nyasaye* in the Son and in the Holy Spirit, which (of course) is the way in which we as Christians experience God, it would be legitimate to tarry on what to make of *Nyasaye*.

Interdisciplinary

This is first and foremost a theological discourse on the doctrine of the Trinity. But this cannot be done without paying attention to the cultural-historical developments in the Greco-Roman world of the second and third centuries as contexts of the confessions of the church. Neither can we adequately focus our studies without applying ourselves to logical and critical thinking as tools of reflection as specifically as they have been applied to distinct philosophical contexts: Neo-Platonism and Hegelianism. Today, because of the difference of the nature of the African metaphysics, it is important that it be considered as a separate and distinct philosophical context. A basic structure of Neo-Platonism helps us to see why people like Augustine, Boethius, and Thomas Aquinas took a certain view of the doctrine of the Trinity. Hegelianism also helps us to understand the recent formulations of the doctrine of the Trinity, especially those of I.A. Dorner, K. Rahner, K. Barth, and even H. Berkhof. Similarly, it is not possible to fully understand the African theologians' view of the doctrine of God if we do not have a proper perspective of the history of Africa and the presence as well as the function of the African conceptual framework.

Theology for the African Continent as a Whole

The theology that we seek to develop is that which understands the historical solidarity of Africa on a continental scale. The conceptual framework of the African Negroes is not shaped according to frontiers fixed by colonization. Anybody seeking to understand the cosmology of the African peoples must first of all comprehend the individual ethnic groups and their genetic relationships. The histories of the African peoples indicate diversity, but such differences must be understood in the context of convergence and reconvergence. In view of this, Olderogge has indicated that there are no fundamental racial and linguistic differences between the two major African Negro groups: the Nilo-Saharan peoples and the Niger-Congo peoples. Even the Khoisan race, whose history has generated difficulties for African historiographers and ethnolinguists, has in time evidently given and taken from a number of ethnic groups falling within the Niger-Congo phylum.

Therefore the doctrine of God that we seek to formulate here does not aim at just one of the four phyla of the African Negroes; on the contrary, we are speaking about a theology for the Niger-Congo phylum of the African peoples, a theology for the Nilo-Saharan group phylum, a theology for the Khoisan phylum, and a theology for the Afro-Asiatic phylum. We can reason this way because movements and interactions between the African peoples in time and space created divergences, but they also created convergences and reconvergences that, as we have argued elsewhere, resulted in a common intellectual crystallizing point for the African Negroes.

African Theology is to be Seen from Within

One cannot speak of African theology without granting it the right to be different (see Tienou, "The Right to Difference," 31). African theology is not constructed with the West, Asia, or Latin America in mind; it is primarily an African theology—as the name suggests—although, like any other theology, it seeks to convey a universal message. To maintain that African theology must be seen from within is not to suggest a theological moratorium. The African church is a part of the universal church, and, therefore, it is only logical that there be active and living theological connections between the two. The connections, however, must be maintained in terms of mutual exchanges and multilateral influences. In order for this to genuinely happen, it is important that the global theological situation should hear and receive some of Africa's contribution to the development of Christian thought.

The Resources

This book is a product of years of reflection on the doctrine of God. My country, Kenya, is overloaded with 'spirit movements' and 'messianic groups.' By 1973 the word *spirit* appeared in 14% of all the denominations within the churches registered with the Kenyan government.[56] Then we also have the problem of 'messiahs.' Well-known 'messiahs' with huge followings are Simeon Ondetto of the Legio Maria Mission,[57] John Owalo of the Nomiya Luo Mission,[58] and Alfayo Odongo

---

[56] D.B. Barret, *Kenya Churches Handbook* (Kisumu: Evangel Publishing House, 1973).

[57] P. Dirven, *Maria Legio: The Dynamics of a break away Church among the Luo of East Africa*. PhD dissertation. (Rome: Pontifica University, 1970).

[58] E. Muga, *African Response to Western Christian Religion* (Kampala: East African Literature Bureau, 1975).

Mango of the Musanda Holy Ghost Church.[59] Of course, the spirit
and messianic movements are not just a Kenyan problem; they are a
problem of African Christianity. Hearing of supposedly Christian leaders like Isaiah Shembe of South Africa,[60] Mapaulos of Malawi, Walter
Matita of Lesotho, and Simon Kimbangu of the Democratic Republic
of Congo,[61]one is compelled to ask the question: What happened to the
Christian view of the Trinity?

Furthermore, the context of my childhood church caused me to
grapple significantly with the problem surrounding the Trinity. This
church, the Church of Christ in Africa, has a very high regard for the
creeds. Since childhood, I recited the vernacular version of the Apostles
Creed at every worship service. When I began theological education,
I started to sense that we recited the creeds without knowing their
true meaning. As an ordained minister, relating the religious thoughts
of our people in their concrete situations to the creeds confirmed my
earlier observation. One area that was and still is a constant bother to
me is how to use the African philosophical symbols to reinterpret the
Christian view of God. I have the impression that although we have the
right doctrine on paper, the worshippers do not really know what the
names God the Father, God the Son, and God the Holy Spirit mean
due to their heritage in African cosmology. Moreover, the church does
not appear to recognize the need to use the metaphysics of the African
peoples in order to express the doctrine of the Trinity.

In addition to being an ordained minister, I have had the privilege of
being a lecturer in systematic theology, first at the Nairobi International
School of Theology and now at Daystar University. In these institutions
of Christian higher learning, both the lecturers and the student popula-
tions come from all regions of Africa. Thus as opportunities opened, I
have had chances to engage in rigorous reflection on what God means
to me as an African believer. My studies at the University of Stellenbosch have been extremely useful in forming my grasp of the doctrine
of the Trinity. My master of theology mini-thesis, *The Doctrine of God in
Contemporary African Christian Thought: An Evaluation of the Extent to Which
African Theology is Trinitarian* (1997), and my doctor of theology disserta-

---

[59] Barret, *Kenya Churches Handbook.*
[60] B.G.M. Sundkler, *Bantu Prophets in South Africa* (Oxford: Oxford University Press,
1961).
[61] M.C. Martin, "The Mai Chaza in Rhodesia" in *African Initiative in Religion.* D. Barret, ed. (Nairobi: East African Literature Bureau, 1971), 106–121.

tion, *The Doctrine of God in African Christian Thought: An Assessment of African Inculturation Theology from a Trinitarian Perspective* (2000), furnished me with the true essence of this book.

Book Format

This book investigates its hypothesis in four parts. Part one discusses the roots of the doctrine of the Trinity as well as the role that the church fathers played in the formulation of the Immanent Trinity. Part two attempts to show how Western theologies have responded to the doctrine of the Trinity as it was formulated by the church fathers. Part three deals with the doctrine of God as it is expressed in African theology. Part four is the original contribution of this book. It articulates the doctrine of the Trinity from the point of view of African metaphysics, and it suggests how the African theological situation may foster the proposal.

Part one of this book is entitled *The Doctrine of the Trinity—The Bible and the Church Fathers*. This part of the study has two chapters. Chapter one discusses the revelation of the Triune God of the Bible. The significance of chapter one lies in demonstrating the point that the doctrine of the Trinity does not have its origin in Hellenism or later European cultures, but that the doctrine has its source in the Bible. This chapter forms the basis of chapter two, which brings the church fathers and their contributions to the emergence of the doctrine of Immanent Trinity into focus. Particular attention is given to the basic aspects of the development of the doctrine and the movement from the Bible to the differentiated language of the creeds. The point of this chapter is to show the type of theological discussions that occurred before the formulation of the doctrine of Immanent Trinity and the role that Greek metaphysics played in the entire process. Whereas knowing the theological issues helps appropriate interpretation of the doctrine for the diverse situations of our own time, understanding the role that the Greek metaphysics played in the formulation of the Immanent Trinity allows us the possibility of using our native thought patterns in order to articulate theological thoughts.

Part two shows how Western theologies have interacted with their own context as they reinterpret the doctrine of the Trinity. Chapter three discusses the 'God as Substance' way of understanding the doctrine of the Trinity that resulted from the influence of the Neo-Platonic concept of 'substance.' This, in a sense, is the most widely held view of the doctrine of the Trinity. At the outset of the missionary century[62] it was the predominant view. Thus the first missionaries to Africa only had this interpretation of the doctrine of the Trinity to bequeath to the African church. Chapter four deals with Trinitarianism conceived from the point of view of Hegelian philosophy. Trinitarianism formulated using the infrastructure of Hegelianism sees 'God as an Absolute Subject.' Chapter five is an attempt by some modern Western theologians who have rejected 'God as Essence' and 'God as Absolute Subject' to recollect the form of Trinitarianism held by the Eastern Church–'God as Community in Unity.' In a sense the significance of this chapter is to indicate that although Western theologies have relied on native metaphysics to articulate their points of view, there are other Western theologians who are of the opinion that the Eastern church's formulation of the doctrine of the Trinity has invaluable merits. Chapter six indicates the 'Pertinent Issues in the Western reinterpretations of the doctrine of the Trinity.' The basic thesis of this chapter is that Western theologies have different models of Trinitarianism that depend on philosophical presuppositions; however, in spite of the differences, they still agree on the significance of the Incarnation, the importance of the concept of *homoousios*, and the need to maintain Christian identity. This is an important lesson for this book. As we have noted with Western theologies, we can use our native metaphysics in the formulation of the doctrine of the Trinity as long as we recognize the significance of the Incarnation, the importance of *homoousios*, and the need to emphasize Christian identity rather than cultural identity.

Part three is the contribution of African thought to the understanding of the doctrine of God. This section of the book identifies the African conceptual framework as an intellectual infrastructure that theology can use in reinterpreting the doctrine of the Trinity for the African context. It also notes gaps and inconsistencies that African theologians bring to the Christian view of God. Chapter seven exposes African metaphysics and challenges theology to take full advantage of it. The issue here is that theology in the West has generally used Neo-Platonism and Hegelianism. In the same way, the African situation can

---

[62] The period that is generally associated with the missionary century is that which runs from 1800 to 1914. An interesting reading in this regard is K.S. Latourette, particularly volume 5 and 6 of his set entitled *A History of Expansion and Christianity The Great Century: The Americas, Australias and Africa*, AD 1800–1914; and *The Great Century: North Africa and Asia*, AD 1800–1914).

constructively use the African conceptual framework to reinterpret the doctrine of the Trinity since it is available, and it is capable of expressing the Christian thought to the African audience. Chapter eight limits itself to the discussions of three African inculturation theologians: Bolaji Idowu, John S. Mbiti, and Gabriel M. Setiloane. The basic proposal of these theologians is that the African people had traditional concepts of God. These concepts were not borrowed from others as if God had left the African people without a witness of his presence. The biblical idea of God, therefore, does not have to be introduced to the African people in a way that is completely unrelated to what they already know. Chapter nine is an evaluation of African inculturation theology's view of God. This chapter recognizes that African inculturation theology is yet to view the doctrine of God as the doctrine of the Trinity, and, in addition, the chapter offers some reasons for the omission. The understanding of this chapter is that, if the reasons for the omission are identified and addressed, then African theology would see the need to develop the doctrine of the Trinity.

The viewpoint in part four is that African inculturation theology must make use of the African conceptual framework to build biblical Trinitarianism. In order for this to take place, chapter ten proposes that we must fully Christianize the African concepts of God and use African metaphysics to explain the new meaning to the African audience. A fully-Christianized concept of God would, for example, understand *Modimo* as the 'Great *Muntu*' manifested by the Son and the Holy Spirit. But having said that God is the 'Great *Muntu*' revealed in the Son and in the Holy Spirit, we must then be in a position to explain how to use African logic or theory of knowledge to interpret that appearance. The chapter suggests an understanding of the doctrine of the Trinity formulated from the point of view of the African thought pattern and challenges the African theological situation in Chapter eleven to critically test and foster the proposal.

PART ONE

THE DOCTRINE OF THE TRINITY: THE BIBLE AND THE CHURCH FATHERS

The perspective in which the believer sees the story of Abraham, through the history of Israel to Jesus, and the history of the church and the history of their own lives, is an occasion for amazement at the continuity of the identity of discussion about God. It is a perspective which does not go against the historian's picture of history, but it can not be gained through studies in the history of religion. It arises out of the present worship of God and exerts pressure towards putting thoughts about the Spirit in the church in a separate mental compartment with the appearance and activity of Jesus and the God of Israel and creator of the worlds.

This separate compartment is the so-called doctrine of the Trinity, which should offer decisive theological help for believers and not ... be a hindrance and an additional difficulty. ... The God who comforts and heals, who brings about liberation and a new creation, is to be found in Israel, in the coming of Jesus and in the sending of the Spirit, with which the doctrine of the Trinity deals.

D. Ritschl in *The Logic of Theology*, 141–143

CHAPTER ONE

AN ANALYSIS OF THE BIBLICAL ROOTS
OF THE DOCTRINE OF THE TRINITY

INTRODUCTION

The issue of the biblical roots of the doctrine of the Trinity relates to the question of the self-revelation of God. As Hendrikus Berkhof has said, in revelation "we perceive not just a something, a segment of a divine mystery, but God himself, his heart, his deepest essence. We see in a mirror and thus do not see God face to face. But what we see in that mirror is God himself."[1] If we know God by revelation, this means that we know him through concrete events and experiences that took place in the past and is recorded in the scripture. The primordial stories are basic, but new events and experiences are added—not to undo the previous ones—but to furnish the community of faith with more penetrating experiences of the One revealed. In these events and experiences (first of all captured in the Old Testament and later occurring in a more profound manner as depicted in the New Testament), we become more acquainted with Israel's God. He is not the God of our own ideas, but the God who calls us to an encounter with him: "Come and see what God has done" (Rom. 10:14–17). As the Bible story unfolds from the Old Testament to the New Testament, we meet the Father, the Son, and the Holy Spirit in a manner that maintains the unity of God.

THE TERM 'TRINITY' AND ITS RELATIONSHIP TO THE BIBLE

The fundamental question is: is the doctrine of the Trinity biblical? We have to deal with the term *biblical*. Just what does it mean to be biblical? The fundamental notion behind the idea biblical is the notion that a word or a concept is an actual fact in the Bible, and because

---

[1] H. Berkhof, *Christian Faith: An Introduction to the Study of the Faith*. S. Woudstra, trans. (Grand Rapids: Eerdmans, 1979), 105.

it is in the Bible it is, therefore, authoritative.[2] The issue that we seek
to address is not semantics; consequently, not the term *Trinity* as such
because theology is not about semantics. The issue is the self-revelation
of God, how the scripture depicts this disclosure, and how the Christian
community experiences that self-revelation. God is both objectively and
subjectively experienced as triune. Thus, a fundamental question is:
Does the term *Trinity* capture the essence of Israel's God as we meet
him in the pages of the Bible? Christian thought has offered diverse
responses to these questions.

The Christian community experiences God in personal terms. C.J.
Webb prefers to call God, who can be experienced in such terms, a
'personal God.' According to him, we can only speak of a 'personal
God' because of "personal relations—of worship, trust, love—between
oneself and God."[3] In the thinking of Otto, this experience, *mysterium
tremendum*, involves a state of awe, an awareness of overpoweringness, an
awareness of energy or urgency expressed in emotion or force, an experience of the Wholly Other, and an attraction element (*fascinans*). Brümmer and Sykes see this experience in the context of Christ. Brümmer
believes that the personal relationship that the Christian has with Christ
forces the Christian to see God as contextualized in Christ.[4] According
to Sykes, the relationship of the believer to Christ is such that the Christian does not only experience Christ as an authoritative exemplar, but
as God himself.[5] And so for Webb, Sykes and Brümmer, the Christian
experiences God each day in personal terms.[6]

Other equally respectable Christian scholars have argued that the
doctrine of the Trinity is mere intellectualism. This group of thinkers
points to the triad formula[7] that they believe was widespread in the

---

[2] K. Greene-McCreight, "When I Say God, I mean Father, Son and Holy Spirit:
On Ecumenical Baptism Formula" in *Pro-Ecclesia* vol. VI, no 3., 1997, 296.

[3] C.J. Webb, *God and Personality* (London: Allen & Unwin, 1920), 70, 73.

[4] V. Brümmer, "The Identity of the Christian Tradition." A paper delivered at the
Faculty of Theology, University of Stellenbosch, 1998, 12.

[5] S. Sykes, *The Identity of Christianity* (Philadelphia: Fortress, 1984), 255.

[6] Often 'experience' is considered to be the opposite of 'revelation,' but experience
can also be used in a more encompassing sense. Used that way, experience is not
merely something subjective; rather, it includes the objective. Everything we know falls
within experience. I cannot be aware of anything outside my experience. Therefore, I
'experience' revelation also.

[7] The concept of the divine triad is by no means peculiar to the Christian faith.
For instance, in the Indian religion we meet Brahma, Siva, and Visnu; in the Egyptian
religion there is Osiris, Isis, and Horus. Besides these historical religions, we also know
that the neo-Platonic view of the Supreme Being or the Ultimate Reality is triadically

Greco-Roman world of the post-biblical era as the source of a Trinitarian view of God. An example here is the South African theologian, Professor Gabriel M. Setiloane. According to Setiloane, the concept of the Trinity is located in the Greek metaphysics and is without biblical base whatsoever. Because of this conviction, Setiloane is of the opinion that the concept of the Trinity is of limited application and is inappropriate as a description of God as the African peoples know him.[8]

Another group of theologians is of the opinion that the doctrine of the Trinity resulted from the Christian misunderstanding of the concept of the 'One and the Many' found among a cross section of religious traditions. A.R. Johnson,[9] for example, argues that the concept of social extension of personality found among the Hebrew and other Ancient Near Eastern cultures could be the explanation for the plurality in the Godhead which the Christian faith uses as one of its arguments for belief in the doctrine of the Trinity. Johnson explains at least four ways one may extend oneself and, therefore, be in a position to influence society for good or evil. They are "the vital power" that reaches "far beyond the mere contour of the body,"[10] "the spoken word" as extension of the one who has spoken,[11] the "name" of an individual is an extension of his personality,[12] and the "house or household" as representing the personality of the man at its head.[13] Extension of personality that is understood in this manner allows Johnson to easily see the Spirit[14] and the Word[15] as mere extensions of Yahweh's personality.

Clearly religious experience, rigorous intellectual reflection, and the problem of the one and the many that is found among different traditional religions are factors that may commend the doctrine of the Trinity. Nevertheless, what makes the doctrine of the Trinity authori-

---

presented as the Good or the One, the Intelligence or the One-Many, and the World-Soul or the One and the Many. To these we could also add the triad associated with Comte's philosophy that speaks of the cultus of humanity as the Great Being, of Space as the Great Medium, and of the Earth as the Great Fetish (see W. Fulton, "Trinity" in *Encyclopedia of Religion and Ethics*. J. Hastings, ed. (Edinburgh: T &T Clark, 1921), 458).

[8] G.M. Setiloane, "Where are we in African Theology?" in *African Theology en Route*. K. Appiah-Kubi and S. Torres, eds. (Maryknoll: Orbis Books, 1979), 65.

[9] A.R. Johnson, *The One and the Many in the Israelite Conception of God* (Cardiff: University of Wales Press, 1961).

[10] Johnson, *The One and the Many*, 2.

[11] Johnson, *The One and the Many*, 2, 3.

[12] Johnson, *The One and the Many*, 3, 4.

[13] Johnson, *The One and the Many*, 4–6.

[14] Johnson, *The One and the Many*, 15, 16.

[15] Johnson, *The One and the Many*, 17.

tative is the fact that it is a description of God as we meet him in the pages of the Bible. The idea 'biblical' or 'scriptural' does not, however, refer only to those words and concepts that are found on the pages of Bible. If we go by this definition of biblical, then we might as well conclude that the doctrine of the Trinity is not biblical because the word Trinity does not appear in the pages of the Bible. However, this is not the way the Christian faith—from the time of the patristic writers until the present—has always defined the term *biblical*. Greene-McCreight explains:

> While it may seem only that the only obvious way to define "biblical" is that which appears on the pages of the Bible, it is apparent that for the orthodox patristic writers, that which counts as "scriptural" and therefore authoritative (the key notion behind the term biblical) encompasses that which is argued, inferred or construed on the basis of the biblical witness read within the guidance of the Rule of Faith.[16]

The concept of the Trinity is not only biblical because it is "argued, inferred, or construed" from the scriptural witness.[17] Rather, as Heick puts it, the doctrine of the Trinity itself:

> ... is the underlying and governing thought of the biblical history of redemption. In addition, the Trinitarian faith expresses a doctrinal experience of the Church, the necessity of which has been tested by the practical needs of piety through centuries. The problem presented itself unconsciously in the baptismal formula of earliest Christianity.[18]

If we reject the term *Trinity* because it does not appear in the pages of the Bible, then we would have to reject a host of other terms as well. An example of a term that falls into this category is *homoousios*. Athanasius obtained *homoousios* from a non-biblical source, but—regardless of this—the term has been accepted as scriptural and, therefore, authoritative even by the critics of the concept of the Trinity on the basis that *homoousios* is "argued, inferred or construed on the basis of the biblical witness."[19] Moreover, translation assumes that if we adhere to the principle of dynamic equivalence we can use the language of non-biblical sources. There is no reason why theology cannot use the language obtained from non-biblical sources to proclaim the truth revealed

---

[16] K. Greene-McCreight, "When I Say God, I mean Father, Son and Holy Spirit: On Ecumenical Baptism Formula" in *Pro-Ecclesia* vol VI, no 3, 1997, 296, 297.
[17] Greene-McCreight, "When I Say God, I mean Father, Son and Holy Spirit," 296.
[18] O.W. Heick, *A History of Christian Thought* (Philadelphia: Fortress Press, 1966), 143.
[19] Greene-McCreight, "When I Say God, I mean Father, Son and Holy Spirit," 297.

in the word of God. Like the word *homoousios*, the word *Trinity* originally came from non-biblical sources; however, it is scriptural and therefore authoritative since it expresses the truth revealed in the biblical witness.

THE BIBLICAL REVELATION OF GOD

Preliminary Observation

When we speak of the biblical revelation of God, we are concerned with the way that the two testaments of the Bible indicate the self-revelation of God. We cannot, however, study and develop the Old Testament's picture of God in isolation from the New Testament's, and neither can we legitimately speak of 'this' as the Old Testament's picture of God and the 'other' as the New Testament's. This procedure has been followed for practical and historical reasons by both Old Testament theology and New Testament theology. However, the practice is theologically questionable. The Bible as a whole is the normative context of interpreting any one of its parts. To fence off one testament and make theological statements from it in isolation is to lead to imbalance. Our articulation of theological statements must, therefore, consider the views of both testaments of the Bible.[20] Our doctrine of God should not only be the Old Testament's construction, and neither should it reject or slight the Old Testament's formation in favor of a supposedly New Testament position. Rather, it should be a comprehensive presentation of the picture of God seen in both testaments of the Bible.

---

[20] Goldingay has explained the nature of the relationship between the OT and the NT in the following terms: "The Old lays the theological foundations for the New and sometimes explicitly looks forward in a hope which the Christian sees confirmed or fulfilled in Christ. The New presupposes this foundation and looks back to Christ, concentrating on what needs to be said in light of his coming, but encouraging rather than discouraging us to do this against the background of OT's broader concerns. Faith in Christ with its background in the NT may provide the pre-understanding for our approach to the OT; but where we find the OT saying something in tension with that pre-understanding, our reaction will be to allow it to broaden the latter, not to accept only what conforms to what we know already. Christ helps us to understand the OT, but the OT helps us to understand Christ." (J. Goldingay, *Approaches to Old Testament Interpretation* (Leicester: Inter-Varsity Press, 1981), 34).

The Trinitarian Vestiges in the Old Testament

The Old Testament indicates what is clearly a progressive self-revelation of God. Immediately from Genesis, early anticipation of the
Trinitarian understanding of God was not only evident but, as Carl
F. Henry has noted, they in fact "… gain increasing clarity in the course
of an enlarging scriptural disclosure."[21]

Us / We Pronouns

A significant, rudimentary intimation of the Trinitarian truth (appearing in the early part of the Old Testament) is the first person plural
pronouns *us* and *our* found in Gen. 1:26. The other places where the
plural, first person *us* is used in reference to God is in the context of the
expulsion of man from the garden of Eden (Gen. 3:22), the confusion of
human language at Babel (Gen. 11:7), and the call of the prophet Isaiah (Isa.6:8). Old Testament scholars understand the plural reference in
these passages in various ways. K.A. Matthews has identified at least
six ways of understanding the plural reference in these passages: "(1) a
remnant of polytheistic myth; (2) God's address to creation, "heavens
and earth";[22] (3) a plural indicating divine honor and majesty;[23] (4) self-
deliberation;[24] (5) divine address to a heavenly court of angels;[25] and (6)

---

[21] Henry, *God, Revelation and Authority*, 195.

[22] The elevated nature of the theology of Gen. 1:1–2:3 cannot allow for remnants of
polytheism. Verse 27 identifies God alone as the creator; consequently, God would have
no reason to address the heavens and the earth.

[23] The honorific plural is debatable since the point of Gen. 1:26, for instance, is not
the majesty of God; rather, the unique relationship between God and man (the issue of
the image of God).

[24] Self-deliberation views depict God as someone in contemplation. This view is
possible—especially in view of the change to the singular in Gen. 1:27. Other passages,
such as Ps. 42:5, 11:43:5, clearly have self-deliberation in view. The difficulty, however,
is that the plural is never used this way in self-deliberations. Cassuto is of the opinion
that the "plural of exhortation" is more likely (see K.A. Matthews, *The New American
Commentary: An Exegetical Theological Exposition of Holy Scripture*, Genesis 1–11:26, vol 1A.
(Nashville: Broadman and Holman Publishers, 1996), n. 175).

[25] P.D. Miller, *Genesis 1–11: Studies in Structure and Theme, JSOTSup 8* (Sheffield: University of Sheffield, 1978, 9–26), strongly argues for this view. As far as Miller is concerned,
the OT warrants the idea of a heavenly court where plans are made and decisions rendered (see Job 1:6–12; 2:1–6; 12:8; 38:7; 1 Kings 22:19–28; Isa. 6:1–8; and Jer. 23:18). The
difficulty with this position is the phrase 'our image.' Could human beings be said to be
created in the image of the angels? Moreover, the theological stance of Gen. 1 is that

divine dialogue within the Godhead."[26] For the first time we see these passages used by the Christian writers in order to prove the activity of Christ and the Holy Spirit in creation in the Epistle to Barnabas (5:5; 6:12). Justin Martyr later expressed similar sentiments.[27] Irenaeus says that God was speaking to his two hands, the Son and the Spirit, when he said, "Let us make man."[28] Of course, the doctrine of the Trinity cannot be derived solely from the use of the plural pronouns in these passages; however, it must be said that a plurality within the unity of the Godhead is clearly indicated by these passages.

The Angel of Yahweh

The earliest books of the Old Testament also speak of Yahweh and the angel of Yahweh in a manner that sees the two as one, yet distinct. In some cases, the angel of Yahweh has divine titles, and he even receives worship (Ex. 23:21). In particular instances, as in the passage just cited, the Old Testament denotes 'angel' in the singular, but at other times the Old Testament clearly refers to angel in the plural (see Gen.18 and 19). The story of Abraham's encounter with the three men at Mamre, for instance, has several oscillations between singular and plural. The story opens with "The Lord (Yahweh) appeared to Abraham" (Gen. 18:1), yet Abraham "saw three men" (Gen. 18:2). He addressed these three men in the singular, "my lord" (Gen. 18:3), although in Genesis 18:4 he continued to speak to them in the plural, "you may all." Interestingly, the mysterious oscillation from singular to plural continues throughout the whole story. Although as Wainwright has noted, since the New Testament never used Gen. 18 in its treatment of the Trinitarian nature of God,[29] it is difficult to rule out any possibility of some seeds of the doctrine of the Trinity here.[30]

God has no antecedent partner with whom he could have created the universe, neither does Gen. 1 mention angels.

[26] Matthews, *The New American Commentary: An Exegetical Theological Exposition of Holy Scripture*, 161.

[27] J. Martyr, *Dialogue with Typho, a Jew. In Ante-Nicene Fathers: Translations of the Writings of the Fathers Down to AD 325* vol I. A. Roberts and J. Donaldson, eds. (Grand Rapids: Eerdmans, 1951) (see particularly the *Dial* 62:1).

[28] Irenaeus, Bishop of Lyons, "Against Heresies." *In Ante-Nicene Fathers: Translations of the Writings of the Fathers Down to AD 325* vol I. (See particularly IV, *Praef.* 4, xx.1; V, i.3, xxviii.4).

[29] A.W. Wainwright, *The Trinity in the New Testament* (London: SPCK, 1962), 28, 29.

[30] This position is not new to Christian scholarship. Wainwright has noted that

The Salvation Story

The salvation story presents the idea of plurality in the unity of God even more clearly. The whole point of the salvation story, which is a direct concern of about half of the Old Testament (narratives from Gen. to Ezra) and an indirect interest of the other half (much of the prophets, some parts of Psalms, wisdom literature, and the prophetic polemics), is to accent the uniqueness of the God of Israel and to bear Israel out as a nation which believes that its God, not gods, controls history.[31] The Old Testament demands that Yahweh alone is "… freely active in history, can alone legitimately claim the title *El-Lohim*, that all other *Elohim* are not such in reality, are nothings; that this Yahweh is the absolute Sovereign Lord," and that absolutely everything depends on him.[32]

Yet this Yahweh is understood by the Old Testament to have a messenger. Prophet Isaiah speaks simultaneously of Yahweh and of his anointed messenger of salvation upon whom is the Spirit of Yahweh (Isa. 61:1 f.). In the words of Henry:

> This messenger is revealed step by step as a distinct divine personality being variously designated as the Word, the Wisdom and the Son of God. While he is said to be "of old," the Mighty God, the Adonai, the Lord of David, Jehovah our righteousness, yet he is to be born of a virgin and to bear the sins of many.[33]

Hypostases of Yahweh

The Old Testament also confers the hypostases, *pneuma*, *sophia*, and *logos* to God. These hypostases are presented not as independent beings, but as personal realities whose existence is somehow integrated with that of Yahweh.[34]

Ambrose held a Trinitarian explanation of the Gen. 18 passage (Wainwright, *The Trinity in the New Testament*, 29). The authorities that Wainwright cites are: *De Spiritu Sancto*, II, Intro.4; *De Excessu fratris Satyri*, II, 96 cf. *De Fide*, I, xiii.80; *De Officiis Ministrorum*, II, xxi.16. Augustine, Ambrose's student, held a clearer Trinitarian view of the Gen. 18 text. As far as Augustine is concerned, all three persons of the Trinity appeared to Abraham (Augustine, *De Trinitate*, III, 25).

[31] Goldingay, *Approaches to Old Testament Interpretation*, 77–79.

[32] K. Rahner, *Theological Investigations I*. C. Ernest, trans. (London: Darton, Longman and Todd, 1965), 93.

[33] Henry, *God, Revelation and Authority*, 197.

[34] Henry, *God, Revelation and Authority*, 197 cf. AW. Wainwright, *The Trinity in the New Testament*, 29–40.

The Spirit

The Old Testament views the Spirit as a person and suggests that he can be grieved (Isa.63:10). It also says that he guides people and instructs them in the ways of Yahweh (Ps. 143:10, Neh. 9:20). Although the Old Testament uses the Hebrew word *ruah*, which is translated 'wind' or 'breath' and which later Judaism would regard as "light," "fire," "sound," or "object which has weight,"[35] it is obvious that the qualities that the Old Testament attaches to *ruah* do not belong to wind, breath, light, fire, sound, or solid bodies. Moreover, the emphasis of the Old Testament's understanding of *ruah* is clearly not about materiality; rather, the emphasis is on the quality of *ruah* as "… power, vitality, activity or life."[36] The Old Testament views this Spirit as generating from Yahweh and as belonging to Yahweh (Jud. 13:25; Is. 32:15; 42:1; 59:21). In some cases the Old Testament goes as far as identifying the Spirit with Yahweh (Ps.139:7). According to Wainwright, the occurrence of Spirit in Psalm 139:7 is "… equivalent to the Presence, which was a term used as a circumlocution for God."[37] In fact, other Old Testament texts separate the Spirit from God—although they closely link him with God as his power, and his breath that gives life, guides, and drives to action (see Ez. 37:9; Jud. 3:10). The fact that the Old Testament identifies the Spirit with Yahweh, while at the same time suggesting that the two are indeed distinct entities, is a point worth noting.

Wisdom

The Old Testament also identifies Yahweh, the deliverer of his people, with Wisdom. The Book of Wisdom 7:25 says the following regarding the relationship of Wisdom to God:

> For she is breath of the power of God,
> And a clear effluence of the glory of the Almighty;
> Therefore can nothing be defiled find entrance into her.
> For she is an effulgence from everlasting light,
> And an unspotted mirror of the working of God,
> And an image of his goodness.

---

[35] W.D. Davies, *Paul and Rabbinic Judaism: Some Rabbinic Elements in Pauline Theology* (London: SPCK, 1970), 183–185.

[36] Davies, *Paul and Rabbinic Judaism*, 183.

[37] Wainwright, *The Trinity in the New Testament*, 30.

According to the Book of Proverbs, Wisdom was brought forth by God (Prov. 8:22). But the Old Testament does not only see Wisdom as having her origin in God, but it also sees her as separate and distinct from God. It is because of this that Prov. 8:30 can speak of Wisdom as being the craftsman at the side of God. During the last four centuries before Christ, the Jews began to see God as transcendent and Wisdom as the explanation for God's activity in the world. Thus Sirach says the following about Wisdom: "I came forth from the mouth of the Most High, and covered the earth like a mist. I dwelt in high places, and my throne was in a pillar of cloud. Alone I have made the circuit of the vault of heaven and have walked in the depths of abyss" (Sir. 24:3). Elsewhere Wisdom is depicted as having been there from the beginning (Sir. 24:9), standing in a close relationship to God (Wis. 8:3), an "initiate in the knowledge of God, and as an associate in his works" (Wis. 8:4). It is no wonder that the term *Wisdom* was taken over by the Christian thinkers as a suitable term for explaining both the nature of Christ and the relationship of Christ to God.

The Word

The Old Testament views the Word of the Lord as an agent for accomplishing the will of Yahweh, thus Ps. 33:6 can say: "By the word of the Lord were the heavens made." This view of the Word enables the Old Testament to ascribe an independent existence to the Word. Isa. 55:11, for example, reports Yahweh as saying: "… so is my word that goes out from my mouth: it will not return to me empty, but will accomplish what I desire and achieve the purpose for which I sent it." Ps. 29 views "the voice" of the Lord in much the same way.

Whereas the Old Testament generally ascribed independent existence to the Word, the Targums[38] sometimes substituted the divine name with the expression "the Word (*Memra*)" and tended to see *Memra*

---

[38] Targum was a custom of giving a running translation of the Hebrew scripture in contexts where the scripture was still read in Hebrew, although the language had long ceased to be a spoken language. At first the Targums were only oral, but later they were written down. Since they were running translations, they gave the sense of the text being read and not of mechanical translation. At the time of the Targums, the Jews had ceased to pronounce the divine name, Yahweh, because of reverence and fear of breaking the third commandment. Because of this, the Targums avoided the name Yahweh and substituted expressions they thought were more appropriate instead (see L. Morris, *The Gospel According to John* (Grand Rapids: Eerdmans, 1971), 119).

more as a surrogate for the divine name Yahweh.[39] Thus, for the Jews, *Memra* was one of the ways in which you could speak about God without using the name. An example of such a case is Exod. 19:17. Morris has observed that our Bible renders this verse as: "And Moses brought forth the people out of the camp to meet God," but the Targum, on the other hand, reads "to meet the Word of God." Some Targums have as many as 320 cases where the divine name has been replaced with "the Word."[40]

The Hebrew concept of *Memra* raises two issues. Philo saw Logos[41] as "a second God" and at other times the concept meant for him "one God in action."[42] However, without going into much discussion we can conclude, in agreement with William Temple, that the Logos:

> ... alike for Jew and Gentile represents the ruling fact of the universe, and represents that fact as the self-expression of God. The Jew will remember that 'by the Word of the Lord were the heavens made', the Greek will think of the rational principle of which all natural laws are particular expressions. Both will agree that this Logos is the starting point of all things.[43]

This Logos, who is 'the starting point of all things,' is—on the one hand—a designation of the Divine, but—on the other hand—Logos is distinguished from the divine (as is evident in such texts as Isa. 55:11; Ps. 33:6; and Ps. 29.) The significance of these observations lies in the fact that the Old Testament's *Memra* allows us to see plurality in the one Godhead: There is God and "a second God."[44]

---

[39] F.H. Albright, *New Horizons in Biblical Research* (London: Oxford University Press, 1966), 45.

[40] A case in point here is the Targum of Jonathan. Morris has noted that this particular Targum is about the books in our Bible from Joshua to II Kings (excluding Ruth) and all the prophetical books (excluding Daniel). In this Targum alone, the divine name is substituted about 320 times by 'the Word' (see Morris, *The Gospel According to John*, 120).

[41] Philo used the term *Logos* about 1,300 times (see W.F. Howard, *Christianity According to St John* (London: Duckworth, 1943), 36 ff.

[42] Morris, *The Gospel According to John*, 121.

[43] W. Tempel, *Readings in St John's Gospel* (London: McMillan, 1939), 4. Several New Testament scholars are of the opinion that John's Logos owes both to Greek and Hebrew sources. Notable examples of such scholars are MacGregor, B.H. Streeter, and F.W. Gingrich (see details of discussion in Morris, *The Gospel According to John*, note 149).

[44] Morris, *The Gospel According to John*, 121.

The Trinitarian Testimonies in the New Testament

The Jewish Idea of Yahweh as Normative

The New Testament accepts the Old Testament's understanding of God and does not raise either the question of God's existence or that of the 'one' and the 'many.' It knows the God it testifies about as the God understood in Old Testament terms. Thus the New Testament believes that the God of Abraham, the God of Isaac, and the God of Jacob is the God who entered into a covenant relationship with Israel—his chosen people—and is the savior that the nations need. This savior is none other than Yahweh himself. The New Testament takes the Old Testament's concept of Yahweh (viewed within the perplexity of the 'one' and the 'many') as its normative, yet unspoken, theological background and the context of its own reconstruction of the doctrine of God.

In a sense, the picture of God in the New Testament is the same as the picture of God in the Old Testament. The exception is that the occurrence of the divine 'plurality' in the former is heightened, intensified, and clarified. The New Testament is not introducing a new and different understanding of God.[45] Instead, it sees itself as performing the necessary and essential task of sharpening the biblical (in this case the Old Testament's) picture of God for the community of faith. In the words of Berkhof, the coming of God to man that we see in the Old Testament is in the New Testament "immeasurably intensified, and thereby given a completion as well: he comes to men in a man, in one who as 'the Son' stands in a unique relationship to him as 'the Father'."[46]

---

[45] John Bright assumes that the New Testament provides a criterion of distinguishing between acceptable and unacceptable aspects of the Old Testament (J. Bright, *The Authority of the Old Testament* (London: SCM Press, 1967), 200, 211–212). John Goldingay believes, however, that "… the New Testament leans, if at all, the opposite way: the question was not whether the OT was Christian but whether the NT was biblical. In reaction to this approach Arnold van Ruler speaks of the OT as the real Bible and the NT being its explanatory glossary" (J. Goldingay, *Approaches to Old Testament Interpretation* (Leicester: Inter-Varsity Press, 1981), 34).

[46] H. Berkhof, *Christian Faith: An Introduction to the Study of Faith*. S. Woudstra, trans. (Grand Rapids: Eerdmans, 1979), 19,20.

One God and Father

The New Testament regards God as one and that this one God is the Father of Jesus Christ. The New Testament passages that describe God as one are Mk. 10:18; 12:29; Matt. 23:9; Jn. 5:44; 17:3; Rom. 3:30; I Cor. 8:4, 6; Gal. 3:20; Eph. 4:6; I Tim. 1:17; 2:5; Jas. 2:19; 4:12; and Jude 25. Whereas these passages speak of God as one, Wainwright has noted that:

> … in eight out of these fifteen passages (Mark 10:18; Matt. 23:9; I Cor 8:6; Gal. 3:20; Eph. 4:6; I Tim 2:5; Jude 25; John 17:3) God is explicitly distinguished from Jesus Christ. In three of the passages (Matt.23:9; I Cor. 8:6; Eph. 4:6) and also in the context of John 17:3, God is called Father.[47]

Although the idea of God as Father is not limited to the Hebrew-Christian tradition, the idea of the fatherhood of God found in the New Testament is derived from Hebrew thought.[48] The title is used in connection with creation (Isa. 64:8), the election of Israel as a nation (Jer. 31:9; Mal. 2:10; Isa.1:2; 30:1; 45:11; Jer. 3:22; Hosea 11:1 and Ex. 4:22), and the anointed king (2 Sam. 7:14; Ps. 2:7; 89:27). Jesus generally referred to God as the Father in the Gospels. Four of these occurrences are in the Gospel of Mark, eight are in the material common to Luke and Matthew, seven are in the material peculiar to Luke, and twenty two in the material peculiar to Matthew.[49] The title is rather frequent in the Johannine writings. In these citations Jesus referred to God using the Aramaic word *abbā*[50] meaning 'my Father.' There is no

---

[47] Wainwright, *The Trinity in the New Testament*, 42.

[48] Schrenk, discussing the title 'Father' in the TWNT, V, has been able to clearly explain that the idea of the fatherhood of God is found in many ancient religions. (1) The early Indian religion regarded Dyaus or Heaven as Father. (2) The Greeks addressed Zeus as 'Father Zeus.' (3) Osiris was said to be the father of Horus. (4) Later Greek philosophy referred to God as the father of men (see the Stoic Epictetus) and the Father of Cosmos (see the later Platonists Numenius and Porphyry) (Schrenk, TWNT, V, pp. 951–956). (5) Plato's *Republic* also allows us to see the title 'Father' as connected to that which he believed to be the absolute reality; namely, the Idea of the Good, while his *Timaeus* assigns the title 'Father' to the Demiurge (see Rep. VI.506e and Tim.41a).

[49] Wainwright, *The Trinity in the New Testament*, 44.

[50] Scholars suggest at least two ways the New Testament uses the Aramaic *abbā* as an address to God. In passages like Gal. 4:6; Rom. 8:15, Matt. 11:16, Luke 10:21, Mark 5:41 and 14:36, *abbā* is used in a determinative sense as in the Greek ὁ πατηρ (the father). In these citations *abbā* suggests the determinative form of *ab* (father). The second usage, the vocative, has generated much debate. Wainwright, for example, argues that the citation in Mark 14:36 indicates that *abbā* is derived from children's baby talk ('daddy', 'papa'). J. Jeremias initially understood *abbā* in this sense, but he later abandoned that line of

evidence in pre-Christian, Palestinian Judaism that an individual Jew ever addressed God as *abbā* since this implied too great a familiarity. Wainwright has, therefore, rightly argued that "when Jesus used *abba* of God he was making a startling innovation. He was claiming a relationship with God that was closer than that which was claimed by any of his countrymen. He was claiming a unique kind of sonship."[51]

It is clear from the New Testament evidence that the New Testament places emphasis on God as the Father of Jesus Christ. This emphasis, viewed in the context of other statements in which the divinity of the Son is affirmed or implied, allowed the Christians to see the Father-Son relationship and therefore a plurality within the Godhead. The Christians, as we see in the Pauline corpus, viewed God as "the Father of our Lord Jesus Christ" (see Rom. 15:6; 2 Cor.1:3; 11:31; Eph. 1:3; Col. 1:3). Although the Christians understood that by the term *abbā* Jesus claimed a unique sonship, they took the liberty and used the term in their prayers. Thus for the Christians, God was related to Jesus in a unique way, but he was also 'our Father' (see I Cor. 8:6; 2 Cor.1:2; Gal. 1:4; etc.).

Jesus Christ as Divine

The New Testament does not see itself as having fabricated the idea that Christ is God. Rather, it sees the idea as having its roots in the text of the Old Testament. We have already seen what the Jews thought of 'Wisdom' and 'Word.' It is no wonder that the Christian thought would apply these titles to Christ. The other Old Testament themes that are equally important in understanding the Old Testament's roots of the divinity of Christ are 'Lord' (the one who has dominion over the created universe), 'Son of God' (he who is divine and has familial relationship with the Father), 'Son of Man' (he who comes to save, serve and judge mankind), 'Christ' or 'the Anointed one' (the one anointed to rule over men), and 'High Priest' (he who appears before God to make intercessions for men). These expressions and other New

---

thought and referred to it as "a piece of inadmissible naivety" (Jeremias, *The Prayers of Jesus* (London: SCM, 1967), 63). The other scholars who understand *abbā* in the sense described by Wainwright are J.G.D. Dunn, *Jesus and the Spirit* (Grand Rapids: Wm. B. Eerdmans, 1975),21–26; *Christology in the making* (Philadelphia: Westminster Press, 1980), 22–23); and M.J. Borg *Jesus: A New Vision* (San Francisco: HarperSanFrancisco, 1987), 45.

[51] Wainwright, *The Trinity in the New Testament*, 45.

Testament terms such as ηικον of God and απαγασμα of God explicitly or implicitly occur in several places in the New Testament.[52]

The titles and the terms are to be viewed as illustrations of the New Testament's position on the identity of Christ and not as proof 'expressions.' They identify Christ with Yahweh, the God of Israel, but without confusing the two. Let us look at the use of 'Lord' as an example. The New Testament does not only call Jesus *Lord*, but it also transfers to Jesus ideas and quotations which originally referred to Yahweh (see Mark 12:35–37 cf. Ps. 110:1; Matt. 7:21; Luke 6:46; Acts 2:21 cf. Joel 2:32 and Rom.10:13; 7:59,60; I Cor. 11:23; 16:22b; Phil. 2:5–11 cf. Isa. 45:23; Eph. 4:8 cf. Ps.68:18; John 12:40,41 cf. Isa. 6:10). Although the scripture uses the term *Lord* in reference to Jesus, it seems to be fonder of the term *Son*. Apparently, the idea of the 'Son' gives the best account of the nature of interaction within the Godhead. The Father-Son relationship does three significant things. First of all, it expresses how both Father and Son were God; second, it expresses the logical priority of the Father without detracting from the divinity of the Son; and finally, it best accounts for the unity of the two persons.[53]

The New Testament texts that expressly call Jesus 'God' are Rom. 9:5, Jn 1:1, 18, 20:28, IJn 5:20, Titus 2:11ff., Heb. 1.8 and 2 Pet. 1.1. What follows are some brief comments on Rom. 9:5, Jn 1:1, 18, 20:18 and Titus 2:11ff. The grammar of Rom. 9:5 indicates that Christ is clearly called God. Scott and Kirk argue that Paul could not have identified Christ with God since to do so would compromise Paul's thought that is deeply rooted in his character and his strict Jewish background.[54] It is difficult to join with Scott and Kirk on this score. The context of Rom. 9:5 indicates that Paul contemplated the rejection of Christ by the Jews. This thought, explains Wainwright, led him to proclaim what he perceived to be the actual identity of Christ; namely, that he was ϑεος (God) and ηυλογετος (blessed).[55] Again there is no doubt that John the evangelist intended from the beginning of the fourth Gospel to identify Christ with God. The fourth Gospel begins with a declaration of the divinity of Christ (Jn 1:1 and 1:18) and ends with the confession of the divinity of Christ (Jn 20:28).

---

[52] C.B. Kaiser, *The Doctrine of God* (London: Marshall Morgan and Scott, 1982), 29–41.

[53] Kaiser, *The Doctrine of God*, 41.

[54] See Anderson Scott, *Christianity According to St Paul*, 274 and Kirk's, *Romans*, 103–104.

[55] Wainwright, *The Trinity in the New Testament*, 54–58.

The study of the Pastoral Epistles yields at least two reasons in
Paul's letter to Titus (2:11–13) why Christ should be called God. (1) The
Pastoral Epistles call both God and Christ 'Savior' (see 1 Tim.1:1, 15;
2:3; 4:10; 2 Tim. 1:8–10; 4:10; Titus 1:3, 2:11–13, 3:4–7). If the title Savior
is given as freely to Christ as it is to God in these Epistles, then there
is simply no reason one would find it strange if the same Epistles called
Christ *God*. (2) The Phrase, 'Great God,' does not occur for the first
time in Titus 2:13. This expression is used of God in the Septuagint
(eg., Deut.10:17; Ps. 85:10; Isa. 26:4; Jer. 39:19; and in Dan. 2:45). The
fact that it is used of Christ in Titus indicates that at some point the
Christians transferred this term to Christ.

The other New Testament passages that explicitly call Christ *God*
are 2 Thess. 1:12; Col. 2:2; Jn 17:3; 1 Jn 5:20; Jas 1:1; Matt. 1:23; and
1 Tim. 1:17. The texts in which Christ is explicitly called God, explains
Rahner, are "… vastly outnumbered by the other texts in which the
New Testament intends to express Christ's divine nature in one way
or another and yet does not make use of the word [theos]."[56] Passages
that call Christ *God* in an indirect way are those that refer to Jesus
as the Son of God, those that use the title *Lord* in reference to Jesus,
those that indicate the worship of Jesus, those that draw the connection
between Jesus and judgment, those that link Jesus to the origin and the
sustenance of Creation, and those that describe Jesus as Savior.

The evidence of the New Testament is that Jesus is known as "God
over all" (Rom. 9:5), as judge and creator (Col. 1:16; 1 Thess.5:2;
2 Thess.2:1–12), as the image of the invisible God (Col. 1:15), and as
Lord in the same way that God is Lord (1 Cor. 12:3). However, although
the New Testament does not hesitate to call Jesus *Lord* and to transfer
to him ideas and quotations that were originally reserved for Yahweh,
it must be noted that it also adequately distances the Father and Christ
(see greetings of Pauline letters; I Cor. 8:5,6; Eph. 4:5,6; Jn 20:28). It
is clear from this manner of speaking of the Son and the Father that
the New Testament authors were aware of the plurality in the Godhead, and that they sought to preserve the divinity of the Father without demeaning the identity of the Son.

---

[56] Rahner, *Theological Investigations I*, 137.

The Holy Spirit as Divine

The Holy Spirit, according to the scriptural revelation, is also called the Spirit of God or the Spirit of Christ (see Rom. 8:9). The New Testament does not introduce his work for the first time; rather, it is already known in Israel by the time of the New Testament. Judges, kings, and prophets are known to have been endowed with the Spirit of God. The Messiah, according to the Old Testament, will receive the Spirit of God (Isa. 11:2), the Spirit of God provides the covenant, and this Spirit will dominate the end time (Joel 2:28). The New Testament does not seek to prove either the existence or the deity of the Holy Spirit. It proceeds from the understanding that the Old Testament teaches the divinity of the Holy Spirit, and that what is said about the Holy Spirit in the Old Testament has either been fulfilled or is about to be fulfilled.

Like the Old Testament, the New Testament sees the Spirit as a person (Isa. 63:10; Ps.143:10, Neh.9:20). The Old Testament uses the Hebrew word *ruah*, which is translated as 'wind' or 'breath' and that later Judaism would regard as "light," "fire," "sound," or "object which has weight."[57] It is obvious, however, that the qualities the Old Testament attaches to *ruah* do not belong to wind, breath, light, fire, sound, or solid bodies. Moreover, the emphasis of the Old Testament's understanding of *ruah* is clearly not materiality; rather, it is the quality of *ruah* as "… power, vitality, activity or life."[58] It is because of this that the New Testament describes the Holy Spirit as a person. Since he is a person, he is called 'Comforter' (Jn 14:26; 15:26; 16:13; and 1Jn 5:6). He speaks (Mark 13:11; Acts 1:16; 8:29; 10:19; 11:12; 13:2; and 28:25), forbids (Acts 16:6), thinks good (Acts 15:28), appoints (Acts 20:28), sends (Acts 13:4), and bears witness (Acts 5:32; 20:23; Rom. 8:16). He prevents (Acts 16:7), cries (Rom. 8:26), leads (Rom. 8:14), and makes intercession (Rom. 8:26). He is also depicted as capable of being deceived (Acts 5:3), tempted (Acts 5:9), resisted (Acts 7:51; 6:10), and grieved (Eph. 4:30).

The New Testament also identifies the Spirit with God in the same way as is seen in the Old Testament (see Jud.13:25; Isa. 32:15; 42:1; 59:21; Ps.139:7). The Apostle John depicts the Holy Spirit as performing a unique function of God, viz the function of judgment (Jn 16:8–11). Paul, in his letter to the Romans, does not only view the Spirit as gen-

---

[57] Davies, *Paul and Rabbinic Judaism*, 183–185.
[58] Davies, *Paul and Rabbinic Judaism*, 183.

erating from the Father, but he also views the Spirit as belonging to
the Father (see Rom. 8:9 ff.). The other reference in which the Spirit
is identified with God is 2 Cor. 3:17–18. The context of this text is Ex
34:34, which speaks of Moses entering the Lord's presence (see 2 Cor.
3:16). There is no doubt that Paul clearly identifies the Spirit with Yahweh in the passage of 2 Cor. 3:17–18. While these examples adequately
illustrate the fact that the New Testament identifies the Holy Spirit with
Yahweh, it is important to note that the New Testament indicates that
the Holy Spirit could be worshipped directly (see Phil. 3:3). The crucial
phrase here is οι πνευμτι θεου λατευοντες, which could be translated
"... who worship by the Spirit of God" (NIV) or "who worship the
Spirit of God." The grammar of the text of Phil. 3:3 in the original
could allow for the second reading since, as Wainwright argues, the
verb λατευω is followed by an object in the dative case—πνευματι θεου,
thus the verse is evidence for the practice of the worship of the Spirit.[59]

While these passages and references identify the Spirit with the
Father, other occurrences separate the Spirit from the Father. A case
in point is 1 Cor. 6:19–20. In verse 19 of this text Paul speaks of the
Holy Spirit "... who is in you, whom you have received from God."
In this passage the Holy Spirit is seen as he who is given and God
as the giver. The other instances where the New Testament obviously
distances the Holy Spirit from the Father are those in which the Spirit
is depicted as speaking, forbidding, appointing, being grieved, and so
on. Occurrences such as these speak of an agent who, though divine as
seen from other Old and New Testament passages, is also adequately
distanced from the Father. The point clearly made by this distinction
is that there is plurality in the Godhead and that the scripture, both
the New and the Old Testament, does not confuse the Father and the
Spirit.

The New Testament does not only speak of the Spirit in a manner
that identifies him with the Father while at the same time putting
adequate distance between the two, it also speaks of the relationship of
the Son and the Spirit in a similar fashion. Again, the New Testament
is not introducing anything new here; in the Old Testament the 'One

---

[59] Wainwright sees this reading as a possibility). He recognizes that Augustine held
this interpretation, and he argues that there is clear evidence for worship—not just
through the Spirit but also to the Spirit. According to Wainwright, the Holy Spirit was
"... worshipped in conjunction with Father and Son" (Wainwright, *The Trinity in the
New Testament*, 228).

Coming' and the Holy Spirit are already linked, and this is done in such a way that the two are not confused (see Isa. 11:2; 42:1; and 61:2). John the Baptist carried the link into the New Testament and spoke of two distinct divine agents; viz the Spirit and the 'One Coming' (Mark 1:8; Matt.3:11; Luke 3:16). The 'One Coming'—namely, Christ—also saw a link between himself and the Spirit. The following passages quote Jesus as speaking about the Holy Spirit: Mark 3:29 cf. Matt.12:31 and Luke 12:10; Mark 13:11 cf. Luke 12:12, 21:15; Luke 11:13; Luke 4:18 cf. Isa.61; and Mark 12:36 cf. Matt. 22:43, Ps. 110:1.

The way in which Jesus testifies about the Holy Spirit in these passages clearly indicates that he has put a reasonable distance between himself and the Holy Spirit, while he has simultaneously brought to surface the divine nature of the Holy Spirit. The apostles, notably Paul, see a close relationship between Christ and the Spirit (see the texts 2 Cor. 3:17–18; Rom. 8:9 ff. and the phrases 'in Christ' and 'in Spirit'). However, what Paul is saying in these references must be seen in the context of the correlation between the Spirit and Christ that is already taught in the Gospels.[60] Thornton has explained the thinking of the apostles on this issue in the following words:

> In St Paul's teaching the parallelism and identification between Christ and His Spirit are so close, that by looking at this side only we might suppose them to be simply identical in all respects, and so conclude that the Two must be taken to be One. If, however, we note the marked differences of Pauline language in describing the functions respectively of Christ and His Spirit, and if we then turn to the teachings of St John about the Paraclete, it will become clear that this simple identification cannot stand. The identification is best understood as that of a mutual interpenetration with divergence of functions.[61]

Perhaps what is also important for our purposes here is the way the New Testament introduces the triad—God the Father, Christ, and the Spirit. Some of the New Testament passages which concretely situate the Holy Spirit in the context of the Father and the Son and make an explicit statement about the divinity of the Holy Spirit are Matt. 28:19,

---

[60] The synoptic Gospels present Christ as having been conceived of the Spirit (Matt. 1:18; Lk.12: 10) and closely links the Spirit with Christ (see Mark 3:29 ff.). John also emphasizes the correlation between Christ and the Spirit (see 1Jn 2:1; Jn 14:16). Paul, as Stauffer notes, leaves no doubt that the Father, the Son, and the Holy Spirit are all "linked in an indissoluble threefold relation" (see Ethelbert Stauffer, *Theos: The Uniqueness of God*, TDNT, 3:107 ff.).

[61] Thornton quoted in Wainwright, *The Trinity in the New Testament*, 220.

Luke 24:49, John 14:16, 17; 15:26; 16:7–11, 12–15, Acts 2:32–33; 38–39;
5:31–32; 7:55–56; 10:38; 11:15–17, Rom. 5:1–5; 8:9–11; 14–17; 14:17–18;
15:15–16; 15:30, I Cor. 2:6–16; 6:11; 6:15–20; 12:3; 12:4–6, II Cor.1:21–
22; 13:13, Gal.4:4–6, Eph.1:3–14; 1:17; 2:18–22; 3:14–19; 4:4–6; 5:15–20,
II Thes. 2:13, Titus 3:4–11, Heb. 2:2–4; 10:29–31, I Pet.:1–2; 2:4–5; 4:14,
I Jn 3:23–24; 4:11–16; 5:5–8, and Jude 20–21. The New Testament does
not only view these associations as formal; this certainly is one of the
ways in which the New Testament seeks to state the divinity of the
Holy Spirit. The divinity of the Holy Spirit is clearly taught in Acts
28:25, where Paul emphasizes to the Jews in Rome that the One who
revealed the divine warning to the prophet Isaiah against the spiritual
callousness of the Hebrews was none other than the Spirit.

Conclusion

The doctrine of the Trinity, as we have noticed, is a teaching that is
deeply rooted in the Bible. The Old Testament has such Trinitarian
vestiges as the first person, plural pronouns, the Angel of Yahweh, the
salvation story, and the hypostasis of Yahweh. The New Testament, on
the other hand, is more explicit on Trinitarianism. In it we find clear
evidence of One God who is worshipped in Three Persons. Yahweh of
Israel is depicted as one God and the Father of Jesus Christ. Christ is
described as Lord, Son of God, Son of Man, the Anointed One, and
High Priest. The Holy Spirit is described as not only generating from
the Father, but he is also identified with and distanced from both the
Father and the Son. Whenever the New Testament describes Christ
and the Holy Spirit as of the same divine nature as the Father, the
indication is that the idea is not a New Testament innovation, but
that it has its roots in the Old Testament. The fundamental issue,
therefore, is not whether the doctrine of the Trinity is scriptural. We
have demonstrated in this chapter that the doctrine of the Trinity is in
fact scriptural. What we see as a major stumbling block is whether we
are prepared to accept the authority of the scriptures on this issue.

CHAPTER TWO

THE EMERGENCE OF THE
DOCTRINE OF IMMANENT TRINITY

INTRODUCTION

What this chapter purposes to explore is the reaction of the early church to the biblical testimony about God and the significance of that reaction to the Christian faith. Perhaps the best place to begin this task is by quoting St. Augustine (extensively) on what he understood as the position of the church fathers who preceded him on the doctrine of God. His book, *De Trinitate*, I, iv, 7 reads as follows:

> All those Catholic expounders of the divine Scriptures, both Old and New, whom I have been able to read, who have written before me concerning the Trinity, Who is God, have purposed to teach, according to the Scriptures, this doctrine, that the Father, and the Son, and the Holy Spirit intimate a divine unity of one and the same substance in an indivisible equality; and therefore that they are not three Gods, but one God: Although the Father hath begotten the Son, and so he who is the Father is not the Son; and the Son is begotten by the Father, and so he who is the Son is not the Father; and the Holy Spirit is neither the Father nor the Son, but only the Spirit of the Father and of the Son, Himself also co-equal with the Father and the Son, and pertaining to the unity of the Trinity. Yet not that this Trinity was born of the virgin Mary, and crucified under Pontius Pilate, and buried, and rose again the third day, and ascended to heaven but only the Son. Nor again that this Trinity descended in the form of a dove upon Jesus when he was baptized; nor that on the day of Pentecost, after the ascension of the Lord, "when there came a sound from heaven, as of a rushing mighty wind", the same Trinity "sat upon each of them with cloven tongues like as of fire", but only the Holy Spirit. Nor that this Trinity said from heaven, "Thou art my Son", whether when he was baptized by John, or when the voice sounded, saying, "I have both glorified it, and will glorify it again;" but that it was a word of the Father only, spoken to the Son; although the Father, the Son and the Holy Spirit, as they are indivisible so work indivisibly. This is also my faith, since it is the Catholic faith.[1]

---

[1] Augustine, Bishop of Hippo, *De Trinitate in Basic Writings of St Augustine*, vol II. E.J. Oates, ed. (New York: Random House Publishers, 1948), I, iv, 7.

As far as Augustine is concerned, the statement given above is his
faith as it is also the Catholic faith. For him, as it was for the Ante-
Nicene and the Nicene fathers, this is also the starting-point of faith;
initium fidei.[2] The fathers began by believing the truth that the personal
coming of God to man in the Old Testament had been realized in
the incarnation of the Son and in the outpouring of the Holy Spirit.
Believing this basic truth, they then proceeded to understand its full
meaning. The fathers saw this truth in the Old and the New Testaments. However, they wished to access it not through the anthropomorphisms of the Judaism of the time, but via the idea of 'substance,'
which was in vogue in the Greco-Roman context of the time, and
which they redefined to express the concept of the 'numerical unity'
of the divine essence in distinction from the "specific unity."[3] The principle of the 'numerical unity' allowed the fathers to articulate, for the
Greco-Roman situation, both the Old Testament's ideas of monotheism and the New Testament's position that this same Yahweh of the
Old Testament faith has revealed himself in the Son and in the Holy
Spirit.

The Problem of the 'Third Race'

The problem of how to define the 'one' and the 'many' in God was
a major theological concern for the early church, but—behind this
concern—we can also see mainstream Christianity struggling with the
question of its own identity. The same fathers who were involved in the
Trinity debate were also involved with the identity question. Justin, Tertullian, Athanasius, the Cappadocians, and Augustine were all aware
that they were not Jews, and the way that they wished to explain the
God they worshiped differed significantly from the perspective that the
Jews held. They also knew that they were Greco-Romans, and they

---

[2] Augustine, *De Trinitate*, I, I, 1.

[3] According to Shedd, 'numerical unity' is distinct from 'specific unity.' The latter
refers to the kind of unity in mankind. "In this case there is division of substance—
part after part of the specific nature being separated and formed, by propagation into
individuals. No human individual contains the whole of the specific nature. But in the
case of the numerical unity of Trinity, there is no division of essence. The whole of the
Divine nature is in each divine person" (Shedd in P. Schaff, *A Select Library of the Nicene
Fathers of the Christian Church*, vol iii (Grand Rapids: Eerdmans, 1956), 20). Of particular
interest here is Shedd's annotation of Augustine's *De Trinitate*, I, iv, 7.

used the infrastructures of that culture to express their belief in the God that they had come to know in Christ. Although the infrastructure of their culture was so important to them, they also maintained that they were not of the Greco-Roman world since the God they knew and worshipped was not θεος as conceived by the Greek thought, but Yahweh of Israel.

The destruction of the Jerusalem Temple in AD 70 and the quelled Jewish revolt of AD 135 (led by Simon Bar Kochba against the Roman power) forced Judaism and Judeo-Christianity to begin to talk about their identities openly.[4] When Judeo-Christianity received its independence from Judaism, (what later became) mainstream Christianity found Judeo-Christianity lacking in the necessary intellectual infrastructure as well as the form of faith that the former wanted to identify with. Therefore, mainstream Christianity did not feel at home within Judeo-Christianity, and so its search for identity continued.

There are two distinct aspects of the concept of Judeo-Christianity that are worth bringing to attention. On the one hand, the concept of Judeo-Christianity represents a complex of heresies that arose out of Judaism but claim Christian identity, and, on the other hand, there is the Judeo-Christianity that was conceived as a "cultural form."[5] As a 'cultural form,' Judeo-Christianity is a whole new system of operation "… with its own particular type of imagination, its own strange manner of conception and mode of speech."[6] And so, in a way, the Judeo-Christian heresies were not only preceded by the cultural form of Judeo-Christianity, but that cultural form also provided the heresies with the necessary intellectual infrastructures. Some of the well known heresies falling under Judeo-Christianity are the Ebionites (Jesus is the greatest prophet but not the son of God), Elkasites (a simple prophet who had many reincarnations), Christian Zealotism (Jesus is an ordinary man; he had nothing to do with the creation of the world as that was done by angels), Samarito-Christian Gnosis, Sethians and Ophites, as well as the Carpocrates (these groups agree on the conception that Jesus was just the son of Joseph and was not in any way different from other men).[7] Given the nature of these sects and the theological posi-

---

[4] Bediako, *Theology and Identity*, 34.

[5] B.J.F. Lonergan, *The Way to Nicea. Dialectical Development of Trinitarian Theology* (Philadelphia: Westminister Press, 1976), 18.

[6] Lonergan, *The Way to Nicea*, 19.

[7] J. Danielou, *The Theology of Jewish Christianity*. J.A. Baker, trans. and ed. (London: Darton, Longman and Todd, 1964), 55–85. See also his *A History of the Christian Doctrine*

tions they advanced, it is obvious that mainstream Christianity had to find a way to distinguish itself.

Apart from breaking with Judaism and later with Judeo-Christianity, the entrance of mainstream Christianity into the Hellenistic world also introduced its own dynamics. The Christian faith soon found itself in a situation where some of the elements of Greek thought that it used in explaining the biblical picture of God heavily influenced the manner in which the faith understood and spoke about God. Some of the Greek concepts which mainstream Christianity used in the task of formulating the doctrine of God for the Hellenistic context are those that connect θεος with the Greek concepts of τιθεμι, θεος, θεορεω, or θεαμαι. The other Greek concepts used in this regard and which influenced the way in which mainstream Christianity understood and spoke about God are the transcendence of θεος, indivisibility of θεος, the idea of the 'Spirit,' and the problem of form.[8]

In some way the use of these Greek ways of understanding θεος facilitated the rise of the Christian heterodox groups such as Gnosticism,[9] Adoptionism,[10] Patripassianism,[11] Sabellianism or Modalistic monarchianism,[12] Subordinationism,[13] Arianism,[14] and Marcionism.[15] Once again the church found itself in a situation which required that it distance itself from the Greek theism as well as from these Christian sects that were born within that framework of the Greek understanding of θεος.

Before the Council of Nicea, vol I. J.A. Baker, trans. and ed. (London: Darton, Longman and Todd, 1964).

[8] G.L. Prestige, *God in Patristic Thought* (London: SPCK, 1952), 1–24.

[9] Gnosticism is the idea that God, the Creator, and the true God are not and cannot be the same.

[10] Adoptionism is the idea that God adopted the man, Jesus, as Son. He never was God from the beginning. One very vocal theologian who advocated adoptionism is Paul of Samosata.

[11] The argument of this position is that if the Son is God he must be identical with the Father. Praxeas has traditionally been identified with this position.

[12] This view sees God as a monad with three successive modes of existence; Noetus and Sabellius are good examples in this category.

[13] Subordinationism sees the Son as subordinate to the Father, and, therefore, he cannot be divine in the same sense as the Father; some well known surbordinationists are Arius, Origen, and Eusebius.

[14] Arianism is the notion that the Father alone is ingenerate. The Son, according to this view, was created at a point in time and, therefore, is *heteroousios*. Arius himself propagated this line of thought.

[15] Marcionism is the view that the Creator God of the Jewish religion is incompatible with the God revealed in Christ.

The fathers did not find the need to distance themselves from both Judaism and Judeo-Christianity, and from Hellenism and the Greco-Roman forms of Christianity strange. In the New Testament writings, the identity of Christianity as a "race, a nation, a people" is evident (see 1 Pet. 2:9). Peter preferred to use 'a race, a nation, a people' in his reference to the Christians. In contrast, Paul speaks about "the Jews, the Greeks, and the community of faith" (see 1 Cor. 10:32 cf. John 4:21 ff.). By the time of the fathers, this triple division on the basis of religion and worship had received acceptance as the basis for developing a distinct Christian self-consciousness in the Greco-Roman context.[16] The triple distinction—Greeks, Jews, and Christians—is already available in the anonymous writing, *The Preaching of Peter*, which dates from the early second century AD; the epistle, *To Diognetus*, which also belongs to the early part of the second-century AD; and in the *Apology* of Aristides that is addressed to Emperor Antoninus Pius. Bediako has noted from these three documents of the early Christian apologetics

> ... that by the middle of the second century AD, the understanding of the Christian faith as "the new. ... third way" of religious apprehension and manner of worship was of considerable influence in Christian centres of thought. Consequently, the triad of the Greeks (Gentiles), Jews and Christians seems to have become "the Church's basal conception of history."[17]

It is clear from these developments that from the time of the apostles, the Christians had consistently looked for their own identity. The formulation of the doctrine of God in Trinitarian terms serves in part as a statement of the identity of the Christian faith in the context of the triad. Based on the doctrine of the Trinity, mainstream Christian faith wished to make it clear to Judaism, to Judeo-Christianity, to Hellenism, and to the various forms of Greco-Roman Christianity that it was different, and that it wished to formulate the doctrine of God within the provisions of the Christian faith it had embraced.

---

[16] Bediako, *Theology and Identity*, 36.
[17] Bediako, *Theology and Identity*, 38, 39.

MONOTHEISM

The Christian and the Talmudic Tradition
know Christianity as Monotheistic

The early church confessed belief in one God.[18] Such a strong identity with the *Shema* (Deut. 6:4) was inevitable since the church began in a Jewish environment, had the chief propagators and many converts from Judaism, took the scriptures of Judaism and saw its own writings as presupposing that foundation, and viewed itself as a Jewish sect. The Apostle Paul in 1 Cor. 8: 5, 6 gives what has been considered a paraphrase of the Jewish *Shema*, which he, as a Jew, must have recited twice a day:

> For even if there are so called gods, whether in heaven or on earth (as indeed there are many 'gods' and many 'lords'), yet for us there is but one God, the Father from whom all things come and for whom we live; and there is but one Lord, Jesus Christ, through whom all things came and through whom we live (1 Cor. 8:5,6; NIV).

In these verses, Paul splits the *Shema* between the Father and the Son in an unprecedented way, but also in a way that seems natural to him. As far as Paul is concerned, the Father is Lord and the Son is Lord, and yet they are not two Lords.

It is not just the Christian faith that saw itself as monotheistic; the Rabbinic thought of the second century also viewed Christianity as monotheist.[19] The issue, which Justin raised to Trypho in the texts cited above, was the existence of ητερος θεος.[20] Skarsaune has summarized the thesis of Justin's argument in the following words: "Christ, not the Father, was the one who appeared in the theophanies of the Old Testament, and that he is to be identified with God's Wisdom, who is spoken of in the Bible as a second divine person, begotten by God, but not separated from him."[21] In response to this thesis, Trypho does not say that that particular position destroys the Christian claim to monotheism,

---

[18] See D.K. McKim, *Theological Turning Points: Major Issues in Christian Thought* (Atlanta: Knox, 1988), 5–6.

[19] See Justin's *Dialogue with Trypho the Jew*; chapter 10—chapter 19; chapter 55—chapter 63.

[20] *Dial.* 55.1.

[21] O. Skarsaune, "Is Christianity Monotheistic? A Perspective on a Jewish / Christian Debate" in *Studia Patristica* vol 29, 357; cf. *Dial.* 56–62, 126–129.

in fact, Typho already believes that the scripture may know a ητερος θεος.[22] Instead, Trypho is portrayed as commending the Christians for retaining the fundamental part of the Torah; namely, the one against idolatry. In *Dialogue* 18.3–19.1 Justin argues that the Christians' readiness for martyrdom that resulted from their rejection of idolatry testifies to the fact that they would keep the whole commandment if they viewed that as necessary. Trypho notes the force of Justin's argument and says: "This is precisely what puzzles us, and rightly so, because, when you endure such things, why don't you observe all other customs (also), which we are now discussing?"[23]

The implication of this submission of the pre-Nicene sources is that the divinity of Christ and of the Holy Spirit does not reject the Jewish understanding of monotheism. In fact, there is a general lack of aware-ness that the admission of the divinity of the Son and of the Holy Spirit may create theological problems to the Jewish concept of monothe-ism.[24] If such awareness were there, Justin would not have raised the issue of ητερος θεος with Trypho, for such a debate would have hurt Justin's case. Trypho, on the other hand, would have raised our atten-tion to the incompatibility of the idea of ητερος θεος with the monothe-ism in his dialogue with Justin since the point of contention would be known to be untrue by everyone. Before Justin, Philo in *Qu. Gen.* II.62 had already written about the *Logos* as δευτερος θεος, and the Jewish thought of the time did not seem to have an issue to raise against such a position.

A third-century Rabbinic statement that is recorded in the *Babylonian Talmud, Megilla* 13a (Socino trans., 74) and attributed to Rabbi Johanan defines whoever rejects idolatry as a 'Jew,' that is "one who proclaims the unity (of God)." Skarsaune has noted a Hebrew wordplay here: "'Jehudi' is modified to 'Jechidi', one who proclaims that God is one, 'echad'. So, the one who proclaims the unity or the one-ness of God is the one who rejects idolatry."[25] According to this criterion, as Skarsaune has noted, the Christians of the third-century church qualify as *Jechidim*. Therefore, the church did not just understand itself as monotheistic;

---

[22] Skarsaune, "Is Christianity Monotheistic?", 362.
[23] *Dial.* 19.1. The argument here as far as Trypho is concerned—if the Christians are willing to die for their monotheistic conviction, they are not only monotheistic but should also observe all the Jewish customs.
[24] Skarsaune, "Is Christianity Monotheistic?", 355.
[25] Skarsaune, "Is Christianity Monotheistic?", 360, 361.

the Jewish faith also included Christianity under monotheism as is indicated in the *Babylonian Talmud, Megilla* 13a.[26]

By the fourth-century we begin to clearly notice that the question of monotheism is not a Jew/Christian problem, but that it is rather an inner Christian problem. Tertullian, for example, writes the book *Adversus Iudaeos* using Justin's *Dialogue* as one of his authorities. Justin had raised the issue of the Trinity earlier in his book, but Tertullian completely ignores the discussion in his argument against the Jews. Instead, he leaves the problem of ητερος θεος and whether the theology of this second divine person and the third divine person threatens biblical monotheism for his other book, *Against Praxeas*.[27] The significance of Tertullian's presentation in *Adversus Iudaeos* is that it helps us to see that the Trinity/Monotheism tension is not a Christian/Jew problem, but that it is an inner Christian problem.[28] The controversy began within Christianity itself and among people who held high offices within the communion of faith.[29] They are the ones who advanced what became known as the Monarchianism of the second and the third centuries and not Judaism.[30] Both Tertullian in *Against Praxeas*, 3 and Origen[31] in *Comm. Ioan.* II.2, themselves firm proponents of separate υποϛταϛεις, are, in fact, on record as having named Christians and not Jews as their opponents[32]

---

[26] A more extensive parallel of this understanding of a 'Jew' is available in *Esther Rabbah* 6:2. H. Freedman and M. Simon, trans. (London, Soncino, 1939), 73f. This understanding of a 'Jew' that included the Christians continues until the start of the 7th century AD. This date coincides with the conclusion of the Babylonian Talmud and the rise of the Muslim empire (see L. Teugels, "The Background of the Anti-Christian Polemics in Aggadat Bereshit" in *Journal of the Study of Judaism*, XXX, 2, 1999 (178–208): note 3).

[27] Tertullian, *Adversus Iudaeus* (An Answer to the Jews translated by S. Thelwal) in *Ante-Nicene Fathers: Translations of the Writings of the Fathers Down to AD 325.* vol. III. A. Roberts and J. Donaldson, eds. (Grand Rapids: Eerdmans, 1951). See also his other writing *Against Praxeas* and *De Carne Christi* D. Holmes, trans., in *Ante-Nicene Fathers: Translations of the Writings of the Fathers Down to AD 325.* vol. III.

[28] Skarsaune, "Is Christianity Monotheistic?", 359.

[29] H.A. Wolfson, *The Philosophy of Church Fathers: Faith, Trinity and Incarnation* (Cambridge: Harvard University Press, 1964), 577.

[30] Wolfson, *The Philosophy of Church Fathers*, 581–585.

[31] Origen, *On the Gospel of John* in *Ante-Nicene Fathers: Translations of the Writings of the Fathers Down to AD 325.* vol. III.

[32] Wolfson, *The Philosophy of Church Fathers*, 581.

The Christian Thought Moved Away from Anthropomorphisms

The period of the early church that corresponds with the Talmudic age of the Jewish history understood the nature of this one God that they worshipped in a corporeal and material sense. It is important to note that the rabbinic sources of the Talmudic age are rich in the same type of anthropomorphic language that we see throughout the Old Testament.[33] As Klein has indicated, "some of the crudest biblical anthropomorphisms are perpetuated and even amplified in the Targums—alongside the common circumlocution and paraphrastic avoidance of human forms."[34] In his conclusion, Klein observes that "the frequency of anti-anthropomorphisms is much smaller than has hitherto been asserted."[35] The point here is that the Rabbis generally thought and expressed themselves within a framework that did not speak about God in abstract terms. This trend was completely reversed by the church fathers.

What seemed to bother the Rabbis was how to conceptualize the transcendence and the nearness of God with respect to the general problems of life. The kind of transcendence they saw in this God made it impossible for them to understand his nearness merely as a:

> general presence and as something inherent in the reality of nature itself. But this transcendence is not experienced as passivity either. This deity is living and active, but as such he must make himself known in the relativity of the phenomenal world; not, however, as a revelation of a static Existence which of necessity permeates the entire world, but in a liberating and guiding acting in which he distinguishes himself from this world.[36]

---

[33] Walker, however, argues to the contrary. For him: "The books of Israel's history and religion took no pains to obviate the appearance of a very distinct anthropomorphic character, but the time came when the main feature of Jewish criticism and exegesis was the anxiety to remove or soften down all references to God that could give rise to misunderstanding in the popular mind ... The clearest expression of this hermeneutic principle is to be found in the Targums, where 'everything was avoided that could lead to erroneous or undignified conceptions of God" (T. Walker, "Targum" in *A Dictionary of the Bible*, vol iv. J. Hastings, ed. (Edinburgh: T&T Clark, 1903), 679). Walker is not alone in this position; other scholars who articulate a similar idea are H. Soligsohn and J. Traub, T. Walker, W. Bacher, E. Schurer, A. Sperber, Y. Komlosh, B. Grossfield, and M. McNamara. For full bibliographical information on these scholars, see Klein, 1982: ix.

[34] M.L. Klein, *Anthropomorhisms and Anthropomorphisms in the Targumim of the Pentatauch with Parallel Citations from the Septuagint* (Jerusalem: Makor, 1982), xxii.

[35] Klein, *Anthropomorhisms*, xx.

[36] H. Berkhof, *Christian Faith: An Introduction to the Study of the Faith*. S. Woudstra, trans. (Grand Rapids: Eerdmans, 1979), 14, 15.

The idea that God is now far away and hidden (but when he breaks into the world of our reality to help he is infinitely closer) is what is achieved by the anthropomorphic language in the Targums, especially in the use of the concept of *Memra*.[37]

In the course of breaking with Judaism and entering into the Hellenistic world, the church fathers clearly moved away from the Talmudic use of anthropomorphic language in putting forth the nature of God. Justin's *Dialogue with Trypho*, chapter 114.3, comments on Ps 8:3 and says: "Your teachers ... think that the Father of the universe, and God unbegotten, has hands and feet and fingers like a compound living creature."[38] Perhaps there could be two reasons why the fathers were against anthropomorphisms. The first reason could be derived from Justin's argument above. The language is incapable of sufficiently emphasizing the utter difference and the complete otherness of 'the Father of the universe' and 'God unbegotten.' This is a scenario which ultimately undervalues the significance of the Incarnation which the fathers saw as a fundamental scriptural truth. It is in the Incarnation alone that God, who is utterly different and completely other, turns himself toward man in order that man may know him. The fathers argued that we know God not because we can relate to the anthropomorphic language, but because he has revealed himself to us in Jesus Christ.

The other reason could relate to the problem of imaging God. Anthropomorphisms tend to image God and may not allow the word to come through clearly. The word, says Berkhof, "comes sovereignly from God, or it does not come at all; it cannot be manipulated or conjured up, but demands total trust and obedience."[39] The fathers argued that, in line with the Old Testament, all images used in speech and thought of God are to be used solely as transparent media through which the word of God may sound and under no circumstance should such a speech image God.[40]

---

[37] See a full discussion on *Memra* in 1.3.2.4.3 of this research. See also M. Kadushin, *Rabbinic Mind* (New York: JTS, 1972); R. Hayward, *Divine Name and Presence: Memra* (Totowa: Oxford Center for Postgraduate Hebrew Studies, 1981), and E.E. Urbach, *The Sages: Their Concepts and Beliefs* I–II. (Jerusalem: Magnes, 1975).

[38] More examples of the fathers' views of the Talmudic anthropomorphisms are in G.G. Stroumsa, "Form(s) of God: Some Notes on Metatron and Christ," HTR 76 (1983), 269–288; esp. 270–273.

[39] Berkhof, *Christian Faith*, 15.

[40] A good example of a Nicene theologian who used this argumentation is Gregory Nazienzen (see *Orations*, 28.12 ff.; 29.2; 31.7; 33.17). It is important to note, however,

The Christian Thought Adopted the Greek Categories

The fathers found a new way of understanding and expressing the uniqueness of this God within the framework of the principle of the Greek μοναρχια (absolute monarchy or sovereignty of God). Some elements of Greek thought that evolved (and which heavily influenced the manner of speaking about God) are those that connect θεος with the Greek concepts of τιθεμι, θεος, or θεαμαι. The other Greek concepts that influenced the direction of the Christian understanding of God are the transcendence of God, indivisibility of God, and the idea of the 'Spirit' as well as the 'form' of God.[41]

The term, μοναρχια, as Prestige explains, "... is a metaphor from kingship.... The Fathers apply the word nearly always to the absolute monarchy of God, and its primary sense of omnipotence. But since the whole significance of omnipotence is that it can be wielded only by one ultimate power, it really comes to mean monotheism."[42] The fathers believed that God described in these terms was a μοναρχια because he was αγενετος, that is 'unoriginated.' The αγενετον, explains Prestige, "exists *per se*: its cause lies within its own being ... it enjoys perfection. To the αγενετον alone belong inherently omnipotence, perfection, creative power and goodness, glory, eternity, causation and wisdom."[43] Thus they understood God, in the words of Theophilus, as the one who has:

> ... no beginning because he is uncreated; he is immutable because he is immortal. He is called God because he established everything on his own steadfastness (Ps 103:5). ... He is Lord because he is master of the universe, Father because he is the maker of the universe, Demiurge

---

that anthropomorphism in and of itself is not a problem in theology. It only becomes a problem when we begin to see God as inherently anthropomorphic and when our language about God is not controlled and adapted by whom God has revealed himself to be. Otherwise, since it is us human beings who must know God, there is a level of anthropomorphism which is ineradicable, or else as Mackintosh once said: "What the conception of God may become when once the life-blood of anthropomorphism has been drained out, we see in the God of Mohammed. The Deity pictured in the Koran is 'like the desert, monotonous and barren, an unfigured surface, unresponsive immensity" (Mackintosh, *The Christian Apprehension of God*, 4th ed., 111).

[41] Prestige, *God in Patristic Thought*, 1–24.

[42] Prestige, *God in Patristic Thought*, 94, 95.

[43] Prestige, *God in Patristic Thought*, 46.

and Maker because he is creator and maker of the universe, most high
because he is above everything, almighty because he controls and sur-
rounds everything.[44]

God could be said to be all of these by virtue of his being: the αγενετον,
the Absolute.

However, the fathers did not only view God as μοναρχια or αγενετον.
Whereas they understood God in these terms, they also emphasized
the fact that He is ineffable (αρρετος). The Greeks acknowledged that
Orpeus, Homer, and Hesiod gave names and genealogies to their gods,
thus they understood their gods as mere names without either deeds or
substance behind them. The Christians acknowledged one God, Yahweh, who has both deeds and substance or individuality of existence.
Yahweh was not given a name by anyone as the Greeks did to their
gods. He is ineffable in that sense. Because he is ineffable in the sense
just stated, they also understood him to be actually uncreated, eternal,
invisible, impassable, incomprehensible, and illimitable—in contrast to
what they saw in the Greek gods.[45] Therefore, it is important to note
that the early church used these terms in a qualified and not in an
absolute sense. The terms served the purpose of preserving the integrity
of Yahweh and distinguishing him and his unique operations. Yahweh,
the God that the Christians worship, is ineffable, does things that can
be identified, and is not just a mere name but has individuality of existence.

THE INCARNATION QUESTION

The Christian Faith's Point of Departure

Whereas the fathers agreed with the Talmudic faith on the issue of
monotheism (which accents μονος), they saw an inner necessity in the
scriptures that led them to read the Old Testament's conception of θεος
differently.[46] In the scriptures, how the fathers saw the Son and the

---

[44] Theophilus quoted in Kaiser, *The Doctrine of God*, 48, 49.

[45] Prestige, *God in Patristic Thought*, 50.

[46] Distinction must be made between Judaism and the faith of the Old Testament.
Berkhof has explained this difference as follows: Judaism "began with the groups who
returned from the Babylonian captivity in the 5th and 4th centuries before Christ, but
did not get its specific structure until after the fall of Jerusalem (AD 70) in the exegetical
methods applied to the OT by the Jewish Scribes, an exegesis and application that is

Holy Spirit required them to say that God became incarnate, suffered on the cross, and redeemed mankind by dying and rising again.[47] The Talmudic faith would have agreed fully with the Christian faith had Christianity simply defined what it came to call the *personae* as three attributes of God. The fathers could not drop the Incarnation even though it was offensive to the Talmudic faith. As far as the fathers were concerned, the strength of the Incarnation lies precisely in its offensive nature. Tertullian's argument with Marcion helps us to see the priority that the fathers attributed to the Incarnation:

> Which is more unworthy of God, which is more likely to raise a blush of shame, that God should be borne, or that he should die? That he should bear the flesh, or the cross? be circumcised, or be crucified, be cradled or be coffined, be laid in a manger, or in a tomb? … The son of God was crucified. I am not ashamed of it, because it seems shameful. And the Son of God dies, it is by all means to be believed, because it is absurd. And he was buried, and rose again; the fact is certain because it is impossible.[48]

What makes the Christian understanding of God unique is the distinct Christian understanding of the doctrine of the Incarnation. We have emphasized *distinct* because incarnation as a concept is available in other religions and philosophies as well. What makes the Christian concept of the Incarnation unique is that by this concept the Christians mean that God endured to be born, to become man, and to suffer. Augustine, for example, argued that the doctrine of the Incarnation is also in the books of the Platonists. He is quick to say, however, that in the same books there is no evidence that "the Word became flesh and dwelt among us."[49] Trypho, in his debate with Justin, accepts the idea of a 'second God,' but he immediately recoils at the idea of the 'second God' becoming man.[50] His answer to Justin is that:

---

embodied in the Talmud which received its definite shape about AD 500. The Talmud may be regarded as parallel of the NT, since both integrate the OT in a new faith perspective" (Berkhof, *Christian Faith*, 22).

[47] In Justin Martyr's, *Dialogue with Trypho*, Judaism is portrayed as having no problems with the issue of a "second God" (see *Dial.* 56.16; 57.1; 58.2; 60.3; 63.1), however, Judaism recoils at the idea that this other God actually became man. In Dial. 68.1 Trypho says: "You are enduring to prove an incredible and almost impossible thing, that God endured to be born and to become man!"

[48] Tertullian, *De carne Christi* 6.1 and 6.4.

[49] Augustine, Bishop of Hippo, *Confessions. In Nicene and Post-Nicene Fathers of the Christian Church.* vol I. Relevant section cited here is vii.9 cf. John 1:14.

[50] Note that Trypho was here in agreement with Philo. Philo, as D.M. Baillie

"You are endeavouring to prove an incredible and almost impossible thing, that God endured to be born and to become man."⁵¹ Thus, as Fulton has clearly observed, "nowhere is the union of God and man so concrete and definite, and so universal in its import as in the Christian religion."⁵² In modern times, C.S. Lewis has made the same point regarding the story of the Incarnation. According to Lewis:

> (The story) is not transparent to reason: We could not have invented it ourselves. It has not the suspicious *priori* lucidity of Pantheism or of Newtonian physics. It has the seemingly arbitrary and idiosyncratic character which modern science is slowly teaching us to put up with in this willingful universe... If any message from the core of reality ever were to reach us, we should expect to find in it just that unexpectedness, that willful, dramatic anfractuosity which we find in the Christian faith. It has the master touch—the rough, male taste of reality, not made by us, or, indeed, for us, but rather hitting us in the face.⁵³

Because of the Christian explanation of the Incarnation, it follows that the Christian formulation of the doctrine of the Trinity is distinct and in a class of its own. One of the difficulties that some African theologians have with the doctrine of the Trinity is the suspicion that the Christian Trinitarianism has its source in Neo-Platonism and may not have anything to do with the Christian revelation.⁵⁴ To the critics of the doctrine of the Trinity, such as Professor Setiloane, we must admit that Trinitarianism is not unique to the Christian doctrine of God. However, we must not forget to also mention that the Christian understanding of the Incarnation gives the Christian understanding of the doctrine of the Trinity a distinct and different flavor altogether.

The θεος question, which dominated the church in its very early stages, was the problem of the Incarnation. The fathers posed the question: "Is the divine that has appeared on earth and reunited man

reminds us, viewed *Logos* as an intermediate being between God and man. This idea of the *Logos* is fundamentally different from the idea of the *Logos* in the New Testament. According to Saint John, *Logos* became flesh, i.e., was both God and man (see Morris, *The Gospel According to John*, refer particularly to n. 143). In fact, Philo was not even sure whether *Logos* was personal or impersonal—he simply never asked this question (see Morris, *The Gospel According to John*, see n. 145).

⁵¹ Justin Martyr, *Dial.* 68.1.
⁵² W. Fulton, "Trinity" in *Encyclopedia of Religion and Ethics*. J. Hastings, ed. (Edinburgh: T&T Clark, 1921), 458.
⁵³ C.S. Lewis, *The Problem of Pain* (London: Centenary Press, 1940), 13.
⁵⁴ G.M. Setiloane, "Where are we in African Theology?" in *African Theology en Route*. K. Appiah-Kubi and S. Torres, eds. (Maryknoll: Orbis Books, 1979), 65.

with God identical with the Supreme divine, which rules heaven and earth, or is it a demigod?"[55] The answer to this question was obvious to the church. Jesus, "... the Redeemer did not belong to some lower order of divine reality, but was God himself."[56] Although the church recognized that the divinity of Christ permeates the entire scripture, it found the following three sets of the scripture particularly helpful in coming to this position: (1) passages of identity which posit simple identity of Christ with God, (2) passages of distinction which distinguish one 'Lord' from another 'Lord,' and (3) passages of derivation which suggest that the Son is from the Father.[57] Consequently, the fathers taught that Jesus, who made God known to the church, is *Yahweh* the God of Israel; the one who gives life, form and value; the one who gives harmony, order, and development.

The Pneumatological Question

The flip side of the Christological problem, however, was the pneumatological question. The fathers posited the problem of the Holy Spirit with the view of Christ as the reference point.[58] Initially the question was: How does the divine that is Christ relate to the Holy Spirit? Later on the fathers accentuated the relationship between the Father and the Holy Spirit. They noticed from the scripture that the Holy Spirit—who operates in the church (gives gifts, sanctifies, empowers, and so on) and in history and, as it were, exegetes the Father—is the very same Spirit of Yahweh who was known in Israel. Their problem was simply how to differentiate the three (the Father, the Son, and the Holy Spirit) from each other.

THE BASIC ISSUES IN THE DEVELOPMENT
OF THE DOCTRINE OF THE TRINITY

As we have demonstrated previously, five stages may be distinguished in relating the Christian concepts of the Incarnation and pneumatology to the idea of monotheism that the church of that time shared with

---

[55] J. Pelikan, *The Christian Tradition*. vol I (Chicago: The University of Chicago Press, 1971), 172.

[56] Pelikan, *The Christian Tradition*, 173.

[57] Pelikan, *The Christian Tradition*, 175.

[58] Pelikan, *The Christian Tradition*, 213.

Judaism. These stages are explained well in W.A. Brown's *Christian Theology in Outline*, 1907.

Formal Identification of the Pre-existent Christ with the Greek Logos

By the time of the apologists, the second person of the Trinity was known as Son, Power, and Wisdom. However, the term that was to play a major role in the development of the doctrine of the Trinity was *Logos*.[59] The fathers employed the *Logos* as a theological term in three distinct ways.

Logos as the Interpretive Revelation and Expression of the Father

Ignatius, for example, held the view that there is one God and that that God has revealed himself through his Son who is known to be his *Logos*, Jesus Christ.[60] Irenaeus taught that the Father is revealed through his *Logos*, the Son, to all whom God wills to be revealed.[61] Origen argued that the idea of *Logos* has the connotation of the capacity to interpret the hidden things of the universe. For Origen, Christ is *Logos* because he interprets the secrets of God's mind and discloses to all other beings the mystery of God.[62] Clement explained that God's *Logos* is his image.[63]

Logos as Wisdom

Justin Martyr taught that the entire human race shares in the *Logos*, and that those like Socrates and Heraclitus who lived with the *Logos* are Christians, even though they may be regarded as atheists.[64] Athenagoras held the view that the Son is the *Logos*, the Mind, and the Wisdom of the Father.[65] Tertullian expounded the idea that, although he

---

[59] Prestige, *God in Patristic Thought*, 116.

[60] Ignatius, Bishop of Antioch, *Epistle to the Magnesians* in *Ante-Nicene Fathers: Translations of the Writings of the Fathers down to AD 325* vol I, section 8.2.

[61] Irenaeus, Bishop of Lyons, *Against Heresies* in *Ante-Nicene Fathers: Translations of the Writings of the Fathers down to AD 325* vol I, sections 2.30.9; 4.6.5; 4.6.6.

[62] Origen, On St John I. 19, iii cf. *De Principiis* in *Ante-Nicene Fathers: Translations of the Writings of the Fathers down to AD 325* vol I, sections I.2.3.

[63] Clement of Alexandria, *Protreptikos* (Address to the Greeks) in *Ante-Nicene Fathers: Translations of the Writings of the Fathers down to AD 325* vol I, sections 10, 98.3.

[64] Justin Matyr, *Apol.* I.46.2.

[65] Athenagoras of Athens, *Supplicatio* in *Ante-Nicene Fathers: Translations of the Writings of the Fathers down to AD 325* vol I, section 24.1.

existed alone before the beginning of all things, God was not really alone because his own reason was with him and this reason was possessed in Himself. According to Tertullian, this reason—God's own consciousness—is what the Greeks call *Logos*.[66]

Logos as the Divine Fiat or Will

The fathers saw a connection between God's *Logos* and his fiat in the Old Testament's accounts of creation. Justin explains that the commandments of Christ are brief and terse because Christ, who is God's *Logos*, is the power of God.[67] In contrast, Hippolytus sees the *Logos* as the causative agency of all that exists.[68]

Eternal Generation of the Logos

Having understood Christ in terms of *Logos*, it is understandable that the historical figure of Jesus Christ would be caught up in the purely speculative Greek style of thinking. The doctrine of the generation of the *Logos* was articulated from the concept of the αγενετος, that is the "unoriginated."[69] The concept of the αγενετος functioned in two ways. In the first place, it explained the eternal fatherhood of God and as such it highlighted the divinity of Christ against Origen's subordinationism or the Arian conception of the Son as a creature. In the words of Athanasius, the Son is the proper offspring of the Father.[70] Since he is the offspring of the Father's being and consubstantial with him, the deity of the Father and of the Son is one and the same.[71] But in the second place, the concept of the αγενετος distanced God from the rest of the created order. The created order has a beginning that is attributed to the 'unoriginated' One.

Also used next to the principle of αγενετον was the idea of χορεω. The technical term χορεω was useful in expressing the nature of the

---

[66] Tertullian, *Prax.* 5.

[67] Justin Matyr, *Apol.* I.14.5.

[68] Hippolytus, *Refutation of all Heresies* in *Ante-Nicene Fathers: Translations of the Writings of the Fathers down to AD 325* vol I, sections 10.33.2.

[69] Prestige, *God in Patristic Thought*, 46.

[70] Athanasius, Bishop of Alexandria, *Contra Arianos* in *Nicene and post-Nicene Fathers of the Christian Church*. Vol IV, see sections 1. 16; cf. *De Synodis* in *Nicene and post-Nicene Fathers of the Christian Church*. Vol IV, 48.

[71] Athanasius, *Contra Arianos*, 1. 9, 39, 58, 61; 3. 4, 6.

immanence of God. God's transcendence had already been captured by the concept of the αγενετον. χορεω literally describes the idea that God 'penetrates,' 'fills,' or 'contains' (χορεω) all things, while he himself is uncontained (αχορετος) by any or all together.[72] However, what is in view in this context is the theological application of the term to the relation of God as he is both in himself and to the world. By this term it was understood that God supports and frames the world not as a monad but as a Trinity. These actions, 'supporting' and 'framing,' are undertaken by the Triune God not merely in the external sense; rather, more in the sense of "permeative sustenance."[73] The entire Godhead took part in this 'permeative sustenance.' Again, the entire Godhead related to the world in this way because the persons of the Trinity are in a relationship of περιχορεςις.

Consubstantiality of the Son with the Father

The concept of the 'intrinsic constitution' or (simply) 'substance,' or the Greek ουςια is what became the theological term for the concept of the one-ness of God. The term ουςια originally came from the Stoics. The Christian thought rejected it as early as Justin (as is evident in Justin's *Dialogue with Trypho*, 128:4.) Origen, however, picked it up and used it. For Origen the meaning was not in the material sense (the way the Stoics used it), but in a new way—a metaphorical usage that accented the individuality of existence. Commenting on Prov. 8:22, Origen maintains that the wisdom of God is an ουςια. In *St. John frag.* 37, he insists that the reason the scripture compares the Holy Spirit to wind is because the Spirit is in fact an *ousia* and not just a divine activity without individuality of existence. Prestige has noted that in commentaries preserved only in Latin translations (*Numbers* 12:1 and *Leviticus* 13:4), Origen applies the concept of a single substance to the divine triad.[74]

By the time we come to Eusebius as evident in *Eccl. theol. 2.23.1*, the Christian thought has begun to teach that there are not two gods, nor two αγγενετα, nor two αναρχα, nor two ουςια but one αρχη. This position compares favorably with Athanasius, who argued that the Father's ουςια is the Father himself. In other words, the Father is his

---

[72] Prestige, *God in Patristic Thought*, 49.
[73] Prestige, *God in Patristic Thought*, 34.
[74] Prestige, *God in Patristic Thought*, 192.

ουϲια as he indicated in *De Synodis*, 34, and ουϲια as such is exhaustive of the whole being of God as articulated in *Contra Arianos*, 4.2.[75] If ουϲια is exhaustive of the whole being of God, then we can understand why the concept of ομοουϲιος of the Father with the Son was crucial in Athanasius' formulation of his Christology.

Athanasius' doctrine of ομοουϲιος (consubstantiality of the persons of the Trinity) is a further development of the concept of ουϲια. While ουϲια connoted God as being, the concept of ομοουϲιος denoted that in God one and the same identical substance "… without any division, substitution, or differentiation of content, is permanently presented in three distinct objective forms."[76] The Son is consubstantial with the Father.[77] To know the Son is to know the Father in his essential nature.[78]

The Son and the Father are one in propriety and peculiarity of nature and in the identity of the one Godhead. The Godhead of the Son is the Father's; whence also it is indivisible; and thus there is one God and none but he. And since they are one, and the Godhead himself is one, the same things are said of the Son as are said of the Father, except his being said to be the 'Father.'[79]

The Holy Spirit, Athanasius argued, is divine because the Spirit has the same oneness in being with the Son as the Son has with the Father.[80] Consequently, the Holy Spirit is consubstantial with the Father and the Son[81] Based on the doctrine of the divine consubstantiality, the fathers developed two important ideas. The first is the idea of oneness in the being and activity of the Father, the Son, and the Holy Spirit. The second was the idea of coinherence. For the fathers, coinherence meant "… a complete mutual indwelling in which each person while remaining what he is by himself as Father, Son or Holy Spirit, is wholly in the other as the others are wholly in him."[82]

---

[75] There are arguments and counter arguments about the authorship of *Contra Arianos* which is believed to have been written anywhere between 356–362 AD. Some believe the work could not have been written by Athanasius.

[76] Prestige, *God in Patristic Thought*, xxix; 168 ff.; 188.

[77] Athanasius, *Contra Arianos*, 1. 9, 39, 58, 61.

[78] Athanasius, *Contra Arianos*, 1. 4–19, 25–34, 2. 57 f.; 3. 1–6; 4. 1–10.

[79] Athanasius, *Contra Arianos*, 3. 5.

[80] Athanasius, Bishop of Alexandria, *Ad Seraponem de morte Arii* in *Nicene and post-Nicene Fathers of the Christian Church*. Vol IV, see sections 2. 3 f.; 3. 1, 3.

[81] Athanasius, *Ad Serapionem*, 1. 4–14, 23 ff., 27.

[82] T.F. Torrance, *The Trinitarian Perspective: Towards a Doctrine Agreement* (Edinburgh: Clark, 1994), 10.

The Idea of the Eternal Distinction Within the Divine Nature

Since Athanasius' concept of the ομοουςιος could not adequately distinguish the Father from the Son, there was need for another theological
model to highlight this distinction. We owe the final statement of the
distinction of the Father from the Son to the Cappadocian theologians
(Basil, Gregory of Nazienzus, and Gregory of Nyssa). By working on
the concepts of the υποςταςις and ουςια, the Cappadocians gave the
needed distinction between the Father and the Son that could address
the issue of tritheism (polytheism) and Sebbalian modalism with new
impetus. They also gave the third member of the Trinity a definite
place and character as a hypostasis in the Godhead, consubstantial with
the Father and proceeding from the Father through the Son.

The term, *ουςια*, (taken from the Stoics and used in an entirely
different way) had helped the fathers and the apologists to capture the
one-ness of God taught by the scripture. How were they now to express
this Divine who evidently was triune? In order to express this Divine
whose one-ness they had expressed in terms of ουςια, the fathers found
the Latin *persona*[83]or the Greek υποςταςις[84] helpful in designating the
persons of the Trinity in the same way as the Greek προςοπον that was
in common usage but was not made a theological term. It is thought
that Tertullian, who brought the term *persona* to the doctrine of the
Trinity, actually adopted it from his Greek contemporary, Hippolytus,
with whom he enjoyed a good working relationship.[85]

The Greeks used προςοπον to denote a concrete representation of
an individual; however, the word never became a theological term.
Tertullian adopted this concept but used the Latin *persona* to express
it. This explains why Tertullian could write phrases such as these: "'…
the Son acknowledges the Fathers speaking in his own *persona*' or '…
whatsoever therefore the substance of the Word was, that I call *persona*

---

[83] The Latin word *persona* described the mask worn by an actor on the ancient
Roman stage. Later it was used of both the actor and his / her part in the play. In
the development of this term, it developed into the idea of the part one plays in social
intercourse generally. The Latins did not use persona as equivalent to 'human beings'
(see C.J. Webb, *God and Personality* (London: Allen and Unwin, 1920), 35).

[84] The literal meaning of the Greek word υποςταςις is 'standing under or below.'
In its metaphorical usage it signified concrete existence as opposed to a mere appearance with nothing solid or permanent underlying it. Used in this sense, υποςταςις is
equivalent to the Latin word *substantia* (see Webb, *God and Personality*, 37).

[85] Prestige, *God in Patristic Thought*, 159, 160.

... and while I recognise the Son, I assert his distinction as second to the Father.'"[86] Latin *persona* in these occurrences means basically the same thing as the Greek προςoπον. In the final analysis the Greek philosophical theology used the term υποςταςις instead of προςoπον in their description of what the Latins called the *personae* of God. It is not clear why υποςταςις was preferred since there is no evidence that προςoπον was ever discredited as a theological term.

The Greek υποςταςις was originally applied to the being or *substantia* of God. However, it was gradually transferred to signify "content or substance of God corresponding to what in case of ordinary objects constitutes their determinate extension."[87] The term υποςταςις was changed, and it no longer meant 'content' or 'substance of God'; rather, it meant person. The identification of υποςταςις with person was itself a revolutionary development as, in the words of Zizioulas, υποςταςις no longer meant 'an adjunct to a being' (as was the case in its earlier application); rather, it becomes a distinctive way in which the being of God exists.[88] In the course of these changes *ousia* (or being) was used exclusively for the unity of the three persons. The point that the Greek context intended to make by using ουςια and υποςταςις in this manner was that in υποςταςις the being of God, or ουςια, achieves 'concrete independence,' 'empirical objectivity,' or simply individuality. Prestige explains:

> ... when the doctrine of the Trinity came to be formulated as one *ousia* in three *upostastaseis* it implied that God regarded from the point of view of internal analysis is one object; but that regarded from the point of view of external presentation, He is three objects; His unity being safeguarded by the doctrine that these three objects of presentation are not merely precisely similar, ... , but, in a true sense identically one. The sum' God + God + God' adds up not to 3 Gods, but simply to God because the word God, as applied to each person distinctly, expresses a Totum and an absolute which is incapable of increment either in quantity or in quality.[89]

The Greeks did not always see the distinction between the 'internal analysis' and the 'external presentation.' In their thought process υπο-

---

[86] Tertullian, *Against Praxeas*, 7.

[87] Prestige, *God in Patristic Thought*, 166.

[88] J.D. Zizioulas, "The Doctrine of the Holy Trinity: The Significance of the Cappadocian Contribution" in *Trinitarian Theology Today*. C. Schwobel, ed. (Edinburgh: T&T Clark, 1995), 39.

[89] Prestige, *God in Patristic Thought*, 169.

ςταςις and *substantia* are mutually exchangeable. This situation presented a critical problem to theology. Moreover, the subtle, historical
roots of υποςταςις and *persona* fueled the confusion. Eastern theology
began the discussion of the doctrine of the Trinity from the reference
point of *persona*—the part played by the Father, the Son, and the Holy
Spirit in the existence of God. Due to its preference for this strategy,
Eastern theology saw the Father as constituting the source and bond
of unity in the Trinity while Western theology saw substance as the
uniting factor.

According to Eastern theology, the Father binds all three persons
together or the *hypostaseis* as one God because the being of God is identical with the being of the Father. The Father is God *simpliciter*. The
Son is God from God and proceeds out of God by eternal generation,
and the Spirit is God from God and proceeds out of God by eternal
spiration. This is also the way that the East distinguished the persons
of the Trinity. Within Eastern theology, theology can speak about the
three hypostaseis; namely, the Father as the Divine *Simpliciter* or Divine
'Fountain,' the Son as eternally generating from the Father, and the
Holy Spirit as proceeding from the Father by eternal spiration. Consequently, the East could argue that there is one God because there is
only One Father, the Divine *Simpliciter*.[90]

The Latins used a less flexible language, *substantia*, and made it their
starting point in articulating the doctrine of the Trinity. For the Latins,
the oneness of God does not rest on the person or hypostasis of the
Father; rather, it rests primarily in the divine essence. According to
Augustine, "the divinity, or to express it more precisely, the Godhead
itself, is the unity of Trinity."[91] For the Latin West, there is one God
because there is one divine essence. What distinguishes the persons
of the Trinity, according to this scheme, are the relationships. The
Father is unoriginated and eternally begets the Son and the Holy Spirit
proceeds from both the Father and the Son. The Latin theology of the
procession of the Holy Spirit from both the Father and the Son is what
developed into the *filioque* debate.[92]

---

[90] V. Lossky, *Mystical Theology of the Eastern Church* (London: James Clarke & Co. Ltd.,
1957), ch 3 especially p. 58.
[91] Augustine, *De Trinitate* 1:8:15.
[92] Augustine, *De Trinitate*, 5:14:15; 15:27:48.

The Concept of the Double Procession

The concept of the double procession, or the *Filioque* (Latin for 'and from the Son'), is a contentious point of Trinitarian doctrine that caused the West and the East to visibly go different ways. Before the *Filioque* debate, patristic theology generally understood the oneness of God in terms of God the Father. The maxim for the Greek patristic theology, in particular, was that "there is one God because there is one Father."[93] For the Eastern theologians this statement did not mean that the Son and the Spirit are any less divine than the Father. Rather, the statement meant that the Father is the 'fountain of the deity.' The Father possesses the divine essence in and from himself alone; whereas, the Son and the Holy Spirit possess it from the Father. The being of the Son and of the Holy Spirit is truly divine. However, it is the Father's being communicated to them by the eternal begetting of the Son and the eternal spiration of the Spirit. Subordination is involved; however, it is not a subordination of essence. It is a subordination of *hypostaseis* or the manner in which the divine essence is obtained.

Clearly at the base of the *Filioque* issue was Augustine's understanding of the divine essence. For him, the idea, *God*, did not directly mean Father, Son, and the Holy Spirit. Rather, as Eugene Portalie has explained, it meant the "more general notion of the Godhead, conceived concretely and personally no doubt, [and obviously] not as any one Person in particular."[94] Having given prominence to essence, the persons for Augustine existed only relative to each other. In other words, the *hypostaseis* were made concrete as persons and distinguished from each other only by their relationship with each other. And so, for Augustine, the Father is personally concrete and distinguished from the Son because the person of the Father is the cause of the person of the Son by the act of eternal generation. The Father is also the cause of the Holy Spirit by the act of eternal spiration. Here Augustine saw two kinds of relationships (Father-Son and Spirator-Spirit) that distinguished Father and Son from each other, and Father and Spirit from each other. But how was the Holy Spirit to be distinguished from the

---

[93] Lossky, *Mystical Theology*, 58.
[94] E. Portalie, *Guide to the Thought of St Augustine* R.J. Bastian, trans. (Chicago: Regnery, 1960), 130, 131.

Son? In an answer to this question, Augustine explained that the Holy
Spirit is caused by the Father as well as by the Son.[95]

As far as Augustine was concerned, the doctrine of the *Filioque* meant
that the Holy Spirit could not be regarded as another Son.[96] The
Eastern theologians saw something of a 'double fountain' of the Father
and the Son in this rather than (what was known as) the Father being
the 'fountain of deity.' But for Augustine there was no inconsistency
here because the unity of God is not in the person of the Father; rather,
it is in the divine essence. For Augustine the divine essence common to
the Father and the Son acted as a single source of the Spirit.[97]

The Greek-Latin debate never really ended. However, the church
fathers on both sides were unanimous that the scripture teaches one
God revealed in three Persons. J.N.D. Kelly summarizes: "The badge
of orthodoxy in the East was one ουσια, three υποστασεις,"[98] while in
the Latin West the 'badge' became one essence or substance, *substantia*,
in three persons, *personae*. The varied terminology that is used indicates
different emphasis; however, theologians and historians of dogma such
as G.L. Prestige and Yves Congar[99] argue that there was a general
consensus. The consensus was the conviction among the fathers that
the God they worshipped was one God, not three. At the same time,
they were prepared to fully recognize the distinct and unconfused
representations or individuations of that one God in the Father, the
Son, and the Holy Spirit.

The Trinity as a Primary Name for God

By the end of the fourth century, 'Father, Son, and the Holy Spirit'
was used as a primary name for God in Christian worship.[100] And so,
the 'Father, the Son, and the Holy Spirit' had become the primary
name for God and not merely a series of metaphors that named the

---

[95] Augustine, *De Trinitate* 5:14:15.
[96] Augustine, *De Trinitate* 15:27:48.
[97] Augustine, *De Trinitate* 5:14:15.
[98] J.N.D. Kelly, *Early Christian Doctrine* (London: Black, 1977), 254.
[99] See Prestige, *God in Patristic Thought*, 235; see also Y. Congar, *I Believe in the Holy Spirit vol ii: The River of Life Flows in the East and in the West* D. Smith, trans. (London: Geoffrey Chapman, 1983), 8, 9.
[100] See R.C. Duck, *Gender and the Name of God: The Trinitarian Baptism Formula* (New York: Pilgrim Press, 1991), 78. Allan Richardson, speaking about the Hebrew understanding of a name, says that a "... name does not merely distinguish a person from

one God.[101] Christians of the time did not see a separation between what God is and what he reveals of himself. Speaking about the context of metaphors that are applied to God, Thomas Torrance warns that: "The One way God has thus chosen in making himself known to us as Father, Son, and Holy Spirit and addressing us in human language specifically adapted to his self-revelation as the Father, the Son and the Holy Spirit sets aside any ways of speaking about him that we may devise and choose for ourselves."[102]

Contemporary theologians seem to agree that the reason God is revealed as triune is because his essential being is triune in the first place. This line of argument is seen in Paul Jewett, Dale Moody, and Karl Rahner. In the words of Jewett, "God makes himself known as Trinity because he is in himself Trinity."[103] Dale Moody reasons that the only reason the economic Trinity corresponds to the immanent Trinity is because "God has revealed his reality."[104] Karl Rahner puts accent

---

other persons, but is closely related to its bearer. Particularly in such powerful persons as deities, the name is regarded as part of the being of the divinity so named and of his character and powers" (A. Richardson, *Theological Wordbook of the Bible* (New York: McMillan, 1957), 157). If we go with the Hebrew understanding of the name of God, then we quickly recognize that the Jews came to avoid using the sacred name *Yahweh* at first, replacing it with *adonai* and later in Rabbinic Judaism by *hassem*, "the name" (H. Bietenhard, "Onoma" in *Theological Dictionary of the New Testament*. G. Kittel, ed., trans. G.W. Bromiley (Grand Rapids: Eerdmans, 1967), 268). To say that the Trinity became the primary name of God is to say that the Christian faith effectively used it as a circumlocution of the proper name of God—*Yahweh* (see Duck, *Gender and the Name of God*, 140).

[101] Some scholars argue that Father, Son, and Holy Spirit is neither a divinely revealed, nor ecclesiastically produced name, but is a metaphorical representation of the Deity. This argument takes the position that all language that is used to speak of God is metaphorical, and that we are free to construct new language or theological models when the old have lost their meaning. A case in point is Sallie McFague's, *Models of God, Theology for an Ecological, Nuclear Age* (London: SCM Press, 1987). She represents the doctrine of God in threefold form as Mother, Lover, and Friend. She argues, "the three metaphors of God as parent, lover and friend form a trinity expressing God's impartial, reuniting, and reciprocal love to the world" (ibid., 91, 92). Other metaphors which have been proposed to take the place of the Father, the Son, and the Holy Spirit are "Creator, Redeemer, Sustainer" (see Gail Ramsaw, "Naming the Trinity: Orthodoxy and Inclusivity" in *Worship* 60 (1986): 492); "Fountain, Offspring, Wellspring" (Duck, *Gender and the Name of God*, 189); "Abba, Servant, Paraclete" (Ramsaw, 'Naming the Trinity', 497); "Of Whom, Through Whom, In Whom" (G. Ramshaw, *God Beyond Gender: Feminist Christian God Language*, Minneapolis: Fortress Press, 1995), 91).

[102] Torrance, *The Trinitarian Perspective*, 140.

[103] P.K. Jewett, *God, Creation and Revelation: A Neo-Evangelical Theology* (Grand Rapids: Eerdmans, 1991), 305.

[104] D. Moody, *The Word of Truth* (Grand Rapids: Eerdmans, 1981), 115.

on the axiomatic unity of the two. He says: *"The 'economic' Trinity is the 'immanent' Trinity and the 'immanent' Trinity is the 'economic' Trinity"* (emphasis in the original).[105] The other theologians who have accepted Karl Rahners' rule, as Ted Peters calls it,[106] are Jurgen Moltmann,[107] Eberhard Jüngel,[108] Alvin F. Kimel,[109] and the feminist theologian, Elizabeth Johnson.[110]

THE CREEDS

The confessional stream of creeds in the Western church indicates that by the fourth century AD the Trinity had become God's name. The Apostles Creed, already in use in the fourth century, defines in absolute, essential terms that the God of the Christian worship is the Father, the Son, and the Holy Spirit. This particular creed was used as a baptismal creed. It indicates that, by this time, the Christians assented to be baptized in the name of the Father, the Son, and the Holy Spirit. The other creed worth mentioning is the Nicene Creed. The Nicene Creed was initially written at the Council of Nicea (AD 325) and was completed at the Council of Constantinople (AD 381). This creed unequivocally affirms the full and equal divinity of the Son and of the Holy Spirit. The most complete formal statement of the Trinitarian doctrine, however, is the creed known as the Athanasian Creed or the *Quicunque vult*.[111]

The *Quicunque Vult* is consistent with both the Apostles Creed and the Nicene Creed. Lohse has observed that it sets forth the import of

---

[105] See K. Rahner, *The Trinity*. J. Doceel, trans. (New York: Seaburg, 1974), 22. For excellent interpretation of Rahner on this, see Catherine Mowry LaCugna, *God for us: The Trinity and the Christian Life*, (San Francisco: Harper SanFrancisco, 1991) 209–241.

[106] T. Peters, *God as Trinity: Revelation and Temporality in Divine Life* (Louiseville: West Minister, 1993), 22, 96–103.

[107] J. Moltmann, *The Crucified God*. R.A. Wilson and J. Bowden, trans. (New York: Harper and Row, 1974), 240, 245.

[108] E. Jüngel, *God as the Mystery of the Universe*. D.L. Guder, trans. (Grand Rapids: Eerdmans, 1983), 368–373.

[109] A.F. Kimel, ed., *Speaking the Christian God: The Holy Trinity and the Challenges of Feminism* (Grand Rapids: Eerdmans, 1992), 201–202.

[110] E.A. Johnson, *She Who Is: The Mystery of God in Feminist Theological Discourse* (New York: Crossroad, 1993), 199–201, 227–228.

[111] For elaborate comments on the creeds of the early church, see J.N.D. Kelly, *Early Christian Doctrines*; his other book, *Early Christian Creeds* (London: Black, 1960); and the other *The Athanasian Creed* (London: Black, 1964).

the earlier creeds "… more profoundly and better than did the fathers themselves."[112] This document, traditionally attributed to Athanasius although composed in Latin and generally known to the Greek East, appeared in Southern France about AD 500.[113] St. Caesarius of Arles, who was a great admirer of St. Augustine, probably wrote this statement. He could have composed this statement either as a test of or as a guide to orthodoxy. There is ample evidence that the statement spread far and wide. At the inception of theological liberalism, the *Quicunque Vult* was still regarded as the standard Christian position on the doctrine of God. Since that time, the use of the document, both as a creed in worship and as standard of theological orthodoxy, has declined tremendously. For example, Bray notes that the creed "… has not been translated by the ICET, nor does it appear in the *Alternative Service Book 1980*, probably because it is little used nowadays."[114]

The decline of the use of the *Quicunque vult* is observable in the African context as well. Here the creed is of prominence in only a few of the historical churches and rarely in indigenous, numerically-superior Christianity. Even in those historical churches where the creed is still available, it is commonplace to notice that the creed is not treated as a theological document that summarizes crucial matters of faith that should be better understood and rightly appropriated. A situation such as this, explains Bray, "… is a pity because despite its length and repetiveness, which are not to our modern taste, the Creed remains the most readily accessible summary of classical orthodoxy."[115] Because of these sentiments, we believe that one cannot provide a basic statement of the doctrine of the Trinity and fail to feature the *Quincunque Vult*. We quote it here extensively, but omit the damnatory and the Christology clauses.

> … We worship one God in Trinity, and Trinity in unity, neither confusing the Persons nor dividing the *divine Being*. For there is one Person of the Father, another of the Son, and another of the Holy Spirit, but the Godhead of the Father, Son, and the Holy Spirit is all one, their glory equal, their majesty co-eternal. Such as the Father is, such is the Son, and such is the Holy Spirit: the Father uncreated, the Son uncreated, and the Holy Spirit uncreated, the Father infinite, the Son infinite, and the Holy Spirit infinite, the Father eternal, the Son eternal, and the Holy Spirit eternal;

[112] B. Lohse, *A Short History of Christian Doctrine* (Philadelphia: Fortress Press, 1966), 54.
[113] Athanasius died in 376 AD, and he wrote in Greek.
[114] G. Bray, *Creeds, Councils and Christ* (Leicester: Intervarsity Press, 1984), 208.
[115] Bray, *Creeds, Councils and Christ*, 175–176.

and yet there are not three Eternals but one Eternal, just as they are not three Uncreateds, nor three Infinites, but one Uncreated and one Infinite. In the same way, the Father is almighty, the Son almighty, and the Holy Spirit almighty, and yet they are not three Almighties but one Almighty. Thus, the Father is God, the Son is God and the Holy Spirit is. God, yet not three Gods but one God. Thus, the Father is the Lord, the Son is the Lord, and the Holy Spirit is the Lord, and yet not three Lords but one Lord.

Because just as we are compelled by Christian truth to confess each Person singly to be both God and Lord, so we are forbidden by the catholic religion to say: There are three Gods, or three Lords. The Father is from none, not made nor created nor begotten; the Son is from the Father alone, not made nor created, but begotten; the Holy Spirit is from the Father *and the Son*, not made nor created nor begotten, but proceeding. So there is one Father, not three Fathers; one Son not three Sons; one Holy Spirit not three Holy Spirits. And in this Trinity there is no before or after, no greater or less, but all three Persons are co-eternal with each other and co-equal. So that in all things, as has already been said, the Trinity in Unity, and Unity in Trinity, is to be worshipped.[116]

Bray notes with satisfaction that the text of this creed "… is well translated and faithful to the meaning of the original."[117]

Conclusion

The question that the modern Christian faith faces is whether it can ignore the doctrinal statements of the early church. This has happened with relative ease in the recent past, as we have seen in the case of the *Quincunque vult*, but it ought not to be so. In the words of Lohse, "an insight which the Christian church has gained, in human weakness and in historically contingent form to be sure, but yet with the help of the Holy Spirit, may and must not simply be discarded as rubbish, nor is it right to make the measure of temporary relevance the measure of dogma."[118] The right approach to this problem is that which insists that the doctrinal statements of the early church must be reinterpreted for our specific contexts.[119]

---

[116] R. Beckwith, *Confessing the Faith in the Church of England* (Oxford: Latimer Studies 9, 1981), 32–33.

[117] Bray, *Creeds, Councils and Christ*, 211.

[118] Lohse, *A Short History of Christian Doctrine*, 15.

[119] For a detailed discussion of the reinterpretation of the creeds, see Lohse, *A Short History of Christian Doctrine*, 12–19. See also D. Tracy, *The Analogical Imagination:*

By insisting on the relevance of the doctrinal statements of the early church for the modern theological situation and for the African context in particular, we are not merely highlighting creeds as important aspects of the Christian heritage that must be recited every time the church assembles. Rather, we are saying that the doctrinal statements of the early church are an important Christian heritage, and, since they are so important, we need to win them for our unique situation and truly make the statements our own. In this regard, we need to categorically state that the African church does not need to formulate the doctrine of the Trinity afresh; as if the church in whose tradition it stands never did anything to that effect. What we need to do in the African context is not to ignore the creeds, but to see them as an important heritage and to reinterpret them for the African context. In the words of Lohse, "… the decisions of the past must be interpreted, i.e., they must be, as it were, translated, if they are to be intelligible in our day."[120] The inevitable question confronting us now is: In what manner may we reinterpret the doctrine of the Trinity for the African situation?

The key to reinterpreting the doctrine of the Trinity is a proper understanding of the development of that doctrine.[121] As we have seen, the doctrine of the Trinity went through definite stages before it be-

---

Christian Theology and the Culture of Pluralism (New York: Crossroad, 1981), 154–119 on the significance of the reinterpretation of religious classics.

[120] Lohse, *A Short History of Christian Doctrine*, 18.

[121] See B.J.F. Lonergan, *The Way to Nicea: Dialectical Development of Trinitarian Theology* (Philadelphia: Westminster, 1976), 1–17. The question of what it is that 'dogmatic development' entails has been in discussion, and, as a result, different responses have been mooted. J.H. Newman believes that the doctrinal content of the Christian church did not unfold in a straight line, but it maintained its identity from its origin to the Roman Catholic doctrine of its time (see H. Berkhof, *Introduction to Study of Dogmatics*. J. Vriend, trans. (Grand Rapids: Eerdmands, 1985), 59). The other model of dogmatic development is found in G. Thomasius. According to Thomasius, the development of doctrine moves from the Greeks (the doctrine of the Trinity and the doctrine of the person of Christ), to the North Africans (the doctrine of man and the doctrine of sin), to the medievalists (the work of Christ), and finally to the Reformers (justification) (Berkhof, *Introduction to Study of Dogmatics*, 59). Clearly Newman and Thomasius seem to agree that succeeding doctrines do not only build on their predecessors, but that the predecessors are in most cases carried forward as foundations for the new doctrine (Berkhof, *Introduction to Study of Dogmatics*, 58). Berkhof agrees with this analysis and argues that in theology as in other classic studies, the new does not render obsolete the previous. Rather, we always "… return to earlier insights, be it never entirely from the same perspective" (Berkhof, *Introduction to Study of Dogmatics*, 60). Lonergan, however, seems to be using 'dogmatic development' in yet another way. For him dogmatic development appears to be about movement from the 'undifferentiated'

came what it is today. Lonergan, in his study of the Christian doctrines, believes that understanding the development of doctrine is useful if contemporary readers are to rightly understand the authority as well as the basic intellectual assumptions and convictions of the conciliar decrees which represent Christian orthodoxy. The issues that Christian orthodoxy sought to clarify were 1) that the Christian faith worships one God; 2) that God has made himself known in the Son and in the Holy Spirit; thus, the three persons are not to be confused and neither may we divide the one Divine Being; and finally, (3) that the Father is from Himself, the Son is eternally begotten from the Father, and the Holy Spirit eternally proceeds from the Father (and the Son). How will African theology explain these issues to the African peoples, who rely primarily on indigenous nomenclature to access developments in their contexts?

---

scriptural picture to the 'differentiated' language of theology. For him what is crucial in dogmatic development is the process of movement from the undifferentiated picture to the differentiated language of theology.

PART TWO

WESTERN THEOLOGIES' RESPONSES
TO THE DOCTRINE OF THE TRINITY

What 'Substance' and 'Subject' are have for centuries determined how Western theologies have understood the doctrine of God. Yet as a "… matter of fact, terminologically speaking, 'substance' and 'subject' have the same meaning. Both are Latin renderings of the Greek 'hypokeimenon'. Substance, substantia, *is essence, that which subsists in itself, the status of the thing in its independence. Subject,* subiectus, *is that which underlies, which is underneath, in which qualities inhere, and which qualities are predicated in propositions. … Philosophical tradition has brought about separation between substance and subject. Substance has retained its original meaning of essence, that which underlies, while subject has come to mean the sum total of perceptions, images and feelings, that is, consciousness."*

N. Rotenstreich, *From Substance to Subject: Studies in Hegel.* The
Hague: Martinus Nijhoff, 1974, 1

CHAPTER THREE

GOD AS ESSENCE

INTRODUCTION

This chapter deals with the influence of the concept of 'substance' seen in the Neo-Platonic philosophy in the reinterpretation of 'one God' as taught by the creeds. There appears to be a clear connection between the Aristotelian doctrine of the 'substance' and Augustine's choice of the abstract concept of the 'Godhead.' This chapter investigates this connection and then seeks to understand how Augustine and his followers would interpret 'one God' and 'three Persons' in view of their Neo-Platonic commitments. Some notable Neo-Platonic thinkers who followed the footsteps of Augustine are Boethius and Thomas Aquinas. Their works, as well as the Christian-Muslim-Jewish debates of the Middle Ages, are very crucial to the view of 'Divinity as essence.'

The doctrine of the Trinity formulated from the perspective of 'God as essence' is important for African Christianity because this is the doctrine of God that the missionaries who planted the church in Africa in the middle and the latter part of the nineteenth century knew and taught. Until now a greater part of the African church interprets the doctrine of the Trinity within the infrastructure of 'God as essence.' The reason for this is partly because the Christian denominations in Africa, the liturgies, the hymns, as well as the theologies that govern beliefs and conduct in the contemporary African situation reflect what was current in the West during the great missionary period.[1]

AUGUSTINE AND NEO-PLATONISM

Many scholars seem to agree that, from its beginnings, Augustinian theology accessed the doctrine of the Trinity through Neo-Platonism.

---

[1] G. Kinoti, *Hope for Africa* (Nairobi: AISRED, 1994), 74f.

Augustine said that—of all the non-Christians—the Neo-Platonists were closest to the Christians.[2] Therefore, it comes as no surprise that Augustine sought to reinterpret the Christian dogma via the Neo-Platonic metaphysics, notably the metaphysics of Plotinus.[3] Turnbull, in clarifying the influence of Plotinus on Augustine, indicates that Augustine did not only directly quote Plotinus five times,[4] but the works of Augustine show a thorough acquaintance with the *Enneads*. Thus, as Turnbull indicates:

> To understand St. Augustine, one must be familiar with the language and ideas of Plotinus from whom he borrowed not only scattered thoughts, but the best part of his doctrine on Soul, on Providence, on the Transcendence of God, on evil as the negation of God, and on freedom; and his theory of time and eternity. It was the 'Platonists' (by which term he designated particularly Plotinus, Porphyry, and Iamblichus) who inspired that impatient desire of his to grasp the Truth, not only by faith but also by reason, since he was confident that in their writings he would find only what was in accord with the Holy Scriptures.[5]

Together with Origen students of Ammonius, Plotinus—a teacher of Porphyry—is widely considered to be the founder of Neo-Platonism. Plotinus' thinking was a result of a complex mix of Plato, Aristotle, the neo-Pythagoreans, and the Stoics.[6] His doctrine of the One provides the prolegomena of the Augustinian understanding of the doctrine of God.

---

[2] R.J. Henle, *St Thomas and Platonism* (The Hague: Martinus Nijhoff, 1954), xiv.

[3] J. Thompson, *Modern Trinitarian Perspectives* (Oxford: Oxford University Press, 1994), 128.

[4] Augustine, Bishop of Hippo. *The City of God*. In Nicene and post-Nicene Fathers of the Christian Church, X, 2; X, 14; X, 16; and *Confessions* in Nicene and post-Nicene Fathers of the Christian Church, VII, x and xvii; and IX, 23–25.

[5] G.H. Turnbull, *The Essence of Plotinus* (New York: Oxford University Press, 1934). See Augustine's own estimation of the Platonists, especially Plotinus, in the following excerpts: "After many centuries and much contention, a philosophy has finally been evolved which in my opinion is entirely true. It is not limited to this world, it reveals another, the Intelligible world" (Augustine, *Contra Academicos*. Translated and Annotated by H.J. O'Meara (New York: Newman, 1951), III, xix, 42). Elsewhere Augustine makes the following observation: "The utterance of Plato, the most pure and bright in all philosophy, scattering the clouds of error, has shone forth most of all in Plotinus who has been deemed so like his master one might think them contemporaries if the length of time between them did not compel us to say that in Plotinus Plato lived again" (Augustine, *Contra Academicos*, III, xviii, 41).

[6] P. Marlan, "Plotinus" in *Encyclopedia of Philosophy*, vol vi. P. Edwards, ed. (London: Colier Macmillan Ltd, 1967), 352.

Plotinus believed that the One is the highest principle and is above being and, therefore, absolutely transcendental (see *Enneads*, VI 9 [9], ch 4, 11.24f. ch 7, 11. 28f.; V 4 [7], ch 1, 11. 4–8; V 2 [11], ch 1). Plotinus further believed that this One is also entirely undifferentiated or without multiplicity (*Enneads*, V 4[7]; VI [9], ch 3, 11. 39–45). Plotinus' doctrine of emanation indicates that he believes in a relationship between the One, intelligence, and the soul. For him, intelligence emanates from the One and the soul emanates from intelligence. In this process the emanating entity does not diminish (*Enneads*, VI 9 [9], ch 9; V 1[10], ch 3, 5–7 cf III 8 [30], ch 8, 1. 11); rather, it remains outside its product while at the same time it is present within it (ibid., VI 4 [7], ch 3; VI 9 [9], ch 7). For Plotinus this emanation is completely involuntary. It is a result of an inner necessity—what is full must overflow, what is mature must beget (ibid, V 4 [7], ch 1, 11.26–41; V 1 [10], ch 6, 1.37; V 2 [11], ch 1, 1.8).

Plotinus' doctrine of the One influenced Augustine's formulation of the concept of the 'Godhead,' which for him is the principle of the unity of God. For Augustine, the idea 'God' did not directly mean Father, Son, and the Holy Spirit; rather, it meant the notion of the Godhead or essence (Augustine, *De Trinitate*, 1:8:15). For Augustine, Godhead or essence is completely simple and without multiplicity. As the highest principle, Augustine also emphasizes the 'One' that is described by him as Godhead or essence.

Having given prominence to essence, the persons for Augustine existed only relative to each other. In other words, the υποϛταϛεις were made concrete as persons and distinguished from each other only by their relationships with each other. And so, for Augustine, the Father is personally concrete and distinguished from the Son because the person of the Father is the cause of the person of the Son by the act of eternal generation. The Father is also the cause of the Holy Spirit by the act of eternal spiration. Augustine saw two types of relationships (Father-Son and Spirator-Spirit) that distinguish Father and Son from each other and Father and Spirit from each other. In Augustine's consideration, the problem was how the Holy Spirit was to be distinguished from the Son. In answer to this problem, Augustine explained that the Holy Spirit is caused by the Father as well as by the Son.[7]

---

[7] Augustine, Bishop of Hippo, *De Trinitate*. In Basic Writings of St Augustine. vol II. E.J. Oates, ed. (New York: Random House Publishers, 1948), 5:6, 8, 14, 15. Augustine, from these texts, seems to suggest that to call these subsistent relations 'person' is a mere

Once Augustine had accepted *substantia*—the grammatical term *underlying* or *lying below*—and, thus, the theological term *Godhead* as the beginning point of the Trinitarian debate, he laid a foundation firmly rooted in neo-Platonic reasoning. Augustinian theologians would use this foundation to argue that God is his essence and, in the process, fail to give due prominence to the persons of the Trinity. We see this happening in the thought of Boethius, in the works of the Christian apologetes against the Muslims, and in the works of Thomas Aquinas.

THE CONTRIBUTION OF BOETHIUS

Medieval theology modified the Augustinian usage of *substantia* and updated it with the latest developments in Neo-Platonism. The person who has been credited with this modification is Boethius. Medieval thought, it should be remembered, was taking place at a time when it was widely believed that there was value in Greek thought (Aristotle in particular) that could provide a new lease on life and a true consolation to the depressed medievals. This context was clearly set in the works of Boethius, who was by far the most prolific and influential scholar of the Middle Ages.

Boethius (described as "the founder of the middle ages"[8] or, simply, as "the last of the Romans, first of the scholastics"[9] and equipped with a thorough grasp of Plato and Aristotle) gave an entirely new direction to medieval poetry, music, theology, education, mathematics, classical philosophy, and logics.[10] He saw his task as developing and extending Greek science and thought in order to embrace the latest developments where they did not advance beyond Porphry and his predecessors. Patch explains, "… his manuscripts were copied in comparative abundance. No properly equipped library was without one or more of his works … what he wrote furnished the basis for education in various

---

linguistic usage. In his own words we can speak of persons "so that we not be altogether silent when asked what three, while we confess that they are three" (Augustine, *De Trinitate*, 5:10).

[8] G. O'Daly, *The Poetry of Boethius* (London: Duckworth, 1991), 15.

[9] T. Marsh, *The Triune God: A Biblical, Historical, and Theological Study* (Connecticut: Twenty-third Publications, 1994), 142.

[10] O'Daly, *The Poetry of Boethius*, 8–14.

subjects in the schools and universities during the many centuries until the Renaissance."[11]

Boethius sought to reinterpret the Augustinian being of God who is Father, Son, and the Holy Spirit within the infrastructure of the concept of 'form.' Boethius' understanding of form, however, indicates that he intended to use the concept in its Aristotelian reinterpretation rather than in its Platonic nuance. Consequently, by speaking about form, Boethius is not merely referring to an independently existing real thing or entity as the concept is understood in Plato.[12] Instead, mimicking Aristotle, he takes form as signifying 'universals' made in a particular way. This understanding of the concept of form allows him to struggle with how the particular 'universal' in question stands in relationship to the "concrete individual thing."[13] In other words, he poses the question: How is the universal in question presented concretely? What is the essence of the universal when it is presented concretely? This quest is what is described as a search for 'what is' in Aristotelian thought.[14]

Boethius' Aristotelian thought on 'form' concludes that God is his 'essence' and that 'essence' is the 'form' that he has achieved—the divine substance. This divine substance or divine nature, explains Boethius, is "... form without matter, and is therefore One, and its own essence."[15] Consequently, argues Boethius:

> ... if God be predicated thrice of Father, Son, and the Holy Spirit, the threefold predication does not result in plural number. The risk of that, as has been said, attends only on those who distinguish them according to merit. But Catholic Christians allowing no difference of merit in God, assuming him to be Pure Form and believing him to be nothing else than his own essence, rightly regard the statement "the Father is God, the Son is God, the Holy Spirit is God, and this Trinity is one God", not an enumeration of different things but as a reiteration of one and the same thing, like the statement "blade and brand are one sword" or "sun, sun, and sun are one sun."[16]

---

[11] H.R. Patch, *The Tradition of Boethius: A Study of his importance in Medieval Culture* (New York: Oxford University Press, 1935), 21.

[12] G. Ryle, "Plato" in *The Encyclopedia of Philosophy*. P. Edwards, ed. (London: Collier Macmillan Limited, 1967), 322.

[13] G.B. Kerferd, "Aristotle" in *The Encyclopedia of Philosophy*, 159 cf. A.M.S. Boethius, *The Theological Tractates and the Consolation of Philosophy*. Revised and Translated by H.F. Stewart and E.K. Rand (London: William Heinemann), see section 5,7.

[14] Kerferd, "Aristotle," 159.

[15] Boethius, *Theol. tract*, 11.

[16] Boethius, *Theol. tract*, 15.

And so *'o theos*, in the thought of Boethius, is what is universal to the three *personae*. *'O theos* in this scheme is a 'pure form,' or his 'own essence.' Elsewhere he says that "when we say God, we... denote a substance; a substance that is supersubstantial."[17]

The three persons in the Boethian theology are only individual, concrete expressions of the universal (the essence or substance) with the same attributes as what is universal. Boethius articulates this point thoroughly in the following words:

> Everything that is said of the Divine substance must be common to the Three, and we can recognize what predicates may be affirmed of the substance of the godhead by this sign, that all those which are affirmed of it may also be affirmed severally of the Three combined into one. For instance if we say "the Father is God, the Son is God, and the Holy Spirit is God," then Father, Son and Holy Spirit are one God. If then their one godhead is one substance, the name of God may with right be predicated substantially of the Divinity.

> Similarly the Father is truth, the Son is truth, and the Holy Spirit is truth. Father, Son and Holy Spirit are not three truths, but one truth. If then they are one substance and one truth, truth must of necessity be a substantial predicate. So Goodness, Immutability, Omnipotence and all other predicates which we apply to the persons singly and collectively are plainly substantial predicates.[18]

Here we see the beginnings of the Aristotelian application of the notion of properties of a substance divided into *essential* and *accidental* being applied to God. Boethius would apply the divine attributes to the 'Godhead,' for it is there where the divine substance lies. In other words, God is simple and undifferentiated. He and his substance (or essence) is one and the same. He is his own essence, and the divine essence cannot be "distinguished either by accidents or by substantial differences belonging to a substrate."[19] We will later examine how in the late Middle Ages the divine persons would be discussed as mere attributes.

Boethius traces the concept of 'person' from the idea of 'mask.' He writes that the word "... person seems to be borrowed from a different source, namely from the masks which in comedies and tragedies used to signify different subjects of representation."[20] The Greeks called

---

[17] Boethius, *Theol. tract*, 17, 35.
[18] Boethius, *Theol. tract*, 35.
[19] Boethius, *Theol. tract*, 13.
[20] Boethius, *Theol. tract*, 86f.

these 'persons' or 'masks' προςοπα and the Latins called them *personae*.[21] It is clear that the understanding of person influences Boethius' conclusion on the matter of the simplicity of God. What is original from Boethius' view of the concept of person is that he sees a substance with intelligence behind the mask.

Boethius' own definition of person would be "individual subsistence of a rational nature."[22] Put in another way, Boethius understands person as an individual nature that is endowed with rationality and consciousness. Two things stand out in this definition of person. The first relates to thinking, self-consciousness, or simply rationality. To be a person is to be able to think, to be self-conscious, and to be rational. The second arises from the term *individual nature*. The way Boethius uses this term indicates that he intends true personhood to arise from one's individualistic isolation from others. For Boethius all persons are individual, but only rational individuals are persons. This way of understanding person is peculiar to the patristic thought, which would not pose the question of one's freedom from one's very existence or what is common to human nature.[23] Zizioulas has noted that in the entire "history of the Western thought the equation of person with the thinking, self-conscious individual has become the highest concept in anthropology."[24] The 'God as Subject,' which is the content of the next chapter, takes its perspective from the Boethian concept of person.

---

[21] Boethius, *Theol. tract*, 87; see also Aquinas, *Summa Theologica*, I, q 29, art. 3. This is part of T. Aquinas, *Summa Theologica*. 3 Volumes. Fathers of English Dominican Province, trans. (New York: Benzinger Brothers, inc., 1947).

[22] Boethius, *Theol. tract*, 85.

[23] J.D. Zizioulas, "The Doctrine of the Holy Trinity: The Significance of the Cappadocian Contribution" in the *Trinitarian Theology Today*. C. Schwobel, ed. (Edinburgh: T&T Clark, 1995), 54.

[24] Zizioulas, "The Doctrine of the Holy Trinity," 58 gives some insight into Boethius' definition of person as "individual subsistence of a rational nature." It is this definition that will mark the beginning of the philosophical use of the term *person* (see C.J. Webb, *God and Personality* (London: Allen and Unwin, 1920), 54). Between 'rationality' and 'individuality' there has been a remarkable oscillation of opinions. The notable scholars who have contributed to these debates include Lotze, Bosanquet, Descartes, Locke, and Kant.

Influence of Islam and Judaism in the Middle Ages

Beyond Boethius, the doctrine of the Trinity cannot be discussed without looking at the dynamics introduced by the contrasting contact between Christianity and the new faith, Islam, and by the continued interaction with Judaism. In Boethius we have seen the doctrine of God discussed entirely in terms of substance. Later, during the Enlightenment, the trend would change and the discussions would converge over the idea of personality.

The invasion of Islam and its encounter with Christianity gave the Christian faith reason to reformulate its thought in ways that could effectively counteract the *Kalam*[25] of the Muslim theologians. With the continued interaction between Christian thought and the Muslim *Kalam*, the Jewish-Christian debates on the problem of monotheism were resuscitated once again, and both Judaism and Islam joined hands and defined "one-ness or unity of God as having to do with his non-material and therefore non-composite and non-divisible essence."[26] This comes very close to the position of the Christian-Latin thinkers in the West, who saw the oneness of God as a common substance but emphasized 'the three essential attributes' which belong by necessity to the substance and are one with it.

The Christian-Muslim debates that dated from the early Middle Ages indicate that the Oriental-Christian apologists, using Syriac or Arabic as their primary language, tried to explain to the Muslims the concept of the Triune God using the attributes ascribed to Allah in the Koran.[27] Different Christian apologists, operating from Neo-Platonic metaphysics, chose different attributes as their starting point. The early approach identified the being of God with the Father. Then the Son and the Spirit merely became his attributes. This approach is seen in the Al Kindi's, *Apology*, which introduces wisdom and knowledge

---

[25] *Kalam* is a rationalistic, philosophical theology that was developed by Muslim theologians in the ninth century that applied the categories of Aristotle to the Arabic thought. A standard monograph on this is H.A. Wolfson, *The Philosophy of the Kalam* (Cambridge: Harvard University Press, 1976).

[26] O. Skarsaune, "Is Christianity Monotheistic? A Perspective on a Jewish / Christian Debate" in Studia Patristica vol 29 (340–363), 1957, 348.

[27] H.A. Wolfson, "The Muslim Attributes and the Christian Trinity" in *HTR* 49, 1956, 1–18.

(alternatively life and knowledge) as the two essential attributes that together with the divine substance make a Trinity.[28]

Also noteworthy are instances where the Father is associated with one divine attribute. For example, by 1150–1200 two Muslim works (*Trinitizing the Unity* and *The Book of the Existing World*) explain that the Oriental-Arabic Christians taught that God's essence has the three attributes of power (the Father), knowledge (the Son), and will (the Holy Spirit).[29] There are two reasons why the Christian polemicists chose these attributes. In the first place, the polemicists possessed their Christian heritage that taught the three *hypostaseis* doctrine (which is really shorthand for the divine being as the common substance underlying the 'three essential attributes.') Consequently, they wanted to see how this doctrine could square with the Muslim understanding of God as it was formulated in Aristotelian terms. And second, the Christian polemicists had noticed that although the Muslim *Kalam* recognizes that God had other names, the triad (power, knowledge, and will) still remained central in that theological tradition. The centrality of the triad was based on the understanding that power, knowledge, and will are "the source of all other names... the faculty of power, for example, is the source of names such as the Mighty, the Strong... while the faculty of will is the source of such names as the Forgiving, the Consenting."[30]

The response of the Muslims and the Jews to this type of polemics is interesting. The Kalamic School of the Mutazilites,[31] for example,

---

[28] N.A. Newman, ed., *The Early Christian Muslim Dialogue: A Collection of Documents from the First three Islamic Centuries (632–900)* (Hatfield: Interdisciplinary Biblical Research Institute, 1993), 419,420.

[29] Skarsaune, "Is Christianity Monotheistic?", 343.

[30] T.E. Burman, *Religious Polemic and the Intellectual History of the Mozarabs, c 1050–1200* (Leiden: Brill, 1994), 165.

[31] Mutazilites derive from the Arabic *Mutazilah*, the first Islamic, systematic, theological school that was of tremendous influence in the Islamic world for many centuries. The Mutazilites saw their call as preserving the divine unity. However in pursuing this task, it chose, as Nasr explains; "a rationalistic interpretation of the Divinity which tended to view God more as a philosophical abstraction than as a reality who is the fountainhead of the revealed religion" (S.H. Nasr, "Islamic Conception of Intellectual Life" in *Dictionary of History of Ideas II (638–652)*. P.P. Wierner, ed. (New York: Charles Scribner's Sons, 1973), 641). Mutazilism was challenged at the end of the ninth century by Asharism, an alternative systematic theological school which "opposed the rationalistic tendencies of the Mutazilites, sought to re-establish the concrete presence of God by charting a middle course between 'tashbih' and 'tanzih' or by giving anthropomorphic qualities to God on the one hand, and abstracting all qualities from him on the other hand" (Nasr, "Islamic Conception of Intellectual Life," 642.).

denied the existence of attributes in God altogether.[32] However, the dominant Muslim group in the school of Asharism[33] and the Jews accepted the existence of the attributes, but did not see how any of the attributes could ever exist as Trinitarian *personae*. For instance, Joseph ben Shem Tov, a Jew that wrote during the High Middle Ages, recognizes that the three attributes in the Deity (power, wisdom, and will) that was espoused by Christian apologists corresponded with the Jewish philosopher Hasdai's conclusion that God has the three essential attributes of power, wisdom, and will.[34] The Jews, however, differed from the Christians when they recognized that the Christians did not use the concept of the attributes in the same way. One Jewish polemicist, Judah Arye de Modena, makes this point very clear:

> One cannot deny that God knows and intellectually cognizes Himself and generates from this an intellectually cognized object which he loves. Now the knower is the Father, what is generated from his intellectual cognition is the Son, and His love for it is the Holy Spirit. None of these three things, His cognition, the result of His cognition, and His love, are accidental to God as they are to man, nor are they external to Him. They are essential to the Godhead, and therefore he is one in His substance and His three attributes which they call *personae*.... When however they come and say that these three attributes are distinct, and external to him, and go so far as to say that one of them can do or become something which the other ones will not do or become, e.g. their statement that the Son became incarnate, but not the Father or the Holy Spirit, then this is the difference which completely divides our opinion from theirs.[35]

The Muslims in the Asharism theological camp, which were the dominant group by the time of High Middle Ages,[36] agreed with the Jewish critique of the Christians. They also did not see how the attributes could exist as *personae*. Their reason for rejecting the Christian stand was not theological however. It was their understanding of the Neo-Platonic concepts of essence and attributes that caused their rejection.[37]

---

[32] H.A. Wolfson, *The Philosophy of the Kalam* (Cambridge: Harvard University Press, 1976), 18, 19; 132–143.

[33] Nasr, "Islamic Conception of Intellectual Life," 642.

[34] D.J. Lasker, *Jewish Philosophical Polemics against Christianity in the Middle Ages* (New York: Ktav Publishing House, 1977), 70; cf. Wolfson, *The Philosophy of the Kalam*, 112,113.

[35] Judah Arye de Modena quoted in D.J. Lasker, *Jewish Philosophical Polemics*, 81, 82.

[36] Nasr, "Islamic Conception of Intellectual Life," 641, 642.

[37] Skarsaune, "Is Christianity Monotheistic?", 347.

According to the Neo-Platonic doctrines of essence and attributes, plurality presupposes materiality of the underlying substance.[38] Since God is not material, he cannot be said to be plural. In the course of these Christian-Muslim-Judaism exchanges, the Muslim thinkers of the time understood God in two distinct senses. In one sense, they saw the oneness (or unity of God) in purely abstract terms. Oneness of God, according to this system, had to do with "his *non-material* and non-composite and non-divisible essence."[39] In the contrasting sense, they saw God as a reality and attached to him anthropomorphic qualities that were not to be understood as *personae*.

Later in the Middle Ages, the Christian authors in the Latin West would adopt many of the arguments earlier posited by the Oriental-Arabic-Christian polemicists, who saw the one-ness of God as a common substance with three essential attributes that (by necessity) belong to the substance and are one with it.[40] The method of the Oriental-Arabic Christians would make sense in the West by around 1000 AD. By that time, Aristotle's *Categories* had been rediscovered in the Latin West,[41] and the Latin West also possessed a ready, intellectual culture, which it could use to tackle the persistent substance-attributes problem. Some of the early Latin-Western-Christian thinkers who used the Oriental-Arabic-Christian polemicists' style of constructing the doctrine of the Trinity and employed the substance-attributes model are William of Conches (d. 1145) and Peter Abelard (1079–1142). In these thinkers we see the triad Father = *potentia*, Son = *sapentia*, and Spirit = *voluntas* (in the case of William), and *benignitas* (in Abelard). The same triad occurs in Hugh of St. Victor (1096–1141), except that this time more flexibility is accorded to the Holy Spirit: *bonitas sive benignitas, amor, voluntas*.[42] A similar trend is noticeable in the works of Anselm.

Anselm followed Boethius and preferred to discuss God within the framework of "being."[43] Like Boethius, Anselm's views were unbalanced and tilted towards accenting the plausibility of the Aristotelian

---

[38] Aristotle, *Metaphysics*. W.D. Rose, trans., in vol. 8 of *The Works of Aristotle* translated into English, J.A. Smith and W.D. Ross, eds. (Oxford: Oxford University Press, 1912–1952). See particularly XII.8.1074A.

[39] Skarsaune, "Is Christianity Monotheistic?", 348.

[40] Lasker, *Jewish Philosophical*, 13–20.

[41] R.W. Southern, *St Anselm: A Portrait in a Landscape* (Cambridge: Cambridge University Press, 1990), 48.

[42] Lasker, *Jewish Philosophical*, 63, 64, 68,207, n. 177.

[43] Kaiser, *The Doctrine of God*, 96.

dialectic over and above the historical ideas revealed in the scripture. Anselm's method of arriving at the knowledge of God proceeded as follows:

> ... we have a hierarchy of being, the apex or limiting term of which is God. In one sense, the limiting term is not just another member of the hierarchy; so we may say that God is not a being. In another sense, however, God is the only real member of the hierarchy, in as much as all the others derive their existence from him; so we may also say that he is the only truly existing being. On balance, then, it is best to call him 'Supreme Being' (*summa essentia*) in order to express both the continuity and the discontinuity between him and all the created beings. Similarly he is the Supreme Life, Supreme Wisdom, and supremely whatever else it is better to be than not to be.[44]

THE CONTRIBUTION OF THOMAS AQUINAS

The understanding of Thomas Aquinas' interpretation of the Latin West's doctrine of God cannot be abstracted from the philosophical and theological developments that were taking place in the Latin West of the high Middle Ages. We have already analyzed the renewed interest in Aristotle from the time of Boethius until 1000 AD. Although he was a theologian, it is common knowledge that Aquinas' understanding of Aristotle is not inferior to that of Averros or Maimonides'; the great Muslim and Jewish Aristotelians.[45] In addition to the renewed interest in Aristotle, there was also an on-going interaction between the three monotheistic faiths: Christianity, Judaism, and Islam. The significance of Aquinas is that he explained his unique faith (Catholic faith) in the light of his Aristotelian frame of thought during a period that already had tremendous interest in Aristotle. What is of particular interest to us here is his long journey through the complex Aristotelian attributes-essence problem that ends where he (of necessity) formulated the doctrine of the economic-immanent Trinity.

Aquinas begins his investigation into the nature of God by radically modifying the Aristotelian conception of simplicity of substance. Theologians and philosophers such as Augustine and Boethius had taught that primary substances are "(i) self-subsistent entities which are (ii) impredictable subjects of predication (or bearers of qualities), (iii)

---

[44] Kaiser, *The Doctrine of God*, 87.
[45] Henle, *St Thomas and Platonism*, 7.

capable of persistence through qualitative change, and (iv) in a special way unitary or simple."[46] However, in the sixth chapter of his *On Being and Essence*, Aquinas separates substance into three distinct categories: divine, spiritual, and material.[47] Aquinas sees the spiritual and the material categories as finite beings that have some aspects in common and fall within the same logical genus as both created spirits and bodies. The divine substance, however, is of an entirely different nature from that of bodies and of created spirits. There is only one divine substance; the identity of which is God.[48] By saying that the identity of the divine substance is God, Aquinas is appealing to the Aristotelian doctrine of the simplicity of substances: no substance consists of substances, or to put it in another way, "the substance of a thing is that which is peculiar to it."[49] In this particular case, the divine substance is peculiar to God.

The argument of Aquinas—that the divine substance is God—is further buttressed by the Aristotelian connection between substance and form. We have seen what substance is.[50] However, like Boethius, Aquinas understands form as the process in which primary substances are made.[51] Based on this understanding of the concept of form, Lamont explains the theory that Aquinas posits in the following words:

> ... all there is to material things is their forms and the matter that composes them. Since their matter is the only feature that material things possess besides their form, it can only be their matter that makes them different from their forms. If a thing is immaterial [and God is immaterial], there is no feature of it that can make it different from their forms. To put it crudely and inaccurately, if you subtract the matter, all you will have left is the form. But if immaterial things do not differ from their

---

[46] E.J. Lowe, "Substance" in *An Encyclopedia of Philosophy*. G.H.R. Parkinson, ed. (London: Routledge, 1988, 255–278), 258.

[47] This division allows Aquinas to deal with the theological problem that occurs because of the existence of spiritual beings such as angels, which he includes in his second category, and the reality of the nature of man seen against the background of the spiritual reality in opposition to the nature of man and the rest of the created world. For Aquinas, man is a special case because he has a soul, but at the same time he has an animal body. Whereas Aristotle viewed man in a naturalistic way (Aristotle assumes that all substances are material) and, therefore, put man in the same plane as animals, Aquinas saw man as possessing a soul united with the animal body. According to Aquinas, the human soul, being a spiritual substance, is capable of disembodied existence (see Aquinas, *Summa Theologica*, 1a, xxix, 3–4 cf. Aristotle, *De Anima*).

[48] T. Aquinas, *On Being and Essence*. Translated and annotated by J.J. O'Meara (New York: Newman, 1951), ch.6.

[49] Aristotle, *Metaph.*1038b 9(1)(a).

[50] Lowe, "Substance," 258.

[51] Ryle, "Plato," 322.

forms, they must be identical with their forms. There is no intermediate state between being identical with something and not being identical with it; immaterial things thus are their forms, are forms subsisting
on their own. But God as has been established, is an immaterial being.
Since God is immaterial, he is identical with his form.[52]

Why is Aquinas introducing the problem of form in his discussion?
The simple and most obvious reason is that the relationship between
matter and form is the context within which the Aristotelian thought
deals with the problem of identity.[53] For Aristotle, primary substances
are made of something, i.e., their 'matter.' The manner in which they
are made of this matter is their form. Aquinas wants to make it clear
that God is a 'primary substance' although he is not made of matter.
He is 'made' of divine substance, and that divine substance is an
immaterial being that is entirely different in nature from that of bodies
or even of created spirits. Since the divine substance is immaterial and
completely other, we must locate God's identity not in what we can
know of the divine substance, but in the divine form. The immaterial
divine substance is organized in a manner that does not connote any
relationship to anything in any way other than to God.

Having dealt with the problem of substance, matter, and form,
Aquinas now turns his attention to the issue of 'essence.' Aristotle deals
with the issue of essence at length in his *Metaphysics* book Z. In this document, Aristotle develops two related ideas. In the first, he raised the
notion that substances persist through qualitative change. This belief
led him to the second issue; namely, that properties of substances divide
into the essential and the accidental. E.J. Lowe believes that the Aristotelian doctrine of essence is best captured in the relationship between
the notion that matter persists through qualitative change, and the idea
that substance can be divided into the essential and the accidental.
Essence understood in these terms, argues Lowe, logically leads to the
view that "the *essential* properties of a substance (collectively constituting its *essence*) are those which, by its very nature, it cannot cease to
have without thereby ceasing to be (so that their loss or gain involves
a *substantial* change); loss or gain of an accident in a substance, on the
other hand, constitutes only qualitative change."[54] Therefore by raising

---

[52] J. Lamont, "Aquinas on Divine Simplicity" in *The Monist*. Vol 80, no 4 1997 (521–
538), 526.
[53] See Aristotle, *Metaphysics*, books Z and H, cf. Aquinas, *Summa theologica*, 1a, xxix,
3–4.
[54] Lowe, "Substance," 258.

the problem of essence in the context of the divine substance, one (in effect) raises the question: What is the essential property of the divine substance? In other words: Why is *this* substance God? The divine substance is God because the essence of God is present in the substance.[55] And what is the essence of God? To this question Aquinas' answer is existence.[56]

What does Aquinas mean by saying that the essence of the divine substance is 'existence'? By this statement Aquinas seems to be positing the view that God is a necessary being in whose very nature it is to exist. His existence cannot depend on anything external; rather, it is necessary as that is his nature. Existence is he, and he is existence. In other words, it is not the case that God could have failed to have existence; his existence is his essence. God is 'He Who Is' (*Qui est*), and 'He Who Is' is the most proper name for God.[57]

According to Aquinas, although essence and existence are identical in God, the human mind cannot comprehend this identity because the divine essence cannot be known as it is in itself. In the thought of Aquinas, man cannot comprehend the divine essence because God is an immaterial being of an entirely different nature. However, we can comprehend the statement, "God exists."[58] We arrive at the knowledge that he exists, not through his essence, but through his effects.[59]

The final explanation of the relationship of essence and existence is found in Aquinas' cosmological proofs of God. The first starts from movement in the world and arrives at a concept of the *primum movens* [first cause of movement].[60] The second proceeds from effects in the world and arrives at the concept of the *causa prima* [first cause of change].[61] The third starts from the potential being of all things and arrives at the concept of the *ens per se necessarium* [something which must be].[62] The fourth begins with the gradation of beings in the world and arrives at the concept of the *maxime ens* [something which causes in

---

55 Aristotle, *Metaphysics*, 1041a 4.
56 Aquinas, *On being*, ch.6.
57 Aquinas, *Summa theologica*, I, 13, II; cf. *Summa Contra Gentiles*. First published in 1956 as *On the Truth of the Catholic Faith*. A.C. Pegis, J.F. Anderson and V.F. Bourke, trans. (Notre Dame: University of Notre Dame Press, 1975). See sections I ch.22).
58 Aquinas, *Summa Theologiae*, I, 86–88; *Summa Contra Gentiles*, I ch. 3.
59 Aquinas, *Summa Theologiae*, I ch 11; cf I *Distinctio* 3 q 1: a.2.
60 Aquinas, *Summa Theologica*, I, q. 2, a. 3.
61 Aquinas, *Summa Theologica*, I, q. 2, a. 3.
62 Aquinas, *Summa Theologica*, I, q. 2, a. 3.

all other things their being].[63] Finally, the fifth starts from the order
of the world and arrives at the concept of someone with the highest
intellectus.[64] To these five definitions Aquinas adds in each case: *"et hoc
dicimus Deum"*—[and this we call God].

These proofs allowed Aquinas to understand the divine nature as the
moving, causing, necessary, pure, and intelligent Being. Thus God, as
essence, has become conceivable as the highest substance. God is the
highest substance, or, in the words of Aquinas, "He [God] is supremely
being ... since he is Being itself." The "name He Who Is, is the
most proper name of God ... for it does not signify some form, but
being itself."[65] To God—who is thus named—can be predicated such
attributes as almighty, omnipresent, omniscient, unchanging, infinite,
and incomprehensible. As Berkhof has observed, these "omni-, un-,
and in-, words" have dominated the doctrine of God for centuries
because they gave expression to both the exaltedness and the firmness
that people sought to find in God.[66]

After Aquinas has discussed the existence and attributes of God
under the rubric of what has become known in theological circles as
De Deo Uno, the Godhead as the nature common to the three persons,[67]
he turns to the Trinity—*De Deo Trino*.[68] This approach, which separates
the immanent Trinity from the economic Trinity, has in a way been
considered the universal standard. Rahner argues "one cannot however
appeal to tradition for the now standard division and order of the
two treatises. It only came into general use since the *Sententia* of Peter
Lombard were replaced by the *Summa* of St Thomas."[69]

Aquinas says: "As the Godhead is God, so the divine paternity is
God the Father, who is a divine Person."[70] What is interesting, however,
is Aquinas' understanding of 'divine Person.' For him, the divine Person
signifies a relationship that subsists in the divine essence, "person means
relation."[71] This is clearly a standard Augustinian position. In Aquinas'

---

[63] Aquinas, *Summa Theologica*, I, q. 2, a. 3.
[64] Aquinas, *Summa Theologica*, I, q. 2, a. 3.
[65] Aquinas, *Summa Theologica*, I, q. XI, a. 4; q XIII, a. 11.
[66] H. Berkhof, *Introduction to the Study of Dogmatics*. J. Vriend, trans. (Grand Rapids: Eerdmans, 1985), 93.
[67] Aquinas, *Summa Theologica*, I, qs. 1–26).
[68] Aquinas, qs. 27–43).
[69] K. Rahner, *Theological Investigations IV*. K. Smyth, trans. (London: Darton, Longman and Todd, 1966), 83.
[70] Aquinas, *Summa Theologiae* I, q. 29, art. 4.
[71] Aquinas, *Summa Theologica*, I, q. 29, art. 4.

consideration, a divine Person is actually an internal relationship within the simple divine essence, the Godhead.

The Father *is* the 'principle,' not *from* a 'principle.' Clearly, Aquinas uses the concept principle to signify "that whence another proceeds,"[72] thus paternity.[73] Aquinas prefers to discuss the Son as Word. The Son alone is called the Word of God;[74] he proceeds from God and this procession is called generation.[75] "Word implies relation to creatures. For God, by knowing Himself knows every creature ... because God by one act understands Himself and all things, His one only Word is expressive not only of the Father, but of all creatures."[76] Turning to the Holy Spirit, Aquinas explains that the Holy Spirit is the procession of "love in God."[77] This position is similar to what Augustine had taught. In the words of Augustine, "Scripture teaches us that he is the Spirit neither of the Father alone, nor of the Son alone, but of both; and so his being suggests to us that mutual love by which Father and Son love each other."[78] The way this procession of love is distinguished from the 'other procession' is by what Aquinas calls "relations of opposition."

> It must be said that the Holy Spirit is from the Son. For if the Spirit was not from the Son, he could in a way be personally distinguished from Him. ... For it cannot be said that the divine Persons are distinguished from each other in any absolute sense; for it would follow that there would not be one essence of the three persons since everything that is spoken of God in an absolute sense, belongs to the unity of essence. Therefore it must be said that the divine persons are distinguished from each other only by the relations. Now the relations cannot distinguish the Persons unless they are relations of opposition. This appears from the fact that the Father has two relationships; by one of these he is related to the Son, by the other to the Holy Spirit. But these two relationships [generation and spiration] are not relations of opposition [to each other], and therefore they do not make two Persons, but belong only to the one Person of the Father. So if in the Son and the Holy Spirit there were two relations only, by which each of them was related to the Father, these relations would not be relations of opposition between Son and Spirit. .... It would follow from this that since the Person of the Father is one, therefore the Persons of the Son and the Holy Spirit would be one Per-

---

[72] Aquinas *Summa Theologica*, q. 33, art. 1 & 4.
[73] Aquinas *Summa Theologica*, q. 33, art 2.
[74] Aquinas *Summa Theologica*, q 34, art. 2.
[75] Aquinas *Summa Theologica*, q. 27, art. 2.
[76] Aquinas *Summa Theologica*, q. 34, art 3.
[77] Aquinas, *Summa Theologica*, q. 27, art. 4.
[78] Augustine, *De Trinitate*, 15:17:27; cf 6:5:7.

son, because their two relations of opposition [Sonship and Spirithood] would only be with the Father's two relations [generation and spiration]. But this is heretical; it destroys faith in the Trinity. Therefore the Son and the Holy Spirit must be related to each other by relations of opposition. Now there cannot be in God any relations opposed to each other, except relations of origin.... And opposite relations of origin are to be understood as of a *principle*, and of what is *from the principle*. Therefore it is necessary to say that either the Son is from the Holy Ghost; which no one says; or that the Holy Spirit is from the Son, as we confess.[79]

Aquinas' image of God is the dominant position within modern Catholicism. Main-line Protestantism also identifies with Aquinas' way of understanding God, as is clearly evident in the Belgic Confession. As Berkhof has noted, the Belgic Confession Article I "... offers a definition of God by means of abstract omni- and in- words, and it is only from Article 17 onward that the love of Christ comes to be central—without however allowing this confession to modify the definition of God given in Article I."[80] This situation results from viewing God more in the context of *quid sit*—as a 'being'—and, obviously, as contemplated within an abstract framework rather than from seeing him as he is revealed in the scripture.

Basic Characteristics of 'God as Essence'

Puts Emphasis on the Transcendence of God

God perceived within an abstract framework is inapproachable. God understood, according to this model, is seen as so simple and undifferentiated that not much thought is given to the fact that, in his desire to be known, God has in fact revealed himself as 'One' yet 'Three.' Barth already gave a detailed analysis of what it means by God revealing Himself in Jesus Christ in his CD II/1, part IV: "The Reality of God" (Chapters 28–31). In chapter 28, Barth defines God as the one who loves in freedom.[81] Elsewhere, Barth says:

---

[79] Aquinas, *Summa Theologiae* I q. 36, art. 2.

[80] Berkhof, *Introduction to the Study of Dogmatics*, 94.

[81] K. Barth, *Church Dogmatics I/1*. G.T. Thompson, trans. (Edinburgh: T&T Clark, 1975); *I/2* Second Edition; *II/1* Parker, Johnston, Knight and Haire, trans. (Edinburgh: T&T Clark, 1975); and *IV/1*. For this particular reference, see CD II/1, part IV, 257–321.

> Who God is and what is to be divine is something we have to learn where God has revealed himself … we may believe that God can and must only be absolute in contrast to all that is relative, exalted in contrast to all that is lowly, active in contrast to all suffering, inviolable in contrast to all temptation, transcendent in contrast to all immanence, and therefore divine in contrast to everything human, in short that [God] can and must be only the 'wholly other'. But such beliefs are shown to be quite untenable, corrupt, and pagan, by the fact that God does in fact be and do this in Jesus Christ.[82]

Berkhof rightly sees in these thoughts a crucial theological factor that provides the much-needed bridge between the theological concepts of transcendence and immanence or, as he calls it, "condescendence." God who loves in freedom is an involved God and is never transcendent in an absolute sense of the word. In Berkhof's own words, "transcendence is not abstracted from condescension as was traditionally done, nor opposed to it as is in Luther. Transcendence realises itself in condescension. Revelation is fully disclosure and actualization of essence."[83] This has meant for Berkhof and other 'Divinity as Absolute Subject' theologians that the traditional manner of speaking about God, taken from the early reinterpretations of the doctrine of the Trinity, be reworked so that the Christian doctrine of God may reflect the one God known to us through the Son and the Holy Spirit.[84] This reworking of the traditional way of speaking about God involves balancing transcendence and condescendence, and unity and particularity because particularity helps us to see the unity in its proper perspective and condescendence focuses our attention on transcendence. The result of such a picture of God should be a theology which understands, as Migliore has explained, that:

> … the unity of the triune God is not a mere mathematical oneness but a living unity which includes diversity; the steadfastness of the triune God is not a dead immutability but a dynamic constancy of character and purpose that includes movement and change; the power of the triune God is not raw omnipotence but the sovereignty of love that is incomparably strong even in weakness; the grace of the triune God is righteous and the righteousness of this God is gracious; the omniscience of the triune God is not trivial "know-it -all" but the deep wisdom of God that includes the foolishness of the cross.[85]

---

[82] Barth, CD IV/1:186.
[83] Berkhof, *Christian Faith*, 110.
[84] Berkhof, *Christian Faith*, 105–147.
[85] D.L. Migliore, *Faith Seeking Understanding* (Grand Rapids: Eerdmans, 1991), 74.

Indicates Transition from the Economic Trinity to the Immanent Trinity

The doctrine of God that we see during the Middle Ages and the Scholastic period is that which has clearly moved from the Trinity of experience—described in other terms as the economic or dispensational Trinity—to the essential, immanent, or ontological Trinity. The major motivation of the Christian thinkers of this time seems to be how to bring the Aristotelian categories within the precincts of Christian thought. It is not surprising, therefore, that Harnack could describe the doctrine of the Trinity formulated during this general period as "the high school of logic and dialectic."[86] Due to the pressure to conform to the Aristotelian logic and dialectic, the doctrines of God formulated during this time are clearly void of the concreteness of the divine persons that we meet in the pages of the scripture.

Thus instead of meeting Jesus, His Father, and the Holy Spirit in distinct but inter-related ways, we meet 'three pure relationships' that in reality cannot be described by the term *person* (Augustine) or three *upostaseis*, each of whom is individually described as "substance of a rational nature" (Boethius). The one God is no longer Yahweh, but 'Pure Form,' 'Being,' or 'Essence' explained in tight Aristotelian logic. In a sense, concern for the regulation of the theological language has become the primary concern and the language must measure up to the requirements of the intellectual culture within which the conversation takes place. Of course, there is nothing wrong with the theological language suiting the requirements of the context within which the theological conversation is taking place. What is wrong, however, is when the emphasis is no longer theology, but philosophy; when what matters is not the truth *per se* but the tight logic which by itself is merely a means. This twist in emphasis is unfortunate and strange to those who have experienced God and have known Him personally.

Severing the Son and the Holy Spirit from the Context of the Trinity

In his essay, "Christology and the Trinitarian Thought," Christoph Schwöbel argues that modern Christology is in a state of crisis. The crisis has to do with the methodological principles seen in three sets of antimonies. The first antimony is whether Christ is to be understood

---

[86] A. Harnack, *History of Dogma* vol.vi. A.B. Bruce, ed. (London: William and Norgate's Publications, 1910), 183.

"from above, from below, from the historical reality of the person of Jesus of Nazareth, or from the ultimate being of God." The second antimony has to do with what has been called 'the ugly broad ditch' that separates the present from the past. The main problem here is whether the Christological methodology is to proceed from the historical Jesus or from the modern Christian experience of faith. The last and the final antimony is whether the Christological question focuses either on his being or his significance.[87] However, the question is: How did these antimonies arise? What is responsible for them? Many reasons could account for the rise of these antimonies. In the thought of Schwöbel, the antimonies are a result of neglect of Trinitarian logic in Christological formulations.[88] The seeds of this neglect are already present in Aquinas, who was visibly uneasy with the speculative tradition of the construction of the doctrine of the Trinity and, as a result, he constantly moved between the economic Trinity and the immanent Trinity.[89] The problem with Aquinas' methodology is that it has given us a theological heritage that sees the Father, the Son, and the Holy Spirit without seeing the three in the context of the Trinity.

Describes a Deity Which is One, Simple, Impersonal Being

Augustine, as we have seen, was clearly uneasy with the idea of the divine persons. For him the divine essence was the crucial factor and persons, according to that scheme, are merely relationships within that essence. For Augustine, as is the case with Aquinas, "relations take a secondary place to the unity and are understood logically and not ontologically."[90] Because of this situation, Gunton observes that Augustine cannot "make claims about the being of particular persons, who, because they lack distinguishable identity tend to disappear into the all-embracing oneness of God."[91] Of course, the divine persons have relationship, but they cannot simply be reduced to relationships. Moreover, a relationship must have concrete objective content, but the Augus-

---

[87] C. Schwöbel, "Christianity and Trinitarian Thought" in *Trinitarian Today: Essays on Divine Being and Act* (Edinburgh: T&T Clark, 1995), 113–119.

[88] Schwöbel, "Christianity and Trinitarian Thought," 120.

[89] W.C. Placher, *Domestication of the Trancendence: How the Modern Thinking about God Went Wrong* (Louisville: Westminster John Knox Press, 1996).

[90] J. Thompson, *Modern Trinitarian Perspectives* (Oxford: Oxford University Press, 1994), 129.

[91] C. Gunton, *The Promise of Trinitarian Theology* (Edinburgh: T&T Clarke, 1991), 42.

tinian relationship lacks this. Instead what we see is relationship contrasted to the other two, what Aquinas would call relationships of opposition. The Holy Spirit in Augustine, as in Aquinas, is the mutual love of Father and Son. The Spirit is thus not given due concreteness and, moreover, how the Spirit is the mutual love of the Father and the Son is not argued from either the perspective of the economy or from the God's involvement with the eschaton.[92]

Boethius, articulating Augustine for his audience, lived only a few generations from Augustine, but understood the idea of three persons as a reiteration of one and the same thing, much like the statement "'blade, and brand, are one sword' or 'sun, sun and sun are one sun'."[93] We see a similar commitment in the context of the Christian-Muslim-Jewish debates of the Middle Ages.

The debates among the Christians, Muslims, and Jews of the Middle Ages indicate that the Christian apologists of the time gave priority to the divine unity and wished to explain the plurality in terms of attributes. The issue that the Christians focused on is what the three monotheistic faiths of the Old Testament had in common rather than how the Christian faith is distinct from the other two. In the final analysis, the eagerness of the Christian thinkers to prove that the Christian faith was monotheistic by the use of the Aristotelian concept of substance and the doctrine of attributes only resulted in the them coming up with a deity which is one simple undiversified being, more or less like the Muslim Allah or the God of the medieval Jewish thinkers. The Aristotelian concept of substance is clearly incapable of providing a structure for formulating diversity in deity. As Skarsaune has noted, there is no known Christian thinker who tried to defend the Aristotelian formulation of the doctrine of the Trinity without finding themselves in troubled waters.[94]

Conclusion

The 'God as essence' model of the Trinity clearly uses the infrastructure of Neo-Platonism to reinterpret the doctrine of the Trinity. Augustine's idea of 'Godhead' was influenced by Plotinus' concept of the 'One' as

---

[92] Gunton, *The Promise of Trinitarian Theology*, 51.
[93] Boethius, *Theol. tract*: 15.
[94] Skarsaune, "Is Christianity Monotheistic?", 353.

the highest principle. Boethius perfected Augustine's notion of 'God-head' for the Middle Ages. There is no doubt that the theology of Aquinas has continued to be of tremendous influence in the church. It should be noted, however, that Aquinas followed the path that Augustine blazed and Boethius improved.

The basic characteristics of God as essence that we noticed in this chapter can partly be explained by the nature of the metaphysics chosen by Augustine, Boethius, and Aquinas. For these thinkers, Neo-Platonism was an appropriate intellectual system of reinterpreting the Christian orthodoxy. Boethius wanted to prove to his readers that the Aristotelian ontology was the appropriate medium of articulating reality. Other Middle Age and Scholastic theologians such as Benedict of Aniane, John Scotus Erigna, Anselm, Abelard, and Albertus Magnus were all derailed by their respective commitment to the Aristotelian description of being. The question that we must pose here is: Do we have to use Neo-Platonic infrastructure in reinterpreting the Christian view of God, or are there other options? Perhaps, as Thompson once asked: "… is it not possible to begin with one personal God who is at one and the same time personally Father, Son, and Holy Spirit? Unity and threeness are both equally ultimate in the Trinity."[95]

---

[95] Thompson, *Modern Trinitarian Perspectives*, 130.

CHAPTER FOUR

GOD AS AN ABSOLUTE SUBJECT

INTRODUCTION

This chapter deals with the 'God as an absolute subject' paradigm of formulating the doctrine of the Trinity. The key theologians associated with the position of God as an absolute subject are Barth and Rahner. Although both Barth and Rahner[1] are not widely used within African theological circles, their notion of God as an absolute subject could be very significant to the traditional Africa that already understands God as a being that is both 'Supreme' and 'Personal.'[2]

THE BEGINNINGS OF 'SELF-CONSCIOUSNESS'

The context of God as an absolute subject reinterpretation of the doctrine of the Trinity was during the rise of the eighteenth century Enlightenment as a cultural period in Western society. It includes the general coldness to Plato and Aristotle that provided the impetus for an alternative model of constructing reality.[3] The medieval cosmology was patterned as below:[4]

---

[1] Within the African Christian situation, Barth is known as a neo-Orthodox theologian, and he is, therefore, not read either by the African liberals or the evangelicals, who together form the largest share of African Protestantism involved in formal theology. Rahner is still regarded as a prodigal son within Catholicism and little is known about him within African protestant circles.

[2] See Part 3 of this research, particularly the contributions of J.S. Mbiti, B. Idowu, and G.M. Setiloane.

[3] Note that the 'coldness to Plato and Aristotle' referred to here does not mean that Platonism died in the West prior to the rise of Idealism. Platonism has never died in the West because if it did we would not have discussed the 'God as Essence' in this work. In fact, other branches of philosophy believe "... that modern philosophy has done little else than write footnotes to the Greek" (H. Berkhof, *Introduction to the Study of Dogmatics*, 58). What happened with the rise of Philosophical Idealism was the arrival of an alternative, or a rival pattern, of constructing reality hitherto unknown to the Western mind.

[4] D.J. Bosch, *Transforming Mission: Paradigm Shift in Theology of Mission* (Maryknoll: Orbis Books, 1991), 263.

God

↓

Church

↓

Kings and Nobles

↓

People

↓

Animals, Plants and Objects

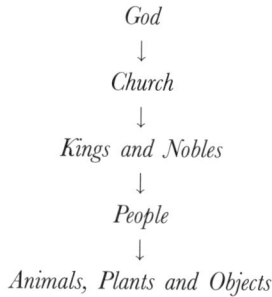

Gradually, but without any conscious awareness of what was unfolding, some sections of Western society moved away from this cosmology. They went through a paradigmatic change so that, by the time of Bacon and Descartes, radical anthropocentrism was deeply entrenched and philosophy in these sections no longer addressed substance, essence, or form as the basis of existence or 'first cause without being caused.' Instead it addressed 'ideas' and the connection between the reality of the ideas and the subject, 'I,' who holds the ideas.

This was a complete paradigmatic change: a movement away from the method which philosophy had hitherto employed to an entirely new way of constructing reality. This new way of looking at reality became known as Idealism. Idealism concerned itself primarily with ideas and in a derivative sense with what it considered ideal. In this context, idea meant "… any and every object of which any human mind is at any time aware."[5] This change of ideas not only meant change to focus on the "… 'copies' in the mind of objects outside,"[6] but it also meant positing a theory of knowledge in which the subject is sure of the existence of the self, the "I"; the object of consciousness (the 'idea'); and consciousness[7] itself. This phenomenon is what Idealist philosophy calls 'self-consciousness.'

---

[5] R.F.A. Hoernle, *Idealism as a Philosophical Doctrine* (London: Hodder and Stoughton Ltd, 1924), 3.

[6] Hoernle, *Idealism as a Philosophical Doctrine*, 34.

[7] The German technical term for consciousness is *Bewustsein*. *Bewustsein* indicates consciousness of an object or just intentional consciousness. The addition of the pronoun *selbst* (self) gives *selbstbewust*, which refers to consciousness, knowledge, or awareness of oneself. The emphasis here is not necessarily on the I (who is conscious as contrasted to the external world of objects); rather, it is on seeing the external world of objects as the product, the possession, or the mirror image of the I (see M. Inwood, "Hegel" in *The Blackwell Companion to Philosophy*. Bunnin and Tsui-James, eds. (Oxford: Blackwell Publishers, 1996), 61–63).

Self-consciousness as a philosophical quest began with Descartes' *cogito ergo sum*. By this expression Descartes did not just mean that he was sure of his own being, the existence of himself, or the I. He also meant that knowing or being conscious of his own existence was a fundamental basis of affirming the existence of the external reality and the existence of a perfect being.[8] Fichte understood 'self-consciousness' in much the same way as Descartes. He called it the "... the primordial, absolutely unconditioned first principle of all human knowledge."[9] While Descartes and Fichte maintained self-consciousness as a necessary inference in talking about external reality, Kant used it to make philosophy aware of the fact that the external reality, which is the object of consciousness, is somewhat related to the nature of the I or the subject that knows it. He graphically expressed this doctrine in the preface to the second edition of *Critique of Pure Reason* in the following terms:

> Hitherto it has been assumed that all our knowledge must conform to objects. But all attempts [for instance, to account for the possibility of objective knowledge] have, on this assumption, ended in failure. We must therefore make trial whether we may not have more success in the task of metaphysics, if we suppose that objects conform to our knowledge.[10]

The point of Kant, as Kain has explained, is that "... all objects are objects-of-my-consciousness they have been constituted by my consciousness and unified by my consciousness."[11]

Hegel took this thought and developed it further. As he clearly writes in Chapter IV of the *Phenomenology of the Spirit*, self-consciousness "... has a double object: One is the immediate object ... which however for self-consciousness has the character of a negative; and the second, viz., itself, which is the true essence."[12] As Kain has explained, Hegel's view of the object as negative means "... that in itself, the object is taken to be nothing—but a thing-for-my-consciousness. Self-consciousness takes itself to be the thing of significance. 'I' is what is important and essen-

---

[8] D.J. Butler, *Four Philosophies and their use in Education and Religion* (New York: Harper and Brothers Publishers, 1950), 269, 270.

[9] J.G. Fichte, *Science of Knowledge* (New York: Meredith, 1970), 93.

[10] I. Kant, *Critique of Pure Reason*. N.K. Smith, trans. An Electronic Edition. Courtesy @ Pilgrave Macmillan, preface to Second Edition, xvi. (http://humanum.arts.cuhk.edu.hk/Philosophy/Kant/cpr/.)

[11] P.J. Kain, "Self-Consciousness, the Other and Hegel's dialectic of Recognition." *Philosophy and Social Criticism*, vol 24 no 5, 1998 (105–126), 106.

[12] G.W.F. Hegel, *Phenomenology of the Spirit*. A.V. Miller, trans. (Oxford: Clarendon Press, 1977), 105.

tial; the object is nothing but a thing-for-me."[13] In the words of Inwood, the external object is primarily the product, the possession, or the mirror image of the subject I.[14]

This theory of knowledge provided an entirely different philosophical structure upon which theology and the doctrine of God was henceforth recognized. An alternative thought structure was necessary because the Enlightenment rejected the medieval cosmology and the issues that were articulated with the framework of that cosmology as the guiding light. This meant that if eighteenth century man were to continue to speak intelligently of God, he would necessarily do so from an intellectual position that was not only current but also acceptable to the native context. This is the basis upon which the theory of self-consciousness was adopted by theology and used in the latter's task of formulating the doctrine of God.

THE DOCTRINE OF GOD WITHIN THE SCHEME OF 'SELF-CONSCIOUSNESS'

In the theory of self-consciousness, God is understood as an absolute subject. How is this concluded? Again, the Cartesian argument is useful. Descartes, as Butler explains:

> ... was sure of his own being, but since he is equally sure that his being is imperfect and incomplete, he is convinced that there is another being beside himself which is complete and perfect. He asks what could possibly be the cause in him of this idea of perfect Being. In answering his question, he holds that imperfect being could hardly be the cause, because it is repugnant to think of a lesser causing a greater as it is to think of nothing causing something. And Descartes himself who possesses the idea, is an imperfect being. Therefore, he holds that perfect Being must exist beyond his own mind, and must be the cause of the idea of perfect Being in his mind.[15]

Descartes knew this absolute subject or personality as 'perfect Being.' Other Idealists called the Absolute Subject the 'Self,' 'Universal mind,' 'Reality,' 'Reason,' or 'Spirit.' Whatever they called the Absolute Subject, it is clear that they meant God.[16] They did not regard them-

---

[13] Kain, "Self-Consciousness," 106.
[14] Inwood, "Hegel," 61.
[15] Butler, *Four Philosophies*, 269, 270.
[16] Nicholas of Cusa used the term *absolute* in referring to God as early as 1440.

selves as Christian theologians (although their inclination to religion is well documented); rather, they viewed themselves as secular poets and thinkers, and so they saw no reason for employing the theologically restricted term *God* that was current within the Christian orthodoxy.

The argument, it is understood, is that all subjects posit[17] themselves as objects and are conscious of this activity. God as an absolute subject also posits himself as an object, and he is also conscious of that activity. To view God in this manner has far-reaching implications for the orthodox Christian doctrine of God. God is now understood according to the terms of the Idealists; namely, 'One Subject, Three Modes or Subsistences' rather than according to the orthodox terms of 'One God, Three Persons.' Dorner, Barth's mentor on the concept of 'modes of being,' explains the relationship between the 'modes' and the 'subject' in the following terms:

> In the trinitarian process of the life and spirit of God, absolute personality is the eternal present result; so the self-conscious God, who desires and possesses himself, is also present in such a way in each of the divine distinctions that these—which would not in themselves and individually be personal—yet participate in One of the divine modes, each in its own way. But as the absolute divine personality is the single constitution of the three divine modes of being which participate in it and has its understanding in them, as they have theirs in it, so this same divine personality which, in its ultimate relationship and according to its nature, is holy love, is also the single constitution and the highest power of all divine characteristics.[18]

After that the term received wide acceptance as an expression for God in philosophical circles. Hegel used the term to refer to God within philosophical circles. He explained his preference for the term as arising from the fact that it was generally accepted as a philosophical expression of the concept of God, but this time the term was shorn of anthropomorphic presuppositions (Inwood, "Hegel," 27).

[17] The term *posit* is from the German *setzen*, but Inwood has noted that in the philosophical usage it has been heavily influenced by the Greek *tithenai, tithesthai* ('to place,' 'to affirm,' 'to assume'). It primarily indicates the assumption or presupposition, the assertion or affirmation, or simply the affirmation of (the existence of) an entity (Inwood, "Hegel," 224).

[18] I.A. Dorner quoted in J. Moltmann, *The Trinity and the Kingdom.* M. Kohl, trans. (London: SCM Press, 1981), 241. Isaak August Dorner was a German Protestant theologian who sought to interpret Kantian and post-Kantian thought in terms of traditional Lutheran doctrine. The best known of the English translations of his many works is *History of the Development of the Doctrine of the Person of Christ,* 5 vol. (1861–1863). Among the English versions of Dorner's writings that strove to mediate the liberal-conservative controversy within 19th-century German Protestantism are *History of Protestant Theology,* 2 vol. (1871), *System of Christian Doctrine,* 4 vol. (1880–1882), and *System of Christian Ethics* (1887).

In this scheme of things, God the Father is understood to be the subject; the Father alienates himself, externalizes himself, or posits himself
as an object by producing the Son; and the Holy Spirit is the self-
consciousness of the Father with respect to the relationship he has with
the object of his reflection; namely, the Son.[19] The Father is the I. In
this thought, he is what is important and essential, viz the true essence.
The Son is the object posited by the I, the true essence, and—in that
sense—a 'thing for me,' the I. The Holy Spirit is the consciousness
itself, the consciousness of the subject I, the Father—the means by
which the Father is conscious of the object he posits, viz the Son. This
way of speaking renders the term *persons* as an equivalent of *upostaseis*
as found in Christian orthodoxy superfluous. All there is is one absolute personality or one Personal God. The Father is the essential mode
of that One Personal God, the Son is simply the Father as posited by
Himself, and as such a mode of the Father, and the Holy Spirit is the
Father's mode in which He is conscious of Himself as the real essence
and Himself as the object.[20]

BARTH AND RAHNER: ILLUSTRATIONS OF THE IDEALIST CONSTRUCTION OF THE DOCTRINE OF GOD

Self-Revelation / Self-Communication

The Idealist account of the doctrine of God was not only present
within the Christian thought of the eighteenth and nineteenth centuries. Protestantism and Catholicism have possessed concrete idealistic
doctrines of God in our own time. The modern, influential Protestant
and Catholic scholars that are known for articulating the doctrine of
God from the Idealists' philosophical standpoint are Karl Barth and
Karl Rahner respectively. Both Barth and Rahner view God as having
one center of consciousness, and, therefore, as one subject with the ultimate capacity to reflect on himself and at the same time is aware of the
nature of that reflection. This Idealist self-consciousness underpins their
respective explanations of the Christian doctrine of God. Although in

---

[19] Inwood, "Hegel," 613, 614.
[20] Barth, CD I/1:359.

this instance, Barth—as a theologian—preferred the theological term *self- revelation*, and Rahner preferred *self-communication*.[21]

Barth preferred the term *self-revelation* because in his theology "God is … independent of everything that is not he. God is whether everything else is, or is not, whether it is in this way or some other. If there is something other, it cannot precede God, it cannot place God in dependence upon itself."[22] For God to be known, he must reveal himself, and this he decisively did in the Incarnation throughout which he remained the divine subject.[23] Rahner chose the term *self-communication* because he believes in a form of self-communication of God. According to Rahner, a divinized subjective orientation was already built within us. This disposition allows us to have a transcendental experience of the absolute, which he also calls the "mystery, one and the nameless." As far as Rahner is concerned, this is the way we come to know God.[24] He prefers to call the Son and the Holy Spirit the "two processions" or "self-communications" of God. These two are, for Rahner, mystery itself.[25] Consequently, for Rahner the offer and the possibility of grace is given with human nature itself.[26]

Barth's View

Barth begins his articulation of the doctrine of the Trinity from commitment to the position that God's revelation is "God alone, wholly God, God himself." The basic explanation of this premise is that God reveals himself as Yahweh. He alone is the revealer, and, moreover, He is wholly revelation. He himself is what is revealed.[27] For Barth, "God cannot reveal anything more certain, more specific, more living

---

[21] It is important to note that these terms *self-revelation* and *self-communication* also indicate the difference between these two theologians. For Barth, the concept of self-revelation emphasizes the fact that God cannot be known except as he has revealed himself. Rahner uses self-communication to indicate what he believes is the capacity of all men to know God. Rahner's concept of self-communication would play a major role in his theology of the 'anonymous Christ.'

[22] Barth, CD II/1:308.

[23] Barth, CD I/2:131 ff.; cf CD II/1:516 ff.

[24] K. Rahner, *Foundations of Christian Faith: An Introduction to the Idea of Christianity*. W.V. Dych, trans. (New York: Crossroad, 1978), 44, 53; c f TI IV:50, 106.

[25] K. Rahner, *Theological Investigations* [TI] IV. K. Smyth, trans. (London: Darton, Longman and Todd, 1966), 72.

[26] Rahner, *Foundations*, 149.

[27] Barth, CD I:87–95; J. Moltmann, *The Trinity and the Kingdom*, 140.

than himself. Any emptiness or abstraction that we might first feel when hearing the term 'God' is on our side."[28]

By God, Barth means the Father. The Father is the subject, the I. As the I, Barth understands the Father as the *principium* of deity.[29] For Barth, the Father's being *principium* of deity, or the divine fountain, means that he is the mode of God's "... existence in which he is the originator of his other modes of existence."[30] Barth graphically describes the Father as this "... thing, the type, origin, knowledge, will in God, in which he distinguishes Himself from Himself, from which proceeds the other thing, to wit the copy, outcome, word, decision; in short this fact that he can relate Himself as Creator and as our Father to one distinct from Himself outside of Him."[31] With the view that God means the Father and that the Father is, in fact, the *principium* of deity, Barth reached the conclusion that God is the one personal God in the mode of the Father, in the mode of the Son, and in the mode of the Spirit.[32]

The following words of Barth indicate how he viewed Christ:

> If we wish to state who Jesus Christ is ... we must also state or at least make clear—and inexorably so—that we are speaking of the Lord of Heaven and earth, who neither has nor did have any need of heaven or earth or man, who created them out of free love and according to his very own good pleasure, who adopts man, not according to the latter's merit, according to his own mercy, not in virtue of the latter's capacity, but in virtue of his own miraculous power. He is the Lord who ... never ceases in the very slightest to be God, who does not give his glory to another. In this, as Creator, Reconciler and Redeemer, He is a truly loving, serving God. He is the King of all kings just as when he enters into the profoundest hiddenness in 'meekness of heart.'[33]

What Barth means in the above excerpt is not entirely clear until we find other places where he understands Christ as simply another mode of the Father. In Barth's own words, Christ—the Word of God—meets us as the Father himself "... but in another way, in a different way of being."[34] He is the Father's revelation and nothing more or less. The

[28] Barth, CD I:89.
[29] Barth, CD I:111, 114, 119.
[30] Barth, CD I/1:451.
[31] Barth, CD I/1:452.
[32] Barth, CD I/1:359.
[33] Barth, CD I/2:133.
[34] Barth, CD I/1:498.

Father is wholly and utterly in His revelation that is in Jesus Christ.[35] In Jesus Christ, the Father "… sets and gives to be known not something, be it the greatest and the most significant, but Himself exactly as He posits and knows Himself."[36] Elsewhere Barth describes the eternal Logos as "… the eternal Word of the Father who speaks from all eternity, or the eternal thought of the Father who thinks from all eternity, the Word in which God thinks Himself, or expresses Himself by Himself."[37] Thus Barth views the Son merely as the self-revelation of the One Subject—the Father.

The Holy Spirit is understood by Barth simply as "participation" of the Father and the Son, "the common factor between the mode of existence of God the Father and God the Son, … What is common to them as far as they are the Father and the Son." He is the "Communion," the act of "committyness" of the Father and the Son.[38] Elsewhere he gives this 'participation,' 'communion,' and 'committyness' the love flavor, so that the Father and the Son are viewed as participating in each other on the ground of love. Love, it is emphasized "… is the essence of the relation between the Father and the Son."[39] The Holy Spirit in Barth's theology is therefore merely a correlation between the Father and the Son—the correlation being love. From this position Barth was able to argue that the Holy Spirit is love itself, and the basis of the theological statement "… God is love and love is God."[40]

Barth refuses to use the term *persons* as equivalent to the three *upostaseis*. As far as Barth is concerned, the concept "'Person' as used in the church doctrine of the Trinity bears no direct relation to personality."[41] Thus Barth assigns personality to the unity of God.[42] The reason Barth abandoned the word *person* is because, for him, the term suggests that God has three centres of consciousness. Thus:

> Barth, believing that the word inevitably suggested "three centres of consciousness" individualistically conceived, suggested the abandonment of the word *person* in connection with God's threeness, and preferred to speak of three mutually related modes (or ways) of being the one personal

---

[35] Barth, CD II/1 74, 75.
[36] Barth, CD I/1:476.
[37] Barth, CD I/1:499.
[38] Barth, CD I/1:527.
[39] Barth, CD I/1:480.
[40] Barth, CDI/1:488.
[41] Barth, CD I/1:351.
[42] Barth, CD I/1:351.

God. In so doing, he was attempting to mediate between Eastern and Western traditions, for the expression is borrowed from the Cappadocian Fathers who used both the term *person* and the term *modes of being* in an ontological and not a psychological sense.[43]

Rahner's View

In contrast, Karl Rahner's Idealist interpretation of the doctrine of the Trinity is deeply motivated by his commitment to the position that there can never be a distinction between God as Godself (the immanent Trinity), and God as he relates to us (economic Trinity). For Rahner, the immanent Trinity is also the economic Trinity, and the economic Trinity is also the immanent Trinity.[44] This axiom means that we can understand God's pre-temporal identity as being identical with the economic Trinity evident in the history of salvation. In other words, the appearing of the Son and the coming of the Holy Spirit are constitutive in the identity of God. We therefore cannot conceive of the eternal identity of God without considering the Son and the Holy Spirit.[45]

When the term *God* is mentioned, Rahner believes that what is pictured is the Father. The Father here is the God proper.[46] Rahner explains that:

> ... when the New Testament thinks of God, it is the concrete, individual, uninterchangeable Person who comes into its mind, who is in fact the Father and is called so that inversely, when it is being spoken of, it is not the single divine nature that is seen, subsisting in three hypostases, but the concrete Person who possesses the divine nature unoriginately, and communicates it by eternal generation to a Son too and by spiration to the Spirit.[47]

The Father expresses or communicates only by speaking his Word.[48] The Word uttered, Logos, is none other than Jesus Christ the Son, whom he imparts "... as his own personal self disclosure"[49] or "... concrete self-disclosure."[50] The utterance and the incarnated Christ

---

[43] B.C.C. *The Forgotten Trinity: The Report of the B.C.C. Study Commission on Trinitarian Doctrine Today* vol I. (London: British Council of Churches, Interchurch House, 1989).

[44] Rahner, *Theological Investigations*. Also *Theological Investigations* [TI] IV.

[45] C.E. Braaten, *Our Naming of God: Problems and Prospects of God-Talk Today* (Minneapolis: Fortress Press, 1981), 4.

[46] Rahner, TI I, 126–148.

[47] Rahner, TI I, 146.

[48] Rahner, TI IV, 93.

[49] Rahner, TI I, 96.

[50] Rahner, TI I, 100.

are seen here as having a necessary relationship. In Rahner's own thought, "… the Word is essentially the expressible, he who can be expressed even in the non-divine, being the Word of the Father, in whom the Father can express himself and freely exteriorize himself, and because, when this takes place, that which we call human nature comes to being."[51] For Rahner, this 'exteriorizing' of the Father also means 'the indissoluble, irrevocable' presence of the Father in the world as "salvation, love, and forgiveness, as communication to the world of the most intimate depths of the divine reality itself."[52] The Word, the Logos, is the Father made visible, exteriorized, or revealed for the sake of man and his salvation. Therefore, Jesus Christ is just the Father as he reveals himself.

In this scheme, the Holy Spirit is understood to be the mutual love that exists between the Father and his Logos, or, put in another way, the love between the Father and his exterior self.[53] He simply is that deep intimacy and fondness that the Father has for his Logos and which the Logos has for the Father. Rahner's position on what to make of the Holy Spirit is very close to Augustine's. In the words of Augustine:

> Whether the Spirit is the unity of both [Father and Son], or the holiness, or the love, or whether he is the unity because he is the love, and the love because he is the holiness, it is manifest that he is not one of the two [Father and Son], because he is the one through whom the two are joined, through whom the Begotten is loved by the Begetter, and loves him who begot him, and through whom…. they are 'keeping the unity of the Spirit in the bond of peace', which we are commanded to imitate by grace, both towards God and towards each other … And therefore they [the Persons of the Trinity] are not more than three: One [the Father] who loves him [the Son] who is from himself, and one [the Son] who loves him [the Father] from whom he is, and Love itself [the Spirit]. And if this last one is nothing, how can God be love? If this last is not substance, how can God be substance?[54]

It is clear that Rahner does not view the Holy Spirit as a distinct ontological reality that answers to the term *person*. This is because he believes that the concept person cannot be predicated to the Holy Spirit, whom he sees as a mere correlation between the Father and the Son.

---

[51] Rahner, TI I, 93.
[52] Rahner, TI I, 49.
[53] Rahner, TI I, 96.
[54] Augustine, *De Trinitate* 6:5:7.

In the thought of Rahner, therefore, we find a one subject God who refuses to be expressed in the classical Nicene terms of *One Substance* and *Three Persons*. Instead, Rahner proposes that God be understood as one subject and three distinct modes or relative ways in which God subsists.[55] To sum up: "The one and the same God is given for us as Father, Son- logos, and Holy Spirit, or the Father gives himself in absolute self-communication through the Son in the Holy Spirit."[56] As far as Rahner is concerned, the term *person* means "that which subsists as distinct in a rational nature."[57] For Rahner, subsistence involves distinction, particularity, concreteness, and relationship. What the traditional language of the doctrine of the Trinity calls person must, according to Rahner, mean "three distinct manners of subsisting."[58]

BASIC CHARACTERISTICS OF THE 'GOD AS ABSOLUTE SUBJECT'

Modalistic in Nature and Thus Substitutes the Term 'Mode' in Place of 'Person'

Here both the Son and the Holy Spirit have no independent existence of the kind that we see in the scripture. Instead, they are depicted as mere modes of the Father. In effect, there is only 'one Subject divinity,' and that one Subject is none other than the Father. The Son is simply 'alienated,' 'externalized,' or 'posited.' He who alienates, externalizes, or posits himself is the Father, who is the subject. The object, viz the Son, is what is alienated, externalized, or posited. The Holy Spirit is the relationship of love between the Father (subject) and the Son (object). This one Subject divinity manifests himself first as the Father; then as the Son—the 'one Subject' divinity (the Father) thinking about himself; and finally as the Holy Spirit—still the one Subject divinity (the Father), but presented as he is enjoying thinking about himself.[59]

In effect, both the Son and the Holy Spirit do not really exist except in the mind of the Father, for Christ is at the bottom line only 'the Father as he is thinking about Himself' and the Holy Spirit 'the Father

---

[55] Rahner, TI I, 95, 96; cf. K. Rahner, *The Trinity* (London: Herder, 1970), 103 ff.
[56] Rahner quoted in Moltmann, *Trinity*, 147.
[57] Rahner, *The Trinity*, 104 n. 25.
[58] Rahner, *The Trinity*, 109.
[59] O.W. Heick, *A History of Christian Thought* (Philadelphia: Fortress Press, 1966), 189.

enjoying thinking about himself.' What occurs is that two experiences of the Father—thought and love—are isolated, presented successively, and interpreted as the Son and the Holy Spirit respectively.[60] It is clear from this model of understanding the doctrine of God that the one divine subject acts and receives. Personhood is transferred from the υπoςταςεις to the one divine Subject. The υπoςταςεις are merely modes of the one Subject. The question that we must raise at this point is whether theology sees its role as providing models and metaphors for the Christian orthodoxy or as deriving them from the Christian orthodoxy. The issue, as Brümmer has written, is that:

> Systematic theologians do not create models for God. They derive them from the religious traditions in which they stand. For the Christians the Bible is the classic text of their tradition and as such the classic source of metaphors and models in terms of which they understand the meaning of their lives and the world. In the tradition of the church these models have been actualised, interpreted, reinterpreted, developed, and amended in many ways throughout the ages and handed down in many ways from person to person and from generation to generation.[61]

It is understandable that the theological models may lose their original force in the process of being "actualised, interpreted, reinterpreted, developed, and amended,"[62] and as they get transmitted in different ways from one person to the other and from one generation to the next. Barth, Rahner, and H. Berkhof see this as having happened to the term *person*. However, the solution is not to reject the term. In fact, if this line of argument were to be followed, theology would have no model and metaphor to discuss since virtually no theological concept has been spared of abuse. Rather, theology has the twin task of preserving the concepts as they are in the Christian story and reinterpreting them for the new situations of reception in terms that are not only consistent with their meaning in their native contexts, but which are also intelligible to the receiving situation.

---

[60] J. Moltmann believes that Barth and Rahner have been betrayed by their idealistic heritage that insists that it is the subject that acts and receives. For Barth and Rahner, " ... the subjectivity of acting and receiving is transferred from the three divine Persons to the one divine subject. But viewed theologically this is a late triumph for the Sabellian modalism which the early church condemned. The result would be to transfer the subjectivity of action to a deity concealed 'behind' the three Persons" (Moltmann, *The Trinity*, 139).

[61] V. Brümmer, "Metaphorical Thinking and Systematic Theology." An unpublished paper delivered at the Faculty of Theology, Universisty of Stellenbosch, 1998, 13.

[62] Brümmer, "Metaphorical Thinking," 13.

God Presented as a Monad

Trinity as a theological term makes sense only in the context of speaking about the plurality (three-ness) in the Godhead. The one Subject divinity, as we have just seen, articulates the plurality in modalistic terms. According to this model, the one Subject divinity (the Father) expresses himself successively in his other modes (the Son and the Holy Spirit). However, even if we grant that the Son, a mode of the Father, is understood as an individual, we still would have only two individuals in the Godhead: The Father and the Son. But deep in us we know that the Son, according to this thought, is not really distinguished from the Father, and therefore the former has no individuality of his own. As such, both the individuality and the deity of the Son are effectively ruled out. His individuality and deity are accented, but only in name.

The one Subject divinity model does not view the Holy Spirit as an individual at all. He is viewed in this model simply as a correlation of the Father and the Son, the consciousness of the Father, the 'mutual intense passion' and 'love' between the two, the 'communion' between the two, and anything else that explains the relationship between the Father and the Son. We have already seen what Barth and Rahner think about the Holy Spirit. Moltmann agrees with them, but discusses the Holy Spirit as mere "… condition which allows the Son to shine in the Father and transfigures the Father in the Son, … the consciousness of the divine life which facilitates … the sacred feast of the Trinity."[63] In this instance, the individuality of the Holy Spirit exists only in name. Under circumstances such as these, one cannot possibly speak about the Trinity. Trinity is what it is only if we are talking about the Father, the Son, and the Holy Spirit as distinct persons but one God. In that case, the unity and the particularity of God are upheld in the terms that the Father is God, the Son is God, the Holy Spirit is God, yet not three gods but One God. The theological term *Trinity* ceases to make sense at the moment we lose focus of this distinction and particularity, or demote one of the members of the Godhead

---

[63] Moltmann, *The Trinity*, 173–176.

CONCLUSION

The God as an absolute subject theology is of the opinion that behind the three Persons is one Subject who acts and receives. This, in effect, transfers personhood from the υποςταςεις to the one divine subject. Because of this transfer, the Idealistic theologians have proposed that the term *person* should be abandoned altogether when making reference to the Trinity, and in its place the term *mode* be instituted. The reason for this change is clearly not the need to be more biblical. The reason is to align theology with the contemporary Western notion of person. Person for the modern Westerner is no longer simply an individual with rationality, but rather the subject I who is conscious.

The God as an absolute subject theology reinterprets the doctrine of the Trinity within the infrastructure of the Idealistic philosophy. Scholars such as Barth and Rahner see this interpretation as adequate to the Western context that constructs its reality from the viewpoint of Idealism.

However, I believe that there are two important contributions of the God as an absolute subject model of interpreting the Trinity. The first addresses the issue of the unity factor in the Trinity. The concept of the one God in the Trinitarian formula is not a static concept that can be represented by the concept of substance. One God is Yahweh—the God of Israel. The second contribution is in questioning the relevance of Neo-Platonism in certain cultural contexts. Before the rise of Idealistic philosophy, it was simply believed that Neo-Platonic metaphysics owned copyright to expressions of truth. In order to give the modern Western world the doctrine of the Trinity that matches their current thought pattern, Barth and Rahner did not need the Neo-Platonic system. What seems to be important is this question: How can I use the infrastructure of the thought pattern current in the situation of reception to express a theological truth without compromising the latter?

CHAPTER FIVE

GOD AS COMMUNITY IN UNITY

INTRODUCTION

Much of the present discussion about the doctrine of the Trinity in the Western context debates the 'God as essence' in opposition to the 'God as an Absolute Subject.' Generally, contemporary Trinitarian scholars seem to view God as essence as obsolete. The focus is trained on how Barth and Rahner responded to God as essence and what to make of their proposal; namely, God as an absolute subject.[1] This general shift in focus has led to the acceptance of the view that the immanent Trinity is the economic Trinity and vice versa.[2]

Although a large number of contemporary Western Christian thinkers operate with the God as an absolute subject model, there is evidently a growing interest in a third model: "God as community in unity" or simply "God as Father, Son, and Holy Spirit in eternal correlation, interpenetration, love and communion which make them one sole God."[3] The Western scholars who seek to understand the doctrine of the Trinity within this model generally take their point of departure from the concept of *homoousios* as it is understood by John Calvin, Gregory of Nazianzen, and Athanasius.[4]

---

[1] P. Collins, "A Critical Review of Recent Writings in the Field of Trinitarian Theology" in *Epworth Review*. vol. 24, 1997, 95–99; W. McWilliams, "Trinitarian Doxology: Jurgen Moltmann on the Relation of Economic and Immanent Trinity" in *Perspectives in Religious Studies*, 1996.

[2] See J. Moltmann, *The Trinity and Kingdom*, xi; R.E. Olson, "Trinity and Eschatology: The Historical Being of God in Jurgen Moltmann and Wolfhart Pannenberg," in *Scottish Journal of Theology* 36 (1983): 219–220; P.K. Jewett, *God, Creation and Revelation: A Neo-Evangelical Theology* (Grand Rapids: Eerdmans, 1991), 305; Moody, *The Word of Truth*, 115; and G.D. Kaufman, *Systematic Theology* (New York: Scribner's, 1968), 250–252.

[3] D. Brown, *The Divine Trinity* (London: General Duckworth, 1985); T.F. Torrance, *The Trinitarian Perspective*; L. Boff, *Trinity and Society* (Wellwood: Burns & Oates, 1988).

[4] Torrance, *The Trinitarian Perspective*, 21–76.

Motives for Renewed Interest
in 'God as Community in Unity'

Some of the leading Western Christian thinkers who seek to understand
the doctrine of the Trinity from the viewpoint of God as community in
unity are J. Zizioulas and J.J. O'Donnell.[5] The Orthodox theologian
John Zizioulas makes a candid enquiry into the *plurality model* of the
Cappadocian tradition. He particularly enquires into the understanding of personhood in that tradition. Like O'Donnell, Zinzioulas appeals
to Richard of St. Victor who understands personhood in the same way
as the Cappadocian fathers. Richard of St. Victor understands personhood from the concept of *existence*, which Collins explains as "being in
relation." This understanding opposes the *unity model* of the Augustinian
tradition that espouses a "unitary psychological modeling of the Godhead and of personhood."[6]

Collins has noted that there are different reasons why a growing
number of modern Western Christian thinkers are opting for the God
as community in unity model of understanding the doctrine of the
Trinity.

> One reason is that the social model of the Godhead of the Eastern
> tradition is seen as that which most closely reflects the primary data of
> the human experience of divine activity. Another is that the Trinity seen
> as being-in-relation offers a paradigm for the human community over
> against such notions as hierarchy and patriarchy. This in turn provides
> models and metaphors for those seeking political, liberation and feminist
> theologies.[7]

---

[5] J. Zizioulas, *Being as Communion: Studies in Personhood and the Church* (Crestwood:
St. Vladamir's Seminary Press, 1985); his article, "On Being a Person—Towards an
Ontology of Personhood" in *Persons, Divine and Human*, 1991; and his other article, "The
Doctrine of the Holy Trinity: The Significance of the Cappadocian Contribution." See
also J. O'Donnell. *The Mystery of the Triune God* (London: Sheed and Ward, 1988), 101.

[6] Collins, "A Critical Review of Recent Writings in the Field of Trinitarian Theology," 97. Other interesting contributors to the Divinity as community in unity model
of interpreting the doctrine of the Trinity include Y. Congar, *I Believe in the Holy Spirit,
vol. III: The River of Life Flows in the East and in the West.* D. Smith, trans. (London: Geoffrey Chapman, 1983); McFadyen, *The Call to Personhood, A Christian Theory of the Individual
in Social Relationships*, 1990; C.E. Gunton, *The One, The Three and the Many, Creation and
the Culture of Modernity* (Cambridge: Cambridge University Press, 1993); and Boff, *Trinity and Society.* Other significant contributors in this field are Brown, *The Divine Trinity*;
and T.F. Torrance, *The Trinitarian Faith* (Edinburgh: Clark, 1988) and *The Trinitarian
Perspectives.*

[7] Collins, "A Critical Review of Recent Writings in the Field of Trinitarian Theology," 95.

David Brown strongly argues against the Augustinian tradition summarized in the *unity model* and proposes the *plurality model* of the Cappadocian tradition instead. His basis for making this claim is the position that the essential Christian experience of God is the personal communion with Father, Son, and the Holy Spirit. Consequently, he concludes that the plurality model "is a more basic datum than [the] ultimate unity. This is one of the most important new perspectives that
modern historical investigations of the New Testament has revealed,
but so far it has been inadequately taken into account in discussions
of the doctrine of the Trinity."[8] T.F. Torrance also defends the plurality
model.[9] According to Torrance, the concept of *homoousios* led Athanasius and, consequently, the Cappadocians to see the Godhead as a plurality of three persons in one *ousia*. Leonardo Boff places the idea of the
perichoresis at the very center of his understanding of the Godhead. As
far as he is concerned, the concept of the *perichoresis* provides a pattern
for human social existence. He writes: "… the Trinitarian communion
between the divine Three, the union between them in love and the
vital interpenetration, can serve as a source of inspiration, as a utopian
goal that generates models of successively diminishing differences. This
is why I am taking the concept of perichoresis as the structural axis of
these thoughts."[10]

The Idea of the Divine Perichoresis

The concept of the divine *perichoresis* or 'God as community in unity'
is connected to the idea of the divine substance (*homoousis*) as expressed
in each person. According to Athanasius, "We are allowed to know the
Son in the Father, because the whole Being of the Son is proper to the
Father's being.… For whereas the form of Godhead of the Father is
in the Being of the Son, it follows that the Son is in the Father and
the Father is in the Son."[11] Athanasius further amplifies this thought
when he explains that "the Son and the Father are one in propriety
and peculiarity of nature and in the identity of the one Godhead. The
Godhead of the Son's is the Father's; whence also it is indivisible; and

---

[8] Brown, *The Divine Trinity*, 287.
[9] Torrance, *The Trinitarian Faith* and *The Trinitarian Perspectives*.
[10] Boff, *Trinity and Society*, 6–7.
[11] Athanasius, *Contra Arianos* 3.3.

thus there is one God and none other but he. And so since they are
one, the Godhead himself is one, the same things are said of the Son
as are said of the Father."[12] Speaking elsewhere about the Holy Spirit,
Athanasius remarks that the Spirit, unlike creatures which are found
only in separately determinate localities, is omnipresent and therefore
must be God; moreover, the Spirit must also be in the Son, and the Son
is established to be in the Father.[13]

For Athanasius, the concept of *homoousios* did not just mean the
intercommunication of the properties of the persons as well as the
oneness in being and activity of the persons of the Trinity. The idea
of the *homoousios* also meant coinherence. And so, besides existing in the
unity of being and activity, the Divine Persons were also understood
to be existing in "a complete mutual indwelling in which each Person,
while remaining what he is by himself as Father, Son or Holy Spirit, is
wholly in others as the others are wholly in him."[14]

Hilary has made an input into the development of the doctrine of the
divine *perichoresis* as well. For Hilary the starting point is God's nature.
The Father contains all things, but can be contained by none. The
Son is a perfect offspring of the Father, and he is endowed with the
properties that are in the Father.[15] Elsewhere Hilary argues that the Son
is derived wholly from the whole of his Father's nature. Consequently,
he has the whole of his Father's nature, and thus he abides in the Father
because he is God.[16]

Whereas Athanasius and Hilary emphasized the fact that the Father
is in the Son, the Son in the Father, and the Spirit in both, Basil
argued strongly for the use of the phrase 'with' in preference to 'in' in
describing the Divine Persons.[17] Gregory of Nyssa approached the issue
from the conception that the Divine Persons mutually 'contain one
another.' Previously Athanasius had used the concept of omnipresence.
Gregory of Nyssa posed the question: If the Father is perfect and fills all
things, what is left for the Son to contain? Gregory of Nyssa's response
is that the Father and the Son are receptive and permeative (*choretikos*)

---

[12] Athanasius, *Contra Arianos* 3.5.

[13] Athanasius, *ad Serap.* 3.4; 4.4.

[14] Torrance, *The Trinitarian Perspective*, 10.

[15] Hillary, Bishop of Poictiers. *De Trinitate. In Nicene and post-Nicene Fathers of the Christian Church.* vol IX. Relevant sections 3.1; 2, 4.

[16] Hillary, *De Trinitate*, 9.69.

[17] Basil 'the Great'. *De Spirit Sancto. In Nicene and post-Nicene Fathers of the Christian Church.* vol IX. Relevant section is *de Spir. sanct.* 63.

of one another. The idea 'containing one another' is understood in the sense of the mutual envelopment of one another.[18] According to Gregory Nazienzen, "each of the Divine Persons is entirely one with those with whom he is conjoined, as he is in himself, because of the identity of being and power that is between them. This is the reason for the Oneness so far as we have apprehended it. If this reason has force, thanks be to God for the insight; if it is not, let us seek a stronger one."[19]

What could be considered a later development of the doctrine of the divine *perichoresis* is found in Pseudo-Cyril. We here quote Prestige's rendering of the understanding of this anonymous author: "We assert that each of the three possesses a perfect hypostasis ... but maintain one ousia, simple, final, ... perfect, in three perfect hypostaseis; so again ... we call the Holy Trinity one God ... the three hypostaseis; they are united ... not so as to be confounded, but so as to adhere ... to one another, and they possess co-inherence in one another without any coalescence or commixture."[20]

Interestingly, John Calvin's understanding of the doctrine of the Trinity is in the same continuum as Athanasius', Hilary's, Gregory of Nyssa's, and Gregory of Nazienzen's. Like these early fathers, Calvin emphasizes the oneness of the being of the incarnate Son with the being of the Father.[21] Moreover, for Calvin the issue is not just the oneness of the being of the incarnate Son with the being of the Father; it also has to do with the oneness of agency and power between them. For Calvin this means that one cannot simply separate what the Son does from what the Father does. He believes this ontological oneness is of crucial significance to the entire Christological debate[22] To the question of why the Holy Spirit is divine, Calvin has the same response.

---

[18] Gregory, Bishop of Nyssa. *Against Sabellius*. In *Nicene and post-Nicene Fathers of the Christian Church* See *adv. et Sab*.12; 266.

[19] Athanasius, Hilary, Gregory of Nyssa, and Gregory of Nazienzen all understood *homoousios* as conveying the concept of the coinherence of the three persons in the one identical being of God. However, patristic theology owes the term *perichoretic relation* to Gregory of Nazienzen, who applied it to the way in which the Divine. (See Gregory Nazienzen, *Oratio*. In Nicene and post-Nicene Fathers of the Christian Church. vol IX. Relevant sections are *Oratio*. 31.16, see also 31.14; cf 25.16, 26.19, and 42.15ff.18.42).

[20] Prestige, *God in Patristic Thought*, 297–298.

[21] J. Calvin, *Institutes of Christian Religion*. Translated and annotated by F.L. Battles (London: Collins. 1986), translation of the original 1559 edition. See *Institutes* I.13.7–11; cf. Gregory Nazienzen, *Oratio*, 30.18; 31.6; 33.16; 38.7; 45.3; Athanasius, *Contra Arianos*, 4.15–24.

[22] Calvin, *Institute*, I.13.12–13.

For him the Holy Spirit is divine because of his subsistence in God. He says, "the Holy Spirit does not act from outside of God or apart from him, but from within God."[23]

Having established the divinity of the Son and of the Holy Spirit in a style that is clearly reminiscent of what we see in the church fathers, Calvin continues and places his own approval on the doctrine of the divine *perichoresis*. On this issue he says the following:

> A certain distinction of the Father from the Word, and of the Word from the Spirit, is clearly pointed out by the Scriptures—but the very magnitude of the mystery warns us of the great reverence and sobriety with which we must proceed in examining this. I am immensely delighted by the statement of Gregory Nazienzen: 'I can not think of the One without immediately being surrounded by the radiance of the Three; nor can I discern the Three without at once being carried back to the One'. Accordingly let us not allow ourselves to imagine a Trinity of Persons in such a partitive way that our thought is not immediately bought back to that Unity. The words 'Father', 'Son', and 'Spirit' certainly import a real distinction—let no one think that they are mere epithets by which God is variously designated from his works—it is a *distinction*,[24] however not a division.[25]

This understanding of the Divine Persons and their interrelationship led Calvin to articulate the doctrine of God as follows:

> When we profess to believe in one God, under the name of God is understood one simple Being… in which we comprehend three Persons or hypostaseis; and whenever the name of God is employed indefinitely … the Son and Spirit, no less than the Father, are indicated. However when the Son is joined to the Father, relation is introduced… and so we distinguish between the Persons. But because the properties of the Persons carry an order with them… having to do with beginning and origin… in the Father, whenever mention is made of the Father and the Son together, or of the Father and the Spirit together, the name of God is peculiarly ascribed to the Father. In this way the unity of Being is retained, and regard for order is preserved, but which in no way derogates from the Deity of the Son and the Spirit.[26]

---

[23] Calvin, *Institute*, I.13.14 ff.; cf 1 Cor.2.9 ff.; 3.16; 6.19; 2 Cor.6.16; Acts 5.3; 28.25; etc.

[24] Calvin makes it clear that the distinctions are not to be traced back to the Incarnation; rather, they existed antecedently and inherently in the one Godhead. The Incarnation only made the distinctions recognizable (Calvin, *Institute*, I.13.17–21).

[25] Calvin, *Institute*, I.13.7; cf. Gregory Nazienzen, *Oratio*, 40.41.

[26] Calvin, *Institue*, I.13.20.

Clearly, Calvin's doctrine of the Trinity revolves around the Father as the "Divine *principium*"[27] as well as the eternal distinctions and interrelations of the Divine Persons.[28] Here we see the whole Trinity comprising three, inseparable, consubstantial persons indwelling one another, and the Holy Spirit proceeding from the Being that is common to the Father and the Son.

The scholars who understand the doctrine of God within the structures of 'God as community in unity' do not see what is common to the Father, the Son, and the Holy Spirit as a substantial reality. As far as the God as community in unity theologians are concerned, the unity factor in the context of the Trinity is love. According to this model, God is each of the Divine Persons—Father, Son, and Holy Spirit—sharing in divine love. Hall has described this phenomenon as: "… personal, communal, loving, and altruistic. In a wonderful divine surprise, God within his own being as one God, exists as a living relationship of love between Father, Son and Holy Spirit. Hence the God celebrated and adored in Christian worship exists and has always existed as a communion of infinite, self-giving love. There is no solitary God lurking behind the divine persons."[29]

---

[27] Calvin prefers to use the term, *pricipium divinitatis*. By this term he meant that Christ is not from himself; he has a beginning in the Father. He is quick to add, however, that the *prinicipium divinitas* has to do with order and position and not ontological priority (Calvin, *Institute*, I.13.6, 18, 20–25). For Calvin, the Father is not merely the 'Divine *arche*' that we see in the Cappadocians for deity can never be derived. Christ is divine—both because of the *homoousios* and because he is the Son. One Being of God is wholly common to the Father and the Son (Calvin, *Institute*, I.13.2, 7f., 23) and, on the other hand, "unless the Father were God, he could not be the Father, and unless the Son were God, he could not be the Son, thus his Being is without *principium*, but the *principium* of his person is God himself" (Calvin, *Institute*, I.13.25).

[28] Unlike the Cappadocians, Calvin accepts the Western understanding of the procession of the Holy Spirit. For Calvin, far from interfering with the utterly simple unity of God, it serves to prove that the Son is One with God the Father because he constitutes one spiritual being with him. The Spirit is not something other than the Father and is different from the Son because he is the Spirit of the Father and of the Son (Calvin, *Institute*, I.13.19). Calvin does not limit the Spirit to the person of the Holy Spirit; rather, he uses it in a sense which refers to the entire spiritual being of God. Since the spiritual being of the Father is shared by the Son and the Holy Spirit, the procession of the Holy Spirit must be from this common being (Calvin, Institute, I.13.2, 19f., 24, 29).

[29] Hall, "Adding Up the Trinity," 26–28.

Basic Characteristics of 'God as Community in Unity'

Gives Emphasis to the Divine Persons

The traditional formula, 'One God and Three Persons,' is understood in a personal way. The doctrine of God understood within the model of God as community in unity comes from the view that the Father is the 'Divine fountain' or, as Calvin puts it, the *principium divinitas*. Here God is not defined abstractly; rather, the One Being is *Yahweh*—the 'I am.' The God as community in unity model upholds the view that Father, Son, and the Holy Spirit are not mere epithets by which God is variously designated.[30] Rather, the Father, Son and Holy Spirit refer to God as he exists in himself, and as he has revealed himself though Jesus Christ and the Spirit.[31]

Defines Person as a Being in Relationship

In the philosophy of the church fathers, substance or nature refers to the *what* of something. Thus human nature or substance refers to the nature of all human beings. There is nothing unique about it. For the church fathers, however, person has to do with the question *how* and can only be predicated of one being in an absolute sense. Man, for example, is only an image of God. He is subject to limitations of space and time; however, he is called to exist in the way God exists. The image of God in man has to do with how to exist in the way that God exists. Man, according to this philosophy, is free to "affect the how of his existence either in the direction of the way (the *how*) God is, or in the direction of *what* his, i.e. man's nature is." Man can live either according to the human nature or in the way God exists—that is, in the image of God's personhood.[32]

For the church fathers, person is, therefore, the how or the way of being of God himself. God does not exist in isolation; he exists in a

---

[30] Calvin, *Institute*, I.13.7.

[31] A significant paradigmatic change in the understanding of both Christ and the Holy Spirit is worth noting here. The locus of the divinity of the Son and of the Holy Spirit is not the possession of a divine nature, nor the act of objectifying God; rather, it is the relationship of the Son and the Holy Spirit to the Father. And so here is a paradigm shift, not from substance metaphysics to metaphysics of self-consciousness, but a shift to the metaphysics of relations.

[32] Zizioulas, "The Doctrine of the Holy Trinity," 55.

communion. The Father exists in love and relationship with the Son and the Holy Spirit. Yet in this relationship there is also the question of the personal identity that should not be lost to view. The names Father, Son, and the Holy Spirit do not merely indicate personal identity in the divine interrelationship. Besides this obvious function, the names also provide us with a model of how we as persons may exist with God, with fellow human beings, and with the rest of God's creation.

Understands the Unity Factor as Love

According to this view of understanding God, the essence of God has no substantial content. God's essence is not even considered to be the Father as we saw in the Divinity as absolute subject model. Instead, the Divinity as community in unity views the essence of God as love. The epistemological basis of this position is that God has shown this love to us in Jesus Christ through the Holy Spirit. The incomprehensible mystery of the divine nature "… is the wondrous communion of love demonstrated and communicated to us in Jesus Christ."[33]

Conclusion

God as community in unity presents us with a fundamental issue for modern theology—the need to revisit the divine plurality we see in the New Testament and its implications for Christian thought, worship, and social action. The New Testament's picture of the Divine Persons helps us to put into perspective the Father who sent the Son, and who is involved with us through the Holy Spirit. God is not detached from the world. In spite of conflicts, wars, disease, hunger, poverty, and the cruelty of socio-political systems, we can be sure that God in the Father, the Son, and the Holy Spirit is an ever present reality.

This perspective of understanding the Trinity also refocuses our attention to the biblical meaning of the term *person*. *Person*, according to the Bible, is not an isolated individual with rationality seeking to pre-serve an autonomous self, as the Western world would have it. Rather, as far as theology is concerned, to be person is to have the image of God and thus to exist according to the way in which God exists. Once

---

[33] Hall, "Adding Up the Trinity," 28.

again we are reminded that God is not a lone being lurking behind the Divine Persons. Rather, as Hall says, God's existence itself is "… personal, communal, loving and altruistic."[34] This is possible because the Divine Persons are, in the first place, not isolated individuals, but persons in relationship with one another.

[34] Hall, "Adding Up the Trinity," 28.

CHAPTER SIX

ISSUES IN THE WESTERN REINTERPRETATIONS

INTRODUCTION

The attempts of Western Christian thought to reinterpret the Christian understanding of the doctrine of God could be placed into three distinct groups: God as essence, God as an absolute subject, and God as community in unity. Each group or model of interpretation has its own unique philosophical presuppositions. The God as essence school is clearly operating within neo-Platonic structures, God as an absolute subject comes from German Idealism, while God as community in unity seeks to function within the same conceptual framework as the church fathers.[1] The philosophical commitments of reinterpreting the doctrine of the Trinity by each of these schools have significantly affected their respective theological outcomes. However, in spite of the differences in philosophical commitments and theological outcomes, there are common threads that run across the three models.

---

[1] Of particular interest to God as community in unity theologians is the way Athanasius, Gregory of Nazienzen, and John Calvin understood the concept of *homoousios*. They also follow the church fathers' definition of person as 'being in relation.'

DIFFERENCES OF WESTERN MODELS OF
INTERPRETING THE DOCTRINE OF GOD

Divinity as Essence	*Divinity as one Subject*	*Divinity as Community in Unity*
God is understood in abstract terms. When one says God, what is meant is the impersonal 'essence,' or 'substance' of God, the Godhead. Substance is therefore the locus of divinity.	God is viewed as the ultimate subject. When one says God, what is meant is the Father. The other members of the Trinity are only real as long as the Father is real. They are but mere modes or extensions of the Father.	God is the relationship existing between the persons of the Trinity. When one says God, what is meant is the *koinonia*, the *perichoretic* relationship with which the three divine persons are ultimately linked and in which they exist. God has no true being, no ontological content, apart from communion (*koinonia*). Relationship of the Father, the Son, and the Holy Spirit is the locus of divinity.
Persons of the Trinity are understood as pure relations. The Father is the Father because he is unbegotten, the Son proceeds from the Father, and the Holy Spirit 'spirates' from the Father through the Son. The Son is the Son because he is begotten of the Father, and the Holy Spirit is who he is because he proceeds from both the Father and the Son. The Divine Persons are thus not made concrete in the sense we see in the divine economy.	Is not at ease with the idea of the Divine Persons. Instead the concept *person* is applied to the Father alone, the Son is merely the Father as externalized, and the Holy Spirit is the 'Self-Consciousness' of the Father regarding his relationship with the Son.	Divine Persons are not adjunct to the divine essence. Free persons are essential to the constitution of true being, and the persons are said to be free because they affirm their identity by means of *perichoresis*.
Uses the philosophical infrastructure of Neo-Platonism.	Uses the philosophical infrastructure of Idealism.	Insists on returning to the philosophy of the church fathers.

Divinity as Essence	*Divinity as one Subject*	*Divinity as Community in Unity*
Accepts the notion of *filioque*	Accepts *filioque*.	Historically this point of view rejects *filioque* because of its very strong links with Eastern theology. However, like Calvin, it is possible to hold this point of view without rejecting the *filioque*.

From the features displayed in the table above, it is clear that the three schools have features that make them unique and distinct in their approach to reinterpreting the doctrine of the Trinity. Historically, God as an absolute subject began as a reaction against God as essence, and God as community in unity sees itself as a resuscitation of the, hitherto, moribund Cappadocian heritage. The result has been an attempt by each of the positions to distance itself from the other two as far as possible. The discrepancy of this style of presentation is that the question of which model is to be taken is posed in terms of either or as the readers are confronted with a situation which has only three options—God as essence, God as an absolute subject, or God as community in unity.

As we look at these models, we are confronted with the question: Which model is adequate, and for what context is it adequate?[2] These models may not be entirely adequate for the African context; however, we cannot deny that they have tremendous merits. Over the years theology has known only these models of reinterpreting the doctrine of the Trinity. Furthermore, the survival of theology as a credible discipline during the heyday of Neo-Platonism or the time of German Idealism has historically been pegged to the willingness of theology to accept and constructively make use of Neo-Platonism and German Idealism respectively. The rise of the God as community in unity model in the present time has no doubt given the church a new interest in the doctrine of the Trinity. Although these models of understanding the

---

[2] Vincent Brümmer suggests criteria for determining the adequacy of theological models. According to him, "all of these are necessary and none of them is sufficient. These are (1) consonance with tradition, (2) comprehensive coherence, (3) adequacy for demands of life, and (4) personal authenticity" (V. Brümmer, "Metaphorical Thinking and Systematic Theology," an unpublished paper delivered at the Faculty of Theology, University of Stellenbosch, 1998, 13).

doctrine of the Trinity are different, they have a common interest in the incarnation question, the concept of the *homoousios*, and the identity debate.

ISSUES COMMON TO THE THEOLOGICAL MODELS

The Incarnation

Undoubtedly, how Western contexts understand the doctrine of God has been influenced by the historical concept of the Incarnation. From the time of the church fathers, Western theologies have generally recognized that God became incarnate, suffered on the cross, and redeemed mankind by dying and rising again. It is on the basis of acknowledging the gravity of the Incarnation that the fathers articulated such concepts as the *ageneton, homoousios,* and *upostaseis* (see chapter 2).

Of course, the concepts of the *ageneton* and *upostaseis* (in particular) have generated a lot of debate within Western theology. The church fathers—such as Athanasius, Hilary, and the Cappadocians—saw the *upostasis* of the Father as the *ageneton*. They called the Father the 'divine fountain.' This term was later rendered, especially in the works of John Calvin, as *principium divinitas.* Augustine differed with this definition and held a view of the Godhead that led him to see the *ageneton* as belonging to the divine essence that is common to the three persons of the Trinity. With the different definitions of the *ageneton* came different views of the *upostasis*, as we saw in part 2 of this research. However, regardless of how Western theologies explain the *ageneton* and *upostaseis,* there is no indication that the theologies question the basic principle of the Incarnation. God as essence, God as an absolute subject, and God as community in unity clearly differ on how to understand substance, essence,[3] or *hypostaseis*;[4] however, they all agree that their goal is to articulate the truth that God became man and lived among us at a point in history.

---

[3] God as essence understands the unity factor as substance or essence; God as absolute subject views the unity factor as the Father, while God as community in unity sees love the unity factor.

[4] Person in God as essence is hypostatic relation; in God as absolute subject person is mode, whereas in God as community in unity to be person is to exist in a community governed by the principle of love.

The Concept of the Homoousios

In addition to agreeing on the basic issue of the Incarnation, it also is apparent that Western theologies have no problem with the basic concept of *homoousios*. According to Athanasius, "We are allowed to know the Son in the Father, because the whole Being of the Son is proper to the Father's being.... For whereas the form of Godhead of the Father is in the Being of the Son, it follows that the Son is in the Father and the Father is in the Son."[5] Elsewhere, Athanasius amplifies this thought when he explains that "the Son and the Father are one in propriety and peculiarity of nature and in the identity of the one Godhead. The Godhead of the Son's is the Father's; whence also it is indivisible; and thus there is one God and none other but he. And so since they are one, the Godhead himself is one, the same things are said of the Son as are said of the Father."[6] Talking about the consubstantiality of the Holy Spirit and the Father, Athanasius says that the Spirit, unlike creatures which are found only in separately determinate localities, is omnipresent and therefore must be God. Moreover, the Spirit must also be in the Son, and the Son is established to be in the Father.[7]

There is not much difference between the statements of Athanasius cited above and those we find in the standard Augustinian theology (see *Quincunque Vult*). Reformed theology pioneered by John Calvin indicates a similar viewpoint. Calvin clearly emphasized the oneness of the being of the incarnate Son with the being of the Father.[8] In the process, Calvin also stressed the oneness of agency and power between the Father and the Son. For Calvin, one cannot separate what the Son does from what the Father does. There is an ontological oneness which is of crucial significance to the entire Christological debate[9] and the Pneumatological discussions.[10]

In summary, the Western theologies, as is evident in the *Quincunque Vult* and in the works of John Calvin, seem to see the concept of

---

[5] Athanasius, *Contra Arianos* 3.3.

[6] Athanasius, *Contra Arianos*, 3.5.

[7] Athanasius, *ad Serap.* 3.4; 4.4.

[8] Calvin, *Institute of the Christian Religion*, I.13.7–11; cf. Gregory Nazienzen, *Oratio. In Nicene and post-Nicene Fathers of the Christian Church*. Relevant sections 30.18; 31.6; 33.16; 38.7; 45.3; see also Athanasius, *Contra Arianos*, 4.15–24.

[9] See Calvin, *Institute*, I.13.12–13.

[10] Calvin, *Institute*, I.13.14 ff.; cf 1 Cor. 2.9 ff.; 3.16; 6.19; 2 Cor. 6.16; Acts 5.3; 28.25; etc.

homoousios as a phenomenon in which "each of the Divine Persons is entirely one with those with whom he is conjoined, as he is in himself, because of the identity of being and power that is between them."[11] Gregory Nazienzen, who authored the statement quoted above, went on to add "... this is the reason for the Oneness so far as we have apprehended it. If this reason has force, thanks be to God for the insight; if it is not let us seek a stronger one."[12]

The Identity Problem

There is no doubt that Westerners seek to understand the doctrine of God from a Western point of view. The attempts by the approaches of God as essence, God as an absolute subject, and God as community in unity to interpret the doctrine of God are clearly done from philosophical positions that are Western in origin and character. Neo-Platonism and Idealist philosophy are ways in which the West has reinterpreted its reality. For the sake of relevance, theology must make critical use of the intellectual culture of the situation of reception to convey universal theological statements.

Besides utilizing thought patterns native to the Western environment, Western theologies have maintained their discussion of the doctrine of God within Christian boundaries. It must be noted that the Western peoples had native gods. The ones whose memories have lingered long are Wodan, god of the dead; Donar, god of thunder and the sky; and Tyr, god of war.[13] However, in the thought of a Westerner today, God is not Wodan, Donar, or Tyr; the Christian faith took the class word *god* from the Teutonic thought and filled it with new content.[14] Regardless of the differences between the models of interpretation, the doctrine of God in the Western theologies are efforts by the Western church to understand the God who has revealed himself in Christ and is present in the Spirit.

---

[11] Gregory Nazienzen, *Oratio.* In 31.16, see also 31.14.
[12] Gregory Nazienzen, *Oratio* 31.16, see also 31.14; cf 25.16, 26.19, and 42.15 ff.
[13] E.W. Smith, *African Ideas of God* (London: Edinburgh Press, 1950), 35.
[14] Smith, *African Ideas of God*, 35.

Conclusion

The doctrine of God in Western Christian thought is a complex matter. In a sense, it has remained at the center of the Christian thought since the inception of the Christian faith. The study of the doctrine of the Trinity Western theologies leads us to the following observations:

1. That theology is clarified using the native metaphysics. Barth's view of the doctrine of the Trinity is different from Thomas Aquinas', not because either of the two sought to be less biblical. Similarly, T.F. Torrance's view of the Trinity is fundamentally different from either Barth's or Aquinas'. The reason for the differences is located in the philosophical system that each of these thinkers employed in the interpretation of the doctrine of the Trinity. Whereas Aquinas used the philosophical infrastructure of Neo-Platonism, Barth and Torrance use the conceptual framework of German Idealism and of the church fathers respectively.

2. That the content of theology must come from the Christian faith. In dealing with the doctrine of the Trinity, the Western experience seems to give clear thought to the concept of the Incarnation, prominence to the idea of *homoousios*, and locates the identity question within the Christian faith. The philosophical system we choose to use must adequately explain what the Christian message means by one God who is made known in three persons.

3. The Western church is part of the universal church. We cannot take the theological developments in the Western church for granted. The West interprets the doctrine of God in ways that only the West can do. The God as essence, God as an absolute subject, and God as community in unity views clearly utilize Western patterns of thought. This can make it difficult for peoples outside of the Western culture to fully grasp the interpretations, but it also challenges those cultures to make use of their own thought patterns to articulate their theology.

PART THREE

THE DOCTRINE OF GOD IN AFRICAN INCULTURATION THEOLOGY

"Christianity is not only not a local religion, but it has adapted itself to the people wherever it has gone. No language or social existence has been any barrier to it; and I have often thought that in this country [Africa] it will acquire wider power, deeper influence and become instinct—with a higher vitality than anywhere else."

P. Bleyden quoted in K. Bediako, *Christianity in Africa*, 13

THE AFRICAN CONCEPTUAL FRAMEWORK

INTRODUCTION

The question of how the African constructs his reality is relevant to our study of the doctrine of the Trinity. From part two of this research, it is clear that major reinterpretations of the doctrine of the Trinity within Christian orthodoxy have been affected by the infrastructure of the philosophical system that was used. Africans do not construct their reality from the viewpoint of either Neo-Platonism or Philosophical Idealism. African people differ from other people in that they have another way of thinking. This chapter discusses how African people think and organize their reality. The purpose of this is to establish the manner in which the Africans are likely to interpret and therefore access the doctrine of the Trinity.

African cosmology researchers have indicated that African people organize their reality according to a specific thought pattern (see Prologue). This discovery is crucial for at least three issues. In the first place, it indicates that African people have their own unique way of viewing and interpreting reality, and that that 'way' was not loaned from some foreign quarter of the globe. The peoples studied by Tempels, Griaule, Dieterlen, Kagame, Jahn, and Mbiti are Africans. The findings of these scholars clearly indicate that we are dealing with a conceptual framework that is indigenous to Africa and receives recognition among the four African Negroid phyla, viz the Khoisan, the Nilo-Saharan, the Afro-Asiatic, and the Niger-Congo. Having a unique way of making sense of reality also means that the Africans have a right to express universal ideas in ways that best suit their circumstances and experiences.

Besides indicating that the patterns of thought are not loaned, the essence of the patterns signifies that the African mind has never been a *tabula rasa*. Contrary to the thought within the missionary enterprise of

the nineteenth and the early twentieth centuries,[1] the African peoples
have always had religion and morals, and Africa was not as dark and
ignorant as it was depicted.[2] Writing in the nineteenth and the early
twentieth centuries, anthropologists and theologians have indicated that
the image of Africa that was received in Europe was substantially different than the situation on the ground,[3] and that the African mind was
never *tabula rasa*. Such an admission is important because this doctrine
was, as Teresia Hinga explains, the reason the "... missionaries were
rather ruthless in their destruction of the African way of life... Behav-
ing ... like a bull in a 'China shop'—they dismissed aspects of African
culture as primitivity, and their spirituality as so much superstition,
fetishism, animism."[4] In any case, as W. Robertson Smith once wrote:

> No positive religion that has moved man has been able to start with a
> *tabula rasa* to express itself as if religion was beginning for the first time; in
> form if not in substance, the new system must be in contact all along with
> the old ideas and practice which it finds in possession. A new scheme
> of faith can find a hearing only by appealing to religious instincts and
> susceptibilities that already exist in its audience, and it cannot reach these
> without taking account of the traditional forms in which religious feeling
> is embodied, and without speaking a language which men accustomed to
> these forms can understand.[5]

---

[1] From Bediako's analysis it is clear that the missionary thinking in relation to Africa
contributed to the general European outlook on Africa. The motive of the Christian
mission to Africa, Bediako believes, is the humanitarian involvement with a "totally
inferior people," people who were thought to be completely 'other' than the Europeans. Christianity, according to these early missionaries and the general European
presupposition, was not just doing the work of evangelization. It was also seen as the
'mighty lever' to elevate the mind of the 'savage' and the 'primitive' Africans (see Bediako, *Theology and Identity*, 230–234; A.F. Walls, "Black Europeans, White Africans: Some
Missionary Motives in West Africa" in D. Baker (ed.), *Religious Motivation: Biographical
and Sociological Problems of the Church Historian* (Cambridge: Cambridge University Press,
1978), 339–348; and T. Hinga, "Inculturation and the otherness of Africans: Some
Reflections" in *Inculturation: Abide by the Otherness of Africa and the Africans*. eds. P. Turkson
and F. Wijsen (Kampen: Uitgeversmaatschappij JH KOK, 1994).

[2] A. Hastings, *Church and Mission in Modern Africa* (London: Burn and Oates, 1967),
60.

[3] See, particularly, W. Schmidt, *The Origin and Growth of Religion: Facts and Theories*.
H.J. Rose, trans. (London: Mathuen and Co. Ltd., 1931); and A. Lang, *The Making of
Religion* (London: Longmans, Green and Co., 1909); also significant is E.W. Smith (ed),
African Ideas of God (London: Edinburgh House, 1950). The importance of Smith's work
is that it draws from the conclusions of several researches conducted in the nineteenth
century and the early twentieth century.

[4] Hinga, "Inculturation and the otherness of Africans," 12.

[5] W.R. Smith, *Lectures on the Religion of the Semites* (London: A & C Black Ltd., 1923),
2.

Moreover, it is important to highlight the fact that the African thought pattern is complex and well-developed enough to take on matters that require logic, creativity, and critical thinking. Therefore the African people, even in their traditional contexts, are not intellectual neophytes. Thus we may not deny the African people any form of truth on the grounds that the idea is too tough for them. On the contrary, it is crucial that we understand the African interpretation of reality in order that we may use it to access the message from outside. Placide Tempels underscored the seriousness of this point when he warned that: "If we do not employ as our interpreter the forms of Bantu thought to propagate our truths, Bantu philosophy will fall back upon itself and the rift between African and white will suffer further cleavage, becoming wider and wider."[6]

A.F. Walls calls this phenomenon in which the conceptual vocabulary of the culture of reception is used to convey a Christian idea "symbol theft."[7] This concept of symbol theft originally came from Origen who argued that the Christians must make use of the resources in the heathen world and employ them for the worship and glorification of God.[8] In symbol theft, the proselyte model is abandoned in favor of the convert model. Highlighting the difference between the proselyte model and the convert model, Walls writes:

> To become a proselyte is to give up one set of beliefs and customs and take up those of another people. To become a proselyte involves the sacrifice of national and social affiliations. It involves a form of naturalization, incorporation into another milieu. But once the transition has been made, all the norms of conduct are set out; the way forward is safe. Precedent is built into the proselyte model; the proselyte inherits the accumulated experience of others.

> To become a convert, in contrast, is to turn, and turning involves not a change of substance but a change of direction. Conversion, in other words, means to *turn what is already there in a new direction*. It is not a matter of substituting something new for something old—that is proselytizing, a method which the early church could have adopted but deliberately chose to jettison. Nor is conversion a matter of adding something new

---

[6] P. Tempels, *Bantu Philosophy* (Paris: Présence Africaine, 1959), 117.

[7] A.F. Walls, "Old Athens and New Jerusalem: Some Signposts for Christian Scholarship in the Early History of Mission Studies" in *International Bulletin of Missionary Research*, October, 1997 (146–153), 149.

[8] Origen, *Philokalia—Origen's Letter to Gregory Thaumaturgus*. In *Ante-Nicene Fathers: Translations of the Writings of the Fathers Down to Ad 325* vol. IV., xii, 2.

to something old, as a supplement or in a synthesis. Rather Christian conversion involves redirecting what is already there, turning it in the direction of Christ. That is what the earliest Jerusalem believers had already done with their Jewish inheritance. Turning that inheritance toward Messiah Jesus transformed the inheritance but did not destroy its coherence or its continuity. On the contrary, it produced a model of thought and life that was Christian because Jesus was at its center; yet it remained essentially and inalienably Jewish.[9]

Thus when we as Africans become Christians, our African inheritance is transformed but not destroyed. It is this inheritance that is then redirected in the direction of Christ. We need to know the nature of our African inheritance, but such knowledge will only help us to better explain our Christian faith. For instance, this chapter deals with African metaphysics. We do not study how the African peoples construct their reality in order to offer the theology of the African traditional religions. Our purpose is to make the native cultural and intellectual resources with which we may give the Christian faith better grounding and clarification available.[10]

The Nature of the African Conceptual Framework

As is evident in recent philosophical and anthropological writings, the question of what is African cosmology / philosophy—or, simply, how does an African organize the totality of his experience—has generated a lot of interest. These writings are largely preoccupied with, as Imbo has noted, "... discussions of whether an African cosmology / philosophy exists, how it is to be defined, what distinguishes it from Western philosophy, whether it is oral or written, and whether it can be accessible to non-Africans or is so unique that only Africans can

---

[9] Walls, "Old Athens and New Jerusalem," 148.

[10] In taking such a view we are aware that we will be criticized for refusing to accept the African traditional religions in their own terms. It is not that we are not taking the African traditional religions seriously; we are, and that is why we believe the African Christian must understand the dynamics of the African traditional religions. What we are saying is that an African Christian has converted from the African traditional religion; the African traditional religion is his previous religion. Understanding how the African religion operates helps him in a different direction—to clarify the nature of his new faith. As a Christian, there is no way I can suspend my evangelical motive when dealing with the African traditional religions.

understand it."[11] Different participants in this debate have influenced the discussions through different responses and underlying assumptions about the nature of African cosmology / philosophy. It is because of these different responses and underlying assumptions that African cosmology / philosophy or conceptual framework has been defined and classified in different ways.

The way that the African organizes his reality has traditionally been classified according to the scheme of Henry Odera Oruka. This scheme identifies four categories of African philosophy.[12] The categories are ethnophilosophy, philosophic sagacity, nationalist-ideological philosophy, and professional philosophy. The other classification, which has some significant following, is the tripartite scheme offered by Samuel Oluoch Imbo, himself a former student of Henry Odera Oruka. According to Samuel Oluoch Imbo, there are three trends in African philosophy; namely, the ethnophilosophical approaches, Universalist definitions, and the hermeneutical orientations.[13]

The interest of this book is the category of African philosophy which Henry Odera Oruka calls 'ethnophilosophy' and which is known to Samuel Oluoch Imbo as 'ethnophilosophical approaches.' Our reason for interest in ethnophilosophy is that the African theology that we are dealing with is recognized as part of that literary movement that believes that the Africans are rational human beings, and that they have a right to put their thoughts differently. This is also the focus of ethnophilosophy and so, in a sense, African theology is a subsection of the larger literary movement called ethnophilosophy.[14]

---

[11] S.O. Imbo, *An Introduction to African Philosophy* (New York: Rowman and Littlefield Publishers, 1998), xi.

[12] H.O. Oruka's "Four Trends in Current African Philosophy," a paper presented at the William Amo Symposium in Accra, Ghana, July 24–29, 1978, gives a clear presentation and definition of each of the four trends of the scheme. The other place where he has given a considerable attention to this scheme and an elaborate definition of each of the four trends is his *Sage Philosophy: Indigenous Thinkers and Modern Debate on African Philosophy* (Leiden: E.J. Brill, 1990), 1–10.

[13] Imbo, *An Introduction to African Philosophy*, 34–37.

[14] Tienou in his article "The Right to Difference," *AJET* 9:1 (1990) has noted that African theology and "Bantu philosophy" have the same preoccupation; viz "… the rediscovery of African identity and the recapture of historical initiative" (T. Tienou, "The Right to Difference: The Common Roots of African Theology and African Philosophy" in *Africa Journal of Evangelical Theology* 9.1, 1990 (24–34), 31). Tienou argues that since notable African philosophers are also theologians / churchmen (P. Tempels; J.S. Mbiti and A. Kagame, for instance), it is clear that African theology should not be studied without African philosophy.

The writers of the brand of the African philosophy that became known as ethnophilosophy[15] were, as Tienou has noted:

> … motivated by the desire to include the Africans in the category of rational human beings. For this the different writers appealed to the Africans' right to difference. Their thought, though not Western, was nevertheless rational. Their philosophy though different and collective, was no less philosophical than the works of Western thinkers. The proponents of African Personality, *Negritude*, Bantu philosophy, and African cultural unity all seem to posit a general and collective African thought.[16]

Whereas Tienou has given the motive for and historical context of the rise of ethnophilosophy, it is Imbo who has given us its identity. According to Imbo:

> The core of ethnophilosophy is its function as a descriptive anthropology. In contrast to a discursive, analytical philosophy, ethnophilosophy treats as philosophy the indigenous cosmologies, the traditional beliefs such as those about supernatural beings and magic. Beliefs, myths, and cosmology are believed to be interwoven into the complex ritual practices that are the manifestation of philosophy. Though unwritten and unsystematized, the rituals and systems of belief nevertheless form an intricate

---

[15] Ethnophilosophy is a term coined by the opponents of a group of poets, philosophers, anthropologists, and theologians. Some well known thinkers who have been classified as ethnophilosophers are Placide Tempels (his book, *Bantu Philosophy*, ignited the debate about African philosophy. In this book Tempels takes the view that philosophy is a collective property of all the individuals in a culture; it is their lived experience. His method is to extrapolate to the Bantu and the African what he observes among the Baluba of the lower Congo.), Alexis Kagame (articulates a philosophy very similar to that of Tempels. He studied the Kinyaruanda laguage to work out a philosophy of being. His chief contribution is in the conclusion that people who speak the same language share abstract philosophical concepts. Kagame expresses these thoughts in *La Philosophie Bantu-Rwandaise de l'etre, 1956* and in *Aperception Empiriquede Temps*, 1976. See also detailed analysis of Kagame's thoughts in Apostel's *African Philosophy*, 1981 and in Imbo, *An Introduction to African Philosophy*, 1998), John S. Mbiti (he takes an approach that is ethnophilosophical in a straightforward sense, see especially his *African Religions and Philosophy*), Cheickh Anta Diop, *Precolonial Black Africa* (Trenton: Africa World Press Edition, 1987), Leopold Sedar Senghor (he posits for Africans, and indeed for all black people, a different way of apprehending the world. For him there must be a distinctly African epistemology with its own methodology of comprehending reality. See his *On African Socialism*, M. Cook, trans. (New York: Praeger, 1964), and Ogotemmeli (he is a sage of the Dogon people of the Southern Mali; his contribution is in the exposition of the Dogon mythological thinking. In 1933 he had 33 days of conversation with a French ethnologist, Marcel Griule. This conversation resulted in Griaule's book, *Conversations with Ogotommeli* (London: International African Institute, 1946). All these thinkers treat the indigenous cosmologies as philosophy and see the philosophers' task as consisting of laying bare the belief systems and ethnological concepts.

[16] Tienou, "The Right to Difference," 29.

web that guides the people in making sense of their lives. Through the description of the rituals and beliefs, the cosmology and the religious worldview of the people can be reconstructed.[17]

As Tienou has noted, ethnophilosophy whether of the African personality and the *Negritude* nuance or of the Bantu philosophy and the African cultural unity nuance[18] "... all seem to posit a general and collective African thought."[19] That there is a general and collective African thought has not really been admitted by the universalist trend in African philosophy.[20] However, to put things in the terms suggested by the Universalists is to overreact. The fact is that there is indeed something unique about African thought forms. This has been forcefully argued by the ethnophilosophers, and the African philosophers that are concerned with the hermeneutical question.[21] The point, there-

---

[17] Imbo, *An Introduction to African Philosophy*, 55.

[18] The African philosophers seem to be dividing ethnophilosophy into two distinct categories, the writings which discuss the Bantu philosophy or the African cultural unity philosophy (Tempels, Kagame, Mbiti, Diop, and Ogotemmeli) and the writings which expose the Negritude movement or the concept of the African personality (Senghor and Cesaire.) Whereas the writers of Bantu philosophy seem to be cheering the African cosmology as a breakthrough, a unique and collective African way of interpreting reality, the Negritude writers locate the discovery elsewhere—it is to be found in the way the Negro / African reasons, he / she reasons by soul and emotion. And so for the Negritude scholars, the gift of emotion is the center of the African culture.

[19] Tienou, "The Right to Difference," 29.

[20] The works of Kwesi Wiredu, Paulin Hountondji, Peter Bodunrin, and Henry Odera Oruka generally differ in the details they cover; however, they all take the view that philosophy must be an objective and universal enterprise. Their emphasis is that the African thought must take its rightful place alongside the thoughts of the other peoples of the world, and, consequently, it must be free to be involved with logic and other procedures common to all philosophy. Houtondji argues that what makes African philosophy African is not that the philosophy is about some unique African experiences or truths, but that it is Africans engaged with universal philosophical problems; see his "Reason and Tradition" in *Philosophy and Culture*. Oruka and Masolo, eds. (Nairobi: Bookwise, 1983), 136–137. For Wiredu, "... there are no African truths only truths—some of them about Africa" (see K. Wiredu, *Philophy and an African Culture* (Cambridge: Cambridge University Press, 1980) and K.A. Appiah, *In my Father's House: African in Philosophy of Culture* (New York: Oxford University Press, 1992), 104). Odera, on his part, distinguishes between philosophy in a debased sense and philosophy in a strict sense. Philosophy in a debased sense limits itself to traditional worldviews, while philosophy in the strict sense is concerned with hidden assumptions, implications, and contradictions in life. See his *Sage Philosophy*. For him, the ethnophilosophers are guilty of mistaking culture for philosophy.

[21] The African philosophers in the hermeneutical tradition seem to be the peace brokers between the ethnophilosophers and the so-called professional philosophers. Notable African philosophers in this category are Tsenay Serequeberhan (see his *African Philosophy: The Essential Readings* (New York: Paragon House, 1991), Marcien Towa (see

fore, is that ethnophilosophy is still of great significance in as far as
it has the capacity to provide a well considered framework for understanding and explaining Africa's contemporary reality, viz the linguistic,
the religious, and cultural aspects of Africa's reality.[22]

African inculturation theology views philosophy as a system of beliefs
about the various regions of our experience, gives meaning to these different regions, and relates them to each other. If philosophy is understood in this way, as Apostel explains, "... the picture drawn by [the
ethnophilosophers] is indeed the picture of such a total integration
and thus, of a philosophy."[23] African inculturation theology believes
that Africa has many peoples, and that these peoples view and organize their realities in essentially one and the same way. For African
inculturation theology, therefore, Africa in reality does not have 'many'
cultures, but has 'one' culture. The many cultures seen across Africa
are, according to this point of view, just 'dialects' of a common culture, 'the African culture.' The basis of this position is the view that the
four phyla of the African Negroes are different; however, the differences
must be seen in the context of historical processes of convergences and
reconvergences. Due to the reality of the convergences and reconvergences, any worthwhile scientific study on the African peoples and their
languages yields no significant emphasis on the diversity of the people
and their languages.

his "Conditions for the Affirmation of a Modern Philosophical Thought" in *African Philosophy: The Essential Readings*, 1991) and Okondo Okolo (see his "Tradition and Destiny:
Horizons of an African Philosophical Hermeneutics" in *African Philosophy: The Essential
Readings*, 1991). Generally, these philosophers agree that there is something of significance both in the ethnological considerations and in the universalist abstractions, but
they insist that philosophy must move beyond preoccupation with these considerations
and utilize them in formulating solutions to Africa's contemporary problems.
[22] As Apostel has explained, it is possible for one to accept the view that philosophy
is basically a developed system of deductively related propositions. If one goes by
this view, then the ethnophilosophers are mistaken. However, if philosophy is "...
a system of beliefs about the various regions of our experience giving meaning to
these different regions and relating them to each other, then the picture drawn by
[the ethnophilosophers] is indeed the picture of such a total integration and thus, of
a philosophy" (L. Apostel, *African Philosophy: Myth or Reality?* (Gent: E. Story-Scientia,
1981), 14).
[23] Apostel, *African Philosophy*, 14.

Models of the African Conceptual Framework

Placide Tempels' Model

Renowned ethnophilosophers, such as Alexis Kagame, J. Jahn, John S. Mbiti, and Cheick A. Diop, seem to agree that Tempels, Griaule, and Dieterlen made significant contributions to the understanding of the African concept of existence or being. Of course, these scholars are not just following Tempels, Griaule, and Dieterlen.[24] They have done their own serious research and have, in the face of vilification, agreed with Tempels and his company (albeit with modifications).[25] Tempels' African cosmology could be explained by the following summary form:

1. The existence or the essence of anything is its being a force. To understand what 'force' means, one must pay attention to the African people's notion of life and death. The African people view life and death not as absolute concepts, but as relative concepts that are to be

---

[24] It should be remembered that the study of African cultures which stressed the metaphysical dimension of the African concept of 'being' was not only done by Tempels; others who made significant contributions by 1946 are Griaule (see *Conversations with Ogotommeli*, 1948), Dieterlen, and Maya Deren. Since the translation of Tempel's book into French in 1945, the book generated more debates than the works of either Griaule or Dieterlen. Consequently, Tempels became the best known of the three. The Tempels' book that we are using here is the 1959 edition of the original book that was published in 1945. It should be noted that these four different authors (Tempels—a Belgian monk, 1945; Griaule—a French ethnographer; Ogotommeli—an African sage, 1946; and Maya Daren—an American author, 1953) came to the conclusion that although the African peoples are different, their conceptual frameworks agree with one another.

[25] Apostel's *African Philosophy* (1981) and Masolo's *African Philosophy in Search of Identity* (1994) explain that Kagame was the first African scholar with solid preparation in philosophy and knowledge of the African ways to give Tempels' hypothesis a better grounding. Besides, they observe, he was also an established scholar of Bantu languages. With this background, Kagame was able to uncover the same concepts that Tempels proposed even though he used a different approach: the analysis of Bantu languages. J. Jahn's book, *Muntu* (1961), adopts the categories of Kagame and sticks to Tempels' concept of force (pp. 99 ff.). Mbiti's African *Religions and* Philosophy (1969) sees Tempels' book as having opened "... the way for a sympathetic study of African religions and philosophy" (p. 10). Mbiti does not particularly agree with Tempels' idea of "the vital force," but the ontology he proposes (p. 16) resembles that of Tempels and Kagame. Diop does not come out clearly in support of Tempels' cosmology; however, he vigorously argues from the foundations of an African historiography that Africa is and has always been different, and that Africans do not need to be embarrassed by that difference, see his *Precolonial Black Africa* (1987).

seen together. Life in this sense is a dynamic process of increase or decrease in 'vital force.' Under this system of thought, one enjoys a state of well being when his/her life force is strong and is said to be dying when his/her life force is diminishing. Therefore, it is in this sense that Temples can say "... force is the nature of being, force is being, being is force." The notion "force," explains Tempels, replaces the Bantu "being" as found in Western ontology.[26]

2. Every force is specific, thus different beings are characterized by different intensities and types of forces, and yet they are in a relationship of interdependence.[27]

3. Each force can either be strengthened or weakened. "... one force that is greater than another can paralyse it, diminish it or even cause its operation totally to cease, but for all that the force does not cease to exist. Existence which comes from God cannot be taken from a creature by any created force."[28]

4. The universe is a hierarchy of forces or beings according to their strengths. (1) Above all forces is God—he gives existence to other forces, (2) then come the first fathers and founders of clans—they constitute an important chain binding men to God, (3) then the dead of the tribe, (4) man, (5) animal, (6) vegetable, and (7) mineral. Beings occupying a higher place in the hierarchy and can directly influence beings of lower rank.[29]

Tempels believes that the Bantu know God as "great *Muntu*," the "great person," the "great, powerful Life Force."[30] Elsewhere he describes God as a "supreme wise man, who knows all things, who established at the deepest level the kind and nature of their forces. He is force itself, which has force within itself, has made all other beings, and knows all forces."[31]

---

[26] Tempels, *Bantu Philosophy*, 49–55.
[27] Tempels, *Bantu Philosophy*, 58–61.
[28] Tempels, *Bantu Philosophy*, 57.
[29] Tempels, *Bantu Philosophy*, 66–69.
[30] Tempels, *Bantu Philosophy*, 28.
[31] Tempels, *Bantu Philosophy*, 39. Note that Placide Tempels does not say that the Africans understand God as merely a force. Rather, the Africans view God as the 'great *Muntu*,' the powerful person and force from which all other things flow. *Muntu*

Alexis Kagame's Model

When Alexis Kagame began his studies at the Gregorian University in Rome (1951–1955), Tempels' African cosmology had already created two camps: the pro-Templesians and the anti-Templesians. Whereas the pro-Templesians held that Tempels' ideas about the African conceptual framework were appropriate and defendable, the anti-Templesians charged that Tempels had made a bad use of philosophy.[32] In view of this debate, the pro-Templesians brought in new African thinkers with solid preparation in philosophy to corroborate and to clarify certain aspects of Tempels' construction of the African conceptual framework.

Kagame was the first renowned African philosopher to take up this task. Kagame, like Tempels, maintains that being is force in the African thought,[33] that every force is specific,[34] that each force can either be strengthened or weakened,[35] and that the universe is a hierarchy of beings or forces.[36] His main contribution to an understanding of Tempels' view of the African cosmology, however, is the development of a theory of categories. He does this in two of his fundamental philosophical works: *La Philosophie bantu-rwandaise de l'etre* (1956) and *La Philosophie bantu comparee* (1976).[37]

---

is not merely a force, but it has intelligence and might be described as mind or a neuter supreme consciousness (see J. Jahn, *Muntu: An Outline of the New African Culture* (New York: Grove Press, 1961, 105); cf. E.G. Parrinder, *Africa's Three Religions* (London: Sheldon Press, 1969), 27f.). Works of scholars such as P.M. Steyne, *Gods of Power: A Study of Beliefs and Practices of Animists* (Houston: Touch Publications, 1989) which come from the commitment that the 'animists' understand God as force (see pp 40, 41) are, therefore, way off line.

[32] D.A. Masolo, *African Philosophy in search of Identity* (Bloomington: Indiana University Press, 1994), 84.

[33] Tempels, *Bantu Philosophy*, 58–61.

[34] Tempels, *Bantu Philosophy*, 49–55.

[35] Tempels, *Bantu Philosophy*, 57.

[36] Tempels, *Bantu Philosophy*, 66–69.

[37] I was not able to access these books due to limitation in French language. However, there is much literature on Kagame's thoughts. Notable and competent works giving full exposition of the two monographs of Kagame are D.A. Masolo, *African Philosophy in search of Identity*, 102; E.G. Parrinder, *Africa's Three Religions* (London: Sheldon Press, 1969), 26, 27; J.S. Mbiti, *African Religions and Philosophy* (London: Heinemann, 1969), 10, 11; J. Jahn, *Muntu: An Outline of the New African Culture*, 96–120; and L. Apostel, *African Philosophy*, 70–84. Of these authors, the ones I found most thorough are D.A. Masolo and J. Jahn.

The first book focuses on the Banyarwanda (the Bantu of Rwanda) and explicitly utilizes linguistic facts to arrive at the same conclusion as Tempels. The second book basically moves the first work beyond the limitations of Banyarwanda. Here Kagame argues that from concrete evidence, viz linguistic consideration, one can speak with authenticity of a philosophy or a way of conceiving being or existence that belongs to the Bantu in general.[38] Kagame believes this way of conceiving being or existence is embodied in the *Ntu* metaphysics[39] that features in four distinct categories or aspects of power in the Bantu thinking.

The categories proposed by Kagame are as follows:

Umuntu—this category denotes life forces with intelligence (men, spirits, the living dead).

Ikintu—this category refers to subordinated powers of things, objects, or simply animals, plants, and minerals. All these are, of course, beings without intelligence.

Ahantu—this category describes the power of place and time.

Ukuntu—this category suggests the manners (modalities) in which power acts (quality, quantity, relation, action, passion, position, and possession). (see Masolo, *African Philosophy*, 87; Parrinder, *Africa's Three Religions*, 27; and Mbiti, *African Religions*, 11).[40]

---

[38] Masolo, *African Philosophy in search of Identity*, 85. The significance of the linguistic consideration is the view that language and thought are often identified with one another. Historical narratives and peoples' cosmology are contexts and forms of thought. Language is the medium through which the thought is expressed. P. Diagne notes, however, that "linguistics can be used to see beyond the evidence of thought, beyond the conceptual apparatus used in a language and the oral or written evidence, to the history of men and their civilization" (P. Diagne, "History and Linguistics" in *General History of Africa Volume I: Methodology and Prehistory*. J. Ki-Zerbo, ed. (California: UNESCO, 1981), 233).

[39] Jahn explaining Kagame's concept of *Ntu* says: "NTU is the universal force as such, which, however, never occurs apart from its manifestations: Muntu, Kintu, Hantu, and Kuntu. NTU is Being itself .... NTU is that force in which Being and beings coalesce .... If we said that NTU was a force manifesting itself in man, beast, thing, place, time, beauty, ugliness, laughter, tears and so on, this statement would be false, for it would imply that NTU was something independent beyond all these things. NTU is what Muntu, Kintu, Hantu, and Kuntu all equally are. Force and matter are not being united in this conception; on the contrary, they have never been apart. NTU expresses, not the effect of these forces, but their being" (Jahn, *Muntu*, 101).

[40] Masolo, *African Philosophy in search of Identity*, 87; Parrinder, *Africa's Three Religions*. 27; Mbiti, *African Religions and Philosophy*, 11. Kagame (see Apostel, *African Philosophy*, 70–84) explains that *Umuntu* and *Ikinitu* relates with the Aristotelian category of substance, *Ahantu* with the Aristotelian category of place and time, and *Ukuntu* with the six other Aristotelian categories (quantity, quality, relation, action, passion, position, and possession.).

Whereas Kagame's ontology gives better grounding to Tempels' hypothesis, it also has its own loopholes. The theologians feel that the categories have squeezed God out of the Bantu's intellectual culture. The fact that God is not among the four categories could mean that God is not even a *Ntu* (he is outside of being or simply that he is a non-being). However, Kagame addresses this by explaining that the name for God is excluded from the categories because name designates a being that is not distinctly separated from personality.[41] God, in this case, is simply understood to be one of the many life forces and therefore not distanced at all from man, spirits, and the living dead. Like Tempels, Kagame could call God "the great *Muntu*," "... the powerful person and force from which all other beings flow."[42]

Whereas God, in this scheme of things, belongs to the category of *Umuntu*, theological thinkers like Mbiti, Idowu, and Setiloane[43] are of the opinion that he must be a different kind of *muntu*. He is the source and the basis of existence of *Ntu* as a whole; other *muntu* are not. He is therefore *umuntu* (personality) in a different class. But even as we say that God is *umuntu*, alongside this affirmation is a strong whisper "and he is not." It is on the basis of this simultaneous belonging and not belonging to the *Umuntu* category that we are able to use the epithet, Great *Muntu*, for God.[44] The others in this category are *muntu*, but the appellation *great* does not apply to them.

---

[41] Masolo, *African Philosophy in search of Identity*, 90.

[42] Parrinder, *Africa's Three Religions*, 27. Since we shall not give specialized attention to Kagame's concept of God, let us give here the most important metaphysical characteristics of God as captured by Kagame. The characteristics are: "(i) God as an external existent: God does not form part of the four metaphysical categories and, therefore, is on the outside of created or qualified beings -NTU; He is external. (ii) God as the Creator: God is considered as the existent which puts the existence [Fr. *l'exister*] of beings -NTU—there, and confers upon them the property of reproduction and activity. (iii) God as the conserver [Conservateur]: the actual existence of beings is thought to be regulated [begin and end] by his decision" (Masolo, *African Philosophy in search of Identity* 92).

[43] The next chapter gives detailed analysis of what these three thinkers say regarding the place of God in African cosmology. It is important to note that these are not the only scholars who have works on the African concepts of God. The other notable scholars are J.B. Danquah, *The Akan Doctrine of God* (London: Frank Cass, 1968); E.E. Evans-Pritchard, *Nuer Religion* (London: Oxford University Press, 1956); and G. Lienhardt, *Divinity and Experience. The Religion of the Dinka* (Oxford: Clarendon Press, 1961).

[44] Mbiti's major contribution to the African cosmology is his inclusion of a separate category for God. His standard presentation of the African reflection about God is his book, *Concepts of God in Africa*. This book, Mbiti explains, contains "... all the information I could find in writing and otherwise, on African reflection about God"

John S. Mbiti's Model

The cosmology that John S. Mbiti proposes has the following five categories:

1. *God* as the ultimate explanation of the genesis and sustenance of both man and all things.
2. *Spirits* that are made up of superhuman beings and the spirits of men who died a long time ago.
3. *Man*, including human beings who are alive and those about to be born.
4. *Animals and plants*, or the remainder of biological life.
5. *Phenomena and objects without biological life.*[45]

Mbiti believes that this ontology is a complete unity in two senses: First, none of the categories can either be removed or destroyed, and, second, there is a thread running through all the five categories. Mbiti explains this unity in the following words:

> To destroy or to remove one of these categories is to destroy the whole existence including the destruction of the Creator, which is impossible. One mode of existence presupposes all the others, and a balance must be maintained so that these modes neither drift too far apart nor get too close to one another. In addition to the five categories, there seem to be a force, power or energy permeating the whole universe. God is ultimate source and controller of this force, but the spirits have access to some of it, a few human beings have the knowledge and ability to tap, manipulate and use it, such as medicine-men, witches, priests and rainmakers, some for good and others for the ill of their communities.[46]

A point worth noting here is that Mbiti expresses an ontological hierarchy that is similar in many ways to those suggested by Tempels, Kagame, Jahn, Mulago, and Bahoken.[47] He has, in fact, split Kagame's *Umuntu* into three distinct categories: God, spirits, and man. He has also

---

(J.S. Mbiti, *Concepts of God in Africa* (London: SPCK, 1970), p. xiii) and besides it covers the concepts of God as found among over 270 ethnic groups of Africa. Mbiti's goal here is to demonstrate beyond Tempels and Kagame that the Africans do conceive of God in a substantive manner.

[45] Mbiti, *African Religions and Philosophy*, 16.
[46] Mbiti, *African Religions and Philosophy*, 16.
[47] Masolo, *African Philosophy in search of Identity*, 119; Parrinder, *Africa's Three Religions*, 25–29.

combined Kagame's *Ukuntu* and *Ahantu* into what he calls "Phenomena and objects without biological life."[48]

In contrast to Tempels, Kagame, Mulago, and Bahoken, his interest is not in philosophical speculation. Rather, he is interested in the experiences of man as the African cosmology situates him at the center of the universe and how, in every day situations, that man relates to God, spirits, fellow men, animals, plants, and the non-biological world. In Mbiti's own words, "... God is the Originator and Sustainer of man; the spirits control the destiny of man; man is the centre of this ontology; the animals, plants and natural phenomena and objects constitute the environment in which man lives, provides means of existence and if need be, man establishes a mystical relationship with them."[49] Mbiti helps us to grasp the idea that this "Originator and Sustainer" is in fact *Umuntu*, but of a different kind of existence. He is *Umuntu* (personality), but he is not a human being. The African peoples are able to make this distinction because personality in the African nomenclature can describe God, divinities, spirits, the living dead, and human beings.

CONCLUSION

The Task

The task before us is to process the end results of the historiographies and the anthropological and the linguistic studies that describe the nature of African intellectual culture. This step is crucial if we are going to take advantage of the conclusions in the construction of theology for African audiences. The question then is: What have the investigations yielded? To this question we can advance four responses.

The African Peoples Have a Common Conceptual Framework

Recent historiographies and anthropological and ethnolinguistic studies done by J. Ki-Zerbo, P. Diagne, J.H. Greenberg, D. Olderogge, and others indicate that the different shades of cosmologies shown here are in fact representative of African patterns of thought.[50] Although they

---

[48] Mbiti, *African Religions and Philosophy*, 16.

[49] Mbiti, *African Religions and Philosophy*, 16; cf. Parrinder, *Africa's Three Religions*, 25–29.

[50] See the following authors: J. Ki-Zerbo, "General Introduction" in *General History*

are different, the cosmologies indicate fundamental similarities. This conclusion buttresses the contributions of the older scholars, such as Tempels, Kagame, Jahn, Mulago, Bahoken, Mbiti, and Idowu, who argued for the cultural unity of the African peoples. As early as 1945, Tempels' book, *Bantu Philosophy*, emphasized the fact that the African peoples have a common system that makes sense of their reality. This observation was also made by Marcel Griaule, Dieterlen, and Ogotommêli in *Conversation with Ogotommêli* (1946), and later on by an American author, Maya Deren, in *The Living Gods of Haiti* (1953). Kagame and the other African scholars agree with these early observers, and, moreover, they have given the necessary academic grounding to their findings. Because of this unity in conceptual framework, it is possible to speak about African metaphysics.

The African Conceptual Framework is Well-Developed

Individual Africans, regardless of their station, function within an intellectual culture that is developed enough to consider matters that require logic, creativity, and critical thinking.[51] Today, conventional anthropology claims that there is no connection between race and intelligence. Moreover, linguistics has now admitted that the theory of language hierarchy, according to which the pure Negro languages settled at the bottom rung of the ladder, had no scientific foundation. Contributing to this debate, UNESCO argues that the only bases for classification are physical and physiological, and that there is no scientific evidence that groups of mankind differ in their innate mental capacities.[52]

---

of Africa; Diagne, "History and Lingusitcs"; Olderogge, "Migration and Ethnic and Linguistic Differentiations"; and Greenberg, "African Linguistic Classification."

[51] According to Jahn, the African pattern of thought has support from modern science. He explains, "… modern science does in fact conceive the world as a world of forces, although it still grossly underrates the forces of the spirit … Perhaps African philosophy could even add something of its own to this conception" (Jahn, *Muntu*, 118).

[52] UNESCO. *Declaration on Race and Racial Prejudice*. Adopted and proclaimed by the General Conference of the United Nations Educational, Scientific and Cultural Organization at its twentieth session on 27 November 1978. See articles 2 and 3.

Article 2

1. Any theory which involves the claim that racial or ethnic groups are inherently superior or inferior, thus implying that some would be entitled to dominate or eliminate others, presumed to be inferior, or which bases value judgements on racial differentia-

Consequently, it is important that research should highlight the African intellectual culture and how it works. A significant beginning point is the African peoples' notions of 'being' and 'person.' Tempels, for example, recognizes that the African peoples explain what the Westerners call 'being' in terms of 'force.' Temple explains that force, "... is the nature of being, force is being, being is force." Tempels believes that 'force' is the African equivalent of what the Western ontology calls 'being.'[53] Jahn sticks to Tempels' concept of force, but defines it with Kagame's *Ntu*. For Jahn:

> Everything there is must necessarily belong to one of these four categories and must be conceived of not as substance but as force. Man is a force, all things are forces, place and time are forces and the 'modalities' are forces. Man and woman (category Muntu), dog and stone (category Kintu), east and yesterday (category Hantu), beauty and laughter (category Kuntu) are forces and as such are all related to one another. The relationship of these forces is expressed in their very names, for if we remove the determinative the stem NTU is the same for all the categories.[54]

---

tion, has no scientific foundation and is contrary to the moral and ethical principles of humanity.
2. Racism includes racist ideologies, prejudiced attitudes, discriminatory behaviour, structural arrangements and institutionalized practices resulting in racial inequality as well as the fallacious notion that discriminatory relations between groups are morally and scientifically justifiable; it is reflected in discriminatory provisions in legislation or regulations and discriminatory practices as well as in anti-social beliefs and acts; it hinders the development of its victims, perverts those who practise it, divides nations internally, impedes international co-operation and gives rise to political tensions between peoples; it is contrary to the fundamental principles of international law and, consequently, seriously disturbs international peace and security.
3. Racial prejudice, historically linked with inequalities in power, reinforced by economic and social differences between individuals and groups, and still seeking today to justify such inequalities, is totally without justification.

Article 3
Any distinction, exclusion, restriction or preference based on race, colour, ethnic or national origin or religious intolerance motivated by racist considerations, which destroys or compromises the sovereign equality of States and the right of peoples to self-determination, or which limits in an arbitrary or discriminatory manner the right of every human being and group to full development is incompatible with the requirements of an international order which is just and guarantees respect for human rights; the right to full development implies equal access to the means of personal and collective advancement and fulfillment in a climate of respect for the values of civilizations and cultures, both national and world-wide.
[53] Tempels, *Bantu Philosophy*, 49–55.
[54] Jahn, *Muntu*, 100 f.

Force never occurs apart from its manifestations.[55] To the contrary, force and its manifestations—whether matter or modalities—have never been apart.[56] Force is not just the African equivalent of the Western idea of being. It might be accurate to say, as Kagame's categories make it clear, that force is a substantial quality in some beings. The difference between beings, however, is based on degrees of forces.[57] Thus God, fathers and founders of clans, the dead of the tribe, man, animals and plants, as well as rocks differ because of *Ntu* from the highest to the lowest in that order. Even within a class there are differences. For example, no two men are identical because of genealogy, and in some individuals the force is 'strong' whereas in others it is 'weak.'

A human being in the African conceptual framework is a union of shadow, body, and force.[58] When a man dies, his biological life is over. The union of body with force, which Jahn refers to as *magara*,[59] also ceases, but the life force remains. What remains is what Tempels calls the "genuine *Muntu* (person)." Tempels says that he "always heard the old men say that man himself goes on existing, he-himself, the little man who sits in hiding behind the outwardly visible form, the *muntu* that went away from the living ones."[60] This genuine *Muntu* is said to be "a tributary of the Supreme Vital Force."[61] When the Sotho-Tswana speak of person being the tributary of God, they mean, "a person is something divine, sacred, weird, holy."[62] To be person is to reveal God[63] and to be part of a community. In the words of Mbiti:

> In traditional life, the individual does not and cannot exist alone except corporately. He owes his existence to other people, including those of past generations and his contemporaries. He is simply part of the whole. The community must therefore make, create or produce the individual;

---

[55] Tempels, *Bantu Philosophy*, 49–55; cf. Jahn, *Muntu*, 101 f.

[56] Jahn, *Muntu*, 101.

[57] Tempels, *Bantu Philosophy*, 58–69; cf. Masolo, *African Philosophy in search of Identity*, 88.

[58] Jahn, *Muntu*, 107.

[59] Jahn, *Muntu*, 107.

[60] Tempels, *Bantu Philosophy*, 28.

[61] G.M. Setiloane, *African Theology: An Introduction* (Johannesburg: Skotaville Publishers, 1986), 42.

[62] Setiloane, *African Theology*, 13.

[63] B. Idowu, *Towards an Indigenous Church* (London: Oxford University Press, 1965), 19.

for the individual depends on the corporate group. ... Whatever happens to the individual happens to the whole group, and whatever happens to the whole group happens to the individual. The individual can only say: 'I am, because we are; and since we are therefore I am'. This is a cardinal point in the African view of man.[64]

This definition of person persists, as is evident in a recent five-month legal struggle over the burial of a prominent Nairobi advocate, Mr. Silvanus Melea Otieno.[65]

> A prominent Nairobi advocate, the leading African criminal lawyer in Kenya, Mr SM Otieno, died suddenly of a heart attack. When his wife had announced plans over the radio to bury her late husband at his farm near Nairobi, his clan objected. His clan claimed that Mr Otieno should not be buried by his wife near Nairobi but by his clan according to customary law at his ancestral home. The protracted legal struggle lasted five months while the body of the deceased lay unburied in the city mortuary. The story became top news in Kenya with thousands crowding the law courts daily and the newspapers giving the story extensive front-page coverage. The story became the chief topic of conversation for thousands. The daily narrative brought suspense and surprise, such as when Mrs Otieno announced that she had been born again. And in the end the Nairobi All Saints Cathedral refused to hold the SM Otieno funeral service at the cathedral as the clan had desired. For five months there were suspense and surprises. At first Mrs Otieno was granted permission by the Judge to bury her late husband but the burial was stopped by a counter injunction from the deceased man's brother. A full trial ensued with the judge awarding burial rights to the clan. Thereafter Mrs Otieno took the matter to the Court of Appeals which handed down its decision five months later, giving the body to the clan for customary burial.[66]

At the heart of this case was a fundamental question: What is a human being? According to the Luo, a human being is body and soul or simply *Umuntu* in community of origin. The Luo believe that in the event of

---

[64] Mbiti, *African Religions and Philosophy*, 108 f.

[65] Although Dr. Gehman has given an accurate account of this case, he has not given it the right interpretation. I come from the same village as S.M. Otieno. As far as the clan was concerned, it was not a Kikuyu-Luo tussle, neither was it a wrangle between the customarily law and the common law as Gehman indicates. It was a question of how the Luo define *person* and whether the modern African society would give that view a hearing. The success of the case in the Kenyan Court of Appeals indicates that there is nothing repugnant about the Luo definition of person.

[66] R.J. Gehman, *African Traditional Religion in Biblical Perspective* (Kijabe: Kesho Publications, 1989), 15 f.

death, the soul (*chuny*) continues to live. The Kenyan Court of Appeals was satisfied with the view that if Mr. Otieno were not given a decent customary burial by both his wife and his clan his soul (*chunye*) would haunt not just Mrs. Otieno and her children, but the entire Umira-Kager clan also. The Kenyan Court of Appeals explained that the ruling was not in any way repugnant to justice and morality.

God is the Starting Point of the African Conceptual Framework

Above all forces or forms of existence is God. Tempels describes him as the "great, powerful Life Force."[67] According to Kagame, he is the first cause of all things or beings—*Ntu*.[68] He is not *Ntu* itself, but the "'Great Muntu, First Creator and First Begetter in one."[69] It is logical that in Mbiti's view of the African cosmology God should be in the number one place since he is the ultimate explanation of the genesis and sustenance of both man and all things.[70] According to Laurent Magesa, the place God occupies in the cosmology is very important. Because of this place, argues Magesa, "human beings can speak of their own existence, let alone their tradition."[71] The existence of the African peoples is linked to God. Consequently, the traditional African peoples believe that if God does not exist, then the reality outside of him also does not exist. In the words of Idowu, all things would have fallen to pieces if God did not exist.[72]

THE CHALLENGE

These investigations have yielded the understanding that the African peoples have a common conceptual framework, that the conceptual framework is well-developed, and that God is the starting point of that intellectual framework. Therefore, unlike during the missionary period

---

[67] Tempels, *Bantu Philosophy*, 28.
[68] Masolo, *African Philosophy in search of Identity*, 91.
[69] Jahn, *Muntu*, 105.
[70] Mbiti, *African Religions and Philosophy*, 16.
[71] L. Magesa, *African Religion: The Moral Traditions of Abundant Life* (Maryknoll: Orbis Books, 1997), 40.
[72] B. Idowu, *African Traditional Religion—A Definition* (London: SCM Press, 1973), 104.

that K.S. Latourette has called the "the Great Century," today African theologians do not have to divert in order to deal with the image of Africa in the mind of the West.[73] How will these findings help us in formulating the doctrine of God?

[73] K.S. Latourette uses this expression to describe the massive missionary efforts in the period between 1800 and 1914. See (particularly) volume 5 and 6 of his works entitled, *A History of Expansion of Christianity (The Great Century: The Americas, Australasia and Africa,* A.D. 1800–1914; and *The Great Century: North Africa and Asia,* A.D. 1800–1914).

CHAPTER EIGHT

THE NOTION OF GOD AMONG THE AFRICAN PEOPLES: THE ACCOUNTS OF B. IDOWU, J.S. MBITI, AND G.M. SETILOANE

INTRODUCTION

The doctrine of God in African inculturation theology has primarily been an attempt to isolate and understand the divine category of African cosmology. The diagram below captures the divine category and how it relates to other areas of existence with African cosmology.

Category 1 *God* The ultimate explanation of the origin and sustenance of both man and all things
Category 2 *Spirits* Made up of superhuman beings and the spirits of men who died a long time ago
Category 3 *Man* Human beings who are alive and who are about to be born
Category 4 *Animals & Plants* Or remainder of biological life
Category 5 *Phenomena & Objects without Biological Life*

According to the African cosmology modeled above, Category 1 describes God. God as he is understood and captured by this model is not an idea or a concept. God is a person, the Great *Muntu*, who relates to the other categories of existence in specific ways.

This chapter investigates the conclusions of renowned African inculturation theologians: Bolaji Idowu, John S. Mbiti, and Gabriel M. Setiloane. It would have been ideal to investigate every possible work by African inculturation theologians on the doctrine of God. However, desirable as such an undertaking would be, it is simply not practical. No one who studies African theology doubts the significance of Bolaji Idowu and John S. Mbiti in the development of African inulturation theology.[1] For many years Gabriel M. Setiloane has been a lone voice in South Africa as far as inculturation as a model of theology is concerned. Other African theologians in the South African context preferred black theology. Including Setiloane's contribution allows us to see that the need to express the Good News using the infrastructure of the African metaphysics was not only performed by the Africans north of the Limpopo, but that the Africans in southern Africa also raised their voices.

B. Idowu: God of Africa is the God of the Christian Faith

Knowledge of One God is Universal among the African Peoples

In this section, the basic issue that Idowu deals with is the knowledge of God. Idowu departs from Andrew Lang[2] and Father Wilhelm Schmidt as demonstrated in his article, "God," that was published in *Biblical Revelation and African Beliefs*, 1969, 18. The two scholars, Andrew Lang and Father Schmidt, are known for their firm stand against Tylor's doctrine of animism that—for a long time—was considered as the standard explanation of the origin of religion.[3] As far as Lang is concerned:

---

[1] See the estimation of Idowu and Mbiti in Bediako's book, *Theology and Identity*.

[2] A. Lang, *The Making of Religion* (London: Longmans, Green & Co., 1909).

[3] Tylor's theory of the origin and development of animism and religion goes through the following steps: (1) The primitive forms the first idea of something different from the body. He realizes that there is a body, and something else, an incorporeal principle of life, the soul. From the idea of the soul arose the belief in continued existence of the soul after death and in transmigration. (2) Then came the belief that all other things also consist of a body and a soul; in that sense man was therefore related to and not different in nature from the rest of the world. (3) Then there arose ancestor worship. (4) The principle of disembodied spirits was also applied to nature. Various parts of the world were animated by the spirits; thus worship of water, rivers, sea, etc. (5) From this developed a higher polytheism. (6) From this we then get the rule of one supreme divinity. (7) Monotheism, according to Tylor, arises in three ways: (a) raising

The religion of the Negro may be considered by some as a particularly rude form of polytheism and may be branded with the special name of fetishism. It would follow, from a minute examination of it, that—apart from the extravagant and fantastic traits, which are rooted in the character of the negro, and which radiate therefrom over all his creations—in comparison with the religion of other savages it is neither very specially differentiated nor very specially crude in form.

But this opinion can be held to be quite true only while we look at the outside of the Negro's religion, or estimate its significance from arbitrary pre-suppositions, as is the case with A Wuttke.

By a deeper insight, which of late several scientific investigators have succeeded in attaining, we reach, rather, the surprising conclusion that several of the *negro races*—on whom we cannot yet prove, and can hardly conjecture, the influence of more civilized people—in the embodying of their religious conceptions are further advanced than almost all other savages, so far that, even if we do not call them monotheists, we may still think of them as standing on the boundary of monotheism, seeing that their religion is also mixed with a great mass of rude superstition which, in turn, among other peoples, seems to overrun completely the purer religious conceptions[4]

In conclusion, Lang warns against the attitude towards the "savages" that denies them any religion except "devil-worship" and the bias which leads researchers to look only for "traces of a pure primitive religious tradition."[5] What researchers must note, explains Lang, is the "reciprocal phenomenon: missionaries often find a native name and idea which answers so nearly to their conception of God that they adopt the idea and name in teaching. Again on the other side, the savages, when first they hear the missionaries' account of God, recognise it … for what has always been familiar to them."[6]

Father Schmidt did his study among the Indo-Europeans, the Amerindians, the Pygmies of the Congo, the Semites, the southern primordial culture (comprising the peoples of southern Africa), those of Southeast Australia, and the Arctic ancient culture.[7] His studies led him to the conclusion that belief in and worship of one Supreme Deity is uni-

---

to divine primacy one of the gods of polytheism; (b) a crowd of gods or pantheon with the king as the supreme deity; (c) the universe may be conceived of as animated by one greatest, all-pervading divinity, an *anima mundi* (see W. Schmidt, *The Origin and Growth of Religion: Facts and Theories.* H.J. Rose, trans. (London: Mathuen & Co Ltd, 1931), 73–77.

[4] Lang, *The Making of Religion*, 219; italics mine.
[5] Lang, *The Making of Religion*, 228, 229.
[6] Lang, *The Making of Religion*, 229.
[7] Schmidt, *The Origin and Growth of Religion*, 185–195, 258–260.

versal among primal peoples.[8] In his own words: "This Supreme Being is to be found among all the peoples of the primitive culture, not indeed everywhere in the same form or the same vigour, but still everywhere prominent to make his dominant position indubitable."[9] For Schmidt, the belief in the Supreme Being is not a product of interaction with 'modern' cultures, nor did the so-called primitives borrow it from the missionaries. Rather, belief in the Supreme Being encircles the whole earth like a girdle, and it clearly is "an essential property of whatever ancient human culture existed in the very earliest time ... before the individual groups had separated from one another."[10]

Whereas the Supreme Being—as advocated by Andrew Lang and Father Wilhelm Schmidt—is central to Idowu's formulation of the doctrine of God, his understanding of revelation is decisive. Of course, Schmidt had asserted that belief in God "encircles the whole earth like a girdle," and that that belief "is an essential property of whatever ancient human culture existed in the very earliest times." But for Idowu the explanation of this old, widespread belief is the Creator God.[11] Quoting DeWolf, Idowu writes, "it is God who is directly made known rather than ideas about him,"[12] and the God that Idowu is talking about is the God as revealed also in the biblical religion;[13] the God who "so loved the world that He sent His only begotten Son to redeem" it (see Jn. 3:16).

> For the Creator Spirit who like a mother bird sat upon the primor-dial chaos and out of that chaos of non-existence brought forth order, cohesion, meaning and life has certainly left the mark of His creative activity upon the created order. This is the primary stage of revelation— something through which the Creator is revealed. Then He created man in His own image—a rational being, intelligent will, someone address-able and therefore responsible (response-able): someone to whom God could communicate His revelation ... and with whose spirit the Divine Spirit could have immediate communication. We can deny this primary revelation only when we rob the created order of its revelatory quality and relieve man of his inherent capability to receive divine communica-tion.[14]

---

[8] Schmidt, *The Origin and Growth of Religion*, 257.
[9] Schmidt, *The Origin and Growth of Religion*, 257.
[10] Schmidt, *The Origin and Growth of Religion*, 260f.
[11] B. Idowu, *Towards an Indigenous Church* (London: Oxford University Press, 1965), 25.
[12] B. Idowu, "God" in *Biblical Revelation and African Beliefs*. Dickson and Ellingworth, eds. (London: Lutterworth Press, 1969), 20.
[13] Idowu, *Towards an Indigenous Church*, 24.
[14] Idowu, *Towards an Indigenous Church*, 19.

Having agreed with Lang and Schmidt on the nature of the Supreme Being, and having opted for the concept of revelation in the terms defined by DeWolf, Idowu arrives at the conclusion that God cannot be confined in any way. "His realm is the whole universe. All peoples are his concern. And he has revealed himself primarily to them all, each race apprehending the revelation according to its native capability."[15] According to Idowu, "God is One, not many; and that to the one God belongs the earth and all its fullness. It is this God, therefore, Who reveals Himself to every people on earth and whom they have apprehended according to the degree of their spiritual perception, ... as those who have had practical experience of him."[16] Appealing to the biblical witness, Idowu reasons as follows:

> On the basis of the Bible taken as a whole, however, there can only be one answer. There is only one God, the Creator of heaven and earth and all that is in them; the God who has never left Himself without witness in any nation, age or generation; Whose creative purpose has ever been at work in this world; Who by one stupendous act of climactic self-revelation in Christ Jesus came to redeem a fallen world.[17]

Consequently, for Idowu, there has to be what Kwame Bediako has spoken of as "[Idowu's] persistent affirmations of the continuity of God from the African pre-Christian past into the present Christian experience."[18] His study of the African divine names, such as *Olodumare*,[19] *Orise*, *Chukwu*, and *Odomankoma*,[20] indicates two things that are crucial to him. First, the study allows him to conclude that God, as known to the Africans, is not "a loan-God from the missionaries."[21] Second, the study allows him to conclude that the God who communicated with the Africans is the same God that the Christian encounters in the pages of the Bible. Because of the study of the names, *Orise*, *Chukwu*, and *Odomankoma*, Idowu can connect the words of Ps. 104:29, 30 and Acts 17:28 without difficulty.[22]

---

[15] Idowu, Towards an Indigenous Church, 20; B. Idowu, Olodumare: God in Yoruba Belief (London: Longman, 1962), 31.

[16] Idowu, *Olodumare: God in Yoruba Belief*, 31.

[17] Idowu, *Towards an Indigenous Church*, 25.

[18] Bediako, *Theology and Identity*, 281, 284.

[19] Idowu, *Olodumare: God in Yoruba Belief*, 30–56.

[20] Idowu, "God," 24–26.

[21] Idowu, "God," 29.

[22] Idowu, "God," 26.

God is Real to African Peoples

One of the ways by which Idowu underscores the fact that God is real to the Africans is by doing a detailed study of the names that African people call God. In the words of Idowu, "it may not be possible in every case to arrive at the primary meaning of a principal name of the Supreme Being, but the praise names, titles or epithets always throw much light upon the people's ideas".[23] The point that Idowu wishes to make here is articulated in his *Olodumare: God in Yoruba Belief* (1962).

In *Olodumare: God in Yoruba Belief* (1962), Idowu explores the full range of the meaning of *Olodumare* and the other names by which the Yoruba call this Supreme Being. The name *Olodumare*, a Yoruba name for God, carries the idea of "One with whom man may enter into a covenant or communion in any place and at any time, one who is supreme, superlatively great, incomparable and unsurpassable in majesty, excellent in attributes, stable, unchanging, constant, reliable."[24] This *Olodumare* is also called *Olofin-Orun* and *Olorun*. According to Idowu, the three names "Olodumare, Olofin, and Olorun are sometimes run together in urgent ejaculation: *L'oju Olodumare! L'oju Olofin! L'oju Olorun!*—In the presence of Olodumare! In the presence of Olofin! In the presence of Olorun!— The one deity is thus called by a three-fold name to express intense emotion or urgent appeal."[25]

The Yoruba conceive of *Olodumare* anthropomorphically.[26] He is the Creator, "the owner of the Spirit," or "the owner of Life,"[27] and even the divinities owe their existence to him.[28] They were either "engendered by Him or they emanated from Him."[29] "He is King";[30] "He is

---

[23] Idowu, "God," 25.

[24] Idowu, *Olodumare: God in Yoruba Belief*, 36.

[25] Idowu, *Olodumare: God in Yoruba Belief*, 36, 37.

[26] Idowu, *Olodumare: God in Yoruba Belief*, 21 cf. 39.

[27] Idowu, *Olodumare: God in Yoruba Belief*, 39 f.

[28] Note that to the worshipping minds, the divinities are real; in some cases the divinities are but conceptualizations of attributes of *Olodumare*. There are also those who have outgrown the divinities; to such people, all reality is concentrated on *Olodumare* (Idowu, *Olodumare: God in Yoruba Belief*, 63).

[29] Idowu, *Olodumare: God in Yoruba Belief*, 62.

[30] Idowu, *Olodumare: God in Yoruba Belief*, 40.

Omnipotent";[31] "He is All-wise, All-knowing, All-seeing";[32] "Judge";[33] "He is Immortal";[34] and "He is Holy."[35]

Regarding the problem of the 'One and the many' posed by the incidence of the realities of the divinities among many African peoples, Idowu points out that (in some cases) the divinities are later additions.[36] In instances where they have become real, he argues that the difficulty exists only for "the casual observer" who ought to see them as but manifestations of One God.[37] However the worshippers who have access to the African religions know and believe the supremacy of One God.[38] The attitude of the Yoruba worshipper, for example, is that:

> Olodumare has portioned out theocratic administration of the world among the divinities whom He brought into being and ordained to their several offices. By the function of these divinities, and the authority conferred upon them, they are "almighty" within certain limits. But their "almightiness" is limited and entirely subject to the absolute authority of the Creator Himself.[39]

In view of the presence of divinities, are we then to view the African religions as polytheistic? Idowu answers this question in the positive. For him, polytheism is an inappropriate description of the African traditional religions. He says: "African traditional religion cannot be described as polytheistic. Its appropriate description is monotheistic, however modified this may be. The modification is, however, inevitable because of the presence of other divine beings within the structure of the religion."[40] Idowu calls this kind of religion "primitive monotheism"[41] or "diffused monotheism." Otherwise, it is described as a type

---

[31] Idowu, *Olodumare: God in Yoruba Belief*, 40 f.
[32] Idowu, *Olodumare: God in Yoruba Belief*, 41.
[33] Idowu, *Olodumare: God in Yoruba Belief*, 42.
[34] Idowu, *Olodumare: God in Yoruba Belief*, 42–46.
[35] Idowu, *Olodumare: God in Yoruba Belief*, 46 f.
[36] Idowu, *Olodumare: God in Yoruba Belief*, 202.
[37] Idowu, *Olodumare: God in Yoruba Belief*, 62.
[38] Idowu, *Olodumare: God in Yoruba Belief*, 141 cf vii.
[39] Idowu, *Olodumare: God in Yoruba Belief*, 49.
[40] B. Idowu, *African Traditional Religion—A Definition* (London: SCM Press, 1973), 168.
[41] Idowu, *Olodumare: God in Yoruba Belief*, 202. The concept of "primitive monotheism" or "diffused monotheism" applied to the African context may be traced to the middle of the nineteenth century. In his book, *The Religious System of the Amazulu* (Routledge and Kagan Paul, 1870), Henry Callaway talks about *Unkulunkulu* as the Supreme Being and the *Amadhlozi* or *Amatongo* (the throng of sprits worshipped by the Zulu) (see pp. 1, 3, 26–31). Andrew Lang, commenting on Callaway's observation, notes that the Zulus recognize one Supreme Being; however, they continue to have daily interaction

of monotheism where "the good Deity delegates certain portions of His authority to certain divine functionaries who work as they are commissioned by Him."[42] The functionaries may be seen, in the words of Kwame Bediako, as "manifestations or refractions of a single God."[43] Idowu is not the first theologian to use these terms in reference to religion in the African context. This term had been in use since the nineteenth century. And so by the time Idowu is speaking about "primitive monotheism" or "diffused monotheism" in his book, *Olodumare: God in Yoruba Belief* (1962), he is not writing about a unknown concept. Rather, he is giving his own scholarly approval to what previous scholars had clearly articulated.

---

with "serviceable family spirits, who continually provided an excuse for a dinner of roast beef" (A. Lang, *The Making of Religion* (London: Longmans, Green & Co., 1909), 209–210). Other examples of African peoples who were known to hold 'primitive theism' by the beginning of the twentieth century include the Dinkas of Sudan (refer to the Supreme Being as *Dendid*), the Wayao of Central Africa (*Mulungu* or *Mlungu*), the Tshi-speaking peoples of Gold Coast (*Nyankupon*), and the Fiorts (*Nzambi Mpungu*) (Lang, *The Making of Religion*, 211–229). Edwin W. Smith's book, *African Ideas of God* (London: Edinburgh House Press, 1950), is yet another significant contribution on both the issue of the 'one and the many' as well as on the problem of 'loan God.' Smith and the authors who contributed to this volume were unanimous on the fact that the African peoples in their traditional contexts had ideas of the Supreme Being and that none of those ideas were borrowed from outside. In the mid-1950s and at the beginning of 1960s the problem of the 'one and the many' in the African context once again caught the attention of E.E. Evans-Pritchard, *Nuer Religion* (London: Oxford University Press, 1956) and G. Lienhardt, *Divinity and Experience. The Religion of the Dinka* (Oxford: Clarendon Press, 1961) respectively. In his study of the Nuer of Sudan, Evans-Pritchard had noted that the Nuer believed in the 'Spirit' (*Kwoth*) and 'spirits' (*kuth*). In the words of Evans-Pritchard: "The inference we can draw from this in considering the spirits of the air is that they are not thought of as independent gods but in some way as hypostases of the modes and attributes of a single God... The spirits of the air are, nevertheless, being Spirit, also God. They are many, but also one. God is manifested in, and in a sense is, each of them. I received the impression that in sacrificing or in singing to an air spirit, Nuer do not think that they are communicating with the spirit and not with God. They are, if I have understood the matter correctly, addressing God in a particular spiritual figure or manifestation" (Evans-Pritchard, *Nuer Religion*, 49,51).

   The study of Godfrey Lienhardt among the Dinka yielded a similar conclusion. "All Dinka assert that Divinity is one, *nhialic ee tok*... Yet *nhialic* is also a comprehensive term for a number of conceptions which differ considerably from each other... This unity and multiplicity of Divinity causes no difficulty in the context of Dinka language and life" (Lienhardt, *Divinity and Experience*, 56).

   [42] Idowu, *Olodumare: God in Yoruba Belief*, 62 cf. W. Schmidt, *The Origin and Growth of Religion*, 262–282.
   [43] Bediako, *Theology and Identity*, 288.

God among Other African Peoples

In considering how the other African peoples understand God, Idowu finds "a common thread, however tenuous in places, running through-out the continent."[44] Two reasons can explain this position. In the first place, Idowu—like Schmidt—believes that belief in one God "encir-cles the whole earth like a girdle and that it 'is an essential property of whatever ancient human culture existed in the very earliest time. ... before the individual groups had separated from one another."[45] This is so because "God's self-disclosure is, in the first instance, to the whole world and that each race has grasped something of this primary revela-tion according to its native capability."[46] In this regard, he agrees with the explanation of H.H. Farmer, who is, of course, writing about what he understood to be the persistence of monotheism in the context of the "polytheistic primitives." Farmer writes:

> a polytheistic form of religious belief was an inevitable stage in the unfolding of man's awareness of, and dealings with, God; nevertheless such polytheism, in so far as there was in it anything of living religion at all, was never so to speak *mere* polytheism: there were powerful monothe-istic trends within it, and these we take to bear witness that the one living and personal God was making Himself known, keeping a grip on men, even through a polytheistic scheme of belief and ritual. Moreover, this implicit sense of the one living God, I have suggested, when it became explicit, did so in a form conditioned by the general mental level and by the polytheistic system of ideas; it took the form of a belief in the one High God who is Supreme over all and to whom all other supernatural powers are therefore subject. In this also we can see the self-disclosure of God in a form appropriate to man's stage of development and historical situation. Belief in the High God was the primitive man's way of appre-hending, and responding to, and expressing, the self-revealing pressure upon him of the one God.[47]

Second, for Idowu, the phonetic similarities in some of the names for God among a variety of African peoples could also indicate that we are dealing with a variation of the same name. It is easy for him to reach this conclusion since he already believes in one cradle, not only

---

[44] B. Idowu, *African Traditional Religion—A Definition* (London: SCM Press, 1973), 103.

[45] Idowu, "God," 18.

[46] B. Idowu, "Introduction" in *Biblical Revelation and African Beliefs*. Dickson and Ellingworth, eds. (London: Lutterworth Press, 1969), 12; cf. B. Idowu, *Towards an Indigenous Church*, 25.

[47] H.H. Farmer, *Revelation and Religion: Studies in the Theological Interpretation of Religious Types* (London: James Nisbet and Company Ltd., 1954), 108f.

for the African peoples but also for the entire human race. He is also a firm believer in one God.[48] In his book, the *African Traditional Religion*, he considers the issue of one God and goes on to argue that "in Africa, the real cohesive factor of religion is the living God and that without this one factor, all things would fall to pieces. And it is on this ground, especially this identical concept, that we can speak of the religion of Africa in the singular."[49] For Idowu, the proper names for God—like *Yamba* that occurs in parts of Nigeria and noticed in the form of *Yambe*, *Yembe*, or *Ndyambi* in the Cameroons and the Congo, and as *Onyame* or *Nyame* among the Akan of Ghana and the Nilotic peoples of the greater Sudan[50]—cannot be explained by coincidence. However, he is not the only one raising this argument. Commenting on *Nyambe*, Smith has noted that the name appears in:

> ... its various forms: Nzambi, Nyambe, Ndyambi, Dzambi, Tsambi, Yambe, Sambi, Zam, Monzam etc. This God's name is spread over a very large area of Western Equatorial Africa, from the Cameroons to the Northern border of Bechuanaland, and from the Atlantic Coast to the middle regions of Belgian Congo. ... The name is used in at least twenty-five versions of the Holy Scripture.[51]

The concern of Idowu is clearly not just phonetics. He wants to categorically state that the African peoples have an identical way of speaking about God. For him the variation of the same name indicates that although each ethnic group used the name for deity that was part of the vocabulary of that community, the African peoples believed that the same God extended beyond any territory to the whole world.

Idowu is thoroughly frustrated by the "too many stay at home investigators," and those who go out into the field and "often find it difficult to leave at home their own preconceived notions" regarding their own theory of "the high gods of the primitive peoples."[52] As far as Idowu is concerned, "these scholars have furnished us with an unnecessary, artificial pluralism. For they do not hesitate to concede to each nation, people, or 'tribe', its own 'high god', with the result that the whole place

---

[48] Idowu, *Towards an Indigenous Church*, 25.

[49] Idowu, *African Traditional Religion—A Definition*, 104.

[50] Idowu, *African Traditional Religion—A Definition*, 103f.; Idowu, "God" in *Biblical Revelation and African Beliefs*, 26; E.W. Smith, *African Ideas of God* (London: Edinburg House Press, 1950), 157.

[51] Smith, *African Ideas of God*, 156.

[52] Idowu, "God," 18f.

is overrun with 'high gods' of various brands."[53] To say that the "whole place is overrun with 'high gods' of various brands" is, in the opinion of Idowu, to make a grave error of theological judgment. Only one God has revealed himself to all peoples of the world, and the various African peoples have apprehended the revelation of this God according to their respective native capabilities.[54] Moreover, from the position of the anthropologists and ethnolinguists, one cannot simply look at the African peoples as tribes and therefore assume that since there is great diversity the same must also apply in the context of God language.

J.S. Mbiti: African Concepts of God as Preparatio Evangelica

Preliminary Comments

In his works, Mbiti seeks to indicate that the African concepts of God could be viewed as *preparatio evangelica*. He demonstrates his point by employing a series of metaphors that traditional African societies use to talk about the divine. The metaphors used by Mbiti range from simple anthropomorphic descriptions to theriomorphic and physiomorphic descriptions of the divine. The basic premise of Mbiti's methodology is that the traditional Africans and the early Israelites had many commonalities. For Mbiti, this could mean that traditional Africa shared the verbal cotext[55] of the metaphors used to describe the divine with the early Israelites. As far as Mbiti is concerned, the traditional Africans and the early Israelites cherished the same concepts of God, used the same metaphors to describe the divine, and systematized the concepts and metaphors into comparable theologies. In order to demonstrate his point, Mbiti isolates a large number of terms, metaphors, and similes that are used to describe God in traditional Africa, and he uses them in a way that reminds one of the of the occurrence of the same symbols in the Old Testament.[56]

---

[53] Idowu, "God," 19.

[54] Idowu, "God," 20.

[55] Verbal cotext refers to "the users' sign-context that act as a rule narrowing down the meaning of metaphors and similes employed" (M.C.A. Korpel, *A Rift in the Clouds: Ugaritic and Hebrew Descriptions of the Divine* (Munster: Ugarit–Verlag, 1990), 79.

[56] But in doing this, is not Mbiti creating an African image of God which in actual fact exists nowhere in Africa? It is true that Mbiti has been accused of pasting bits and

TRADITIONAL AFRICA'S ANTHROPOMORPHIC
DESCRIPTIONS OF GOD

Human Properties

The Body

Generally, God is viewed as a person with a spiritual body and will.[57] However, nobody has seen him, and it is fatal to see God (Bambuti, the Lugbara).[58] Since God is known to be a person, every African language and people has a personal name for him.[59] He has a personality, and in this personality there is a will that governs the universe.[60] He has eyes, mouth and saliva, nose, ears, beard, wings, belly, and blood. Thus God wills, sees, speaks, eats, smells, and hears. People of one ethnic group see themselves as one because they all have "one continuous blood from the originating blood of the great source of that blood."[61]

---

pieces together taken from all over Africa. This view was articulated by Okot p'Bitek. As far as p'Bitek is concerned, African scholars such as Mbiti, Idowu, Danquah, Busia, Kenyatta, and Sengor are "intellectual smugglers" who have draped the African gods in "awkward Hellenic garments." He adds that "the African deities of the books … are creations of students of African religions. They are all beyond recognition to the ordinary Africans in the countryside" (O. p'Bitek, *Religion of the Central Luo* (Nairobi: East African Literature Bureau, 1971), 7, 46, 47, 50, 80, 88). Given his attitude to Christianity, can p'Bitek's criticism of the African scholars' opinion on what the African peoples make of God be accepted without validation? Okot p'Bitek, for example, denies that the traditional African ever knew anything about a Creator God and believes that this is the result of missionaries' soliciting (p'Bitek, *Religion of the Central Luo*, 62), if he slipped on this, why should we believe the previous claim? Is it not true that God who is not a Creator God is the creation of p'Bitek and is "… beyond recognition to the ordinary Africans in the countryside"?

In my opinion, p'Bitek's criticism of Mbiti and the other African scholars is unfair. Mbiti, like Idowu and Danquah, is interested in demonstrating the fact that the African peoples also had something of the self-revelation of God. Moreover, the notion of "pasting bits and pieces taken from all over Africa" assumes a fundamental diversity of the African Negroes, an argument which modern anthropologists, ethnolinguists and African historiographers have taken issue with (see the Prologue of this research). The diversity of the African peoples is a fact that must be accepted; however, it should not be accepted at the expense of the fundamental unity of the African Negroes, which is a direct result of the historical processes of convergence and reconvergence.

[57] Mbiti, *African Religions and Philosophy*, 37.
[58] Mbiti, *Concepts of God in Africa*, 25; Mbiti, *Introduction to African Religion*, 48.
[59] Mbiti, *Introduction to African Religion*, 43.
[60] Mbiti, *African Religions and Philosophy*, 37.
[61] Mbiti, *Concepts of God in Africa*, 95.

God does not have a material body; rather, he is believed to be a spiritual being, and, as such, some peoples simply call him "the Great Spirit, the Fathomless Spirit, the Ever-present Spirit or the God of wind and Breath."[62] As spirit, no one can make an image of him. In the words of Mbiti, "there are no images or physical representations by African peoples, this being one clear indication that they consider him to be a spiritual being."[63] Neither can God be confined to space and time. He is the "Great Spirit," the "Creating Spirit and the Saving Spirit," and the "Protecting Spirit" who made all the spirits in the universe (the Shona, the Ashanti, the Ewe, the Kagoro). He is like wind; he comes and goes (the Ga, the Bena, and the Banyarwanda). The Nuer word for God is spirit; thus they believe his essence is spirit. It is the spirit of God who empowers the rainmakers and the medicine men.[64] Thus the African peoples admit that they know some of the activities and manifestations of God, but nothing of his essential nature.[65]

The spirits of people who were once leaders, heroes, warriors, clan founders, and other outstanding personalities go through some form of *theosis* and are pictured as being close to God.[66] As the prominent personalities die, they progress into a spiritual status that points in the direction of a progressing association with God. This is the reason that prominent personalities ascend (without question) to the level of intermediaries.

Intellectual Capacities

God knows, thinks, and remembers all. He is the wise one (Zulu, Banyarwanda, and Yoruba). The rationale for worship and sacrifice is so that God may remember and—if he wills—may change his mind. The Nuer thinks that God created the universe through thought and imagination.[67] Man is wise, but only in a limited manner. Absolute wisdom belongs to God and is part of his nature.[68] In order to clearly present the idea of omniscience, Mbiti explains that the African peoples "speak of God as the All-seeing and the all-hearing, the Watcher of

---

[62] Mbiti, *Introduction to African Religion*, 53.
[63] Mbiti, *African Religions and Philosophy*, 34.
[64] Mbiti, *Concepts of God in Africa*, 23 f.
[65] Mbiti, *African Religions and Philosophy*, 35; Mbiti, *Introduction to African Religion*, 53.
[66] Mbiti, *Introduction to African Religion*, 72.
[67] Mbiti, *Concepts of God in Africa*, 97.
[68] Mbiti, *Concepts of God in Africa*, 3.

everything, the All-seer, and the Discerner of hearts."[69] Wisdom, in the words of Mbiti, commands great respect in the African societies. Therefore, to say that God knows all things is to confer upon God the highest possible place of honor and respect. God also has a will that governs the universe and the fortunes of mankind, and against this will man can do nothing.[70]

Emotions and Morality

God is said to be merciful and kind (the Akamba, the Banyarwanda, the Ila, the Herero, and others). As a general rule, he exercises his will justly. For many people, God is always right.[71] He cannot be charged with offence. His kindness and mercy are known and experienced in situations of difficulty. God rejoices, and his smile is the reason for good health and prosperity, whereas his displeasure can only bring misfortunes, sickness, and death.[72] He is essentially good. He averts calamities, provides rain, and causes people, animals, and the fields to be fertile. He is holy, and he loves.[73]

Moving and Working

God is the strong one (Yoruba, Ngombe); he is irresistible (Zulu), able to alter the natural laws and completely destroy both people and objects (the Abaluhya, the Shona). He is the source of power (the Akan, the Ashanti). God commands the created world, and they obey (the Bambuti, Banyarwanda). Even the rulers and the moral codes receive their powers from God; he is the one "who gives or breaks dignities" (Banyarwanda, Zulu, the Lugbara).[74] In the African mind, power is viewed "hierarchically in which God is at the top as the omnipotent, beneath him are the spirits and natural phenomena, and lower still are men who have comparatively little or no power at all."[75]

---

[69] Mbiti, *Introduction to African Religion*, 50.
[70] Mbiti, *African Religions and Philosophy*, 37.
[71] Mbiti, *African Religions and Philosophy*, 37 f.
[72] Mbiti, *Concepts of God in Africa*, 97.
[73] Mbiti, *African Religions and Philosophy*, 37 f.; cf. Mbiti, *Introduction to African Religion*, 48–50.
[74] Mbiti, *Concepts of God in Africa*, 8–11; J.S. Mbiti, *Introduction to African Religion*, 50.
[75] Mbiti, *African Religions and Philosophy*, 32.

Although God is understood to be powerful in the absolute sense, he is perceived to be capable of allowing himself to come within reach of man. He eats and drinks. This provides the basis for offerings and sacrifices. God plays, sleeps, and walks. There are specially designated places where the divine rests, i.e., mountains and clouds (the Shona and the Agikuyu). God's rest may take the form of either sleep or recuperation (the Nandi). When he is asleep he does not answer prayers and requires mediation (the Karamoja).[76]

Social Relations

Other Divinities and Demigods

God is alone. He has no companions (the Herero, the Agikuyu). Other peoples have the concept of the 'one but many' (the Shilluk and the Vugusu). Mbiti discusses this phenomenon as the divinities and the demigods. The Yoruba has a pantheon of divinities—the *abosom* through whom God manifests himself. Other communities also have pantheons of divinities.[77] As far as Mbiti is concerned, the idea of divinities and demigods has nothing to do with what could be considered polytheism in the African traditional religions. For Mbiti the African traditional religions are monotheistic. What has been described as divinities and demigods are "personifications of God's activities and manifestations." They could also rightly be called nature spirits, deified heroes, and mythological figures[78] that function as intermediaries between God and man.[79] According to Mbiti:

> … the idea of the intermediaries fits well with the African view of the universe, which holds that the invisible world has its own life and population. The life of this invisible world is in some way higher than that of man, but God is higher still. In order to reach God effectively it may be useful to approach him by first approaching those who are lower than he is but higher than the ordinary person.[80]

---

[76] Mbiti, *Concepts of God in Africa*, 95 f.; Mbiti, *Introduction to African Religion*, 48.

[77] The other communities which have a concept of the divinities are the Bakene, the Babuti, the Banyoro, the Barundi, the Basoga, the Dinka, the Edo, the Fon, the Ga, the Ganda, the Gofa, the Idoma, the Igbo, the Indem, the Itsekiri, the Mao, the Songhay, the Suk, the Sukuma-Nyamwezi, the Teso, the Tumbuka, the Vugusu, the Walamo, the Ashanti, the Zinza, and the Zulu (Mbiti, *Concepts of God in Africa*, 117–121).

[78] Mbiti, *Concepts of God in Africa*, 117.

[79] Mbiti, *Introduction to African Religion*, 63.

[80] Mbiti, *Introduction to African Religion*, 63.

This explanation is close to the position of K.A. Busia. He explains:

> There is the Great Spirit, the Supreme Being, who created all things, and who manifests his power through a pantheon of gods; below these are lesser spirits which animate trees, animals, or charms; and then there are the ever present spirits of the ancestors (*nasamnafa*), whose constant contact with the life of man on earth brings the world of the spirits so close to the land of the living.[81]

Family

God is viewed as the universal creator-father. "Over the whole of Africa creation is the most widely acknowledged work of God."[82] The metaphors used in this regard include excavator, hewer, carver, creator, originator, inventor, architect, potter, and fashioner.[83] God alone is described as the one who fathered the world, owns it, and cares for it, and before he fathered the world there was nothing. Moreover, he is the unfathered Father of the divinities, of the forefathers, and of all men. Still he is distinct from the divinities, men, and forefathers because he is not one of them. Being unfathered father means that he is understood to be self-existent. "He is made by no other, no one beyond him is" (Bacongo). He was the first, has always been in existence, and will never die. He came of Himself into being. He is he who speaks by himself, thus he is the speaker and the hearer, and the subject and object at the same time (the Bambuti, the Banyarwanda, the Zulu, and the Bena).[84]

He is also known to be a personal father to whom men may turn. What he created he sustains, provides for, and rules over.[85] Besides his relationship with man and the rest of the creation as father-creator, God is also said to have a family of his own where he is either the head of the family or as an elder brother. The Dogon talk of Nommo, 'the Son of God.' The Ganda speak of God and his two sons, but they also believe that God is the father of gods. Other communities view God as

---

[81] K.A. Busia, "The Ashanti of Gold Coast" in *African Worlds*. Daryll Forde, ed. (London: Oxford University Press, 1963), 191.

[82] Mbiti, *African Religions and Philosophy*, 39.

[83] Mbiti, *Introduction to African Religion*, 44.

[84] Mbiti, *Concepts of God in Africa*, 19f.

[85] Whereas traditional Africa generally thinks of God as father, a few communities with matrilineal system of descent (the Nuba, the Ovambo, and the Shona) refer to God as mother (Mbiti, *Concepts of God in Africa*, 91–93; cf. Mbiti, *Introduction to African Religion*, 44–47).

having either a younger brother (the Bari, the Tiv, the Vugusu, and the Suk) or a younger sister (the Dorobo).[86]

Balance of Power

The African peoples that have strong monarchical systems of governance view God as king and lord.[87] God is the great king who reigns over and owns all things, visible and invisible; has absolute power; maintains order in the sky, earth, and underworld; and may not be approached directly but only via intermediaries.[88] Since God is king and lord, he is also viewed as master, thus he controls the destinies of all things (the Banyarwanda, the Shongay, the Barundi), helps and teaches (the Banyarwanda, the Ganda, the Baluba, the Barotse, the Meru, the Shilluk, the Tswana, the Vugusu, the Mende, the Tiv, and the Lodagaa), and, moreover, he gives material things as well as life as the most precious gift.[89]

God is also associated with justice, punishment, and retribution. He is the ultimate dispenser and judge, thus he gives to each person his own portion, punishes those who commit wrong, and intervenes in human affairs. God punishes individuals through illnesses, calamities, misfortune, barrenness, or death. God's help is sought during war and in almost every case (among the peoples who believe in divinities) there is at least one divinity of war (the Ankore, the Banyoro, the Ga, the Ganda, the Itsekiri, and the Yoruba).[90]

Misfortune, Disease, and Death

For some reason, many African peoples attribute afflictions to God. He is thought to cause afflictions, allow them to happen, or is in some way connected with them. God is thought to cause epidemics, calamities, destruction, death, pests, and cattle diseases (the Ambo, the Azande, the Bambuti, the Bongo, the Bavenda, and the Suk). In some cases, the personifications of God may be responsible for certain types

---

[86] Mbiti, *Concepts of God in Africa*, 114–116.

[87] This is seen among the Banyarwanda, the Barundi, the Edo, the Baluba, the Twi, the Akan, the Bachwa, the Babuti, the Indem, the Ngoni, the Agikuyu, the Yoruba, the Zulu, the Bena, and the Chagga, among others (Mbiti, *Concepts of God in Africa*, 71–73).

[88] Mbiti, *Concepts of God in Africa*, 71–73.

[89] Mbiti, *Concepts of God in Africa*, 73–76.

[90] Mbiti, *Concepts of God in Africa*, 76–79.

of afflictions. The personifications or the manifestations of God are known to send smallpox, spiritual illnesses, bubonic plague, and death.[91] Whereas God is associated with afflictions, he is also known to be the deliverer and savior from evil. He always delivers those in trouble, the ill, the poor, and the weak.[92]

Accessories of Life

Habitation

God is self-existent. He is of himself. He came into being by himself (the Zulu, the Bambuti, and the Agikuyu). Beyond this God there is nothing. God "is the most abundant reality of being, lacking no completeness."[93] He transcends all boundaries; he is omnipresent everywhere and at all times.[94] He even defies human conception and description. He is simply "'the Unexplainable', as the Ngombe like to call him."[95] God's presence is met everywhere at once just like water, air, and wind (the Karanga, the Bena, and the Kono). His presence stretches beyond human imagination. He is a being in the wind, invisible, but certainly present (the Lango, the Nuer, and the Shilluk).[96] According to the Ila, the omnipresence of God is captured by the saying "God has nowhere or nowhen, that he comes to end."[97]

Certain objects, events, and phenomena are particularly associated with the presence of God—even though God is present everywhere simultaneously. The Gikuyu, the Lango, the Xhosa, and the Sonjo associate the presence of God with hills and mountains. The Banyarwanda associate the presence of God with 'every terrifying place'; the Herero with rain, lightning and thunder; while the Gisu, Ganda and Amba associate his presence with a cock that is supposed to be seen when there is lightning. God's manifestations are also said to be in dangerous situations such as fighting, journeys, and encounters with wild animals. People are cautioned to avoid such situations (Lango). God's presence is

---

[91] Mbiti, *Concepts of God in Africa*, 80–87.
[92] Mbiti, *Concepts of God in Africa*, 82 f.
[93] Mbiti, *African Religions and Philosophy*, 33; cf. Mbiti, *Introduction to African Religion*, 52.
[94] Mbiti, *Introduction to African Religion*, 51.
[95] Mbiti, *African Religions and Philosophy*, 33.
[96] Mbiti, *Concepts of God in Africa*, 5, 6.
[97] Mbiti, *African Religions and Philosophy*, 31.

also manifested in the sexual encounter between a wife and a husband, and thus is the explanation for conception.[98]

Time

However, in terms of time, God is seen as a being in and beyond the past, yet he is there now and men can reach him. He is present now as he was in ancient times. He endures forever (the Akan and the Tonga). He antedates the forests, and he thunders from the beginning (Ngombe, Zulu). Thus God is transcendent beyond all things in temporal comparison.[99] But whereas he is temporally transcendent, he is also quite immanent. He stretches over and beyond the *zamani* period, yet he is also near and close to men.[100] In his immanence he could be dangerous (the Lugbara, the Turu, and the Lango); therefore, people avoid close proximity with the divine. Although God is conceived as immanent, there is no evidence of pantheism.[101]

Other Traditional African Descriptions of God

Theriomorphic Descriptions

The Old Testament occasionally uses the picture of mammals (the bull—Gen. 49:22–26, Num. 23:22, 24:8, and the lion—Hos. 13:7 f. cf. 2 Sam. 17:8, Prov. 17:12, Lam. 3:10), birds (Deut. 32:11, Ex. 19:4, Psa. 91:4, Isa. 31:5), and winged creatures such as the cherubim (Psa. 18:11, II Sam. 22:11) and the seraphim (Isa. 6, Isa. 14:29, Ezek. 1 cf. Ezek. 11:22 f.) to describe God. The African people occasionally describe God theriomorphically. Generally, the African people understand that God gave animals to man and caused them to be under the power of man either as brothers or as food. However, there are instances where animals are used either as metaphors of God or as his manifestations.[102]

---

[98] Mbiti, *Concepts of God in Africa*, 7, 8.

[99] Mbiti, *Concepts of God in Africa*, 12, 13.

[100] Mbiti, *African Religions and Philosophy*, 32.

[101] Mbiti, *Concepts of God in Africa*, 16, 17.

[102] In the following instances, animals—such as the buffalo (the Lango), the zebra (the Shona), the lion (the Turu), the leopard (the Lango), the hyena (the Lugbara, the Turu), the sacred snakes (the Banyoro, the Bari, the Bemba, the Gisu, the Turu, and the Zala), and the eagle (the Herero and the Bavenda)—are used as metaphors of God. There are also instances where theriomorphic animals received sacrifices either because they are considered manifestations of God, or because they are his messengers and they

Physiomorphic Descriptions

According to traditional African views of reality, what we regard as the inanimate and neutral physical reality could harbor divine presence. Under consideration here are cosmology; geology, geography, and hydrology; trees and plants; and natural phenomena.

Cosmology

In the words of Mbiti, practically all the two hundred and seventy peoples he studied in his *Concepts of God in Africa* (1970) associate God with the heavens, sky, or firmament. A number of the African peoples understand that God lives in the heavens or the sky. Some people personify the sun and view it as a divinity (the Amba, the Azande, the Fon, the Meban, the Sandawe, the Akan, the Nandi, and the Afasure among others). Mbiti makes it clear, however, that in spite of the personifications and the rather loose associations, he never came across a situation where the sun was considered to be God and God to be the sun.[103]

The moon is also personified and considered to be a divinity by some peoples (the Akan, the Amba, the Fon, and the Sandawe). A number of the peoples associate the moon with God in different ways. The moon is one of the two eyes of God (the Balese, the Sidamo); it symbolizes God (the Turu); it has the signs of God (the Watumbatu); it belongs to God, and God shines in it (the Nuer). Observance of the new moon is reported among many peoples (the Banyoro, the Nuer, and the Ingassana).[104]

Geology, Geography and Hydrology

Rain is generally viewed as a gift of God and the ultimate good. Thus if it does not rain then God is said to be meting out his punishment. In the words of Mbiti, the view that rain is a "source of happiness, the basis of man's physical security, and a symbol of spiritual well-being and social order"[105] can be applied to all African peoples. Some peoples

---

are close to him. Cases in point are the mantis (the Lesotho Bushmen), the snakes (the Zulus), and the hyenas (the Giryma) (Mbiti, *Concepts of God in Africa*, 98–108).

[103] Mbiti, *Concepts of God in Africa*, 129–134.

[104] Mbiti, *Concepts of God in Africa*, 134–137.

[105] Mbiti, *Concepts of God in Africa*, 137.

personify rain and view it as a divinity (the Bushmen, the Elgeyo, the Igbo, and the Suk, among others). Others closely associate God with rain (the Beir, the Didinga, the Idoma, the Iyala, the Maasai, the Nuba, the Suk, and the Piti), and sometimes rain is seen as a manifestation either of God himself or of his power (the Nuer, the Agikuyu, the Tiv, and the Ila).[106]

Thunder is said to be produced by God (the Herero, the Kuku, the Lokoiya, the Suk, and the Zulu) and a manifestation of his immanence. Thus God is said to thunder (the Ila), and, in some cases, thunder is described as God's manifestation (the Nuer and the Shona), his movement (the Agikuyu, the Zulu, and the Ila), and a manifestation of his anger and power (the Tiv, the Watumbatu, and the Yoruba).[107] Hurricanes, hail, and thunderstorms are generally viewed as manifestations of God's anger and may indicate that God is arming himself (the Shona, the Tonga, the Zulu, the Watumabatu, the Yoruba, the Bambuti, the Tswana, and the Zulu).[108]

Some peoples use wind to describe some aspects of God. His omnipresence, in particular, is described using the metaphor of wind. Thus he is described as being like moving air or wind (the Lango, the Ga, the Shilluk, and the Vugusu). High wind may be considered as either a manifestation of God (the Turu), a vehicle by means of which God travels in great power (the Bavenda), or as a punishment (the Tswana).[109]

Floods and cloudbursts are associated with God. In some cases it is believed that God's presence can be felt in springs, rivers, pools, and lakes (the Lugbara, the Lango, the Turu, the Shona, the Azande, the Banyoro, the Ganda, the Haya, the Sukuma-Nyamwezi, and the Yoruba). Some rivers are thought to be divinities, as in the case of river Tano (the Ashanti) and the Nile (the Shilluk), and waterfalls are considered manifestations of God (the Nandi and the Gisu).[110]

Many of the peoples have a concept of sacred stones or rocks. For these people, the stones or the rocks are associated with God either as his abode or as his manifestation. Others believe that the mountains and hills are the places where the immanence of God is

---

[106] Mbiti, *Concepts of God in Africa*, 137–139.
[107] Mbiti, *Concepts of God in Africa*, 139–141.
[108] Mbiti, *Concepts of God in Africa*, 142.
[109] Mbiti, *Concepts of God in Africa*, 141–142.
[110] Mbiti, *Concepts of God in Africa*, 145–148.

most intense (the Agikuyu—Mt. Kenya, the Lango—Mt. Agoro, the Bavenda—Matoba hills, Jumjum—Jebel Tunya, the Shona—Matopo mountians).[111] Mountains, hills, and other high standing earth formations in a way give a concrete manifestation of God's presence and his being.[112]

There are divinities of metals among the Edo, the Yoruba, and the Itsekiri. Desolate places and wastelands also have some significance in the African peoples' description of God. The Shona made the Zimbabwe ruins a sacred place long before the Europeans 'discovered' the land of the Shona. The Turkana diviner-to-be retires into a desert area for an extended period of time before he begins to practice. The Lugbara do not go to desolate places for fear that God in his immanent aspects resides in such places.[113]

Trees and Plants

The forests are generally associated with God. This explains why a number of peoples have sacred groves where religious ceremonies are performed (the Agikuyu, the Akamba, the Meru, the Butawa, and the Igbo). Sometimes the forests are thought to be occupied by spirits or divinities. The Herero speak of 'the tree of life,' while the Bambuti, the Chagga, and the Meru speak of 'the forbidden tree.' There is also the idea of sacred trees. The Akamba, the Egede, the Agikuyu, the Meru, and the Tonga offer sacrifices and prayers under a fig tree. Many peoples have a concept of sacred trees.[114] The sacred trees symbolize God's immanence. The Banyarwanda, for example, believe that God lives in every big tree. The Idoma view the white silk-cotton tree or the fig tree as symbolizing God. The Lango, the Lugbara, and the Luo associate God with certain trees. In contexts where divinities are understood to be a reality, trees are viewed as their temporary abode (the Ashanti).[115]

---

[111] Mbiti, *Concepts of God in Africa*, 148–151.

[112] Mbiti, *African Religions and Philosophy*, 55.

[113] Mbiti, *Concepts of God in Africa*, 148–151.

[114] The Barundi, the Batawa, the Beir, the Murle, the Gisu, the Igbo, the Galla, the Masongo, the Teita, the Toposa, the Sonjo, and the Ngombe all have a concept of sacred trees (J.S. Mbiti, *Concepts of God in Africa* (London: SPCK, 1970), 109–113).

[115] Mbiti, *Concepts of God in Africa*, 109–113.

Natural Phenomena

Having shown us the connection that traditional Africa makes between God and phenomena such as wind, thunder, lightning, flood, and storm, Mbiti also lets us see how traditional Africa uses the metaphors of light, fire, smoke, day, night, heat, cold, colors, and numbers to describe God. Traditional Africa associates God with light, brilliance, and heat. This is the reason many African peoples have names which are similar for both God and the sun. God is also associated with heat.[116] The Ila believe that heat indicates that God is much too hot. Whereas he is associated with light and brilliance, he also assumes the rhythm of day and night. The immanence of God by day is indicated by light, while his immanence by night is associated with the moon, darkness, and coolness. When it is cool, God has granted his peace and deliverance from evil (the Nuer and the Luvedu).[117] The Fon connects God's aspects of motherliness, gentleness, rest, and joy with both the moon and the night.[118] For some people, the night symbolizes a time of communication and contact with God in a way that benefits the human community (the Nuba), but for others the night symbolizes shame, fear, and punishment (the Meru).[119]

Some peoples believe that God is black (the Maasai). The Maasai believe that originally there were four gods—the black god (very good), the white god (good), the red god (bad), and the blue god (neither good nor bad), but now the only God that remains is the black God. The Dinka and the Vugusu associate suffering and misfortune with a black divinity. The Agikuyu and the Yoruba associate God with absolute whiteness. Whiteness is the phenomenon by which the Vugusu distinguish between God and other divinities.[120] Numbers do not constitute a significant way of describing God. The only occurences that Mbiti discusses are those that indicate their significance in the reverence of God, punishment, creation stories, and bad omens.[121]

---

[116] The peoples who have names similar for both God and the sun are the Afasure, the Ankore, the Ashanti, the Chagga, the Chawai, the Dorobo, the Elgeyo, the Ingassana, the Luo, the Nandi, the Sonjo, the Akan, and the Pyem (Mbiti, *Concepts of God in Africa*, 133).

[117] Mbiti, *Concepts of God in Africa*, 154.

[118] Mbiti, *Concepts of God in Africa*, 134.

[119] Mbiti, *Concepts of God in Africa*, 154.

[120] Mbiti, *Concepts of God in Africa*, 155.

[121] Mbiti, *Concepts of God in Africa*, 156, 157.

G.M. Setiloane: The African Concept of God as *Mysterium Tremendum et Fascinans*

Setiloane's Point of Departure

The point of departure of G. Setiloane's understanding of God con-
currs with what Rudolf Otto has in his book, *The Idea of the Holy*, called
mysterium tremendum et fascinans.[122] According to Setiloane, the African
peoples cannot agree with a kind of theology that explains the essence
of the divine completely and exhaustively in the kind of rational attri-
butions we see in Western theologies. What the African peoples believe
in, explains Setiloane, is a divine *Modimo* in Sotho-Tswana who, on the
one hand, is *mysterium tremendum* and, on the other hand, is *fascinans*.[123]

For Setiloane, numinousness is a basic theological truth that must
never be forgotten in formulating the doctrine of God.[124] Theology
needs to understand God not just rationally, but it also needs the
mysterium tremendum and the *fascinans*. These two concepts (the *mysterium
tremendum* and the *fascinans*) applied to God, explains Otto, convey the
idea of:

> … the daunting and the fascinating, now combine in a strange harmony
> of contrasts, and the resultant dual character of the numinous conscious-
> ness, to which the entire religious development bears witness, at any
> rate from the level of 'demonic dread' onward, is at once the strangest
> and most noteworthy phenomenon in the whole history of religion. The
> demonic-divine object may appear to the mind as an object of horror
> and dread, but at the same time it is no less something that allures with
> a potent charm, and the creature, who trembles before it, utterly cowed
> and cast down, has always at the same time the impulse to turn to it, nay
> even to make it his own. The 'mystery' is for him not merely something
> to be wondered at but something that entrances him; and beside that in
> it which bewilders and confounds, he feels a something which captivates
> and transports him with a strange ravishment, rising often enough to the
> pitch of dizzy intoxication; it is the Dionysiac-element in the numen.[125]

---

[122] R. Otto, *The Idea of the Holy*. J.W. Harvey, trans. (London: Penguin Books, 1923),
19f.; cf. G.M. Setiloane, "MODIMO: GOD Among the Sotho-Tswana" in *Journal of
Theology for Southern Africa*, Sep 1973 No 4, 1973 (6–17), 6; and G.M. Setiloane, *The Image
of God among the Sotho-Tswana* (Rotterdam: A.A. Balkema, 1976), 77.

[123] Setiloane, *The Image of God among the Sotho-Tswana*, 77; Otto, *The Idea of the Holy*,
26–55.

[124] Setiloane, *The Image of God among the Sotho-Tswana*, 78.

[125] Otto, *The Idea of the Holy*, 45.

Since God is *mysterium tremendum* and *fascinans*, Setiloane wants to see such elements as "awefulness," "overpoweringness," "energy or urgency of the numinous" perceptible particularly in the "wrath," "the wholly other," and fascination[126] associated with the understanding of God. These elements, Setiloane believes, are clearly noticeable in the Sotho-Tswana concept of God.

The Sotho-Tswana word, which Setiloane finds useful in conveying the concept of *mysterium tremendum* and *fascinans*, is *selo*.[127] In Sotho-Tswana, *selo* is described as *selo se se boitshengang, sa poitshego, se se tshabegang, se se mashwe* ("a fearful, awful, ugly, ugly, monstrous thing"). Setiloane emphasizes that there is nothing malevolent or malicious in these adjectives.[128] When *selo* is applied to *Modimo*, it conveys what Otto calls *Ungeheuere, poitshego* which is translated as the "monstrous" or "weird."[129] Therefore *Modimo* is "described as *selo*, 'thing,' 'monster.'"[130] Since *Modimo* is *selo*, 'thing,' Setiloane proposes that God be designated with the pronoun *It* rather than *He*.[131] The real reason why Setiloane proposes *It* is because whenever the Sotho-Twsana speak about *Modimo*, they do not have a person in mind.[132] The concept *selo* is apparently too intense for person, although it is used of chiefs. *Modimo* understood as *selo* explains why *It* had to be approached through *badimo*, and neither could *Its* name be used so freely.[133] Setiloane explains that the Sotho-

---

[126] Otto, *The Idea of the Holy*, 19–55.

[127] Setiloane, "MODIMO: GOD Among the Sotho-Tswana," 6, 7.

[128] G.M. Setiloane, *The Image of God among the Sotho-Tswana*, 78f. The Sotho-Tswana word *selo* is not "a mere neuter, but, in the right context, an attribution of excellence appearing in the praises of chiefs" (Setiloane, "MODIMO: GOD Among the Sotho-Tswana," 15). The word *selo* literally means 'beast'; however, when applied to a chief it conveys the notion of "strength and power and almost horror which properly attach to a chief... even when he is most just and most considerate of his people's need and opinion" (Setiloane, "MODIMO: GOD Among the Sotho-Tswana," 15). Because of this factor, Setiloane prefers to spell the Sotho-Tswana name for God in capital letters.

[129] Setiloane, *The Image of God among the Sotho-Tswana*, 78f.; G.M. Setiloane, *African Theology: An Introduction* (Johannesburg: Skotaville Publishers, 1986), 33.

[130] Setiloane, "MODIMO: GOD Among the Sotho-Tswana," 6f. cf. Setiloane, *African Theology*, 22f.

[131] Setiloane, "MODIMO: GOD Among the Sotho-Tswana," 6f.

[132] Setiloane, *African Theology*, 25, 27.

[133] W.C. Willoughby's book, *The Soul of the Bantu*, explains that *Modimo* has to be approached through the *badimo* (the ancestors) because he is "too great to be approached by the mortals" (W.C. Willoughby, *The Soul of the Bantu* (London: SCM, 1928), 206ff.). Setiloane notes, however, that "despite the dangers of direct approach, IT can be called upon in mortal danger" (Setiloane, *The Image of God among the Sotho-Tswana*, 84).

Tswana felt that the missionaries did not recognize the greatness of
Modimo enough because they used his name so freely.[134]

With these considerations, Setiloane has wondered whether:

> What the missionaries have offered to Africans is not GOD but the
> god of the Europeans, who may well—perhaps rightly—be discarded
> with the coming of political independence and the reassertion of African
> culture which is its ideological counterpart. Indeed, the whole discussion
> in the West—focused in 'Honest to God' and the "Death of God"
> theology—suggests that the West itself has lost the image of God as
> "mysterium tremendum et fascinans", and deals, at the best, with a
> "creator absconditus", a god of the gaps, or a saviour of individual souls
> destined for a pie in the sky.[135]

Regardless of this concern, Setiloane continues to hold the conviction that "the Black man still believes that Christianiy comes from
God (Modimo), so he clings to it although his mind is in a state
of revolt against Western Christianity."[136] According to Setiloane, the
Africans never disagreed with the missionaries in their description of
God because when the missionaries talked about God, it was as is
they were telling the Africans "an old story with which they were quite
familiar but have now half forgotten."[137] The familiarity was most evident in the attributes. The attributes of God as he had revealed himself to the Africans, and the attributes of the God that the missionaries
preached were so similar that the Africans agreed to a simple identification of the God they had known with the God of the missionary
message.[138]

Qualities and Names of Modimo

Modimo *is One*

The Sotho-Tswana knows *Modimo* only in the singular. In the words of
Setiloane, that *Modimo* is one is a "statement so obvious as to seem

---

[134] The Sotho-Tswana still regard the use of the name *Modimo* as taboo. For example,
when *Modimo* forms part of a personal name as it stands, the part having the word is
avoided in everyday use of the name, "eg a child whose name is 'Tiro-ya-Modimo', the
work of MODIMO, would ordinarily be called simply 'Tiro'" (Setiloane, *The Image of
God among the Sotho-Tswana*, 235).

[135] Setiloane, *The Image of God among the Sotho-Tswana*, 229.

[136] Setiloane, *African Theology*, 29.

[137] E.W. Smith quoted in Setiloane, *African Theology*, 28.

[138] Setiloane, *African Theology*, 26.

absurd. MODIMO. ... has no plural without a radical change of meaning. There is no being whom they could begin to compare with IT. Nor would it occur to them that IT was any other than THAT called, in neighbouring societies, by other names."[139]In performing an etymology of the word *Modimo*, Setiloane comes to the conclusion that:

> The missionaries were looking in a wrong place for the etymology of 'Modimo'. The word initially had nothing to do with *godimo...* or *lego-dimo*. The prefix *Mo* of the word is a prefix of the Third Class of the table of nouns in African languages, called the '*Mo–Me* Class'. There is a whole number of nouns in this class, which do not take the plural form. Such nouns are names of 'invisible, intangible objects often describing natural phenomena ...' for example *Mollo*: fire, *Mosi*: smoke, *Mmuwane*: mist, *Monyo*: dew, *Ngwedi*: moon, *Mokoodi*: rainbow, etc. This regulation applies to equivalents of these words in all African languages. The root or stem of the word—*dimo* is a derivation of a local permutation of the original African stem—*dzimu*. All African philologists, agree that the correct translation of—*dzimu* is 'spirit or pertaining to spirit'. African colleagues from Central and Equatorial Africa, Zaire, Congo (Brazza), Cameroon and Fenade Po where the word '*mudzimu*' exists in its original form do confirm that even in present day usage it is ascribed to things of the Spirit.[140]

There are *badimo*, but the *badimo* are ancestors, the living dead, and are not to be confused with the Divinity.[141] They, therefore, belong to the category of persons, and they are experienced as such, although they share in the 'essence of *Modimo, BoModimo*.' Since they share in *BoModimo* along with humans, the levels of intensity of the numinous in them is much higher than that found in man.[142]

Modimo *is Supreme Being*

The Sotho-Tswana expresses the supremacy of *Modimo* by using a number of titles and praise names. Notable titles and names used in this regard include: "*hla'a-Macholo*" (ancient of days); "Modimo *wa borare*" (of my forefathers—thus the forefathers know *Modimo* better); "*Na Choeng Tsa Dithaba*" (whose abode is on the highest peak of the

---

[139] Setiloane, "MODIMO: GOD Among the Sotho-Tswana," 9 f.; cf. Setiloane, *The Image of God among the Sotho-Tswana*, 80.

[140] Setiloane, *African Theology*, 24.

[141] Setiloane, *African Theology*, 17.

[142] Setiloane, *African Theology*, 19.

mountains); "*Mong'a Tschle.*" (owner or master of all, Lord).[143] By supreme the Sotho-Tswana do not mean 'supreme being among other
beings.' In contrast, they believe that *Modimo* "is Being, from whom all
particular beings derive. Through badimo, IT is concerned in all life."
The focus of these peoples is not on "Supreme"; the emphasis falls on
"Being."[144]

Modimo *is Not a Man*

When speaking about *Modimo*, the Sotho-Tswana do not have human
being in mind. Setiloane notes that the "one quality of MODIMO that
nearly approaches a human quality (but far surpasses all human manifestation, thereby rendering MODIMO numinous) is being associated
with 'penetrating insight into men and things' as if it had some human
cognition."[145] On account of this "cognition," the African people know
that *Modimo* has personality, although as Smith says, he is "in sharp
distinction from everyone and everything else. … He is a being who
is not human, and never in the recollection of men was human."[146]
Rather, *Modimo* is *moya* (spirit). But although *Modimo* is *moya*, this *moya*
is to be understood in the sense of power and energy ever going on.
Consequently, *Modimo* can be explained by Placide Tempels' concept of
Force Vitale, but understood in the sense in which Vincent Mulago has
explained *Participation Vital* that expresses the energy that is ever active,
initiating action, and maintaining interaction.[147]

Modimo *is Invisible, is Everywhere and is Involved With Everything*

No man has seen *Modimo*. In a sense he is unknown. He is not even
as tangible as the wind, yet he is experienced at all points. Quoting
Otto, Setiloane explains that the Sotho-Tswana experience *Modimo*
in ways other than "the world of senses."[148] But although *Modimo* is
wholly other and is experienced in ways other than senses, *Modimo*
is still known to be manifested in lightning and thunder; however,

---

[143] Setiloane, "MODIMO: GOD Among the Sotho-Tswana," 10.
[144] Setiloane, *The Image of God among the Sotho-Tswana*, 227.
[145] Setiloane, *African Theology*, 25.
[146] Smith, *African Ideas of God*, 21 f.
[147] Setiloane, *African Theology*, 28.
[148] Setiloane, "MODIMO: GOD Among the Sotho-Tswana," 13; Setiloane, *The Image of God among the Sotho-Tswana*, 80.

these are but manifestations of *Modimo*. The manifestations are not to be confused with *It*.[149] Since *Modimo* is *motlhodi*, he is involved in everything and so *It* controls everything "even in the last resort natural disasters of *baloi* (sorcerers), and IT is affected by offences against the natural order."[150] Thus the order needs to be restored once it has been disturbed.

Modimo *is the Source*

The term used here to convey the concept of source is *motlhodi*.[151] This word refers to "the source, originating in unrecorded time, of the stream of life which flows into the indeterminate future and is ever returning to its source."[152] *Modimo* is the "Creator, Originator, and cause of all things."[153] To the Sotho-Tswana it is obvious that "man is only because MODIMO is," and men are in a relationship because the "eternal I creates in a relationship a plurality of thous." Man is himself numinous, but the numinousness is derived from *Modimo*.[154] A saying which truly expresses the numinousness of personhood is "*Motho ke Modimo*." By this expression the Sotho-Tswana mean "the mystery that the human is a portion, a tributary of the Supreme Vital Force (*Modimo*) itself."[155] Elsewhere Setiloane explains that:

> The human person is that Energy or Force, that is Modimo—Divinity. The word used to describe the human person in this saying is the same as that employed to describe the mysterious, all pervasive Energy-Force which is in fact the *source of life*. It expresses in a very pithy and exact manner that a person is something divine, sacred, weird, holy; all qualities of Divinity (Modimo).[156]

---

[149] Setiloane, "MODIMO: GOD Among the Sotho-Tswana," 10; cf. Setiloane, *The Image of God among the Sotho-Tswana*, 82 f.

[150] Setiloane, "MODIMO: GOD Among the Sotho-Tswana," 13; cf. Setiloane, *The Image of God among the Sotho-Tswana*, 82 f.

[151] Setiloane, "MODIMO: GOD Among the Sotho-Tswana," 13; Setiloane, *The Image of God among the Sotho-Tswana*, 80.

[152] Setiloane, *The Image of God among the Sotho-Tswana*, 81.

[153] Setiloane, *The Image of God among the Sotho-Tswana*, note 27.

[154] Setiloane, *The Image of God among the Sotho-Tswana*, 226 f.

[155] Setiloane, *African Theology*, 42.

[156] Setiloane, *African Theology*, 13.

Modimo *is in the Sky but Vividly Associated with the Earth*

Modimo dwells in the sky,[157] yet he is also said to be living in a hole in the bowels of the earth.[158] What is captured here is simultaneous transcendence and condescendence of God. When God is distant, he is very distant, but when he is near he is very near.

Modimo *Wills Good to Mankind and Preserves Justice*

No one can change the purposes of *Modimo*. The *badimo* are asked to appeal to *It* in times of need and calamity. No evil comes from *Modimo*. However, he may occasionally inflict pain to "draw attention to a disruption of harmony by man." Rain and harvest are his gifts.[159] *Modimo* does not only will good, he does this because his very being embodies "life together and relationships between persons and peoples."[160] In order for the community to be together, *Modimo* binds it with justice. *Modimo's* justice is *wa makgon the'a kgodi's kgokgo* (steadfast and fixed like granite).[161]

Modimo *Acts Through Badimo Yet He is Readily Available to Those in Need*

The normal way in which *Modimo* acts is through the *badimo*. The *badimo* are the intermediators. However, it is understood that *Modimo* can "intervene directly to draw attention to the breach of taboos."[162] The intervention may take the form of such calamities as drought, hail, locusts, and plague that *It* alone can avert.[163] Yet the emphasis does not fall on the individual.

---

[157] Setiloane, "MODIMO: GOD Among the Sotho-Tswana," 11–13; Setiloane, *The Image of God among the Sotho-Tswana*, 81.

[158] Setiloane, "MODIMO: GOD Among the Sotho-Tswana," 12; Setiloane, *The Image of God among the Sotho-Tswana*, 82.

[159] Setiloane, "MODIMO: GOD Among the Sotho-Tswana," 13, 14.

[160] Setiloane, *African Theology*, 11.

[161] Setiloane, "MODIMO: GOD Among the Sotho-Tswana," 14; Setiloane, *The Image of God among the Sotho-Tswana*, 83.

[162] Setiloane, "MODIMO: GOD Among the Sotho-Tswana," 14; Setiloane, *The Image of God among the Sotho-Tswana*, 83.

[163] Setiloane, "MODIMO: GOD Among the Sotho-Tswana," 14.

Man did not originate as an individual. He came out of a cave "in company with other people and living things". It is the community which demands his first loyalty. All—the noble, the rich, the poor, adults, and children—must bow before its general good. Conflicts and dissentions of course there are in plenty: and this because every I is fully I and every thou fully thou. But those who wilfully reject the common good are 'baloi', the embodiments of evil ....[164]

CONCLUSION

The *what* that the African peoples make of God is perhaps the single area of Christian doctrine that has received immense focus in African inculturation theology. Two reasons could be advanced for this focus: first, African theologians seem to view theology primarily as engaging in discourses on God. But the second, and perhaps the most important reason, is the place that God occupies in African cosmology. We noted in the previous chapter that African cosmology is a hierarchy of beings with the Divine Being occupying the number one place. The Divine Being, in the thought of Africans, is number one because he is the ultimate explanation of the genesis and sustenance of man, and the rest of the created order. In that sense, he is the ultimate source and controller of 'being' which, as we saw in Tempels and Kagame, is expressed by the African in terms of "force," "power," or "energy."[165]

The following can be considered a summary of African inculturation theology's understanding of God:

1. God is one. There is no other God besides him. Various African peoples knew this God by different names. This one God—known to different African peoples by different names such as *Nyasaye, Leza, Mulungu, Modimo,* and so on—is also the One True God of the Christian worship. He is the creator, the fashioner, and the source. He is all these and more because he is the ultimate being. However, he did not create and leave. As is clearly indicated in the African cosmology, he is involved with the spirit world, the dead of the peoples, the living, the world of animals and plants, as well as with the entire created

---

[164] Setiloane, *The Image of God among the Sotho-Tswana,* 226; Setiloane, *African Theology,* 9–16.

[165] Mbiti, *African Religions and Philosophy,* 16.

universe. God is a spiritual being. He is *moya*; no one has seen him. He has personality (*Muntu*), but he is not human. The African people have always known him as *Umuntu*, the Great *Muntu*, but never as a human being. In the words of Setiloane, God "was always the numinous, *Ungeheure, mysterium tremendum et fascinans* of Rudolf Otto."[166] He has a personal name, life, and consciousness. Because he has personality and is described anthropomorphically, he is worshipped. Sacrifices and prayers are offered to him. It must be noted that in contexts in which the intermediaries are prevalent, there is practically no direct worship of God. Generally, as Kirwen has noted, in such contexts the ancestors, the spirits, and the divinities are the saviors of humanity.[167] On the basis of these evidences, Smith once stated that:

> ... it is a noteworthy fact, vouchsafed for by many missionaries, that when one goes to pagan Bantu one does not have to prove the existence of God. They easily accept the idea of the God of Christianity. As M. Junod says: '... it seems as if one were telling them an old story with which they had been quite familiar but have now half forgotten.'[168]

It seems that for thousands of years the African people have known God as creator and sustainer of all things. For this reason, the preaching of the gospel and the translation of scriptures use African names of God in each area of the continent.

2. As an African Christian thinker, what do I make of the natural knowledge of God that African inculturation theology strongly emphasizes? This is a hard question. However, I am willing to commit myself to the following judgements:

– It is futile to deny the African people a natural knowledge of God. A self-declaration of God to mankind can be recognized in the natural order. However, God himself is not to be encountered in nature and history. God exists above the order of nature and is not immanent within it. The order of nature only shows traces of his reality.

---

[166] G.M. Setiloane, "How the Traditional world-view persists in the Christianity of the Sotho-Tswana" in *Christianity in Independent Africa*. E. Fashole-Luke et al, eds. (Bloomington: Indiana University Press, 1978), 411.

[167] M.C. Kirwen, *The Missionary and the Diviner: Contending Theologies of Christian and African Religions* (Maryknoll: Orbis Books, 1987), 5–8.

[168] Smith, *The Christian Mission in Africa*, 38.

– The self-declaration of God in the order of nature is objectively real. What is revealed—however little—is God himself. Nevertheless, the knowledge of God acquired from the natural order is subjective and questionable. First, what we know of God from the natural order must be subjective and unreal because our sinful condition does not allow us to have a neutral attitude towards God. Second, our finitude as creatures means that we cannot grasp the full sweep of God's self-revelation. Moreover, the fact of the hiddenness of God means that we will not have a full knowledge of him for this moment. Full knowledge of God is reserved for the eschaton.

– The fact that the African people knew God from the natural order means that they cannot hide behind the excuse that they have no knowledge of him. The African peoples have perceived the self-revelation of God. As Calvin once said, this natural knowledge must be distinguished from the saving knowledge. The natural knowledge "exists solely for the purpose of making us inexcusable."[169] As is the case among other peoples, the African peoples have turned what they have perceived of the self-revelation of God away from God and towards creatures, spirits, and divinities.

– Since it is impossible for all people to finally come to a true knowledge of God by themselves, the final outcome of the natural knowledge of God should lead us to the praise of God's self-revelation in Jesus Christ our savior. For the African people to view God as savior of mankind is to present them with an overwhelming truth. This is because the savior such as we see in Christ is nowhere in the African cultural milieu. According to J.S. Mbiti:

> ... Our myths look back to the creation of the world, the early man, the coming of death into the world, the separation between God and men, heaven and earth. There is nothing that looks towards the future, nothing to be awaited and nothing to be expected in the future apart from the rhythm of day and night, birth, initiation, marriage, death, and entry into the company of the departed.[170]

---

[169] J. Calvin. *Calvin's Works* (*Corpus Reformatorum*). Baum, Canitz, and Reuss, eds., vols 1–59 (Brunswick 1863–1890) (London: Edward Arnold, 1983), 49, 24; 49, 326; 48, 327.
[170] J.S. Mbiti, "Some African Concepts of Christology" in *Christ and the Younger Churches*. ed. G.F. Vicedom (London: SPCK, 1972), 60.

Of course, as Calvin argues:

> ... the preaching of the cross is not compatible with human reason, yet
> we must accept the same in all humility if we desire once more to enter
> into relationship with God our Creator (from whom we are estranged) in
> such a way that He again becomes our Father.[171]

This is the message for the African people as it is for the other peoples
of the world as well. Nowhere is this captured more truthfully than in
the doctrine of the Trinity.

---

[171] Calvin, *Institutes*, II, 6, 1; cf II, 6, 4.

CHAPTER NINE

MOVING BEYOND THE AFRICAN
NOTION OF GOD: CLEARING GROUND FOR
THE DOCTRINE OF THE TRINITY

INTRODUCTION

The question that this chapter seeks to address is of utmost importance to this research. African inculturation theology is Christian theology. As such, it has the moral obligation to articulate Christian theology for the African Christian population. The chief agents in this task are, of course, the African Christians themselves. They are the ones who already operate within the cultural language into which Christianity is to be translated. They are the ones who raise the questions, provide the experience of having lived with the questions, and struggle with different answers. Indeed, it is the humble African Christians who, at the end of the day, recognize the solutions that are "genuine, authentic, and commensurate with their experience."[1] However, as Schreiter has explained, the professional theologian also has a role:

> ... the professional theologian serves as an important resource, helping the community to clarify its own experience and to relate it to the experience of other communities past and present. Thus the professional theologian has an indispensable but limited role. The theologian cannot create a theology in isolation from the community's experience; but the community has need of the theologian's knowledge to ground its own experience within the Christian traditions of faith. In so doing, the theologian helps to create the bonds of mutual accountability between local and world church.[2]

The basic question is whether the efforts of professional African theologians have helped the African Christian population to articulate an understanding of the God that we encounter in Christ. The answer to this question is a simple "no." The doctrine of God in African incul-

---

[1] R.J. Schreiter, *Constructing Local Theologies* (Maryknoll: Orbis Books, 1985), 17.
[2] Schreiter, *Constructing Local Theologies*, 18.

turation theology (1) uses the comparative interpretation of the scripture, which simply highlights the similarities between the African concepts of God and the Christian view of God; (2) is built upon a cultural identity paradigm, which in principle is responsible in this context
for emphasis on how the African peoples understand God rather than
on God revealed in Christ; and (3) has never attempted to utilize the
native philosophical symbols as medium for the Christian message. In
this chapter we seek to understand how these factors have hindered
the formulation of an understanding of the God that we encounter in
Christ for the African context and make suggestions on the way forward.

THE COMPARATIVE INTERPRETATION OF THE SCRIPTURE

In his monograph, *Bible and Theology in African Christianity*, John S. Mbiti
identifies at least three ways that African Christianity interacts with
scripture. He identifies these ways as "written theology," "oral theology," and "symbolic theology."[3] Kwame Bediako has also drawn our
attention to what he calls "the living roots of the church" or "oral theology," and "academic theology."[4] The 'roots' of the church are the ways
in which the church interacts with the scripture. Knut Holter identifies
two contexts in which African inculturation theology interacts with the
Bible: "the popular context" and "the academic context."[5]

Whether in the popular context or in the academic context, scholars seem to agree that African biblical interpretation is characterized
by two significant considerations. These considerations are "the use
of comparative methods that focuses on correspondence between the
Bible, especially Old Testament, and the religio-cultural and socio-
political realities of Africa" and the search for and "emphasis on relevance."[6] African inculturation theology is not the first to introduce the

---

[3] J.S. Mbiti, *Bible and Theology in African Christianity* (Nairobi: Oxford University Press,
1986), 46 f.

[4] K. Bediako, *Christianity in Africa: The Renewal of a non- Western Religion* (Edinburgh:
Edinburgh University Press, 1995), 59 f.

[5] K. Holter, "Popular and Academic contexts for Biblical Interpretation in Africa."
Paper delivered at University of Stellenbosch, Department of Old and New Testaments' International Workshop, 14–15 May 1999.

[6] V. Zinkuratire, "Method and Relevance in African Biblical Interpretation." An
unpublished paper delivered at the University of Stellenbosch, Department of Old
and New Testaments' International Workshop, 14–15 May 1999, 1; cf. D. Tutu, "Some

"comparative method" (or the direct literal reading) and the search for "relevance" into the task of biblical interpretation. This was also the conventional mode of translation that was employed by the first translators of the Bible into the African vernaculars[7] and was widely used by the Protestant Reformers.[8] According to this method, a word like *Nyasaye* (God in the Luo of Kenya) is used in the Luo translation of the Bible in a manner that allows a Luo reader to assume that *Nyasaye* has the same meaning in the Bible as it has in the traditional context.

Although the comparative method of biblical interpretation allows the African theological enterprise to see the relationship between the biblical revelation and the African traditional worldviews in at least three ways: comparative or corroborative, corrective, and suppletive,[9] the use of the method confronts one with three fundamental problems. First, it does not highlight the areas of divergence between the biblical testimony and the concept as it is presented by the culture of reception. Of course, the Christian's view of God and the African concepts of God show many similarities. However, there are fundamental differences that must not be overlooked. The African concepts of God, for example, have no incarnation element. God, for our people, is *Moya* (Spirit), but this *Moya* is never seen as a distinct hypostasis of equal divinity with God. There is the issue of plurality of God among our people; however, our plurality is explained in the context of divinities. Our plurality of God is therefore fundamentally different from the plurality of God we see in the Bible.

Second, exclusive use of the comparative reading of the scripture has the effect of short-circuiting much of the theological developments and controversies that the doctrine of God has gone through in the past 2000 years. The theological developments, such as the ones that took place from the second to the fourth centuries, and the struggles of the Reformation era are easily ruled out as irrelevant. Sometimes it is argued that the theological issues debated by the church over the centuries are too abstract for the African mind. A notion such

---

African Insights and the Old Testament" in *Journal of Theology for Southern Africa*, no. 1 Dec. 1972, 16–22, 1972.

[7] E.W. Smith, African *Ideas of God*, 35; cf. Z. Nthamburi and D. Waruta, "Biblical Hermeneutics in African Instituted Churches" in *The Bible in African Christianity: Essays in Biblical Theology*. H.W. Kinoti and J.M. Waliggo, eds. (Nairobi: Acton Publishers, 1997), 47.

[8] Bediako, *Christianity in Africa*, 60.

[9] Zinkuratire, "Method and Relevance in African Biblical Interpretation," 1.

as this is unfortunate. The problem in the African church is not its inability to link with and to enter into the discourses that have gone on in the history of the church over the years.[10] The problem is that the African church, due to excessive use of comparative hermeneutics, has not effectively participated in the story of the church. The African church is part of the universal church. We (in Africa) must exploit the scriptural witness as well as the resources of all Christian ages and places. Our voice should rise with those of the other Christians elsewhere in affirming the fundamental teachings of the Christian faith.

The third problem with the exclusive use of comparative hermeneutics is that it does not allow the culture of reception to benefit from the suppletive and the corrective use of the scripture. The lead role in this case is given to the culture of reception rather than to the scripture. The scripture raises issues, but the theologians legitimize the issues on the basis of corresponding presence in the cultures of reception. What is not available in the cultures of reception is dismissed as irrelevant and inappropriate.

For instance, take Setiloane's notion of *selo*. The *selo* model of understanding God is typical of Sotho-Tswana. Its basic thrust is the view that God is a "fearful," "awful," "ugly," or "monstrous or weird thing."[11] Setiloane believes that this model for God cannot be challenged and that all other models for God that are seen in Christian theology are, in fact, depictions of the god of the Europeans.[12] The other examples are seen in the emergence of Christologies based on titles that are specifically African in origin or emphasis. Some of the images used for Christ are friend, liberator, elder brother, ancestor, king / chief, elder, healer, and master of initiation.[13] The fundamental problem with these Chris-

---

[10] H.O. Oruka, "Sagacity in African Philosophy" in *African Philosophy*. Serequeberhan, ed. (New York: Paragon House, 1991), 49 f.

[11] Setiloane, *The Image of God among the Sotho-Tswana*, 78 f.; Setiloane, *African Theology: An Introduction*, 33.

[12] Setiloane, *The Image of God among the Sotho-Tswana*, 229.

[13] G.C. Oosthuizen, *Post Christianity in Africa* (London: C. Hurst, 1968), 129, 133 f.; B.G.M. Sundkler, *Bantu Prophets in South Africa* (Oxford: Oxford University Press, 1961), 200. Some of the literature on Christology in the African scene include: G. Thomas, *An African Tree of Life* (New York: Maryknoll, 1990); J.D.K. Ekem, *Priesthood in Context: A Study of Akan Traditional Priesthood in Dialogue Relation to the Priest-Christology of the Epistle to the Hebrews* (Hamburg: Lottbek, 1994); U.C. Manus, *Christ, the African King: New Testament Christology* (New York, Bern, 1993); T.A. Mofokeng, *Crucified Among the Cross Bearers* (Maryknoll: Orbis, 1994); J.S. Pobee, ed. *Exploring Afro-Christology* (Paris: Peter Lang, 1992); R.J. Schreiter, ed, *Faces of Jesus in Africa* (New York: Maryknoll, 1991); E.B. Udoh, *Guest Christology: An Interpretive View of the Christological Problem in Africa* (New York: Peter

tologies is that Christ is not discussed in the context of his divinity. The reason he is not discussed in the context of his divinity is because, among most of our cultures, one can speak about a person of significance such as Christ as friend, liberator, elder brother, ancestor, king / chief, elder, healer, and master of initiation, but never as God. Yet the tone of the scripture is clear—Christ is God. This hermeneutic model chooses to not offend our cultures. In such innovations, where then is the offending nature of the gospel?

The Problems Raised by the Paradigm of Reflection

The Nature of the Paradigm

There are two distinct issues here. The first is the problem of cultural identity. The theologians began their reflection within the paradigm of cultural identity, and they have found it rather difficult to steer the discussions back to the basic Christian precepts. The second problem is the focus on the African concepts of God. It is clear that combining the issue of cultural identity and focus on the African concepts of God place the African inculturation theology within a paradigm that makes it structurally difficult to raise and address the idea of the Trinity with passion.

The Cultural Identity Issue: The Theologians Response

Historically, reflection within African inculturation theology began at the question of identity. And so the African concepts of God that are available in the works of B. Idowu, John S. Mbiti, G. Setiloane, and other African theologians are partly motivated by the need to draw attention to the religious schizophrenia that until recently characterized African Chrisitanity "and to attempt to remedy it, mainly by rehabilitating Africa's rich cultural heritage and religious consciousness."[14]

Lang, 1988); G.F. Vicedom, ed, *Christ and the Younger Churches* (London: SPCK, 1972); and P.N. Wachege, *Jesus Christ our Muthamaki (Ideal Elder)* (Nairobi: Phoenix Pub, 1992).

[14] D. Tutu, "Whither African Theology?" in *Christianity in Independent Africa*. E. Fashole-Luke et al, ed. (Bloomington: Indiana University Press, 1978), 367.

Kwame Bediako's book, *Theology and Identity* (1992), is a recent example of the seriousness of the issue of identity in the African theological enterprise.

It is common knowledge, as Adrian Hastings has written, that " ... Europeans almost always underestimated the African sense of God in the earlier encounters, being much more struck by the strong consciousness of a wider spirit world—ancestors and natural forces—with its shrines and sacrifices."[15] One does not need to look far to corroborate this statement. In 1668 Olfert Dapper wrote: "No one ... however thoroughly he has enquired, has ever been able to find among the Kaffirs, Hottentots and Beachrangers, any trace of religion or any show of honour to God or the devil."[16] In the nineteenth century, Robert Moffat echoed Dapper when he wrote that Satan:

> ... has employed his agency with fatal success, in erasing every vestige of religious impression from the minds of the Bechwanas, Hottentots and Bushmen; leaving them without a single ray to guide them from the dark and dread futurity, or a single link to unite them with the skies.[17]

Accusations such as these are grave. They need an authority in the field in question to suggest an alternative opinion, if any. In 1950, Edwin W. Smith defended the Hottentots, the Kaffirs [Bantus], the Beachrangers [Khoi], and the Bechwanas when he wrote, "with our large interpretation of religion nobody with any knowledge of these people would venture to say such things about them."[18]

Given the place of Africa on the globe, the quest for identity is certainly a legitimate concern. In his book, *Theology and Identity*, Kwame Bediako has demonstrated that cultural identity has always been crucial in the contextualization of the Christian message. What we must emphasize, however, is that it is possible to affirm our cultural identity without demeaning our Christian identity. In other words, it is possible to affirm our cultural identity and our Christian identity simultaneously. Great theologians such as Athanasius, the Capaddocians, Augustine, Aquinas, Calvin, and (closer to our time) Barth clearly had a firm grasp of their own culture. Nevertheless, their Christian identity forced

---

[15] A. Hastings, *Church and Mission in Modern Africa* (London: Pall Mall Press, 1967), 51.

[16] O. Dapper, I. Schapera, W. Rhijne, J.G. Grevenbroek, and B. Farrington, *The Early Cape Hottentots, Described in the Writings of Olfert Dapper (1668), Willem Ten Rhyne (1686) and Johannes Gulielmus de Grevenbroek (1695)* (Westport: Negro Universities Press, 1970).

[17] R. Moffat, *Missionary Labours and Scenes in South Africa* (London: J. Snow, 1842), 243.

[18] Smith, *African Ideas of God*, 83.

them to formulate their thoughts in ways that were critical to their own cultures. It is possible for us to refuse to be either subservient or aggressive, but to offer the right interpretation of our cultural heritage to the global theological community without hindering our Christian consciousness.

Focus on the African Notion of God: Some Key Reasons

Failure of Trust

The African inculturation theologians that were studied in the previous chapter clearly set their theological agenda to correct, among other things, the European missionary view that misrepresented, undervalued, and ignored the sense of God and his activity as perceived in African tradition. We noted the concept of *selo* that was proposed by G.M. Setiloane and was taken from the Sotho-Tswana, and the idea of diffused monotheism suggested by both Bolaji Idowu and J.S. Mbiti. The point of these proposals is to state in clear terms that the African peoples thought about God in ways that were no less complex. In fact, according to Idowu, it is the European conceptions of God that may not be trusted. He observed the following in a paper presented at the Consultation of African Theologians in 1966:

> Recent publications in Europe and America have come to indicate how much confusion there is in the minds even of the enlightened Westerners about God. If we take for example some of the writings of Dietrich Bonhoeffer, the writings of Paul Tillich, and *Honest to God* of Dr JAT Robinson, we shall see at least two facts clearly emerging: the fact that the masses of Westerners appear to be losing their sense of God, and Western theology is in conflict because it has become too theoretical: God according to it has become largely an intellectual concept.[19]

Gabriel M. Setiloane, an ally and a great admirer of Idowu, in his book, *Image of God among the Sotho-Tswana*, maintains a similar understanding of the European views of God:

> In the whole discussion of MODIMO [Sotho-Tswana proper name of God], and in what has been said above about the contrast between 'Being' and 'Supreme Being' [see his chapter 6] there is a suggestion that what missionaries have been able to offer to Africans is not GOD

---

[19] B. Idowu, "God" in *Biblical Revelation and African Beliefs*. Dickson and Ellingworth, eds. (London: Lutterworth Press, 1969), 21.

but the god of the Europeans, who may well—perhaps rightly—be discarded with the coming of political independence and the reassertion
of African culture which is its idealogical counterpart. Indeed the whole
discussion in the West—focused in *Honest to God* and the 'Death of God'
theology—suggest that the West itself has lost the image of God as *mysterium tremendum et fascinans* and deals at best, with a *creator absconditus*, a
god of the gaps, or a saviour of individual souls destined for pie in the
sky ... It is indeed suggested that western theologians might go to school
with Sotho-Tswana if the wish to rediscover, in truth, the Yahweh whom
they profess to serve.[20]

The Problem of Appearance

The problem of "appearance and reality" deals with the fact that the
African peoples appeared to outsiders as if they did not have a God.[21]
The problem of appearance and reality can be traced back to the days
of the explorer Stanley. Since then, Africa has been described as "dark,"
"darkest," "a place governed by insensible fetish," and her people as
niggers, "burnt out husks of men with no souls."[22] A famous acting
governor of the Anglo-Egyptian Sudan, Emil Ludwig, once said: "How
can the untutored African conceive God? ... How can this be? ... Deity
is a philosophical concept which savages are incapable of framing."[23]

In agreement with Edwin W. Smith and in contradiction with the
opinion of Emil Ludwig, the position of African inculturation theology is that the African might have appeared less sophisticated and
unschooled according to some standards. However, the reality is that
they are not only capable of thinking about God, but, if they want,
they are capable of thinking about God in abstract and philosophical
terms. Setiloane demonstrates that the Sotho-Tswana's view of God as
mysterium tremendum et fascinans operates at a relatively high degree of
difficulty. In a number of ways, it bears a mark of truth that is miss-
ing in some contemporary Western notions of God.[24] In the thought
of Idowu, the miracle of grace has occurred all over Africa. God's self-
disclosure did not exclude the Africans. God's self-disclosure, which was
to all the races of the world, was also grasped by each of the African
peoples according to their native capacities. Mbiti's book, *Concepts of*

---

[20] Setiloane, *The Image of God among the Sotho-Tswana*, 229 f.
[21] Idowu, *Olodumare: God in Yoruba Belief*, 2.
[22] Idowu, "God" in *Biblical Revelation and African Beliefs*, 10.
[23] Ludwig quoted in E.W. Smith, *African Ideas of God*, 1.
[24] Setiloane, The Image of God among the Sotho-Tswana, 229.

God in Africa), attests to the above statement of Idowu. Mbiti's research, done among more than two hundred and seventy peoples of Africa,[25] indicates that each of the peoples of this continent grasped something of God according to their native capacities.

If God also revealed himself to the African peoples, then a biblical idea of God does not have to be introduced to the African peoples in a way that is completely unrelated to what the Africans already know.[26] This position is not new within the African theological scene. On the contrary, it is an echo of the first African bishop, Bishop Ajayi Crowther, who in his instruction to his clergy said:

> When we first introduce the Gospel to any people we should take advan-
> tage of any prinicples which they themselves admit. Thus though the
> heathens in this part of Africa possess no written legends, yet wher-
> ever we turn our eyes, we find among them, in their animal sacrifices,
> a text which is the mainspring of the Christian faith: 'Without shedding
> of blood there is no remission'. Therefore we may with propriety say:
> 'That which ye ignorantly practise, declare we unto you.' 'The blood of
> Jesus Christ the Son of God cleanseth from all sin.'[27]

The Idea of 'Loan Gods'

In the book, *The Making of Religion*, Andrew Lang criticizes the idea of "loan-gods" from "missionaries and other Europeans." Earlier writers had advanced this idea as the explanation of the concepts of God among what was then known as primitive cultures.[28] By the 1950s the idea of loan-gods had not disappeared, as is evident in Edwin Smith's *African Ideas of God*. In the words of Smith, "certain writers seem to be supremely ambitious to find origins outside Africa for African ideas … and they make great play with verbal similarities."[29] By the time Idowu writes his *Introduction* in 1962, the problem of loan-gods is still real. The

---

[25] Mbiti, *Concepts of God in Africa*, xiii.

[26] Geoffrey Parrinder has noted that serious writers no longer describe the African religions as 'fetishism' and 'animism.' There is much more to the African religions than magical and idolatrous practices. Moreover, the African view of the divine is much more sophisticated than the mere personification of nature which the concept "animism" suggests Parrinder, *Africa's Three Religions*, 25, 26; cf. J.S. Mbiti, *African Religions and Philosophy*, 6–10). Richard J. Gehman sees these terms as based on racism. In Gehman's own words, many of the "… theories are not only out-dated today but are offensive. They are racist and reflect a condescending attitude toward many peoples in the two-thirds world" (Gehman, *African Traditional Religion in Biblical Perspective, 38*).

[27] J. Page, *The Black Bishop* (London: Simpkin, 1910), 282.

[28] A. Lang, *The Making of Religion* (London: Longmans, Green & Co., 1909), xix.

[29] Smith, African *Ideas of God*, 3.

exception is that this time the Africans are supposed to have received the concepts of God from the ancient civilization of Egypt.[30] Idowu rejects the idea that the Africans have always been *tabula rasa*, and that they could not have had their own concepts of God. Echoing Smith, Idowu describes the problem in the following words:

> There have been those who eagerly traced the origin of every element in our native belief and culture to sources outside ourselves. The ancient civilization of Egypt has been irresistible to such investigators, so attractive that it has become impossible for them to think even of breath of our nostrils without going all the way to Egypt for its source![31]

At the[32] very beginning of his book, *Concepts of God in Africa*, Mbiti takes the view that the African concepts of God that he wishes to study "have sprung independently out of African reflection on God."[33] In the works of Professor Setiloane, we recognize that *Modimo* (as God is known among the Sotho-Tswana) is clearly not a loan God. The Sotho-Tswana did not get the idea of *Modimo* from the missionary. What they discovered from the missionaries was that *Modimo* and the God proclaimed by the missionaries had similarities that these African peoples could not ignore.[34] This statement can also be made of other African peoples and their respective concepts of God. If the African concepts of God are loaned from foreign sources, then we can say

---

[30] Idowu, "Introduction" in *Biblical Revelation and African Beliefs. Olodumare*, 3.

[31] Idowu, "Introduction" in *Biblical Revelation and African Beliefs. Olodumare*, 3. Note that the issue here is God's self-revelation. Did God reveal himself to the African peoples, and did the African peoples perceive that revelation? The fact is that God is proclaimed to all men everywhere in nature (Psa. 19:1–6; Rom. 1:20; Acts 14:15–17) and through man's conscience (Rom. 2:14, 15; Acts 17:21; cf. Ecces. 3:11). This basic question must not be confused with what theology discusses as the limitations of the general revelation (Gehman, *African Traditional Religion in Biblical Perspective*, 41, 42; cf. T. Adeyemo, *Salvation in African Tradition* (Nairobi: Evangel Publishing House, 1979), 24, 26).

[32] In his book, *From Fetish to God in Ancient Egypt*, E.A. Wallis Budge argues that the Egyptian concept of God moved in evolutionary phases from animism, fetishism, the god and the goddesses, and finally to the Sun god. According to the religion of Egypt, magic regulated the relationships of the men, the dead, the spirits, and the gods (E.A. Wallis Budge, *From Fetish to God in Ancient Egypt* (London: Humphry Milford, 1934), 3–136). It is interesting that the scholars who take an evolutionary view of the African traditional religions present these religions in a way that is clearly reminiscent of the Egyptian traditional religion (see Philip M. Steyne, *Gods of Power: a Study of Beliefs and Practices of Animists* (Houston, Touch Publications, 1989). Although Steyne's study is wider than the African traditional religions, he clearly sees the Africans as modern day animists and their religion animism.

[33] Mbiti, *Concepts of God in Africa*, xiii.

[34] Setiloane, *African Theology*, 25 f.

that the African cosmology is equally foreign. Although it is possible to make this kind of statement, we do not have the necessary data to buttress it.

The 'African Gods' and the God of the Christian Faith

For some reason, African theology has discussed the doctrine of God in terms of the 'African Gods' and the God of the Christian worship.[35] Was the God known in traditional Africa (Nyasaye, Were, Mulungu, Mungu, Asis, Olodumare, Modimo, Ngai, and so on) the one true God whom we Christians worship? For African theology, the answer to this question is yes.[36] As Professor Mbiti has noted:

---

[35] Note, however, that the focus here is not the divinities or the mediators. The focus is on whether the African religions should be given status of world religion. The proponents of world status for African religions argue that the different African peoples had religions that were as good as Islam, Christianity, and Judaism. Consequently, the 'African Gods' should not be viewed as inferior to Allah, God, or Yahweh. Among the authors who argue for the status of world religion for the African traditional religions is L. Magesa, *African Religion*, 1997:18–28; O. p'Bitek, *African Religions in Western Scholarship*, (Kampala, East African Literature Bureau, 1970), 1–2; F. Eboussi Boulaga, *Christianity Without Fetishes*, (Maryknoll: Orbis Books, 1984), 2, 17. Other prominent authors in this subject are J.M. Ela, *African Cry* (Maryknoll: Orbis Books, 1986); J.P. Brown and S. Perry, trans. *My Faith as an African* (Maryknoll: Orbis Books, 1988); H. Dinwiddy, "Missions and Missionaries as Portrayed by English-speaking Writers of Contemporary African Literature" in Fashole-Luke, *Christianity in Independent Africa*, 426–442.

[36] It is important to note that African evangelical theology disagrees with this position. Some of the African evangelical authors who have discussed this problem are: Byang Kato, *Theological Pitfalls in Africa* (Kisumu: Evangel Publishing House, 1975); L. Nyirongo, *Gods of Africa or the God of the Bible: The Snares of the African Traditional religion in Biblical Perspective* (Potchefstroom: Potchefstroomse Univeriteit vir Christelike Hoër Onderwys, 1997); and Y. Turaki, *Christianity and African Gods: A Method in Theology* (Potchefstroom: Potchefstroomse Universiteit vir Christike Hoër Onderwys, 1999).
    As far as Kato, Nyirongo, and Turaki are concerned, there is a clear discontinuity between the God of the Bible and the 'Gods of Africa.' This position is also shared by David Bosch (D.J. Bosch, "God in Africa; Implications for Kerygma." *Missionalia* vol 1, No 1, pp 3–21, 1973). Bosch, explaining his position, reasons that many African peoples (the Akan, the Mende, the Yoruba, the Nyakyusa, and the Zulu) developed the idea of a primal ancestor into a divine figure (see Bosch, "God in Africa; Implications for Kerygma," 8). As far as David Bosch is concerned, even the name for God and the word for ancestors have a common root in many African languages (Bosch, "God in Africa; Implications for Kerygma," 10). This thought can also be detected in the thought of Harry Sawyer (H. Sawyer, *God: Ancestor or Creator* (London: Longman, 1970)).

... the concept of God is common in both Christianity and African Religion. The Biblical God is not unknown to the African peoples. For thousands of years they have known him as creator and sustainer of all things. For this reason the preaching of the Gospel and the translation of Scriptures use African names of God in each area of the continent. The concept of God is a point of continuity.[37]

The African theologians are not the first to discover this understanding. Smith has explained this trend in the following words:

Christian missionaries in their teachings and translations of Scripture have adopted African names of God. This practice has been criticized on the ground that pagan terms can never express Christian truth. There is a pragmatic sanction for what they do. The Hebrew elohim was a class name covering many supernatural beings. ... When the Hebrew Scripture was translated into Greek, elohim was rendered theos and the sacred personal name Yahwe kurios, 'Lord'. Greek-speaking Christians as well as Jews of the Diaspora accepted these as equivalents ....

Teutonic peoples had their own god-names—Wodan, god of the dead, Donar, god of thunder and the sky, Tyr, god of war. The Christian missionaries took over not these personal names, but the class word god, which denoted (according to the Oxford Dictionary) a superhuman person who was worshipped as having power over nature and the fortunes of mankind; and also an image or other object which was worshipped. Whatever it meant to our Teutonic forefathers it did not mean what it means to us today: Christianity took it and filled it with new content.

Christian missionaries in Africa differ from their predecessors in Europe for they have generally adopted not class names like theos or god but personal names like Nyame, Leza, Nyambe.[38]

When these theologians talk about *Modimo, Nyame, Leza, Nyasaye*, and other African names for God, they are not only intellectually aware, but they also know—at a deeper existential level—that they are discussing the God of the Christian message. That is why these African theologians insist that there is only one God, and that that God has revealed himself to all peoples of the world. Setiloane wrote: "The black man still believes that Christianity comes from God (Modimo) so he clings to it although his mind is in a state of revolt against Western Christianity."[39] Consequently, for African theologians to say that the God the

---

[37] J.S. Mbiti, "Christianity and African Culture" in *Facing the New Challenges—The Message of PACLA, 9–19 Dec 1976*. M. Cassidy and L. Verlinden, eds. (Kisumu: Evangel Publishing House, 1978), 309.

[38] Smith, *African Ideas of God*, 34, 35.

[39] Setiloane, African *Theology*, 29.

traditional Africa knew is not the God we meet in the Christian worship is to deny the very truth of God's word, which insists that God is proclaimed to all men everywhere.[40]

As Hendrikus Berkhof has said, in revelation "we perceive not just a something, an aspect, a segment of a divine mystery, but God himself, his heart, his deepest essence. We see in a mirror and thus do not see God face to face. But what we see in that mirror is God himself."[41] The different African peoples saw *Nyasaye, Ngai, Modimo, Nyambe, Nyame, Leza,* and so on. For example, when a Luo speaks about *Nyasaye,* he is not merely comparing the 'African God' to Yahweh. He is not referring to fate or a primal ancestor with attributes maximized to fit divine status, nor is he thinking of a spiritual mystery, proposition on, or a mere segment of God. He is making reference to the revealing God, God himself. On this issue, even Byang Kato, who is uncompromising on discontinuity, argues that the name the non-Christians give the Supreme Being indicates "man's awareness of the Supreme Being and man's rebellion against God. It also indicates deep search for the Reality in spite of the unconscious flight from Him."[42]

What needs emphasis in the African Christian thought is the fact that whereas *Nyasaye* (a Luo word for God) is referring to God himself, the presence of this name among the Luo people does not mean the Luo captured the full sweep of God. God is more than his revelation, and, moreover, man is both in rebellion and limited by his creatureliness. In the words of Berkhof, *"God's essence transcends his revelation ....* No creature is capable of making the infinite and inexhaustible richness of the essence of God his own. Yet he does reveal his essence to us."[43] Berkhof's statement applies to all peoples of the world. Although we are sinners, we have not lost the image of God so completely that we are left without a trace of it, nor can we argue from the position of the Christian faith that God has not revealed himself to us in nature around us, in our consciousness and in our history. The issue, therefore, is not whether God revealed himself to some peoples of the world and not to others; the issue is whether the different peoples of the world were able to perceive and absorb the fullness of God's revelation. No one can per-

---

[40] See Psa. 19:1–6; Rom. 1:20; 2:14, 15; Acts 14: 15–17; 17:21–31; cf. Eccles. 3:11.

[41] H. Berkhof, *Christian Faith: An Introduction to the Study of the Faith.* S. Woudstra, trans. (Grand Rapids: William B. Eerdmans Publishing Company, 1979), 105.

[42] Kato, *Theological Pitfalls,* 114.

[43] Berkhof, *Christian Faith,* 106. Italics his.

ceive and absorb the fullness of God. God can only be known by God
(see Job 38:2 and I Cor. 2:6–16).

The Problem of the Use of Christian Theological Terms

The last problem is what Idowu calls the "mistake of morbidly shrink-
ing from any suggestions of similarities or identification between one
category of religious terminologies and another."[44] A good example
here is found in the following excerpt of Andrew Lang:

> The phrases 'Creator', 'creative', as applied to Anyambi, or Baime, have
> been described, by critics, as rhetorical, covertly introducing conceptions
> of which savages are incapable. I have already shown that I only fol-
> low my authorities, and their translations of phrases in various savage
> tongues. But the phrase 'eternal' applied to Anyambi or Baime, may be
> misleading. I do not wish to assert that, if you talked to a savage about
> 'eternity', he would understand what you intend. …
>
> With these explanations I trust that my rhetorical use of such phrases as
> 'eternal', 'creative', 'omniscient', 'omnipotent', 'omnipresent', and 'mor-
> al' may not be found to mislead or covertly import modern or Christian
> ideas into my account of the religious conceptions of savages.[45]

Whereas Lang shrinks from using the categories developed by theology
to describe concepts found among the 'savages,' others like Eric Waterhouse condemn those that they think have 'illegitimately' used Christian theological terms to describe the concepts of the Supreme Being
among the primitives.[46] Charles E. Fuller, writing from the same point
of view, suggests that "weighted terms such as omnipotence, omniscience, and eternity are … too interlaced with theological complexi-
ties of the traditions common to Jewish, Moslem, and Christian faiths
to be used in any neutral sense when observing religions external to
these."[47] Fuller goes so far as to suggest that in the African context we
should instead "speak of 'divinity' where reference is made to 'god' or
'gods.'"[48]

Of course, Idowu has made a point that is worth taking seriously. As
Lang, Waterhouse, and Fuller seem to think, it is not true "that other

---

[44] Idowu, *Olodumare: God in Yoruba Belief*, 3.
[45] Lang, *The Making of Religion*, xxii–xxiv.
[46] Idowu, *Olodumare: God in Yoruba Belief*, 3.
[47] C.E. Fuller, "God of African Thought and Life" in *God in Contemporary Thought*
(New York: Learned Publications, 1977), 20.
[48] Fuller, "God of African Thought and Life," 21.

races apart from the Europeans are incapable of apprehending the Deity in those terms. Surely there are no ideas and categories, which are created to be the exclusive monopoly of any particular race. Why should it be impossible for the Deity to reveal Himself to other races and to the Europeans in similar ways?"[49] Why should we be afraid to describe God as he was known to the African in such terms as omniscient, omnipresent, omnipotent, and so forth?

On the Way to the Doctrine of the Trinity

Take a Realistic View of General Revelation

So far African theology has concerned itself with the content of what the African peoples made of the self-revelation of God. Mbiti believes that "African theologians are more or less unanimous in affirming that, God who is known in African religion is precisely the same God who is revealed in the Bible."[50] Prominent African theologians hold this view and include John S. Mbiti (Kenya), Harry Sawyer (Sierra Leone), Bolaji E. Idowu (Nigeria), Samwel G. Kibicho (Kenya), and Gabriel M. Setiloane (South Africa). J.S. Mbiti argues that one of the reasons that Christianity has obtained a large following in the African situation can be attributed to the fact that "... the message of the Bible is the message of the same God our people already knew, acknowledged, and to whom they prayed and offered sacrifices, from generations past."[51] This thought is, of course, in line with the sentiments of Brunner, who believes that:

> Apart from real revelation ... the phenomenon of religion cannot be understood. Even the most primitive polytheistic or pre-polytheistic idolatrous religion is not intelligible without the presupposition of the universal revelation of God which has been given to all men though the creation. Therefore the Apostle, when he explains the nature of the pagan religion, speaks, first of all, of this universal self-manifestation of God to all men without exception through the works of creation and through the writing of the law upon their hearts.[52]

---

[49] Idowu, "Introduction" in *Biblical Revelation and African Beliefs*, 3, 4.

[50] J.S. Mbiti, "Is the Bible in African Religion and African Religion in the Bible?" An unpublished paper delivered at EFSA and University of Stellenbosch, department of Old and New Testaments International Workshop, 14–15 May, 1999, 5.

[51] Mbiti, "Is the Bible in African Religion and African Religion in the Bible?" 6.

[52] E. Brunner, *Revelation and Reason* (London: SCM Press, 1947), 59, 262.

Some of the theologians from the non-African extraction who hold
this view are John V. Taylor, E. Geoffrey Parrinder, Edwin W. Smith,
and Malcolm J. McVeigh—among others.

We cannot deny the fact that the African peoples can and do conceive of God. We must be quick to point out, however, that such conceptions are blurred and of no salvific value. This yes-and-no principle
in the traditional African conception of God could be summarized in
the following words of George Peters:

> [The biblical approach] accepts the absolute predicament of man in a
> realistic manner, acknowledging on the one hand man's rebellion against
> God and his flight from God, hiding himself under the figs' leaves of
> man-constructed and designed religion and culture, -man's barricade
> against all that threatens him including God, ever seeking to perfect
> this covering and to control the power above and beyond him to the
> furtherance of his selfish ends. On the other hand this approach takes
> account of the fact that man lives as creature with an awareness that
> he is away from home, separated from true reality and life, with a
> "feeling of dependence upon the ultimate", with a guilt complex and
> a conscious of deserved judgment. Thus he seeks, gropes, longs to be
> restored to his rightful creature relationship and household membership,
> makes attempts to appease God, the gods, spirits, or powers to reconcile
> himself to or submit and control that which threatens him.[53]

Historically, belief in general revelation was often the symptom and
result of a rejection of special revelation.[54] It is important to note,
however, that general revelation, and scriptural or historical revelation
are not in competition; the two are an integral part of the Christian
message. African inculturation theology is obligated to clarify how God
has been made known to the entire world and to all men without
losing sight of the fact that this God appeared in the flesh. In the

---

[53] Peters quoted in B. Kato, *Theological Pitfalls*, 44, 45.

[54] The nineteenth-century Hegelian notion of the absolute Spirit in the human ego,
reason, and freedom completely opposed the revelation of God in Jesus as the only
source from which we may draw our knowledge of God (G.C. Berkouwer, *General Revelation* (Grand Rapids: Wm. B. Eerdmans: 1955), 11, 12. The increased knowledge of other
religions, including the African traditional religions, resulted in a further generaliza-
tion of revelation. In the words of Berkouwer, "for many the denial of the absoluteness
of Christianity became the background of the dilemma: general or special revelation?
They thought they could see one broad revelation of God in the background of the
various religions, and they hesitated to see the uniqueness and exclusiveness of the revelation in Christ on the basis of *a priori* of faith." (Berkouwer, *General Revelation*, 12). In
the African context the denial of the absoluteness of Christianity has taken the form
conferring world religion status on the African traditional religions.

words of Berkouwer, "only there did God actually become manifest."[55] This manifestation must be understood as a mystery (I Tim. 3:16; Rom. 16:25–26) for in the Son dwells the fullness of the Godhead (Col. 2:9 and Gal. 4:4). He revealed the name of the Father (Jn 17:6); indeed, the Son alone has manifested the Father (Jn 1:18). We cannot simply stop after mentioning that the various African peoples knew God as *Nyasaye*, *Leza, Modimo, Mulungu, Nyame*, and so on. Having mentioned that the Luo, for instance, knew God as *Nyasaye*, we must be quick to add that *Nyasaye* appeared in the flesh.

Discuss Revelation as the Self-Revelation of God

It is unfortunate that at some stage the African peoples were regarded as 'savages' who knew no religion except the worship of the devil. The basis of this position was the assumption that the Africans completely lost the image of God so that no element of it remained. Today it is perplexing to us that such a view of things was ever taken and supported with zeal. The fact of the matter is that, like other peoples of the world, the African people are sinners. The fall did not demonize them. Moreover, the first missionaries found and utilized what Andrew Lang has called the "reciprocal phenomenon" in his book, *The Making of Religion* (1909). According to Lang, in their encounters with the "savages," "the missionaries often find a native name and idea which answers so nearly to their conception of God that they adopt the idea and name in teaching. Again on the other side, the savages, when first they hear the missionaries' account of God, recognise it … for what has always been familiar to them."[56] This idea of the reciprocal phenomenon challenges us to revisit the concept of revelation as it is formulated in the Christian faith, and its implication on how God relates to Africa.

As Hendrikus Berkhof has said, in revelation "we perceive not just a something, an aspect, a segment of a divine mystery, but God himself, his heart, his deepest essence. We see in a mirror and thus do not see God face to face. But what we see in that mirror is God himself."[57] The different African peoples saw *Nyasaye, Ngai, Modimo, Nyambe, Nyame, Leza*, and so on, and yet these are but different dialects of the same term:

[55] Berkouwer, *General Revelation*, 294.
[56] Lang, *The Making of Religion*, 228f.
[57] Berkhof, *Christian Faith*, 105.

God.[58] When a Luo speaks about *Nyasaye*, for example, he is not merely comparing the 'African God' to Yahweh. He is not referring to fate or a primal ancestor with attributes maximized to fit divine status,[59] nor is he thinking of a spiritual mystery, propositions on, or a mere segment of God. He is making reference to the revealing God, God himself. On this question even Kato (who is uncompromising on discontinuity) argues that the name that the non-Christians give the Supreme Being indicates "man's awareness of the Supreme Being and man's rebellion against that God. It also indicates deep search for the Reality in spite of the unconscious flight from Him."[60]

Generally, theology in the African situation has discussed the doctrine of God from the point of view of a series of truths and a number of neat theological propositions derived from the African myths. This could be seen in the titles of Edwin W. Smith's, *The African Ideas of God* (1950), and John S. Mbiti's, *The Concepts of God in Africa* (1970). In these works the emphasis falls not on God who has revealed himself, but on truths about God and what the African peoples say about God.[61] The propositions about God in the African myths pale considerably in comparison to the truth seen in the scripture. Idowu, for example, brings the Yoruba belief that *Olodumare* (God) brought forth *orisa* (divinities) as his ministers to our attention.[62] The scripture does not allow us to make statements like these. However, when we come across statements like these, we recognize an attempt on the part of fallen man—deluded by

---

[58] Idowu, *African Traditional Religion*, 104.

[59] David Bosch argues that among many African peoples, notably the Akan, the Mende, the Yoruba, the Nyakyusa, and the Zulu, a primal ancestor developed into a divine figure (Bosch, "God in Africa; Implications for Kerygma," 8). This thought can also be detected in Harry Sawyer's *God: Ancestor or Creator*. As far as David Bosch is concerned, even the name for God and the word for ancestors have a common root in many African languages (Bosch, "God in Africa; Implications for Kerygma," 10).

[60] Kato, *Theological Pitfalls*, 114.

[61] Interestingly, the African people put focus not on truth but on the God who exists. According to Magesa, it is the "place that God occupies in the order of things that human beings can speak of their own existence, let alone their tradition" (L. Magesa, *African Religion: The Moral Traditions of Abundant Life* (Maryknoll: Orbis Books, 1997), 40). When it comes to the African propositions about the attributes of God, Magesa sees them as having been derived from "human experience of what is good and noble." This point can be interpreted in different directions. It could mean that the African peoples are in fact atheists, and what they say about God are but metaphors maximized to fit divine status. But it could also mean that the African peoples perceive God as silent. This second option is the position taken by this paper.

[62] Idowu, *Olodumare: God in Yoruba Belief*, 60f.

Satan and living within the limitations of creatureliness—to say something about God who is revealed and yet hidden.

What needs to be emphasized in the African Christian thought is the fact that whereas *Nyasaye* is referring to God himself, the presence of this name among the Luo people does not mean that the Luo have captured the full sweep of God. God is more than his revelation, and, moreover, man is both in rebellion and limited by his creatureliness. In the words of Berkhof, "*God's essence transcends his revelation....* No creature is capable of making the infinite and inexhaustible richness of the essence of God his own. Yet he does reveal his essence to us."[63] Berkhof's statement applies to all peoples of the world as well as to the individual African ethnic groups. Although we are sinners, we have not completely lost the image of God so that we are left without a trace of it. Neither can we argue from the position of the Christian faith that God has not revealed himself to us in nature around us, in our consciousness, or in our history. The issue, therefore, is not whether God revealed himself to some peoples of the world and not to others. The issue is whether the African peoples, as well as all the people of the world, were able to perceive and absorb the fullness of the revelation. Of course, as Berkhof says, "no one is capable of making the infinite and inexhaustible richness of the essence of God his own," and the African peoples are no exception to this rule. God can only be known by God (see Job 38:2 and I Cor. 2:6–16).

Indeed it could not be possible for anyone to perceive and absorb the fullness of the revelation of God. This explains the reason why African ideas about God pale in comparison to the truth seen in the scripture. Due to our creatureliness, God chose to employ the modes that come with the earthly life[64] to reveal himself but now, because of the human condition, we need a special revelation in order for us to be certain about the self-revelation.[65] In his interaction with our peoples, God had to accommodate himself to the conceptual forms and the

---

[63] Berkhof, *Christian Faith*, 106, italics his.

[64] Of course, the earthly character of revelation means that the modes that are given with this earthly life are the willing and the necessary instrument of the revelation of God, but equally important is also the idea of the divine accommodation (Calvin, Inst I, x, 2; I, xi; I, xiii, 1). God's revelation is limited by the earthly existence, but as Berkhof puts it his accommodation is not "as if" (Berkhof, *Christian Faith*, 53).

[65] Barth and Brunner have fiercely discussed how the two revelations—general revelation and special revelation—relate to each other. Barth rejects the possibility of general revelation. Brunner, on the other hand, argues that it is because of sin that man has turned general revelation into a caricature. As far as Brunner is concerned, only as

existential traits of our peoples, not just because of our sin, the reality of the forces of darkness, or our creaturely finitude—but also because of the hiddenness of God.[66]

Address the Problem of the Hiddenness of God

There are two sides that we must put into perspective. There is our inability to see God clearly, but there is also the hiddenness of God. The hiddenness of God is not just true outside of special revelation. It is seen within the special revelation as well. Full knowledge of God is a promise that is reserved for the end time.[67] We thus see God, the true God, but in a mirror and not face to face.

The hiddenness of God is not a favorite theme in Christian theology; however, its significance to the overall understanding of the God we have come to know cannot be underestimated. In his works, Thomas Aquinas describes God as the Unknown.[68] Aquinas wrestled with the hiddenness of God so much that he preferred to use knowledge (*scientia*) within the realm of human things and wisdom (*sapientia*) when dealing with divine things.[69] In the thought of Aquinas, no man can know God and love him rightly by his own resources, "it must be given to him from above."[70] Luther reminds us that God remains a mystery even in revelation. For example, Luther noticed in Ezekiel 33:11 that God wills salvation for all, and this is powerfully demonstrated in the weeping, wailing, and groaning of Jesus over the perdition of the ungodly. Whereas this remained true, he noticed that the same God willed some to remain in their sin.[71] As far as Luther is concerned,

---

we see God in Christ can we again understand general revelation and get to be certain that God had previously revealed himself (see G.C. Berkouwer, *General Revelation*).

[66] Barth has given a detailed study of this characteristic in CD II, 1 par. 27,1. Here Barth allows us to see that God is indeed hidden. And as Berkhof puts it, it is because he is hidden that he must be revealed. For Berkhof, revelation accompanies hiddenness in three different dialectical relationships: revelation presupposes hiddenness, revelation reveals hiddenness, and revelation assumes the form of hiddenness (Berkhof, Christian Faith, 53–56).

[67] The indirectness of the revelation of God is taught by such scriptural texts as Jn 1:18, Ex 19:21; Judg 13:22; I Cor 13:12 and Ex 33:18–23. Of course, the scripture allows for a direct vision of God, but only at the end of time.

[68] T. Aquinas, *Summa Theologica*. 3 Volumes. Fathers of English Dominican Province, trans. (New York: Benzinger Brothers, Inc., 1947), see 1a. 3.

[69] Aquinas, *Summa Theologica*, 2a2ae.9.2.

[70] Aquinas, *Summa Theologica*, 1a.38.1.

[71] Luther, *The Bondage of the Will*, 33: 139–140, and 146.

revelation does not solve the divine mystery, instead it confronts us with it. William C. Placher, commenting on Luther's perception of the divine mystery, adds that:

> We cannot imagine how the God of the entire universe will turn out to have been revealed in the crucified Jesus—in that sense God's revelation remains hidden—and yet we believe that this is so. We therefore literally cannot help thinking of a hidden God apart from Christ—and yet we believe that this way of thinking is only a sign of our failure to comprehend the mystery and love of God; for if we did comprehend, we would see how this hidden God has been revealed in Christ.[72]

The hiddenness of God is something of a perplexity to the traditional African peoples also. Although he is hidden, he is not just some vague existential reality.[73] Most African peoples believe, as Klaus Nürnberger explains, that "there is no revelational relationship from him to man, nor is there, except in a few cases, any cultic relationship from man to him. All Africans seems to agree that he is basically unapproachable and aloof—whatever the reasons for this distance may be."[74] David Bosch thinks that "the God of Africa is a silent God and his real essence remains shrouded in mystery."[75] According to the Zulu informants of Bishop Callaway, the *izibongo* (praise names) of *Nkulukulu* were no longer known.[76]

> The oldmen say that *uNkulukulu* is *umVelingqangi*, for they say he came out first; they say he is the *uhlanga* from which all men broke off. The oldmen say that *uNkulukulu* is; he made the first men, and ancients of long ago; the ancients of long ago died; there remained those who had been begotten by them, sons, by whom we hear that there were ancients of long ago who knew the breaking off of the world. They did no know

---

[72] W.C. Placher, *Domestication of the Transcendence: How Modern Thinking about God Went Wrong* (Louisville: Westminister John Knox Press, 1996), 50.

[73] Klaus Nürnberger describes an existential as "a recurring, non-objectifiable, immediate experience like being loved, being doubted, being dependent etc. Existentials are at the root of genuine religious phenomena. They find their verbal expression in, but are also often overgrown by myths, images, philosophical speculations, personifications etc." (K. Nürnberger, "The Hidden God in Africa—Fate and Affliction". *Missionalia*. Vol. 1 No 1, April 1973 (21–31), 21).

[74] Nürnberger, "The Hidden God in Africa—Fate and Affliction," 21. Clearly, Nürnberger has overstated himself here. It is not true that all Africans see God as unapproachable and aloof. This is true only in contexts where there is a strong sense of the intermediaries. David Bosch also fell into the same trap when he argued that the religious experience of the southern Bantus ends effectively with the ancestors (Bosch, "God in Africa; Implications for Kerygma," 9).

[75] Bosch, "God in Africa; Implications for Kerygma," 12.

[76] Smith, *African Ideas of God*, 106.

> *uNkulukulu*; they did not see him with their eyes; they heard it said that *uNkulukulu* was. He came out where men broke off from *uhlanga*. He begat the ancients of long ago. They died and left their children. They begat others, their sons, they died. They begat others; thus we at length have heard about *uNkulukulu*. It was our ancestors who told us the accounts of *uNkulukulu* and of the ancients of long ago.
>
> Tell me if at the present time there are any who pray to *uNkulukulu*? There are none. They pray to the *amatongo* (men who have died).[77]

Although the traditional Zulus recognize the hiddenness of *uNkulukulu*, they view it as a disturbing reality and they look forward to a time when *uNkulukulu* will emerge from his hiddenness.

> This then is what I maintain, if anyone says he understands all about *uNkulukulu*. I say all men would be glad to go to the man who says this to see him and to hear him; for in process of time we have come to worship the *amadhlozi* only, because we knew not what to say about *uNkulukulu*; for we do not even know where we separated from him, nor the word which he left with us. It is on that account then that we seek out for ourselves the *amadhlozi* that we not always be thinking about *uNkulukulu*, saying: "*uNkulukulu* has left us", or "What has he done for us?"[78]

The Lango of Uganda are similar to the Zulu in this regard. The Lango admit that they know nothing of *Gabipiny* (God—literally the one who sees the universe). *Gabipiny* is watching the universe, but from a distance. The Venda do not say much about *Mwali* except that he is the highest in the hierarchy of beings.[79] The Dinka solve the problem of the hiddenness of God by pointing to the mystery of life. A Dinka will say: I do not know the fine details about *Nhialic* (Dinka word for God), but because I have life, I know *Nhialic* exists. Gabriel M. Setiloane explains that no man has seen *Modimo* (Sotho-Tswana word for God). In a sense, *Modimo* is unkown.[80]

Indicate that Hiddenness has been Revealed in the Son and the Holy Spirit

Nyasaye, Ngai, Modimo, Nyame (and the other African names for God) is hidden. The Zulu bemoan the fact that they know very little of *uNku-*

---

[77] H. Callaway, *The Religious System of the Amazulu* (London: Trübner, 1870), 13.

[78] Callaway, *The Religious System of the Amazulu*, 31.

[79] J.A. van Rooy, *The Traditional World View of the Black People in Southern Africa* (Potchefstroom: PU vir CHO, 1978), 5.

[80] Setiloane, "MODIMO: GOD Among the Sotho-Tswana," 13; cf. Setiloane, *The Image of God among the Sotho-Tswana*, 80.

lukulu. The Lango admit that they know nothing of *Gabipiny*. It is amazing that, in spite of there being so many African myths about God, we still find the African peoples admitting that they do not know God. This is not an 'as if' kind of situation. There is no pretence here. The Luo know that there is *Nyasaye*; the Kikuyu are aware that *Ngai* exists; the Sotho-Tswana believe that *Modimo* is, and yet they admit that God is hidden from them. Different philosophies and religions offer explanations for this puzzle. The Christian faith also has its explanation, and only this option is available to Christian theology. The explanation is that only God can reveal himself. In the words of Karl Barth, God's revelation concerns "God alone, wholly God, God himself."[81] The gist of this statement is that "God cannot reveal anything more certain, more specific, more living than himself."[82]

The Son is the revelation of the Father. The Father is "wholly and utterly" in His revelation; that is, in Jesus Christ.[83] He is the Father's revelation and nothing more or less. In Jesus Christ, the Father "sets and gives to be known not something, be it the greatest and the most significant, but himself as He posits and knows Himself."[84] The scripture also refers to the Son as the Word. The Christian faith knows that its God (*Modimo, Ngai, Nyasaye, Olodumare,* and so on) is not silent. How could "the Unexplainable,"[85] "he who has nowhere or nowhen that he comes to end,"[86] "he who thunders from the beginning"[87] be silent? How could he who thinks and remembers all, the *Great Muntu*, who is the ultimate explanation of *muntu* (personality) be conceived of as dead silent? Of course, he is not silent.

The Son is the Word of God. In the beginning was the word, the word was God, and the Word was with God. According to Barth, the Son is the "eternal Word of the Father who speaks from eternity, or the eternal thought of the Father who thinks from all eternity, the Word in which God thinks Himself, or expresses Himself by Himself."[88] Already the African conceptual framework experiences the existential of *Nyasaye*,

---

[81] Barth, *Church Dogmatics I/1*.87–95; cf. J. Moltmann, *The Trinity and the Kingdom*. M. Kohl, trans. (London: SCM Press, 1981), 140.

[82] Barth, *Church Dogmatics I/1*.89.

[83] Barth, *Church Dogmatics I/1*.498.

[84] Barth, *Church Dogmatics I/2*, Second edition, 1975, 476.

[85] Mbiti, *African Religions and Philosophy*, 33.

[86] Mbiti, *African Religions and Philosophy*, 31.

[87] Mbiti, *The Concepts of God in Africa*, 12 f.

[88] Barth, *Church Dogmatics I/2*.527.

Modimo, and *uNkulukulu* in much the same way as the biblical Father. In this case, the African metaphysics recognizes *Nyasaye*, *Modimo*, and *uNkulukulu* not merely as God of Africa, but as the God of Israel. If the existential and the person of *uNkulukulu*, for example, is the same as God of Israel, then the Christian theology demands that we state that *uNkulukulu* has revealed himself in the Son and in the Holy Spirit.

It seems to me that the theology that will be most innovative is that which seeks to explain to the African believers what it means by *uNkulukulu* (for example) revealing himself in the Son and the Holy Spirit. To say that *uNkulukulu* has revealed himself in the Son and the Holy Spirit is not simply to add something to the old beliefs. It is to say what the scripture expects; namely, that God has made himself known in Christ and in the Holy Spirit. This was the Good News to the Jews, and it should not be viewed as less significant when it is applied to God in these discussions. As we reflect on the revelation of God in the Son and the Holy Spirit, we are not only able to hold both the hiddenness / transcendence and the nearness of God together, but we are also able to make a clear statement on the uniqueness of both the Son and the Holy Spirit. For an African who traditionally understood God merely as hidden and transcendent, and who could not access God even through an elaborate doctrine of the intermediaries, nothing can be more revolutionary than the teaching that God has revealed himself in the Son and the Holy Spirit.

Admit the Seriousness of the Intermediaries

In fact, the African idea of the mediators is a direct result of the belief among the African peoples that God is hidden.[89] In other words, the idea of the divinities and intermediaries is the African version of the tower of Babel. Mbiti even sees the idea of the intermediaries as a necessary element of the African cosmology. He argues that:

> The idea of the intermediaries fits well with the African view of the universe, which holds that the invisible world has its own life and population. The life of this invisible world is in some way higher than that of man, but God is higher still. In order to reach God effectively it may be useful to approach him by first approaching those who are lower than he is but higher than the ordinary person.[90]

---

[89] Idowu, *Olodumare: God in Yoruba Belief*, 62.
[90] J.S. Mbiti, *Introduction to African Religion* (London: Heinemann, 1975), 63.

Although Mbiti sees the concept of intermediaries as a reality in the African religious consciousness, he clearly distinguishes the mediators from God.[91] D.C. Scott, writing about *Mulungu* from the point of view of the Nyanja people, says: "... you can't put the plural with God because God is one. There are no idols called gods, and spirits are spirits of people who have died, not gods. ... Hence God is one, is a distinct person, cannot be identified with the powers of nature, nor confounded with spirits in general."[92] The point made by Scott is that the Nyanja people, for example, know of idols or spirits, but they never speak about them in the context of *Mulungu* (God). Dr. Hastings Kamuzu Banda, the former president of Malawi, corroborates S.C. Scott's understanding of the distance that should be maintained between *Mulungu* and the intermediaries. According to him, his people:

> ... never use the plural form of Mulungu at all, for the simple reason that we did not think there were more such Beings than one. ... None of my parents and grand parents used the plural form of Mulungu or Chiuta. They always used the singular form. And they used the word many times within my hearing, especially when we were about to eat the new crop of maize or beans or when there was drought in the country or when there was death in the family. ... The fact that we used the plural form of mzimu [mizimu or aazimu, spirits], but never that of Mulungu (God) makes it plain that we never thought that spirits were gods, as writers are inclined to think. The spirits of the ancestors had to be prayed to, not because they were themselves the deities, but because they were the means of approaching the Deity, who was above everything else, including the spirits themselves.[93]

---

[91] It seems to me that the concept of the mediators in the African traditional religions performs—for the African steeped in tradition—a function that deserves some clarification. According to the definition of Berkhof, religion "is a relationship with the transcendent and the absolute, but man can have such a relationship only through the immanent and the relative" (Berkhof, *Christian Faith*, 14). If we accept this definition of religion and see African religion as religion, then we see a situation where in African religion God is seen as expressing himself in the relative (the mediators) because God is seen to be passive. The implication of this is that, at one point or the other, the traditional African must secure for himself the favors of the mediators. Here is the difference between Christianity and the ATRs. In Christianity God not only expresses himself in himself, but his transcendence and immanence are also seen together. Consequently, the worshipper does not try to secure the favor of God. Rather, God in Christ has come to the Christian worshipper. By the work of the Holy Spirit, the Christian has been brought into communion with God and has no need for 'towers of Babel.'

[92] D.C. Scott, *Dictionary of the Nyanja Language*. Heatherwick, ed. (London: Religious Tract Society, 1929), 348.

[93] Quoted in Smith, *African Ideas of God*, 60.

Regardless of how African thought may explain the idea of the intermediaries, the fact that it presents Christian theology with difficulty
refuses to go away. African Christian thought has not paid sufficient
attention to the problem of the intermediaries. In the past they have
been discussed in the context of the doctrine of God. The problem with
this approach is that it is not possible to adequately isolate them, and
to deal with them for what they are. Kwame Bediako defines them as
"manifestations or refractions of a single God"[94] Bolaji Idowu, dealing
with the problem in the context of diffused monotheism, understands
the mediators as functionaries who work as they are commissioned by
God.[95] These functionaries may be divinities, serviceable family spirits,[96]
the spirits in a general sense,[97] or the living dead.[98] Even evangelicals do
not seem to realize that the (so-called) mediators are not gods, and that
they cannot be studied in the context of God. As a result of our inability
to adequately distance the mediators from God, African theology has
also not been able to see the difference between *Nyasaye*, *Modimo*, etc.,
and Baal.

Presentations such as these miss an important quality of God. God,
as Berkhof puts it, is a "defenseless superior power."[99] God is the
almighty, but in his superior power he retreats to give us room in our
rebellion against him. God gave room to the African peoples, like all
other peoples of the world. But some African peoples, by formulating
the concept of the mediator, preferred to use the freedom to withdraw
from the intended communion with God. This is sin. Men everywhere,
albeit in different ways, use the God-given space for themselves. When
man worships the mediators and abuses his God-given room, it does
not mean that he who gave the room was not God. In the Old Testament we see continual—and often futile—pleading of the prophets;
however, despite Israel's sustained rebellion, nothing was added to or
removed from the Yahweh of the covenant.

The Bible clearly indicates that non-Christians have gods and their
images (ηιδαλον), and the Africans have no need to deny that this is a
truth that is also applicable to the African peoples. The Yoruba recog-

---

[94] Bediako, *Theology and Identity*, 288.
[95] Idowu, *Olodumare: God in Yoruba Belief*, 62; cf. Schmidt, *The Origin and Growth of Religion: Facts and Theories*, 262–282.
[96] Lang, *The Making of Religion*, 209f.
[97] Evans-Pritchard, *Nuer Religion*, 49, 51.
[98] Gehman, *African Traditional Religion in Biblical Perspective*, 54.
[99] Berkhof, *Christian Faith*, 133–140.

nize the supremacy of *Olodumare*; however, they also have innumerable divinities. No one really knows the actual number of the Yoruba divinities since they simply call them *orisa*, meaning "legion."[100] According to Mercier, research has not been able to offer a reasonable account of the divinities of the Ewe of Ghana, Togo, and Dahomey. The divinities among these peoples are too numerous and complex. Generally, belief in divinities is prevalent in West African and some parts of Uganda; however, the belief dwindles to insignificance as one moves into the central part of Africa, eastern Africa, and southern Africa[101] When we encounter divinities, we cannot fail to take them seriously since the New Testament did not ignore them. According to Friedrich Buchsel, the New Testament regards the gods as realities.

> It is evident from 1 Th. 1:9 that they are no gods in comparison with God, and from Gl. 4:8 and R[omans] 1:23 that they are not divine by nature but only products of human sin and folly. But [Paul] seems to see demons behind their worship (1 C[or] 10:19; cf. 8:5) so that we do not have here a purely intellectual dismissal. (Buchsel, 1965: 378).[102]

The apologists also confronted the problem of the intermediaries. Michael Green suggests that the pagan world of the first and second centuries viewed the deities as sons or ministers of God.

> They were accordingly commonly regarded as subordinate agents of the one God. "The one doctrine upon which all the world is united", wrote Maximus of Tyre, "is that one God is king of all and Father, and that there are many gods, sons of God, who rule together with God. This is believed by both Greeks and Barbarians." Thus, ... worship offered to the subordinate deities as ultimately reaching the Supreme God.[103]

Here is a phenomenon very similar to Bolaji Idowu's concept of diffused monotheism. The apologists knew that the divinities obscured pure devotion to and direct worship of God. Thus they confronted the divinities. Our approach to this situation should not be that of denying the involvement of the true God with the African peoples. On the contrary, on this side of God's creation the presence of God is everywhere, but the reality of ηιδαλον (the gods themselves and their images) is also a truth that we cannot deny. Emphasizing that *Nyasaye* (a Luo

---

[100] Gehman, *African Traditional Religion in Biblical Perspective*, 125.

[101] Gehman, *African Traditional Religion in Biblical Perspective*, 124.

[102] F. Buchsel, "εἴδωλον" in Gerhard Kittel, ed., and Geoffrey Bromiley, trans. and ed., *Theological Dictionary of the New Testament* vol. 2 (Grand Rapids: Wm. B. Eerdmans Publishing Company, 1964), 378.

[103] M. Green, *Evangelism in the Early Church* (Grand Rapids: Eerdmans, 1970).

word for God), for instance, is not a god or an image of god, but God himself means that we cannot equate *Nyasaye* with the mediators or the divinities.

Borrow a Principle from the El in Canaan and Quas in Edom

Having made a distinction between *Nyasaye* and the mediators confronts us with the need to admit that the Luo people, and all the African peoples, for that matter, never knew *Nyasaye* as the Father of our Lord Jesus Christ. *Nyasaye*, in the original Luo understanding, seems to fall into the same category as the Edomites' *Quas*[104] or the Canaanites' *El*.[105]

According to Heureux, "Yahweh exhibits an extraordinary number of El characteristics,"[106] and there is no trace of polemic against El in the Hebrew Bible. David Bosch, approaching this observation from another angle, explains that:

> [God] appeared on scene as Yahweh, the wholly other, revealing himself to his people, and yet there was a degree of continuity between him and El. A certain amount of integration took place. Or to put it differently: Yahweh took over El: his names (eg El Elyon, El Shaddai, etc.) and his functions. El was king, creator, judge, the wholly other, the God to whom glory and honour belonged, the owner of heaven, the God of gods in the heavenly court (cf. Psa. 82), the just and the righteous who supported the weak and the under-privileged, the gracious and the merciful God who could also anger, the God of all children of men. All these traits were subsumed and transcended in Yahweh. He revealed himself to Abraham

---

[104] Scholars are of the opinion that the divine name *Quas* is of Arab origin and entered Edom with the incursions of Arab tribes in the 8th and 7th centuries BC (see M. Rose, "Yahweh in Israel—Quas in Edom?" in *Journal for the Study of Old Testament* 4 (1977), 28–34; W.F. Albright, "Islam and the Religions of the Ancient Orient" in JAOS 60 (1940), 283–301; T.C. Vriezen, "The Edomitic deity Quas" OTS 14 (1965), 330–353; and J.R. Bartlett, "Yahweh and Quas: A Response to Martin Rose" in JSOT 5 (1978), 29–38.

[105] C.E.L. Heureux, *Rank Among the Canaanite Gods: El, Baal, and the Rephaim* (Ann Arbor: Scholars Press, 1979); cf. Bosch, "God in Africa; Implications for Kerygma," 12–17. David Bosch argues that from the beginning Yahweh was not completely identical with El. El appeared as Yahweh and yet there was a degree of discontinuity; however, in spite of this, Yahweh took over the names of El and his functions. El, according to David Bosch, J. Blommendaal, Albrecht Alt, B. Gemser, Rolf Rendtorff, Otto Eissfeldt, Georg Fohrer, F.M. Cross, and M.J. Mulder, was the gate through which Yahweh penetrated the Semitic world. According to Bosch, the "Gods of Africa" are like El. They must allow themselves to be taken over by Yahweh or else they are Baal (Bosch, "God in Africa; Implications for Kerygma," 15–17).

[106] Heureux, *Rank Among the Canaanite Gods*, 50, 59.

and Moses as the Wholly Other, but he did this within the context of the religious world of the Semites. ... In this process he adopted many of the traits and names of El. El was the "gate" through which he penetrated the Semitic world.[107]

Commenting on the Edomites *Quas*, M. Rose posits the view that the name, *Quas*, was applied to an already established Edomite god who would at a later stage be identified with the Isrealites' Yahweh.[108] In fact, according to J.R. Bartlett[109] and T.C. Vriezen,[110] *Quas* and Yahweh had similar characteristics. Grounding this argument, J.R. Bartlett says that:

> ... it is quiet remarkable that the Old Testament, while firmly condemning Ammonite Milcom and Moabite Chemosh as 'abominations', neither names nor condemns any Edomite God. This difference in treatment requires explanation. It may be a matter of chance, or of Isreal's ignorance of Edomite belief, but perhaps the most likely explanation is that there was some awareness in Isreal that Yahweh belonged to the Edomite region and that Edomites themselves might be among his worshippers.[111]

As is the case with El and *Quas*, the notion of God among the African peoples indicates a number of similarities with Yahweh. In fact, as Bosch has observed, the translators of the Bible into the African languages, "... experienced no difficulties in finding African 'dynamic equivalents'—for the God of Scripture—Modimo, Nkulunkulu, Thixo, et cetera."[112] This observation can allow us to see the African notion of God as (in some ways) similar to the idea of El or *Quas*. Consequently, we are in a position to distance the African notion of God from Baal, *Milcom*, or *Chemosh*. In view of this, it is important that we reject the line of thought that clamps together the African concepts of God with Baal or his equivalents.

---

[107] Bosch, "God in Africa; Implications for Kerygma," 16; cf. Heureux, *Rank Among the Canaanite Gods*, 49, 50.

[108] Rose, "Yahweh in Israel—Quas in Edom?" in *Journal for the Study of Old Testament* 4, 1977, 31.

[109] Bartlett, "Yahweh and Quas: A Response to Martin Rose" in *JSOT* 5, 1978, 33.

[110] Vriezen, "The Edomitic deity Quas" OTS 14 (1965), 353.

[111] Bartlett, "Yahweh and Quas: A Response to Martin Rose," 33.

[112] D.J. Bosch, "The Problem of Evil in Africa: A Survey of African Views of Witchcraft and of the Response of the Christian Church" in *Like a Roaring Lion*. P. de Villiers. ed. (Pretoria: UNISA, 1987), 40.

African evangelical theology has in the recent past developed terms such as the "Gods of Africa,"[113] the "African Gods,"[114] or the "Gods of power"[115] to sustain the view that the African concepts of God are virtually interchangeable with the idea of Baal in the religions of the ancient near east. The Bible indicates that El, who came to be identified with Yahweh, was a foe of Baal. *Mulungu, Modimo,* and *Nyasaye* as we have seen in the works of Bolaji Idowu, John S. Mbiti, and G.M. Setiloane show a number of Yahweh characteristics. As Christianity becomes rooted in Africa, and as Africans in their millions accept Christianity as their religion, the examples—*Mulungu, Modimo, and Nyasaye*—will be increasingly 'Yahweh-ized.' It is the responsibility of the Christian faith in the African context to tell the African Christians what to make of a 'Yahweh-ized' *Nyasaye, Modimo, and Mulungu.*

CONCLUSION

African theology needs to move beyond the African concepts of God. Until now this has not been possible because African theology has traditionally stuck to the comparative method of biblical interpretation. Moreover, African theology has operated from the cultural identity paradigm that is structurally incapable of articulating the Trinity for the African context. These problems have shielded African theology from addressing the more crucial theological issues such as 'revelation as self-revelation,' 'the hiddenness of God,' 'God as revealed in the Son and the Holy Spirit,' and 'divinities and intermediaries.' A proper understanding of these areas of theology is helpful in laying the foundation for the articulation of the doctrine of the Trinity.

Christ has made a difference to millions of Africans. As Mbiti once said, some Africans have "suffered, some have been tortured and others killed, not because of their belief in God, but for the sake of Jesus Christ and his message of Love, Salvation, Justice, Hope and Peace."[116] The

---

[113] L. Nyirongo, *Gods of Africa or the God of the Bible: The Snares of the African Traditional religion in Biblical Perspective* (Potchefstroom: Potchefstroomse Univeriteit vir Christelike Hoër Onderwys, 1997).

[114] Y. Turaki, *Christianity and African Gods: A Method in Theology* (Potchefstroom: Potchefstroomse Universiteit vir Christike Hoër Onderwys, 1999).

[115] P.M. Steyne, *Gods of Power: A Study of Beliefs and Practices of Animists* (Houston, TX: Touch Publications, 1989).

[116] Mbiti, "Is the Bible in African Religion and African Religion in the Bible?", 6.

Christ that these Christians have suffered for is the Christ that we see in the Bible. If Christ makes such a difference, how is it that at the level of formal theology the Christ event has not affected the African Christians' naming of God?

PART FOUR

FROM THE AFRICAN CONCEPTS OF GOD TO THE DOCTRINE OF THE TRINITY

"Men of Athens, I observe at every turn that you are a most religious people! Why, as I passed along and scanned your objects of worship, I actually came upon an altar with the inscription, TO AN UNKOWN GOD. Well, I proclaim to you what you worship in your ignorance. The God who made the world and all things in it ..."

Acts 17: 22–24; James Moffat's translation of the Bible

CHAPTER TEN

GOD AS THE 'GREAT *MUNTU*' MANIFESTED BY THE SON AND THE HOLY SPIRIT

INTRODUCTION

This chapter takes as its point of departure the statements of the first African bishop, Bishop Ajayi Crowther; the observations of W. Robertson Smith; and the conclusion of Edwin W. Smith. Bishop Crowther in his instruction to his clergy said:

> When we first introduce the Gospel to any people we should take advantage of any principles which they themselves admit. Thus though the heathens in this part of Africa possess no written legends, yet wherever we turn our eyes, we find among them, in their animal sacrifices, a text which is the mainspring of the Christian faith: 'Without shedding of blood there is no remission'. Therefore we may with propriety say: 'That which ye ignorantly practise, declare we unto you.' 'The blood of Jesus Christ the Son of God cleanseth from all sin.'[1]

But in order to implement the above suggestion, one must be willing to reject the doctrine of the *tabula rasa*, and, especially, the form that was applied to the African peoples. Robertson Smith has argued that " … No positive religion that has moved men has been able to start with *tabula rasa*, and express itself as if religion were beginning for the first time; in form, if not in substance, the new system must be in contact all along the line with the older ideas and practices which it finds in possession."[2]

---

[1] J. Page, *The Black Bishop* (London: Simpkin, 1910), 282.
[2] W.R. Smith, *Lectures on the Religion of the Semites* (London: A & C Black Ltd., 1923), 2.

CHRISTIANIZATION OF GOD AS HE APPEARED TO THE AFRICANS

In a sense, what Bishop Crowther and Robertson Smith are concerned with is what the Ghanaian theologian, Kwame Bediako, has described as the Christianization of the African past. Bediako argues that the Christianization of the African past has served a valuable purpose of providing Africans with "cultural continuity."[3] In Bediako's thought, the phenomenon of Christianization has to do with the task of the African Christian thought, which seeks to give the African religious heritage Christian meaning.[4] The main point of Christianization is—for our discussion here—what theology has discussed as the referentiality of God language. When the African says "God" what does he mean? According to Gilkey, we cannot speak about the referent religious language when we have not been able to grasp the reality that we are referencing.[5] In the words of Frederick Ferré, "... without the element of belief in the reality of a referent designated by the theological language, the

---

[3] A similar point has been made by Kraft, who has observed four areas in which the African cultures are already closer to Christianity than European cultures. The areas are: (1) the community aspect of the church; (2) ability to understand most of the Bible (the Old Testament, synoptic Gospels, Hebrews, James, and Peter) whereas the Europeans better understand the Pauline letters written to the present day ancestors of the modern European; (3) moral and ethical practices—examples given here are patience, generosity, politeness, and, generally, "failure in love," which has been seen as the cause of the mushrooming of independent churches; and (4) effective means of communication—use of proverbs, parables, dialogue, and so on. C.H. Kraft, *Christianity in Culture* (Maryknoll: Orbis Books, 1979), 290, 291.

[4] K. Bediako, *Theology and Identity* (Oxford: Regnum Books, 1992), 9f. Note that like Mbiti, Bediako is also moving with the conviction that the African traditional past is part of the *praeparatio evangelica*. Some African scholars such as Okot p'Bitek, Ali Mazrui, Setiloane, Christian Gaba, and Samwel Kibicho argue that to view the African traditional religions as *praeparatio evangelica* amounts to a refusal to look at the latter on its own terms. Okot p'Bitek called this kind of scholarship "intellectual smuggling" (O. p'Bitek, *African Religions in Western Scholarship* (Kampala: East African Literature Bureau, 1970), 88). But perhaps the fiercest critic of the phenomenon of Christianization of the African past is Ali Mazrui. Mazrui, formulating his point of view on the Christianization in the epilogue of p'Bitek's book, writes: "Why should there be a constant search to fit African conceptions of God into notions like omnipotence and omnipresence and omniscience? Why should there be a constant exploration for one super-god in African societies, as if one was trying to discover an inner monotheism in traditional African belief systems? Why should African students of religion be so keen to demonstrate that the Christian God had already been understood and apprehended by Africans before the missionaries came?" (p'Bitek, *African Religions in Western Scholarship*, 125).

[5] L. Gilkey, *Naming the Whirlwind: The Renewal of God Language* (Indianapolis: Bobs–Merril, 1969), 20.

distinctly religious character of this speech is sought in vain."[6] When African Christians speak about *Nyame*, *Modimo*, and *Nyasaye* in the context of Christian faith, they are making reference to Israel's God; the God they have come to know in Christ and in the Holy Spirit.

The issue of Christianization has been criticized by African *and* Western scholars. The African scholars think that the Christianization of the African God language amounts to "intellectual smuggling,"[7] while some Western scholars argue that "pagan terms can never express Christian truth."[8] This type of argument misses the point. When we speak about *Nyame*, *Modimo*, and *Nyasaye*, the interest is not concerned with the term or some theological concept, the interest is God—the One who communicates about himself. Moreover, Christianization has both historical and pragmatic sanction. As Braaten has observed, theology gets into deep trouble when it has no interest in the referentiality of its own God-language.[9] When Greek and other European languages gave the Christian faith their own God names, they were—in their own way—'Christianizing' their indigenous concept of the divine. Christianity took the God names from the cultures and filled them with new content. This is what the Christianization of the traditional African God language sought to achieve.

Christianization of the African concepts of God means that we are prepared to fill the African God reference with Christian content. The implication of this is that *Nyame*, *Leza*, *Modimo*, and *Nyambe* will no longer refer to their respective native referents. The 'Christianized' *Modimo*, for example, will have no need for the *badimo* and will certainly not have to be an *It* since he will have made himself known in the Son. According to Karl Barth, this way of naming God distinguishes the Christian doctrine of God as Christian and must, therefore, be set forth clearly at the beginning of all Christian speech about God.[10]

The trouble with mere Christianization of the African concepts of God without regard for native metaphysics is that the cultures of reception do not know what to make of the Christian content. Michael C. Kirwen, in a discussion with an African diviner, noted that the local

---

[6] F. Ferré, *Language, Logic, and God* (New York: Harper & Brothers, 1961), 160.

[7] O. p'Bitek, *Religion of the Central Luo* (Nairobi: East African Literature Bureau, 1971), 88.

[8] E.W. Smith, *African Ideas of God* (London: Edinburg House Press, 1950), 34.

[9] C.E. Braaten, *Our Naming of God: Problems and Prospects of God-Talk Today* (Minneapolis: Fortress Press, 1981), 23.

[10] Barth, CD I/1:301.

language had no theological words to explain clearly and precisely the basic Christian doctrines. He noted, for instance, that his informant understood his explanation of the doctrine of the Trinity as tritheism.[11] He further observed, "... the very words used by African Christians to express doctrines such as the Trinity seem to have a life of their own and are continually used in contexts in which they have no meaning. The words themselves become the doctrine rather than the keys unlocking the doctrine."[12]

When a Sotho-Tswana, for example, hears that *Modimo* has a Son and both *Modimo* and the Son are worshipped in the Spirit, he processes the message according to Sotho-Tswana metaphysics that could be diagrammed as below:

Category 1
God (Modimo, Leza, Nyambe, etc)
The ultimate explanation of the origin and sustenance of both man and all things
Category 2
Divinities / Spirits / Holy Spirit
Made up of superhuman beings and ancestors (Christ being one of them), and the spirits of men who died a long time ago
Category 3
Man
Human beings who are alive and who are about to be born

An interpretation of this diagram presents us with a disturbing revelation. The three persons of the Trinity occupy two distinct ontological categories. Both the Son and the Holy Spirit belong to category 2 of the African cosmology, and so they cannot be said to be God and to be known by such personal names as *Nyame, Leza*, and *Nyambe*. This is because God and the spirits, ancestors, or divinities cannot participate in one life. God is God, the spirits are spirits, the ancestors are ancestors, and the divinities are divinities. When Christ is said to be

---

[11] Barth, CD I/1: 5–22.
[12] M.C. Kirwen, *The Missionary and the Diviner: Contending Theologies of Christian and African Religions* (Maryknoll: Orbis Books, 1987), 22.

God incarnate, he is simply understood to be a 'superhuman being' paralleling what is known of heroes, the founders of different communities, and ancestors. He may thus be 'divine,' but is just like the other beings in category 2 of the cosmology. He is a "mediator,"[13] but not in any unique way; the divinities, the spirits, and the ancestors play the mediatorial role as well. This could partly explain the reason that African messianic movements easily speak about 'African Christs' without a hint of embarrassment. The Holy Spirit is easily confused with either the spirits or the 'vital force.' The extent of this confusion is easily visible among most of the independent churches and the modern charismatic renewal movements.

Careful Christianization of the African concept of God should first fully accept that God is one. The Africans already know that God is one, and that that God is the explanation of the genesis of man and the entire created order.[14] Moreover, God in the African context is not a static substance or essence, and neither is he mere man on an infinitely magnified scale. On the contrary, he is the "Great *Muntu*,"[15] a 'subject' with the ultimate personality and thus distinct from everyone and everything else.[16] Although God is totally other, the Yoruba understand God, *Olodumare*, as "One with whom man may enter into a covenant or communion in any place and at any time, one who is supreme, superlatively great, incomparable and unsurpassable in majesty, excellent in attributes, stable, unchanging, constant, reliable."[17] It is as the Great *Muntu* with keen interest in his people that God is freely said to be the creator and the sustainer of the created order.

But how is the African Christian to understand the Great *Muntu*? As we have already indicated, the African Christian thought must 'Yahweh-ize' the Great *Muntu* and name him in trinitarian terms. This is a significant point of departure that must be deliberately addressed. The African context, as we have noted, knows monotheism, but the

---

[13] The notion of Christ as mediator can be quite confusing to an African. For us the term *mediator*, when used in the context of the ontological difference between God and man, conveys the idea of an intermediate being between God and man. This is the role played by divinities, spirits, the living dead, and, in some cases, chiefs. The mediatorship of Christ, however, is different. Christ is not a being between God and man; he is Logos who became flesh, in other words, who is both God and man.

[14] Mbiti, *African Religions and Philosophy*, 16.

[15] Jahn, *Muntu: An Outline of the New African Culture*, 165.

[16] Smith, *African Ideas of God*, 21, 22; Setiloane, *African Theology: An Introduction*, 25; and Scott, *Dictionary of the Nyanja Language*, 348.

[17] B. Idowu, *Olodumare: God in Yoruba Belief* (London: Longman, 1962), 36.

idea of God as Trinity is a completely new concept. The beginning of
the concept of the Trinity is the Incarnation. The Trinity is the focal
point in Christian worship and the concept lays the claim that Jesus
Christ is God. This thought is revolutionary to an African worshipper.[18]
Because the African knows God by his name, to tell him that Jesus is
Nyame, *Leza*, or *Nyambe* is similar to telling a Jew that Jesus is Yahweh!
It is met with initial shock, surprise, and denial. But this, to be precise,
is the scriptural position. There is 'another' *Nyasaye* while, at the same
time, not more than one *Nyasaye*. M.C. Kirwen corroborates the basis
of this refusal in his research among a Tanzanian ethnic group whose
name for God is *Kiteme*. God conceived from the point of view of
Kiteme means that "... there is no other God. There is no one else
who approaches, is equal to, or shares Kiteme's power. Kiteme is alone,
without family, without sons, without a community, without a lineage.
Kiteme is totally different and apart from humankind, apart from all
creation."[19] God is in a class of his own. He is above all things or beings,
Ntu. He is the explanation of the existence of *Ntu*.

It follows, therefore, that African theology should—with urgency—
carefully and systematically Christianize the African sense of the Great
Muntu. The first (Kenyan) Luo Bible translators used the Luo concept
of *Nyasaye* as referring to God as he is made known in Christ. Wherever
the term *Father* appears in the text of the Bible, the translators of the
Bible rendered it *Nyasaye Wuoro* (God the Father). Thus the Luo (my
ethnic group) Christians see God (*Nyasaye*) and the Father (*Wuoro*) as
mutually interchangeable concepts.

---

[18] For the African mind the Trinity could as well mean that God created lesser
beings who are godlike and have God's powers but who are subject to God (see Kirwen,
The Missionary and the Diviner: Contending Theologies of Christian and African Religions, 12).
However, what the African mind needs to be convinced of is the fact that the Son is,
in fact, God himself and the Holy Spirit God himself, yet not three gods but one God.
Note that in the mind of an African, the difference between beings is based on degrees
of forces (Tempels, *Bantu Philosophy*, 58–69; Masolo, *African Philosophy in search of Identity*,
88). Above all forces is God. Tempels describes him as the "great, powerful, Life Force"
(Tempels, Bantu Philosophy, 28). According to Kagame, he is the first cause of all things
or beings -*Ntu* (Masolo, *African Philosophy in search of Identity*, 91). He is therefore not *Ntu*
itself, but the "'Great Muntu', First Creator and First Begetter in one" (Jahn, *Muntu:
An Outline of the New African Culture*, 105). Therefore to state that Jesus is God is to say
that Jesus and God have a common force, thus God is the great, powerful life force, but
Jesus is also the great, powerful life force.

[19] Kirwen, *The Missionary and the Diviner: Contending Theologies of Christian and African
Religions*, 15.

In the African context, the concept of the fatherhood of God has a primary connotation of universal creator. "Over the whole of Africa creation is the most widely acknowledged work of God."[20] The metaphors used in this regard include excavator, hewer, carver, creator, originator, inventor, architect, potter, and fashioner."[21] God alone is described as the one who fathered the world, owns it, and cares for it, and before he fathered the world there was nothing. Moreover, he is the unfathered Father of the divinities, of the forefathers, and of all men, but he is distinct from the divinities, men, and the forefathers because he is not one of them. Being unfathered Father means that he is understood to be self-existent. "He is made by no other, no one beyond him is" (Bacongo). He was the first, has always been in existence, and will never die. He came of Himself into being; he is he who speaks by himself, thus he is the speaker and the hearer, subject and object at one and the same time (the Bambuti, the Banyarwanda, the Zulu, and the Bena).[22]

The New Testament regards God as One, and this one God to be the Father of Jesus Christ. The New Testament passages that describe God as one are Mark 10:18; 12:29; Matt. 23:9; Jn 5:44; 17:3; Rom. 3:30; I Cor. 8:4, 6; Gal. 3:20; Eph. 4:6; I Tim. 1:17; 2:5; Jas. 2:19; 4:12; and Jude 25. Whereas these passages speak about God as One, Wainwright has noted that:

> … in eight out of these fifteen passages (Mark 10:18; Matt. 23:9; I Cor 8:6; Gal. 3:20; Eph. 4:6; I Tim 2:5; Jude 25; John 17:3) God is explicitly distinguished from Jesus Christ. In three of the passages (Matt.23: 9; I Cor. 8:6; Eph. 4:6) and also in the context of John 17:3, God is called Father.[23]

Although the idea of God as Father is not limited to the Judeo-Christian tradition, the idea of the Fatherhood of God found in the New Testament is derived from Hebrew thought.[24] The title is used in connection with creation (Isa. 64:8), election of Israel as a nation (Jer. 31:9; Mal.

---

[20] Mbiti, *African Religions and Philosophy*, 39.

[21] Mbiti, *Introduction to African Religion*, 44.

[22] Mbiti, *Concepts of God in Africa*, 19, 20.

[23] A.W. Wainwright, *The Trinity in the New Testament* (London: SPCK, 1962), 42.

[24] Schrenk, discussing the title *Father* in the TWNT, V, has been able to clearly explain that the idea of the fatherhood of God is found in many ancient religions. (1) The early Indian religion regards Dyaus or Heaven as father, (2) The Greeks addressed Zeus as 'Father Zeus,' (3) Osiris was said to be the father of Horus, (4) Later Greek philosophy referred to God as the father of men (see the Stoic Epictetus) and the father of Cosmos (see the later Platonists Numenius and Porphyry) (Schrenk, TWNT, V, 951–956), and (5) Plato's *Republic* also allows us to see the title 'Father' as connected to that

2:10; Isa. 1:2; 30:1; 45:11; Jer. 3:22; Hos. 11:1 and Exod. 4:22), and the anointed king (2 Sam. 7:14; Psa. 2:7; 89:27). In the Gospels, Jesus generally referred to God as the Father. Four of such occurrences are in the Gospel of Mark, eight are in the material common to Luke and Matthew, seven are in the material peculiar to Luke, and twenty two in the material peculiar to Matthew.[25] The title is rather frequent in the Johannine writings. In these writings, Jesus often referred to God as 'my Father.' The Pauline corpus views God as "the Father of our Lord Jesus Christ" (see Rom. 15:6; 2 Cor.1: 3; 11:31; Eph. 1:3; Col. 1:3) and, at times, simply as "our Father" (see I Cor. 8:6; 2 Cor. 1:2; Gal. 1:4; etc.). It is thus that the New Testament puts emphasis on God as the Father of Jesus Christ. This emphasis, viewed in the context of other statements in which the divinity of the Son is affirmed or implied, allowed the Christians to see the Father-Son relationship and therefore plurality within the Godhead.

Although God is primarily viewed as Creator-Father in the African context, it is important to indicate that the idea of fatherhood in the context of the Trinity has a rather different connotation. Fatherhood in the context of the Trinity means that God is the Father of the Son and the Spirator of the Holy Spirit. Fatherhood in this context, therefore, is not used in the sense in which God is our Father and the ultimate explanation of the invisible created world. Rather, fatherhood here means that the Father eternally begets the Son, and the Holy Spirit eternally proceeds from the Father. And, therefore, whenever we use Father for God in the African context, we must always remember to deliberately include the trinitarian fatherhood.

INCULTURATION OF THE CHRISTIAN VIEW OF GOD

Whereas 'Christianization' is significant, the real goal of African theology should be "inculturation."[26] Inculturation as a theological process is a dynamic interaction between the Christian message and the culture

---

which he believed to be the absolute reality; namely, the Idea of the Good while his *Timaeus* assigns the title 'Father' to the Demiurge (see *Rep.* VI.506e and Tim.41a).

[25] Wainwright, *The Trinity*, 44.

[26] T.S. Maluleke argues that positing Africanization as the new task of African inculturation theology, as Bediako does, may not be as ground-breaking as it may seem. He reasons that the proposal is based on juxtaposing Christianization and Africanization (T.S. Maluleke, "Half Century of African Christian Theology" in *Journal*

of reception. In the process of the interaction the Christian message is incarnated in the cultural milieu of the recipients, and the culture is also impacted and changed by the gospel. The concept of inculturation is the equivalent of the Hellenization of the Christian faith from the second to the fourth centuries of the church. Under Hellenization the church utilized the Greek metaphysics to explain the Christian concepts to the indigenous Greek culture. In the process, the gospel was incarnated in the Greek culture, but the Greek culture was also changed by the gospel. A similar principle is clearly noticeable in Augustine, Boethius, and Aquinas, who were attempting to use the Latin metaphysics to convey the Christian view of *divinitas* to the Latin West. Inculturation as a theological strategy for the African context is an effort to use the African metaphysics to explain 'the new content,' viz the Christian interpretation of *Nyame*, *Leza*, *Nyambe*, and *Modimo* to the African audience. This is groundbreaking, and it is yet to be done.

In order to inculturate the Christian view of God into the African conceptual framework, it is important that we first consider the issue of the referentiality of the God language. According to Christian faith, God is the One who has revealed himself in the Son and in the Holy Spirit. This concept is encapsulated in the traditional theological language or formula, 'One God Three Persons.' Having understood the referent designated by the theological language, we then seek to have a thorough understanding of the African conceptual framework. Mugambi warns that if this basic requirement is not met, we are likely to have a "... mutual misunderstanding which would be difficult to reconcile."[27]

For the Africans, being *Ntu* is not just defined substantially. There are categories of existence such as *Ikintu* or the time aspect of *Ahantu* that cannot be defined substantially. The underlying principle here is that

---

of Theology for Southern Africa, 99, 1997 (4–23). But the concern of Bediako is clearly not to place a wall between that which is Christian and that which is African. The point of Bediako is that the Christian thought in the African context has done well to show the areas of continuity between the African culture and the Christian faith. And without taking away this credit, Bediako now urges African theology to engage in a kind of scholarship which utilizes the African conceptual framework to explain the Christain concepts. This, in my opinion, is why Bediako took such pains to explore the significance of the developments of the Christian faith in the second century to modern Africa (see Bediako, *Theology and Identity*, 1992).

[27] J.N.K. Mugambi, *The African Heritage and Contemporary Christianity* (Nairobi: Longman, 1989), 58.

force and its manifestation are inseparably intertwined. God exists in a non-substantial category. Moreover, He is known to be a category of existence that is outside *Umuntu, Ikintu, Ahantu,* and *Ukuntu.* In a way, God is unknown. He is not even as tangible as the wind, yet he is experienced constantly. He is experienced in ways other than "the world of senses."[28] For this reason, some African peoples simply call God "the Great Spirit, the Fathomless Spirit, the ever-present Spirit or the God of wind and breath."[29] Although the African people admit that they know nothing of the substantial nature of God,[30] they insist that this "Great *Muntu*" is "the source, originating in unrecorded time, of stream of life which flows into indeterminate future."[31] Therefore the African peoples do not describe God in substantial terms. In view of this consideration, the term that can best capture the unity factor in the context of the Trinity is the 'Great *Muntu.*'

Person (*Umuntu*) in the African metaphysics is life force.[32] This is what remains when a man dies. Tempels calls it "genuine *Muntu* (person)." Tempels says that he "always heard the old men say that man himself goes on existing, he-himself, the little man who sits in hiding behind the outwardly visible form, the *muntu* that went away from the living ones."[33] Personality in human beings is said to be "a tributary of the Supreme Vital Force."[34] To be person is not just to be divine, sacred, weird, and holy, but to be person is also to reveal God.[35] Moreover, to be person is to be in a community.[36] Archbishop Desmond Tutu puts this point well:

> The African would understand perfectly well what the Old Testament meant when it said, "man belongs to the bundle of life", that he is not a solitary individual. He is linked backwards to the ancestors whom he reveres and forward with all generations yet to be born. … Even today when you ask an African how he is, you usually in fact speak in the plural "How are you?" and he will usually answer, "We are well, we are here",

[28] Setiloane, "MODIMO: GOD Among the Sotho-Tswana," 13; cf. Setiloane, *The Image of God among the Sotho-Tswana,* 80.
[29] Mbiti, *Introduction to African Religion,* 53.
[30] Mbiti, *African Religions and Philosophy,* 35; cf. Mbiti, *Introduction to African Religion,* 53.
[31] Setiloane, *The Image of God among the Sotho-Tswana,* 80.
[32] Jahn, *Muntu: An Outline of the New African Culture,* 107.
[33] Tempels, *Bantu Philosophy,* 28.
[34] Setiloane, *African Theology: An Introduction,* 42.
[35] Idowu, *Towards an Indigenous Church,* 19.
[36] Mbiti, *African Religions and Philosophy,* 108f.

or the opposite; he will not be well because his grandmother is unwell, his vitality will be diminished in so far as one member has reduced life force.[37]

This understanding of 'person' is crucial for theology's formulation of the doctrine of the Trinity. It means that theology relevant for the African context must view person not just as coinciding with 'human being.' Personality in the African context, as we have already indicated elsewhere, can also be applied to God, spirits, and the living dead. Moreover, we cannot just describe person as 'individuals with rationality' (see 'God as subject') or as 'pure relations' (see 'God as essence'). While a person has these qualities, what is determinative is that he is in an existence that is consistent with the way God himself exists.[38]

From the African metaphysics of *Ntu*, the fatherhood of God in the context of the Trinity has several implications. First, it means that we are to continue to view God as "the 'Great Muntu', First Creator and First Begetter in one."[39] The significant metaphysical characteristics of this Great *Muntu* as noted by Kagame include:

(i) God as an external existent: God does not form part of the four metaphysical categories and, therefore, is on the outside of created or qualified beings -*Ntu*; He is external.

(ii) God as the Creator: God is considered as the existent which puts the existence [Fr. *l'exister*] of beings -*Ntu* there, and confers to them the property of reproduction and activity.

(iii) God as the conserver [*Consevateur*]: the actual existence of beings is thought to be regulated [begin and end] by his decision."[40]

Second, the fatherhood of God in the context of the Trinity means two things to an African reader. First, it means that the Father is to be understood as the Divine *principium*. The Father is the *principium* of the persons of the Son and of the Holy Spirit.[41] If the Father is the *principium*, then it logically follows that the Fatherhood of God also means that the Father, the Son, and the Holy Spirit share a common category of existence (*NTU*) that is different from all other beings. It

[37] D. Tutu, "Some African insights and the Old Testament" in *Journal of Theology for Southern Africa*, no. 1 Dec. 1972, 20.

[38] Idowu, *Towards an Indigenous Church*, 19; cf. 'God as community in unity.'

[39] Jahn, *Muntu: An Outline of the New African Culture*, 105.

[40] Masolo, *African Philosophy in search of Identity*, 92.

[41] Calvin, Institute, I.13.2, 7f., 23.

is not only the Father who does not belong to the series of objects for which the African cosmology developed categories; the Son and the Holy Spirit are also not part of the four metaphysical categories which qualify created beings.

In other words, the Father, the Son, and the Holy Spirit belong to the divine category and in this category there is only one existence, the Great *Muntu*. The Sotho-Tswana, for example, refer to this Great *Muntu* (*Modimo*) as "*hla'a-Macholo*" (ancient of days); "MODIMO *wa borarè*" (of my forefathers—thus the forefathers know *Modimo* better); "*Na Choeng Tsa Dithaba*" (whose abode is on the highest peak of the mountains); "*Mong'a Tschlè*" (owner or master of all, Lord).[42] The point of these attributes and names is that *Modimo's* existence is consistent at all points with the nature of *Modimo*, and that there is only one such nature.[43]

Christian theology teaches that the existence of the Son and the existence of the Holy Spirit are consistent at all points with the nature of *Modimo*. But since there is only one such nature, one who shares in that one nature must of necessity be *Modimo* since it is impossible to talk of more than one *Modimo*. Thus we can speak of *Modimo* as having manifested or revealed himself in the Son and in the Holy Spirit. This phenomenon can be diagrammed as follows:

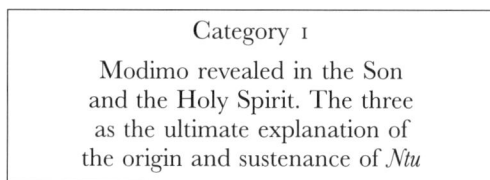

Category 1
Modimo revealed in the Son and the Holy Spirit. The three as the ultimate explanation of the origin and sustenance of *Ntu*

Third, the concept of *Ntu* helps us to grasp the theological ideas of *homoousios*, eternal generation, and procession. To say, for example, that *Modimo* is consubstantial with the Son and the Holy Spirit is to say that the three share *Ntu*. Since there is only one *Ntu* of God, and only

---

[42] Setiloane, "MODIMO: GOD Among the Sotho-Tswana," 10; cf. Setiloane, *The Image of God among the Sotho-Tswana*, 80.

[43] Setiloane, "MODIMO: GOD Among the Sotho-Tswana," 9, 10; cf. Setiloane, *The Image of God among the Sotho-Tswana*, 80. To say that there is only 'one such nature' of *Modimo*, for instance, is to say that God, according to the conceptual framework of the African peoples, is not a count noun. Because of this we cannot, for example, speak about *Modimo* in the plural. We also cannot say 'this is the same God as Modimo or a different God from Modimo.'

an existence within the context of that *Ntu* can be consistent with the existence of God, we can say with Hilary that the Son is a perfect offspring of the Father, and that he is endowed with the properties that are in the Father.[44] Elsewhere Hilary argues that the Son is derived wholly from the whole of His Father's nature (*Ntu*). He has the whole of his Father's nature (*Ntu*), and thus he abides in the Father because he is God. The Bible identifies the Holy Spirit as the Spirit of God and the Spirit of Christ. The Holy Spirit is divine because he only has the nature (*Ntu*) of God shared by both the Father and the Son. Moreover, the individual existence of the Son and of the Holy Spirit is consistent at all points with the only Being (*Ntu*) of the Father, viz the Great *Muntu*. And so the Father is God; the Son is God; and the Holy Spirit is God.

Fourth, whereas the *Ntu* concept may be important in the interpretation of the doctrine of the Trinity by the African audiences, it is worthwhile to note that we cannot apply the concept to the doctrine of the Trinity in an absolute sense. If we applied the concept of *Ntu* in its absolute sense to God, we will understand him as "... the Supreme Vital Force"[45] or simply power *par excellence*. The Great *Muntu* will then be all powerful and exist as the explanation of all powers. This way of understanding God would suffice if we accepted a one-sided transcendental view of God. But the Christian faith does not understand God simply as 'power *par excellence*.' God, worshipped in the Christian faith, brings power and powerlessness together in a profound way.[46] According to Berkhof, God who is present as almighty is also experienced as:

> ... the one who is hidden or angry or provoked or unrecognized. ... That is how we see him present in Isreal.... God's history with Israel is to a large degree the history of a God who sees his plans fail and who repeatedly must react to the hostile or at least disobedient initiative of his partner, without apparently having (or wanting to have) the power to force that partner to his will.[47]

In the New Testament's parables, the almighty God is depicted as a man who has gone on a journey and is absent.[48] The Son, who is the revelation of the Father, refuses to establish his kingdom by

---

[44] Hilary, Bishop of Poictiers. *De Trinitate*. In *Nicene and and post-Nicene Fathers of the Christian Church*. vol. IX. See 3.1; 2, 4.

[45] Setiloane, *African Theology: An Introduction*, 42.

[46] Berkhof, *Christian Faith*, 133–140.

[47] Berkhof, *Christian Faith*, 135.

[48] Mat 24:50; 25:14; and Mk 12:1.

force,[49] and instead renounces power and becomes powerless in order to bring succor to humankind and to the entire creation. According to Paul's letter to the Philippians: "Though he was divine by nature, he did not set store upon equality with God, but emptied himself by taking the nature of a servant; born in human guise and appearing in human form, he humbly stooped in his obedience even to die, and to die upon the cross."[50] On the cross we see the climax of the divine defenselessness. Here God is unable to save himself; the Father is depicted as in complete silence and as having deserted him who is his manifestation, and man triumphs over God by nailing the Son to the cross.[51] The scripture also depicts the Holy Spirit as the source of the power which the Christian has, yet the Holy Spirit is also depicted as defenseless. He must persuade men to accept the salvation of God, and, in most cases, he is resisted[52] and even quenched.[53]

The defenselessness of God—or as we have said here, his weakness—implies a paradigm shift that is important in how we in the African context are to understand the Great *Muntu*. As Great *Muntu* he is all powerful. He is in a different category of existence, and he exists as the explanation for all powers. Yet in the context of the Christian faith we must understand the Great *Muntu* as a 'powerless power.' This is because the powerlessness of God is the expression of his superiority. The scripture is clear that in the weakness of God there is power *par excellence*, viz power that is stronger than man's strength.[54] This is a different way of understanding the power of the Great *Muntu*. He is powerful, but in a different way, in a hidden yet active sense.

We can organize the first category of the African cosmology in the light of the Christian information and have it look like this

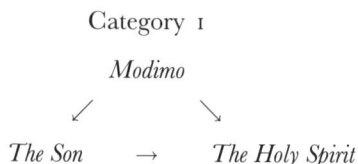

Category 1

Modimo

↙   ↘

The Son   →   *The Holy Spirit*

---

[49] Mat 26:51 f.; Lk 22:38; Jn 6:15; 18:36.
[50] Phil. 2:6–8.
[51] Mk 15:31 f., 34.
[52] Acts 7:51 cf. Isa. 63:10.
[53] I Thess. 5:19.
[54] I Cor. 1:25.

The 'Great *Muntu*' as Community in Unity

The Great *Muntu*, according to the Christian faith, is not a monad. He has existed with the Son and the Holy Spirit from eternity. When the Christian faith speaks about the Son, what is discussed is not the 'son' concept as in the Shona-Ndebele understanding of God, nor the kingship concept found among the Shilluk; neither is it the idea of the *Nommo* (the appointed model of creation) found among the Dogon.[55] The term *Son* in the context of the Trinity refers to Jesus Christ. From eternity the Great *Muntu* has oneness of *Ntu* and activity with the Son and the Holy Spirit. This oneness of *Ntu* within the Christian context should mean at least two things. First, the Son and the Holy Spirit derive from the Great *Muntu* and so the Son and the Holy Spirit respectively have the whole *Ntu* of the Great *Muntu*. Second, the Great *Muntu*, the Son, and the Holy Spirit in fact exist in complete mutual indwelling in which each person (while remaining what he is by himself as the Great *Muntu*, the Son, and the Holy Spirit) is wholly in others as the others are wholly in him.

How is it possible for the Son and the Holy Spirit to exist with the Great *Muntu* in a complete mutual indwelling of each other? Perhaps the African view of 'person' can help us explain this problem of the African mind. The primary meaning of person in the African context is "the genuine *Muntu*."[56] The "genuine *muntu*" in human persons is only a "tributary" of the "Great *Muntu*"[57] or simply a reflection of the "Great *Muntu*."[58] But to say that the Son is a person is not the same as saying that he is a person in the sense that you and I are persons. The "genuine *Muntu*" that you and I have are but tributaries of the "Great *Muntu*." The genuine *Muntu* that the Son has is the Great *Muntu* himself. Thus the Son is a perfect reflection of the Great *Muntu*; the Holy Spirit is a perfect reflection of the Great *Muntu*; and the Father is a perfect reflection of the Great *Muntu*. Thus the Son is a person in the ultimate sense; the Holy Spirit is a person in the ultimate sense; and the Father is a person in the ultimate sense. Just as each of us reveal the nature of the genuine *Muntu*, the little 'tributary' of God in each of us,

---

[55] J.S. Mbiti, "Some African Concepts of Christology" in *Christ and the Younger Churches*. G.F. Vicedom, ed. (London: SPCK, 1972), 58f.

[56] Tempels, *Bantu Philosophy*, 28.

[57] Setiloane, *African Theology: An Introduction*, 13.

[58] Idowu, *Towards an Indigenous Church*, 19.

so the Father, the Son, and the Holy Spirit fully reveal the Great *Muntu*. No one can fully reveal the Great *Muntu* except an ultimate person, and we know of three ultimate persons from Christian theology: the Father, the Son, and the Holy Spirit. Persons cannot exist in isolation. These ultimate persons have always and will always exist in a community.

In his book, the *African Heritage and Contemporary Christianity*, J.N.K. Mugambi recommended that the notion of "… 'persons' in the Trinity should be discarded because in the African mind they are misleading, vague and confusing. … The best and most relevant way to understand the Trinity, we thought, is in terms of the *modes of God's manifestation to Man*."[59] Mugambi rejects the traditional presentation of the doctrine of the Trinity because "Greek philosophical influence was at work in the formulation of the doctrine of the Trinity and most Africans are not acquainted with Greek philosophy." He prefers the "modes of God" because this paradigm does not disturb the "traditional African monotheism."[60] We will not discuss the problem of understanding the Trinity in terms of 'modes of God' here since that has already been dealt with in chapter four of this research. What we need to say now is that the theological term *persons* was not taken from Greek thought. The Father is revealed to us as a person; the Son who fully manifested the Father was revealed to us as a person; and the Holy Spirit too was revealed to us as a person. The term *persons* is constitutive of the concept of the Trinity, and somehow we have to let it disturb the African cultural milieu if need be. As we have seen, there is no reason why we should believe that a doctrine of the Trinity formulated within the African conceptual framework must preclude the use of the term *persons*. In fact, the *Ntu* concept presents the Trinitarian arguments in terms that are very close to the lines of discussion that the church fathers observed.

Father Charles Nyamiti has also attempted to articulate the doctrine of the Trinity. In his book, *Christ as our Ancestor*, Nyamiti argues that God should be seen as "the ancestor," Christ as "the brother ancestor," and the Holy Spirit as the relationship between "the ancestor" and "the brother ancestor." He defines "the brother ancestor" "… as a relative of a person with whom he has a common parent, and of whom he is mediator to God, archetype of behaviour and with whom—thanks to his supernatural status acquired through death—he is entitled to have

---

[59] Mugambi, *The African Heritage and Contemporary Christianity*.
[60] Mugambi, *The African Heritage and Contemporary Christianity*, 75, 77.

regular sacred communion."[61] The concept of ancestors continues to be an issue in African theology; however, it raises fundamental difficulties when used as a model for understanding the doctrine of the Trinity: Are we sons of God in the sense in which Christ is the Son? Did Christ acquire his supernatural status through death? How do we deal with the problem of the referentiality of the ancestor language in African nomenclature? In other words, how can one be an ancestor and be God at one and the same time? These are hard questions for this model of explaining the doctrine of the Trinity. Moreover, this model of understanding the doctrine of the Trinity is very similar to the Idealistic point of view. The only difference that Nyamiti has brought into the discussions is to call the Father, "The Ancestor," and the Son, "The Brother Ancestor." As is the case in Idealistic theology, he reduces the Holy Spirit to a mere relation between "The Ancestor" and "The Brother Ancestor."

IMPLICATIONS OF UNDERSTANDING THE 'GREAT *MUNTU*' AS COMMUNITY IN UNITY ON CHRISTOLOGY AND PNEUMATOLOGY

Christology

Jesus in African Christianity

Christ From Above

Within the African theological situation, we do not often come across a perspective of Christ which begins with 'Christ from above.' Most Christology's done by African theologians prefer either 'Christ from below' or 'Christ from before.' Responding to this situation, Y.A. Obaje proposes that African converts will benefit most from the doctrine of Christ that is formulated from the point of view of 'Christ from above' or 'theocentric Christology.' This Christology, as Obaje explains, emphasizes that "God came in the human flesh as Jesus of Nazareth. There is a God-centred or God-ward approach here to the doctrine of Christ."[62]

---

[61] C. Nyamiti, *Christ as our Ancestor: Christology from an African Perspective* (Gweru: Mambo Press, 1984), 23.

[62] Y.A. Obaje, "Theocentric Christology" in Exploring Afro-Christology" J.S. Pobee, ed. (Paris: Peter Lang, 1992), 49 f.

By proposing a theocentric Christology, Obaje is concerned with the African theologians' tendency to confound the Son with the creatures. However, a theocentric Christology or Christ from above sees the Son and the Father as having a common *Ntu*—the *Ntu* which is known to be God's. Thus, as Calvin would argue, the *Ntu* of God is one, "... hence the whole Godhead is revealed in the flesh."[63] The Son is categorically distinct from the divinities, the spirits, the ancestors, and the rulers because the Son is God. Since he is God, he is the Great *Muntu*, the 'great, powerful Life Force.' Divinities, spirits, ancestors, and rulers are powerful, but their power is derived from the ultimate source—God.

If Christian theology says the Son is divine, as far as the African metaphysics is concerned that statement means that the Son has in common with God "the great, powerful, Life Force"[64] that characterizes only God. In other words, his nature is consistent at all points with the only nature of God, and, like God, he is the explanation of *Ntu*. Due to these factors, the Son is God in the very sense of *Nyasaye*, *Modimo*, *Nyame*, *Leza*, *Nyambe*, and so on. He does not belong to some lower order of divine reality; rather, he is God himself. In the words of Obaje:

> The coming down of God on a long chain from heaven in African myths of human alienation from God must be seen as a perversion of truth and an imperfect understanding of God's self-disclosure as a result of sin. However it is significant for the African convert to know that the very God who used to come down on a long chain from heaven to assist the creatures has finally come in the human flesh as Jesus of Nazareth. ... There is no longer any need for them to return in search of the God of the traditional African worldview. The same God, who indeed is the God of all creation, has finally come in Jesus Christ.[65]

Perhaps the soteriological argument gives us a better view of Christ from above as understood within the framework of the *Ntu* concept. The Son sets us free from the bondage of divinities, spirits, and ancestors because he is God. Cases of exorcism of the possessed[66] by the

---

[63] Calvin, CW, 40, 56.

[64] Tempels, *Bantu Philosophy*, 28; cf. Jahn, *Muntu: An Outline of the New African Culture*, 104 f.

[65] Obaje, "Theocentric Christology," 50.

[66] A.F.C. Wallace has defined possession as "... any native theory which explains any event of human behavior as being the result of the physical presence in a human body of an alien spirit which takes control of the host's executive functions, most frequently speech and control of the sketal musculature" (A.F.C. Wallace, "Cultural Determinants of Responses to Hallucinatory Experience", *AMA Archives of General Psychiatry*, no 1, 1959, 59). According to Wallace, possession is the explanation of such behaviors as (1)

authority of Jesus are numerous in Africa. The Africans understand that one cannot carelessly play with categories that have greater power without experiencing serious consequences. In the words of Tempels, "one force that is greater than another can paralyse it, or even cause its operation totally to cease."[67] The Son causes the powers of divinities, spirits, ancestors, and even of witches to diminish or cease because he himself is the ultimate power. The Son joins us to the Father in his great salvation because as we share in his *Ntu* we share in the only divine *Ntu*, the Great *Muntu* himself.

Although the context of Africa requires that the salvation bequeathed to us by the Son be understood as including freedom from the bondage and influences of the divinities, spirits, and ancestors, it is important that we see the victorious Christ as the manifestation of the defenseless, almighty God. Christ's power cannot be compared to the powers of the divinities, the spirits, or the ancestors. Since he is God, he is almighty. However, there are times when, from a human point of view, it will look like the divinities, spirits, and ancestors have defeated Christ. In situations like these, Calvin advises us to listen to the message of the Holy Scripture and the appeal of the cross of Christ.[68] From the scriptures we learn about the mystery of the cross and the principle that "… the foolishness of God is wiser than men, and the weakness of God is stronger than men."[69]

Even our salvation and the victory that we have won in Christ must be understood in the context of the power and the powerlessness of God. In a context such as Africa, where demons, spirits, disease, and poverty are realities, this way of understanding Christ and his salvation is crucial. In such a context it is very easy to fall into the trap of triumphalistic Christianity. The Son, who himself is the Great *Muntu*, became man so that we in turn can become one with God and live in victory. From a human standpoint, becoming one with God means having full access to power *par excellence*. But the Scripture provides

---

obsessive ideation and compulsive action, (2) hysterical dissociation including multiple personalities, fugues, somnambulism, and conversion hysteria, and (3) hallucinations (ibid: 59,60). J. Beattie emphasizes the individual's state of dissociation, claim to illness, or unusual behavior is attributable to the outside agent who inspires the individual to act in a particular manner or displaces the individuals' personality and acts in its stead (J. Beattie, *Other Cultures* (New York: The Free Press of Glencoe, 1964), 229).

[67] Tempels, *Bantu Philosophy*, 28.
[68] J. Calvin, *Institutes*, I, 18,4.
[69] I Cor 1:25.

us with the way in which we are to understand the divine power.
In contexts of power encounters, the spirits, divinities, and ancestors
will melt away before us, but our joy should be that our names are
written in the book of life. Again we can live as conquerors, enjoying
remarkable abundance, harmony, and peace, but then there are these
warnings: we must not avenge ourselves, and we must be prepared to
suffer.

Christ From Below
In the recent past there has been an emergence of the understanding of Christ based on titles that are specifically African in origin
or emphasis. Some of the titles used include Friend, Liberator, elder
Brother, Ancestor, King / Chief, Elder, Healer, and Master of Initiation. These Christologies seek to establish a relationship between the
historical Jesus, the impression his followers had of him, and the implications of such impressions on the socio-cultural and political history
of modern Africa. The focus of these 'Anthropocentric Christologies'
is twofold. First, they seek to locate the equivalents of biblical titles
for Jesus in local African languages. Second, they intend to posit the
view that God in his humanity identified with our humiliation, sin, and
death. In Christ, God has defeated the spiritual forces and taken all
our diverse sufferings upon himself. Indeed, God is not aloof; rather,
he is with us in our diseases, poverty, famine, political unrests, ignorance, sin, and even death. Because of the socio-cultural and political
climate of the African continent, the African peoples can and do understand Christ as Friend, Liberator, elder Brother, Ancestor, King / Chief,
Elder, Healer, and Master of Initiation and so forth.[70]

Of course, the New Testament gives us a picture of Christ from
below. He was a true man, a Jew by race. As is the case with many
African peoples, he lived in a hostile environment and suffered different
kinds of oppression. According to Zablon Nthamburi:

> For Jesus there is no question of neutrality or compromise in relation to
> evil and injustices. There can be no neutrality in the face of injustices
> and oppression, domination and exploitation. ... We are reminded that
> in Africa there is always a struggle between good and evil, justice and
> injustice, righteousness and unrighteousness. ... We cannot tell victims of

---

[70] A bibliography indicating the contributions of African theologians to Christological debates has been furnished in one of the sections of chapter 9 of this research.

injustice and inhumanity that God is only concerned about their spiritual lives. … We need Christ who in His humanity suffers with us, is deprived with us, fights with us and identifies wholly with our situation.[71]

Clearly, as Nthamburi and the others have stated, there is a place for anthropocentric Christology in African Christianity. Jesus never took a neutral view of evil and injustice in his earthly life, nor did he limit his ministry to the spiritual. He was a rabbi, a prophet, a miracle worker, a sage, a deliverer, a healer, and a protector—along with many other titles. How could he combine so much? The simple answer is that he was all these and more because he did not fit any of these descriptions. He was the Great *Muntu* himself. In the words of Calvin, in Jesus Christ God brings himself "… within the reach of human understanding, humbles himself and makes himself small."[72] African Christianity cannot take this message for granted.

African inculturation theology has identified and applied the equivalents of biblical titles for Jesus in local languages in Christian thought. But how adequate are the equivalents? Should we merely describe Christ as an ancestor, a witchdoctor—*sing'anga par excellence,*[73] or the liberator after the brave warriors and chiefs known by the different African peoples? Of course, as Kwame Bediako has argued, the experience and the actuality of Jesus as intended in the Christian affirmation can inhabit *nana* (Akan word of ancestor), *sing'anga*, and other such words. It is also true, as Bediako argues, that "the exegesis of biblical words and texts is not to be taken as completed when one has established meanings in Hebrew, Aramaic and Greek; instead, the process needs to continue into all possible languages into which biblical faith is received, mediated and expressed."[74] However, Christology and Pneumatology that is formulated by using the equivalents of biblical titles in local languages face us with an acute problem of referentiality that is

---

[71] Z. Nthamburi, "Christ as seen by an African: A Christological Quest" in *Jesus in African Christianity*. J.N.K. Mugambi and L. Magesa, eds. (Nairobi: Acton Publishers, 1989), 58.

[72] Calvin, CW, 55, 227.

[73] Aylward Shorter takes the Chewa word *sing'anga* that describes the traditional specialist in medicine, psychiatry, and religion, and applies it to Christ (A. Shorter, *Jesus and the Witchdoctor, an Approach to Healing and Wholeness* (London: Geoffrey Chapman), 1985).

[74] K. Bediako, "The Doctrine of Christ and the Significance of Vernacular Terminology" in *International Bulletin of Missionary Research*, July, 1998, 110.

deeply rooted in the very consciousness of the African peoples and in the divinity of Christ and the Holy Spirit.

Christ differs from the traditional healer not just in degree, as John Pobee suggests,[75] he differs from the traditional healers in a very fundamental way—he is God; the healers are creations. Similarly, he differs fundamentally from such tribal liberators as Gor Mahia and Okore Ogonda.[76] In view of the fixed hierarchical nature of the African cosmology, we cannot just redirect these titles away from the categories in which they properly belong to Christ. Christ is God; he belongs to the divine category, and so he heals and liberates as God. It is important that we achieve some degree of complete otherness of Christ if we are going to succeed in planting a theocentric Christology in the African Christian consciousness. The traditional healers and liberators are men, and so whatever powers they have are derived from God.

Christ from Before

The notion that views 'Christ from before' is also present within the African Christian scene. Judith M. Bahemuka advances this view in her article, "The Hidden Christ in African Traditional Religion," in *Jesus in African Christianity*. However, an interesting and a more thorough work in this regard is John S. Mbiti's essay, "Is Jesus Christ in African Religion?", in *Exploring Afro-Christology*. In this composition, Mbiti argues that Jesus Christ is in the African religion. Supporting his argument, he uses the sayings of Jesus about himself, theological[77] terms often applied to Christ[78] and the view that Jesus is present in the African religion

---

[75] J.S. Pobee, *Toward African Theology* (Nashville: Abington, 1979), 87, 93, 94.

[76] The Luo, my ethnic group, has myths of the liberators of the tribe. The well-known heroes and liberators among the Luo are Gor Mahia and Okore Oganda.

[77] J.S. Mbiti uses at least five sets of passages to argue his point. (1) The first passage is the one which says that Abraham saw Jesus and rejoiced (John 8). According to Mbiti, if Abraham saw Jesus, what about the Africans who believe in the same God? (2) Jesus is presented in the Bible as the 'Light of the world.' Did he not shine in the African religion also? (3) Then comes the symbol of the 'Good shepherd.' Could we include the followers of the African religion among 'the other sheep'? Did the other sheep know him as their 'Shepherd'? (4) There is also the scriptural teaching of the oneness of Jesus with the Father. Can we not also say that seeing the Father is tantamount to seeing the Son? (5) Last, Mbiti makes reference to the eschatological meal in the Kingdom of God. Among the guests are Abraham, Isaac, Jacob, and all the prophets. We also see there the unidentified throngs of guests, including people from outside of the biblical circle of believers. Will the people who believe in God but are within the context of the African religion be part of the party?

[78] Among the biblical witnesses which Mbiti uses in this regard are the concept of

through the presence of God.[79] The logical conclusion of this argument
is the view that the cosmic Christ saves the African peoples through
African traditional religion.[80]

It is legitimate to understand Christ from the point of view of 'Christ
from before.' Christ's work is seen in man's conscience, in nature,
and in history. Christ could have revealed himself to the pre-Christian
African people if he so willed. God is not confined. However, as Calvin
argued, it is not for us to speculate; rather, we should restrict ourselves
to the channels through which God wills to act towards us. In the words
of Calvin, "… all those who have wished to come to the knowledge
of God have always had to be guided by the same eternal wisdom."[81]
Calvin uses 'wisdom' here in the sense of Logos, the eternal Word of
God. This view of wisdom becomes clear where he argues that "…
among the heathen there has been no revelation of God apart from
Christ as also among the Jews."[82]

But acknowledging that there is no revelation of God apart from
Christ means that we are to understand 'Christ from before' in the
context of the promises of the Old Testament, in the Incarnation, and
the proclamation of the New Testament. The incarnate Son clearly
understood himself as Logos, but he also saw himself in the light of the

---

the "Logos" (Jn 1:1–9, 14), the idea of Jesus as "the savior of the world" (Jn 4:42), the
appearance of "his star in the East" to the Magi who were not followers of the Old
Testament (Mat 2:1–12), the application of the metaphor "rock" to Christ (I Cor 10:1–
4), the notion of Jesus as "the first and the last" (Rev 1:17).

[79] Mbiti argues that the "African traditional religion has not pronounced the name
of Jesus Christ. But we might venture that He is present though the presence of
God. He is the unnamed Christ, working in the insights that people have developed
concerning God, in as far as these insights do not contradict the nature and being
of God as revealed more openly in the New Testament" (J.S. Mbiti, "Jesus in African
Religion?" in *Exploring Afro-Christology*. J.S. Pobee, ed. (Paris: Peter Lang, 1992), 28).

[80] In the contemporary African scene, there is a tendency to see Christ as the fulfiller
of the African traditional religions. From this position, some theologians and movements see God's way with Israel as accidental and therefore, in principle, interchangeable with preparations in the African traditional religions. The logical conclusion of
this position is the argument that African traditional religions can take over the role of
the Old Testament. The problem with this position is that Christ of the New Testament
does not only lose his concrete redemptive function, but he is also reduced to the level
of a mere cosmic principle. This position is clearly indicated in E.E. Evans-Pritchard,
Theories of Primitive Religion (Oxford: The Clarendon Press, 1965), 2, 3. We can deal with
this problem effectively only as we emphasize the non-exchangeableness of the Old
Testament.

[81] Calvin, *Institutes*, IV, 8, 5.

[82] Calvin, CW, 51, 169 ff.

Old Testament (Christ from behind). In view of this, one should accept the place of the cosmic Christ or Christ from before; however, such an acceptance must note that the cosmic Christ cannot be understood apart from the Incarnation and the biblical witness.

Why can we not speak about the cosmic Christ without making reference to the Incarnation and the biblical witness? The simple response is that by speaking about the cosmic Christ we are talking about God. The problem, as Calvin has elucidated it for us, is that "… all we think and speak about God … is but vain folly and empty words."[83] Because of the weakness of the human mind, we cannot fathom and grasp the full sweep of God.[84] Logically, then, in and of ourselves we cannot comprehend the cosmic Christ. If we wish to say anything about God we must be taught by God himself. In this regard, Calvin argues that " … we must go to the Word, in which God is clearly and vividly mirrored for us in his works, and where the works of God are appraised not by our perverse judgments but by the criterion of eternal truth."[85] We personally meet God only in the incarnate Word, not in the 'cosmic Word.' The incarnate Lord, however, is no longer among us. Although he is no longer among us, "… he has left us the word of His witness. As he himself is the mirror of God, so the word of Scripture reflects the grace and truth of Christ."[86] In short, if we wish to articulate any aspect of Christian doctrine, we must be prepared to be students of the Holy Scripture.[87]

Towards a Comprehensive Christology for African Christianity

The Christian faith views Christ as arising 'from above' (Christ as the Word), 'from below' (the application of the methodology of historical investigation), and 'from before' (the Cosmic Christ). To these we could as also add 'Christ from behind' (Christ arising from the Old Testament problematic and giving answer to it).[88] The view taken here is that these four approaches to Christology should be seen as both necessary and complementary. The African Christians need a Christology that allows them to clearly see Christ as the incarnate Lord. They also

---

[83] Calvin, *Institutes*, I, 13, 3.
[84] Calvin, *Institutes*, I, 6, 4.
[85] Calvin, *Institutes*, I, 6, 3.
[86] W. Niesel, *The Theology of Calvin* (Grand Rapids: Baker Book House, 1980), 35.
[87] Niesel, *The Theology of Calvin*, 6, 2.
[88] Berkhof, *Christian Faith: An Introduction to the Study of the Faith*, 267–280.

need a Christology that is structurally capable of addressing Africa's multi-faceted problems. They need a Christology which takes into consideration the significance of Jesus for all ages and all people, and they need a Christology which arises from the biblical problematic. None of the four approaches singled out here can satisfactorily address these needs. If this understanding of Christology is taken for African Christianity, then the four approaches are to be seen as essential to a balanced Christology, and none of them are adequate when taken in isolation.

Pneumatology

Pneumatology is a difficult area in African theology. There are two reasons for this. First, the African people understand God as Spirit (*moya*). It is in view that there is no physical representation of God among the peoples of Africa. Due to this understanding of God, the Holy Spirit is understood as referring to the spiritual (versus the physical) dimension of God. The incarnate Christ, in this case, becomes the physical dimension of God.[89] The second reason is because of the spirits in African cosmology. Most of the African people believe that there are two kinds of spirits: those that were once human (ancestral spirits) and those that were never human.[90] In some communities, for example, the Banyore, Segeju, Lugbara, Sukuma, Alur, Ankole, and the Luo, belief in spirits was so strong that they had cults of spirit mediumship to deal with spirit possession.[91]

The concept of the Holy Spirit presented the first translators of the Bible into the African languages with a special difficulty. There are African words for 'Holy' and 'Spirit' but, as Mbiti explains, "... the combination which gives us the 'Holy Spirit' as part of the Trinity, is specifically Christian heritage."[92] In the context of the Bantus of East Africa, for instance, the Kiswahili word *Roho* was adopted to represent the concept of the Holy Spirit instead of the vernacular words for spirit.[93] The Protestant Acholi of Uganda adopted *Cwiny*

---

[89] J.S. Mbiti, "The Holy Spirit in African Independent Churches" in *Festschrift Guenter* (Wagner: Faculty of Baptist Theological Seminary, 1994), 102, 104.

[90] Mugambi, *The African Heritage and Contemporary Christianity*, 64.

[91] See J. Beattie, and J. Middleton, *Spirit Mediumship and Society in Africa* (New York: Africa Publishing Corporation, 1969).

[92] Mbiti, "The Holy Spirit in African Independent Churches," 103.

[93] Mugambi, *The African Heritage and Contemporary Christianity*, 65.

Maleng (heart), while their Catholic counterparts adopted *Tipu Maleng* (shadow, depiction, and ancestral spirit), and *Maleng* that specifically refer to either physical or ethical purity.[94] Although (from these two examples) the new concept *Roho* and *Cwiny Maleng* or *Tipu Maleng* refer to the third person of the Trinity, the exact reference of the theological terms *Roho, Cwiny Maleng*, or *Tipu Maleng* has remained elusive to many African Christians due to the traditional interferences. Dr. Nathaniel Ndiokwere, in his book *Prophecy and Revolution*, specifically refers to the African independent churches, and charges that among these groups there is a "general confusion caused by misunderstandings of the biblical meaning of the Holy Spirit."[95]

What to make of the Christian doctrine of the Holy Spirit is not just a problem to the African independent churches. It is a problem for the entire of African Christianity, and it can be traced back to the concept of the spirits in African cosmology. Because of the spirits in the African cosmology, a number of African Christians have simply replaced beliefs in spirits by the Christian doctrine of the Holy Spirit.[96] In his study of Pneumatology in the African context, E. Andersson noted this trend when he said that African popular theology has let the doctrine of the Holy Spirit "be the wide gate through which a number of pre-Christian conceptions have entered."[97]

Sundkler believes that African popular theology makes no distinction between the Holy Spirit of the Bible and the concept of power in the traditional African thought.[98] Martin and Oosthuizen also share this view. According to Martin, African popular theology regards the Holy Spirit as power *par excellence*, "… the man in the African traditional religion is most concerned to increase his vital power … so the Zionist is most deeply concerned to get hold of the power of the Spirit."[99] Oosthuizen notes that African popular theology views the Holy Spirit as a simple continuum of the African traditional view of the vital force,

---

[94] H. Behrend, *Alice Lakwena and the Holy Spirits: War in Northern Uganda 1985–1997* (Nairobi: EAEP, 1999), 116.

[95] N.I. Ndiokwere, *Prophecy and Revolution: The Role of Prophets in the Independent African Churches* (London: SPCK, 1981), 257.

[96] See the argument in the article of Behrend, *Alice Lakwena and the Holy Spirits*.

[97] E. Andersson, *Messianic Prophet Movements in the Lower Congo* (Uppsala: Studia Ethnographica Upsaliensia, 1958), 109.

[98] B.G.M. Sundkler, *Bantu Prophets in South Africa* (Oxford: Oxford University Press, 1961), 244.

[99] M.C. Martin, "The Mai Chaza in Rhodesia" in *African Initiative in Religion*. D. Barrett, ed. (Nairobi: East African Literature Bureau, 1971), 113.

the spirits, and ancestors.[100] This point is well demonstrated by the rebel armies called Holy Spirit Movements that are fighting to take control of Uganda and the Sudan, pagan or traditional spirit mediums (*ajwaka* or *ajuoga*), and the Christian mediums.[101]

It is true that some sections of the independent church movement have tended to confuse the Holy Spirit with the spirits. However, to say that all independent churches have fallen into this error is to make a statement that cannot stand the rigor of scientific validation. Allan Anderson, doing studies among the African Pentecostals in South Africa, has observed that:

> African Pentecostalism has Africanised Christian liturgy in a free and spontaneous way that does not betray essential Christian character, and liberates it from the foreignness of European forms. African Pentecostals are among the most committed churchgoers in the townships. They have experienced the living Christ through the power of the Holy Spirit; and their lives have been radically changed as a result. This conversion, or 'born again' experience as the *bazalwane* call it, has so transformed their lives that they do not have any time for traditional practices. Unlike any other church group they have almost unanimously rejected the ancestor cult and traditional divination.[102]

The above observation indicates that not all independent churches have compromised the Christian view of the doctrine of the Trinity. Instead of blaming the independent churches, theology should admit that the church has not always had a strong Pneumatology, and that the African church, in particular, needs to rethink its Pneumatology and have it address the problem of spirits and spirit possessions in the African context.

The African peoples already know that God is *moya* (spirit). Since he is *moya*, he is called the "Great Spirit, the Fathomless Spirit, the Everpresent Spirit, or the God of wind and breath."[103] According to the Ashanti, the Shona, the Ewe, and the Kagoro, God is the saving Spirit and the protecting Spirit who made all the spirits in the universe. The Ga, the Bena, and the Banyarwanda believe that God is like wind. He comes and goes.[104] Of course, as the African peoples believe,

---

[100] G.C. Oosthuizen, *Post Christianity in Africa* (London: C. Hurst, 1968), 129, 133, 134; cf. Sundkler, *Bantu Prophets in South Africa*, 200.

[101] See the argument of Behrend, *Alice Lakwena and the Holy Spirits*.

[102] A. Anderson, *Bazalwane: African Pentecostals in South Africa* (Pretoria: University of South Africa, 1992), 119.

[103] Mbiti, *Introduction to African Religion*, 53.

[104] Mbiti, *Concepts of God in Africa*, 23 f.

God is essentially *moya*. God keeps the order of *Ntu* because in him
is the Great *Muntu*, *moya* who is ever active, initiating action, and
maintaining interaction.[105] The African peoples knew the cosmic Spirit
and understood his operations.[106] But having said that, we must quickly
add that when Christian theology speaks about the Holy Spirit, it is
referring to a specific hypostasis of God who is both active and radically
Christocentric.

Of course, the African description of *moya* as set in the above para-
graph could fit the biblical picture of the Holy Spirit. The Bible depicts
the Holy Spirit as God's active presence in the world, in human history,
and in human experience. As the Great *Muntu*, he sustains the universe.
J.V. Taylor, using the African concept of force (*Ntu*), describes the Spirit
as the life force of creation.

> From within the depths of its being [the Spirit] urges every creature
> again and again to take one more tiny step in the direction of higher
> consciousness and personhood; again and again he creates for every
> creature the occasion for spontaneity and the necessity for choice, and at
> every turn he opposes self interest with a contrary principle of sacrifice,
> of existence for the other.[107]

As sustainer of creation, the Spirit can be said to have power *par excellence*. However since the Spirit is the manifestation of the Great *Muntu*,
we are to understand his power in the context of his powerlessness. He
brings power and powerlessness together in a profound and a different way. This means that he has power *par excellence*, but, at the same
time, some things happen in the world that he sustains that the human
observers may interpret as indicating either his absence or the absence
of his power.

The Holy Spirit as a hypostasis of God is depicted by the Christian
faith as radically Christocentric. This is evident in Luke's Acts 1:8,
which depicts the work of the Spirit as empowering the disciples of
Christ to be "my witnesses." F.D. Bruner sees the *Gospel According to St.
John* as offering the most comprehensive Christocentric approach to the
Holy Spirit. He observes the following:

---

[105] Setiloane, *African Theology: An Introduction*, 28.
[106] Mugambi, *The African Heritage and Contemporary Christianity*, 78.
[107] J.V. Taylor, *The Go-Between God: The Holy Spirit and the Christian Mission* (London:
SCM Press, 1972), 36.

1. It is Jesus who sends "another Paraclete" from the Father to be with the disciples forever in mission (14:16).

2. The Paraclete's special mission will be to teach the disciples "everything" ... that is—as Jesus amplifies—"to remind you of all that I have said to you" (14:26).

3. Jesus promises (in summary) that the Paraclete will "bear witness to me." (15:26).

4. Then, in the most extended discussion of the Spirit in the four Gospels, Jesus teaches the church that the Paraclete will convict the world of three great Christological errors related to sin, righteousness, and judgment—failure to believe in Jesus is the great sin; failure to see that Jesus' career is the meaning of righteousness is the great error; and failure to see that his work defeated the evil one is the great oversight (16:8–11).

5. The Paraclete will guide the church "into all the truth"—not in independence, for, Jesus adds, the Spirit "will not speak on its own, but whatever it will hear [through the Son from the Father] it will say" (16:13).

6. The Paraclete, says Jesus in global summary, "will glorify me, because the Spirit will take what is mine and explain it to you" (16:14).

7. The Holy Spirit, Jesus concludes, will teach the Christocentric truth that, in turn, teaches God, for, as Jesus concludes, when Jesus is talking about "what is mine," he is actually taking about what is God's: "Absolutely everything the Father has is mine, and that is why I could say to you that the Spirit will take what is mine and explain it to you" (16:15).[108]

The full implication of the Spirit's relationship to the Son is soteriology. The Spirit who has a common *Ntu* with both the Father and the Son applies to man's forgiveness and renewal, viz. justification and sanctification on the basis of Christ's finished work. In the words of Berkhof:

> ... the Spirit performs a twofold work in man. The first thing needed is that we know ourselves as unconditionally invited and accepted. We have to give up our distrust, our pride, our covetousness, our holding on to ourselves and start moving in the direction of our true destination. We can do that only through a radical self-condemnation which frees us from ourselves and sets us free to hear our acquittal. Going against our self-sufficiency, we must learn to seek our salvation outside ourselves, in the man who with his obedience stands in our place before God.

---

[108] F.D. Bruner, "The Son is God Inside Out: A Response to Stephen B. Bevans, SVD" in *International Bulletin of Missionary Research*, July 1998, 106.

> But this one man who stands in our place is at the same time the
> firstfruits of a renewed humanity. The Spirit takes us entirely as we are.
> But then he does not leave us as we are. We must begin to resemble the
> new man, we need to be transformed after his image.[109]

The Holy Spirit sets us free from ourselves, our neighbors, and other
categories of existence that fall under *Umuntu, Ikintu, Ahantu,* and *Ukuntu*
because he himself is ontologically superior to these categories. The
Holy Spirit frees us to conform to the image of the Son, who is the
true manifestation of the Father because the Spirit is the Spirit of the
Son and of the Father. Existences that fall under *Umuntu, Ikintu, Ahantu,*
and *Ukuntu* can only decrease or increase ones' vital force, but they
are powerless in as far as freeing and conforming men to the image
of God is concerned. Only the Great *Muntu* can absolutely free men
from *Umuntu, Ikintu, Ahantu,* and *Ukuntu* and orients the freed men to
the Great *Muntu* himself. Since the Holy Spirit does this biune work, he
must be the Great *Muntu.* Again it should be noted that the Holy Spirit
does not always have his way in us. We often resist and even cause him
grief.

CONCLUSION

The doctrine of God in African theology has remained at the level of
the African concepts of God for too long. This chapter has suggested
that the doctrine of God in African theology must remain biblical, but
at the same time it must be explained to the Africans by using the
intellectual tools in the African heritage. We cannot only speak about
the Christian understanding of God as *Nyame, Leza, Nyambe, Modimo,
Nyasaye,* and so on. If we are to understand *Nyasaye* (my mother tongue
word for God) in the Christian context, then, as we have indicated
elsewhere, we have to Christianize the concept of *Nyasaye* and begin
to speak about *Nyasaye Wuoro* (God the Father), *Nyasaye Wuowi* (God
the Son), and *Nyasaye Roho Maler* (God the Holy Spirit). Our picture
of God will have to go through modifications and it will look like
this:

---

[109] Berkhof, *Christian Faith,* 327.

Nyasaye Wuoro

↙   ↘

Nyasaye Wuowi   →   *Nyasaye Roho Maler*

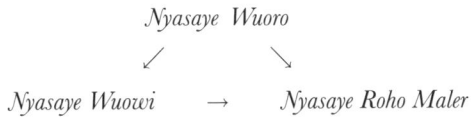

But Christianizing the African concepts of God is not enough. A Christianized African concept that is not explained to the African audiences using African metaphysics can look strange and confusing. Once we Christianize the African concept of God, it is important that we also explain the new nuance using the metaphysics native to the situation of reception.

CHAPTER ELEVEN

FOSTERING THE VIEW OF GOD AS 'GREAT *MUNTU*' MANIFESTED BY THE SON AND THE HOLY SPIRIT

INTRODUCTION

This chapter raises a fundamental, practical problem. It is one thing to propose a line of thought, but it is quite another thing to promote a new thought. One of the basic problems of theology in the context of Africa is that we never really recognize the ground that is already captured. Kwesi Dickson once noted that:

> ... the present stagnation [of theology] may be accounted for by reference to the fact that recent discussants often seem to be unaware of past discussions on the subject. Again and again contributions made at conferences have not been such as to build upon the insights which have already been gained into the subject.[1]

Of course, the neglect of captured ground can be explained by the intensity and speed of change—both at the level of the continent and globally. The other realities that can explain this difficulty are the historical, the practical, the political, the ecclesiastical, and the geographical reasons that have forced the theologies to be done in what Maluleke calls "isolated camps."[2] A possible way to remove the problem of the neglect of the captured ground is by isolating what has already been done and promoting it.

REASONS FOR PROMOTING THE VIEW OF GOD AS THE GREAT *MUNTU* MANIFESTED BY THE SON AND THE HOLY SPIRIT

Roughly four reasons can explain why we need to promote this paradigm of understanding the doctrine of God within the African theological situation. The first reason is the need for African Christians to know

---

[1] K.A. Dickson, *Theology in Africa* (Maryknoll: Orbis Books, 1984), 8.
[2] Maluleke, "Half Century of African Christian Theology," 5.

that the Christian faith understands God in Trinitarian terms. According to the Christian faith, God is the Father who is made known by the Son and the Holy Spirit. It is unfortunate that, as a general rule, Christian theologies view God "… as an abstract unity for reams of pages—the existence of God, the nature of God, the attributes of God—before finally arriving at a (sometimes brief) consideration of the fact that this God is Father, Son, and Holy Spirit."[3] This situation is contrary to the position of the church as it is reflected in the creeds that date from the third and fourth centuries. In the creeds, God is clearly named as the Father, the Son, and the Holy Spirit. African Christians need to know this fact and not be content with either the Christian theologies that view God as a monad or with the traditional African concepts of God.

But our interest is not merely to promote the doctrine of the Trinity. The African theological situation needs a Trinitarian perspective that is both biblical and relevant.[4] Part 2 of this research indicated that Western theologies have articulated theologies from perspectives that are authentically Western. A reading of Western theologies indicates that the West has never lost the intellectual heritage of Western antiquity. The questions for African inculturation theology are: Could we emulate the achievements of Western Christian scholarship at least on the issue of relevance? Is it possible to constructively reject the notion that the color black is a symbol of mediocrity, parasitism, and sterility? Throughout the centuries the West has involved itself in the formulation and the promotion of its own theologies. Christian scholarship in the African context can make full use of African strengths to formulate theology that is appropriate for the African context. Are the African theologians willing to engage in such a task?

The third reason for promoting a doctrine of the Trinity that is formulated from the point of view of the African is the significance of African Christianity to the global church. Christianity is already a major influence in Africa, and it is clearly part of the heritage of

---

[3] N. Needham, "The Filoque Clause: East or West" in *The Scottish Bulletin of Evangelical Theology*, 1997, 161.

[4] It is important to note that African theology has always respected the Bible. Mbiti once declared that "any viable theology must and should have a biblical basis" (Mbiti, *Concepts of God in Africa*, 90). Fashole-Luke is of the opinion that "the Bible is the basic and primary source for the development of African theology" (E.W. Fashole-Luke, "The Quest for African Christian Theologies" in *Mission Trends No. 3: Third World Theologies: Asian, African and Latin American Contributions to a RadicalTheological Realignment in the Church*. G. Anderson and T.F. Stransky, eds. (New York, Grand Rapids: Paulist, Eerdmans, 1976), 141.

contemporary Africa.[5] The statistics of David Barrett indicated that by the year 2000 Africa was to be largely Christian. Mbiti interprets Barrett's statistics of the Christian population in Africa today as amounting to about 370 million or 48.8% of the continent's population of 758 million.[6] In 1956, Roland Oliver noted the geometric progression of Christianity in Sub-Saharan Africa since 1912.[7] It is not surprising that A.F. Walls should believe that, in our own time, there has been a complete change in the center of gravity of Christianity from Europe and North America to Africa.[8] This change of gravity also means that the theology of the twenty-first century may well "depend on what has happened in the minds of African Christians in the interim."[9] But "what has happened in the minds of African Christians" cannot just remain in books and within reach of isolated camps; the proposals should be thorough, interesting, and public enough to warrant wider investigation. How can we contribute to the global theological situation when we ourselves are still wallowing in imported theology?

The fourth reason has to do with the need to urge the African church to be engaged in theological reflection. In a sense, the theologies that the Africans have written have not yet found their way to the roots of the church. Whereas Barrett and Walls have shown us the potential of theology in the African scene, George Kinoti has powerfully described the situation as it is. According to Kinoti:

---

[5] Whereas Mbiti believes that Christianity, Islam, and African traditional religions will continue to dominate Africa (Mbiti, *African Religions and Philosophy*, 262), A.A. Mazrui sees the three religions as a significant part of what properly constitutes the contemporary African heritage (A.A. Mazrui, *The Africans: A Triple Heritage* (Boston: Little, Brown, 1986). The true significance of Mazrui and Mbiti on the question of heritage is the fact that the African heritage can never be thought to be obsolete. There is vast literature which indicates that many Africans actually live at 'two levels.' The most prominent Christian sources on this problem are S.G. Williamson, *Akan Religion and the Christian faith* (Accra: Ghana University Press, 1965); K.A. Busia, *Report on a Social Survey—Secondi-Takoradi*, (London: Oxford University Press, 1950); K.A. Busia, *Africa in Search of Democracy*, (New York: Praeger, 1967); K. Little, "The Mende in Sierra Leone" in *African Worlds*, ed. D. Forde, (London: Oxford University Press, 1963); and G.M. Setiloane, "How the Traditional World-view Persists in the Christianity of Sotho-Tswana" in *Christianity in Independent Africa*, ed. Fashole-Luke (Bloomington: Indiana University Press, 1978).

[6] J.S. Mbiti, "Is the Bible in African Religion and African Religion in the Bible?" Unpublished paper delivered at EFSA and University of Stellenbosch, Department of Old and New Testaments International Workshop, 14–15 May, 1999, 1.

[7] R. Oliver, *The Missionary Factor in East Africa* (London: Longman, 1952), 8.

[8] Walls, "Towards understanding Africa's Place in Christian History," 180.

[9] Walls, "Towards understanding Africa's Place in Christian History," 183.

... there is a sense in which Christianity in Africa is the white man's religion. The denominations we belong to, the liturgies we use, the hymns we sing, the theologies which govern our beliefs and conduct, be they liberal or evangelical, are all made in the West. Most of the Christian books we read originate from the West and are usually written for Western readers. This is not to blame the Western church: it is time to say to the African Christians to begin to think and do things for themselves.[10]

Kinoti's observation is obviously an embarrassment to the 370 million Christians in Africa today.[11] Dick France clearly agrees with Kinoti when he suggests that the African church "needs more teaching and direction from within, not from without. It needs theology, its own African theology. Until this is achieved, ... [theology] will not grow in influence on the new Africa, and it will be increasingly dismissed as a legacy from the colonial past."[12] Who will think for us if we do not accept the challenge to think and formulate theological responses to our questions ourselves?

There is no doubt that African Christianity needs to think and do things for herself if the prediction of Walls is to be a reality.[13] What France proposes here for the African Christians is not just the need to think, but the need to think critically; a kind of thinking that is willing to use the African intellectual resources to serve theology. Critical reflection for African Christian scholarship will mean that we can no longer take our own metaphysics for granted. Then we can engage such cognitive skills as interpretation, analysis, evaluation, infer-

---

[10] Kinoti, *Hope for Africa*, 74, 75.

[11] Note that C.G. Baeta recognized in 1968 that "the figures derived from official church sources, represent far less than the actual numbers of professing Christians" (*Christianity in Tropical Africa* (London: Oxford University Press, 1968), xii). This could be the situation on the ground today as well.

[12] Dick France quoted in T. Adeyemo, *Reflections on the State of Christianity in Africa* (Potchefstroom: Instituut vir Reformatoriese Studie, Potchefstroomse Universiteit CHO, 1995), 5.

[13] How does the missionary or the expatriate fit into this scheme of things? The missionaries and the expatriates are part of the universal Christian community whose role in working out local theologies should be that of removing "... obstacles in the way of the Spirit, and to share its own experience, light and judgment" (L.J. Luzbetak, *The Church and Cultures: New Perspectives in Missiological Anthropology* (Maryknoll: Orbis Books, 1988), 70). In this way the missionaries, the outside experts, and the entire universal Christian community still have an important part to play—the task of bringing to local theology an 'outside' experience that is crucial if the theology is to be saved "... of turning in on itself, becoming self-satisfied with its own achievements" (R.J. Schreiter, *Constructing Local Theologies* (Maryknoll: Orbis Books, 1985), 19).

ence, explanation, and self-regulation from our own conceptual frame-works.[14] The West does this in their theology, why not us? It should be noted that these are not skills that one comes to possess simply by instinct. They come as a result of intensive study, long reflection, persistence, and interest. African Christian thinkers must be willing to apply these virtues to their tasks if they are to foster their own theological proposals and to offer valuable contributions to the global theological situation.

The Method of Fostering the Proposed View of God

Search for an Appropriate Model

The American Catholic theologian, David Tracey, speaks about the 'publics' of theology. His position is that there are three publics of theology—the university, the believing community, and the public arena. The task of theology and of how theology may be fostered in each of these publics differs significantly. If theology has not understood its own public, there is most likely going to be "internal confusion and external chaos."[15] Fostering Trinitarianism within the African theological situation should occur within each of these three publics (the academy, the church, and the community).

It seems, however, that in order to promote the proposed doctrine of God in these publics, we have to devise a model that is equal to the task. In the context of Thambo Mbeki's *African Renaissance*, the Africans are already being called upon to solve their own problems. This call is not just limited to the areas of economics, technology, science, arts, and politics. Mbeki's immediate interest is obviously in the area of politics; however, the call touches all areas of the African existence, including the area of intellectual development. As Mbeki explains:

> In a world in which the generation of new knowledge and its application to change the human condition is the engine which moves the human

---

[14] See P. Facione's article for a detailed analysis of the characterization of the cognitive skills involved in critical thinking (P. Facione, "Critical Thinking: A Statement of Expert Consensus for Purposes of Educational Assesment and Instruction". Research Findings and Recommendations Prepared for the American Philosophical Association, 1989).

[15] D. Tracey, *The Anological Imagination: Christian Theology and the Culture of Pluralism* (New York: Crossroad, 1981), 3, 5.

society further and further away from barbarism, do we not need to recall Africa's hundreds of thousands of intellectuals back from their places of immigration in Western Europe and North America, to rejoin those who remain still within our shore?

I dream of a day when these, the African mathematicians and computer specialists in Washington and New York, the African physicists, engineers, doctors, business managers and economists will return from London and Manchester and Paris and Brussels to add to the African pool of brain power, to inquire into and find solutions to Africa's problems and challenges, to open the African door to the world of knowledge, to elevate Africa's place within the universe of research, the formation of new knowledge, education and information.

Africa's renewal demands that her intelligentsia must immerse itself in the titanic and all—round struggle to end poverty, ignorance, disease, and backwardness inspired by the fact that the Africans of Egypt were, in some instances two thousand years ahead of European Greece in the mastery of such subjects as geometry, trigonometry, algebra and chemistry.[16]

Theology, and especially how we understand God, is obviously one of the areas upon which this call bears significantly. We must move our understanding of God beyond the mere cultural identity debate, and start to view our Christian understanding of God as part of theology's effort to address Africa's intellectual culture. It is also a task which avails Africa's constructive contributions to the global theological situation. The challenge then is: How do we formulate the doctrine of God in a way that is cognizant of the African metaphysics as well as of the questions of Africa, while at the same time contributing to theological knowledge at the global level? Are there well-established and credible methods? Creativity researchers seem to agree on the interactive model. This model of reflection focuses on creativity, critical thinking, and application. These are very important qualities when it comes to formulating, nurturing, and disseminating thoughts.

The Interactive Model

A recent investigation of the elements of the interactive model (Busse & Mansfield) has led to the conclusion that in order to concretely address a problem one has to go through a series of steps similar to those

---

[16] T. Mbeki, "Africa's Renaissance Desperately needs your Help" in *Cape Times*, August 17, 1998.

recommended by Rossman, Wallas, and Dewey. The table below is a summary of the steps in the interactive model as envisioned by these three creativity researchers.[17]

Rossman (1931) *Invention*	Wallas (1926) *Creative Production*	Dewey (1910) *Problem Solving*
1. Need or difficulty observed	1. Preparation (problem stated; information obtained; attitude set toward appropriate solution)	1. A felt difficulty (problem found)
2. Analysis; problem defined	2. Incubation (unconscious generation of potential solutions)	2. Definition and location of difficulty (problem formulated)
3. Information surveyed; possible occurrence of incubation	3. Illumination ('Eureka!' or 'Aha!'- idea emerges from subconscious)	3. Suggestion of possible solution(s)
4. Many possible solutions formulated	4. Verification (evaluation of solution)	4. Development of implications of solution(s) through reasoning.
5. Critical evaluation of solutions; sustained and ongoing incubation, particularly in complex problems		5. Experimental corroboration of conjectural solution
6. Formulation of new ideas, 'inventions,' and solutions		
7. Evaluation and refinement of most promising solution; acceptance of final solution		

The five steps below take important elements not only from Rossman, Wallas, and Dewey, whose inputs are summarized in the table above, but they also take elements from Osborne and Guilford.[18] According to the summaries of Annis and Brown, the five steps of the problem finding / problem solving model involve (1) recognizing or selecting the

---

[17] See R.T. Brown, "Creativity: What are we to Measure?" in *Handbook of Creativity*, J.A. Glover, R.R. Ronning, and C.R. Reynolds, eds. (New York: Plenum Press, 1989), 3–32.

[18] See Dacey's summary of problem solving according to Wallas, Dewey, Osborne, and Guilford. J.S. Dacey, *Fundamentals of Creative Thinking* (Lexington: D.C. Heath, 1989).

problem, (2) clarifying and representing the elements of the problem as
an extended effort to solving it, (3) proposing solutions to the problem
or setting constraints on existing solutions to the problem, (4) testing
and evaluating or restructuring the solutions, and (5) revising, restating,
and re-evaluation or simply verification and elaboration.[19]

Promoting the Proposed Doctrine of God

The steps suggested above are based on the view that theology is a
problem-finding / problem-solving undertaking. This is consonant with
Saint Anselm's definition of theology as *fides quarens intellectum*. In the
recent past, Professor Daniel Migliore resuscitated this line of thought
in his book, *Faith Seeking Understanding*.[20] It is not possible to adequately
understand the meaning of faith without engaging problem-finding and
problem-solving mechanisms. In order for me to understand what my
faith[21] means to me, I must be willing to have and exercise certain
attitudes and sets of skills that have been summarized in the twin
phenomena of creativity and critical thinking by problem-finding and
problem-solving researchers.

The problem-finding / problem-solving approach as a way of promoting the doctrine of God is not only relevant given the situation
of modern Africa[22] and the complex cultural heritage which provides
the matrix within which Africa's concepts of God are embedded, it is
also appropriate because it is the emerging paradigm for understanding
issues that require an enormous amount of creativity and critical think-

---

[19] D.B. Annis, "Fostering Creativity in Philosophy" in *Metaphilosophy* vol. 29 nos 1/ 2,
January – April, 1998, 96–99. See also Brown, "Creativity: What are we to Measure?",
5.

[20] D.J. Louw, however, believes that since theology is science of interpretation and
understanding, it cannot fully be captured by the concept of *fides quarens intellectum*.
For Louw, theology has a three-fold description: *fides quarens intellectum* (faith seeking
understanding of God which is linked to our human quest for meaning), *fides quarens
verbum* (faith seeking different ways of communication and conversing in order to foster
the discourse and encounter between God, mankind and creation), and *fides quarens
actum* (faith seeking different ways of doing the will of God so as to relate the church to
our quest for meaning). D.J. Louw, *Pastoral Hermeneutics of Care and Encounter: A Theological
Design for a Basic Theory of Anthropology and Therapy*. (Cape Town: Lux Verbi, 1998).

[21] As Cantwell Smith has explained, faith can be truly personal: "My faith is an act
that I make myself, naked before God" (W.C. Smith, *The Meaning and end of Religion*
(London: SPCK, 1978), 1991).

[22] See Kinoti, *Hope for Africa*, chapter 2 for a detailed analysis of the modern problems of Africa.

ing.[23] The doctrine of God that we hold and teach must not only be biblical and relevant, it must also show that some critical thinking and creativity has gone into it.[24] The steps below are adopted from the summaries of Annis, Brown, Rossman, Wallas, and Dewey and reworked to suit our purpose.

Step One: Abstract an Account of the Doctrine of the Trinity

In order to abstract an account of the doctrine of the Trinity, one has to have large and fluent knowledge of the Christian doctrine of God. One must not only be in a position to identify the problem areas within the doctrine and deal with the inadequate explanations currently offered within the Christian theological circles, but he / she must also be willing to offer a well-considered explanation of the doctrine of the Trinity. This is where a keen understanding of the historical debates, as well as a good grasp of significant theologians of the church, is crucial.

We (in African theology) must seek to understand what the Bible means by emphasizing one God, while at the same time teaching the divinity of the Son and of the Holy Spirit. We have to search for ourselves how the church fathers understood God when they formulated the creeds that have been inherited by us. The creeds have had rein-

---

[23] Creativity and critical thinking are related. In order to be creative one has to have the skill of critical thinking. Both creativity and critical thinking require the application of the right attitude as well as such largely accepted cognitive skills as interpretation, analysis, evaluation, inference, explanation, and self-regulation (Annis, "Fostering Creativity in Philosophy," 98). Creativity researchers have found that these skills are applied through at least five steps; none of which is adequate in and of itself and all of them are necessary. The steps are: (1) recognizing or selecting the problem, (2) clarifying and representing the elements of the problem as an extended effort to solving it, (3) proposing solutions to the problem, (4) testing and evaluating or restructuring the solutions, and (5) revising, restating, and re-evaluation or simply verification and elaboration (see Annis, "Fostering Creativity in Philosophy," 96–99; Brown, "Creativity: What are we to Measure?", 5 f.)

[24] Note that many 'Creativity' researchers have the view that creativity itself is a special case of problem solving. With creativity one arrives at a novel and a valuable solution to a problem. For example, see Newell, Shaw, and Simon. Creativity, explains Annis, "… involves a complex interaction of various (a) cognitive competencies, traits, processes, and activities, and (b) personality, attitudinal, and motivational traits. Various "environmental" conditions, such as developmental experiences in the family and school as well as in the social and the historical context, also play and important role. Within the cognitive category, creativity requires the development and effective use of a large and a fluid knowledge base, critical thinking, problem solving, decision making, and metacognitive skills" (Annis, "Fostering Creativity in Philosophy," 96).

terpretations in different directions by scholars and faith communities. We cannot bypass these efforts in our own search for a reinterpretation that is appropriate for the African context. If we are going to engage in informed theological discourses with the wider theological fraternity, we cannot afford to short-circuit the contributions to the Trinitarian debate by individual theologians such as Augustine, Aquinas, Calvin, Barth, and many others. To listen to what these theologians say is to function within a universal Christian story. To function within the universal Christian story, or as Vincent of Lerins emphasized in *Commonitorium* II, 1–3, "what has been believed everywhere, always and by all" is not to fall into Eurocentric formation. The African church is part of the universal church; it does not have another story. It is the same universal story that the African theology must identify, listen to, and clarify for the African audience.

Step Two: Find Out How This Account is a Problem to the African Mind

Here we are basically concerned with what Annis calls "problem clarification and representation." We clarify and represent the problem by asking and providing answers to such questions as: "What are the elements of the problem? What are the relevant issues involving it? How is the problem to be represented so that it can be explored and solved?"[25]

The doctrine of the Trinity is a problem to the African mind in at least four ways. In the first place, the doctrine comes to us clothed in either Neo-Platonism or Idealism. We see these models of interpreting reality clearly in the theological terms: 'substance' and 'persons.' As we have demonstrated in this research, the African people do not think in either Neo-Platonic or Idealistic terms. They do not understand the theological concepts 'substance' and 'persons' in the terms of either the Neo-Platonists or the Idealists. The conceptual framework of the African peoples is best captured by the *Ntu* concept, and, as we have already seen, the *Ntu* metaphysics has its own way of understanding substance or being and person. How are we to reinterpret the doctrine of the Trinity for a people whose way of understanding *being* or *substance* and *person* is so different?

---

[25] Annis, "Fostering Creativity in Philosophy," 97.

Then there is the theological problem that is raised by the three persons. As we have indicated in the previous sections, the African cosmology does not allow the African to think in Trinitarian terms. For him God is one, and no one else shares the divine category with him. How do we instill in our people the view that God has made himself known in the Son and the Holy Spirit? How do we help the African Christians to understand that the Son and the Holy Spirit are not just manifestation of the Father in the sense in which the sun and the moon, for example, are manifestations of *Nyasaye*?[26] How do we help the African Christians to know that the Son and the Holy Spirit are not similar to the African teaching about God creating lesser beings who are godlike and have God's powers, but who are subject to God? In other words, how do we teach the theological concept of 'three Persons in one God' to a people whose nomenclature does not seem to allow for plurality in God?

Besides the problem of the 'one and the many' in the God language of the Christian faith, there is also the problem of God-man. Kirwen has captured the difficulty this causes for the God language in the traditional African setting.

> … Kiteme is so different from humanity that it is impossible for human-ity to be joined with God in one life as you teach. How can God be part of his own creation? Do not your teachings about Jesus Christ dilute the true nature of God by bringing God physically into the world of human-ity? Are you trying to say that God was also a human being who was born, ate, slept, suffered, got sick, and died? But what is your point? What does this add to your understanding of God? And to interpret the cruel, inhuman death of Jesus as a sign of God's love makes a mockery of God. Indeed, Jesus' death on the cross reinforces our belief that evil is within the human community and that God has nothing to do with evil. Jesus' death could only be the result of the evil wills of other persons, wills that would not have had any power over God if Jesus were truly God.[27]

The questions that the God language raises in the African context for the Christian view of God-man have been clearly captured by the excerpt above. How do we deal with these questions?

And then there is the problem of the suitability of African terms for the theological enterprise. Are there African terms that can convey

---

[26] M.C. Kirwen, *The Missionary and the Diviner: Contending Theologies of Christian and African Religions.* (Maryknoll: Orbis Books, 1987), 5.

[27] Kirwen, *The Missionary and the Diviner*, 16.

the deep theological issues that are encapsulated in the traditional
Trinitarian formula? Of course, as Lamin D. Sanneh says, the gospel
truth can be expressed in the conceptual forms of every culture.[28]
Kwame Bediako also argues strongly for the significance of the capacity
to transpose the Christian message from its biblical matrix into the
categories of understanding available in the indigenous cultures.[29] As
we have demonstrated, there is no doubt that the doctrine of the
Trinity can be expressed for Africans using the African metaphysics.
But how willing are we to search and locate the necessary intellectual
tools and symbols for this task within our conceptual framework? Will
the tools and symbols gain acceptance among us and within the global
theological situation? In other words, are we willing to be different
and will the global theological fraternity accept the fact that we are
different? Put in another way: Will the African tools and symbols gain
recognition and respect within the global theological situation?

Step Three: Propose Solution(s) to the Problem(s)

The solutions proposed depend, to a great extent, on the nature of
the problems identified. In step two, we noted four problems that the
account of the doctrine of the Trinity poses to African God language.
In a sense, this whole book is an attempt to address these problems. We
have, for example, proposed the following solutions:

1) The African God language as replacement for the Neo-Platonic and
Idealistic nomenclatures. Theology should be willing to do research
into and make use of the infrastructure of the African metaphysics to
express the truth. This is important because how people speak about
the reality around them is hidden in their cultures, and, as Mbiti once
said:

> Without culture, the Gospel can not encounter people. Yet, by its very
> nature, even though expressed and communicated within the limits of
> culture, the Gospel is itself beyond culture. The beyondness of the Gospel
> derives from the fact that God is the author of the Gospel while man is
> the author of culture. Culture makes us very earthly and human, the
> Gospel makes us very heavenly and divine. It is not culture, but the
> Gospel, which has the final say over us as human beings. Yet the Gospel

---

[28] L. Sanneh, *Translating the Message: Missionary Impact on Culture*. Maryknoll: Orbis
Books, 1989.
[29] Bediako, *Theology and Identity*, 426–441.

makes us new people in Christ within the framework of our culture and not apart from it. For that reason, the Gospel and culture are not mutually contradictory or in conflict—since man (and not culture) is the sinner and the Gospel changes man whatever culture makes him to be. ... If we take it that the Gospel is intended for the whole man in the whole world (*oikumene*) and creation ... then the church must take African culture seriously. In the book of Revelation, the final picture of the new creation is one in which, among other things, the people of the whole world, bring into the holy city, the new Jerusalem, "the glory and the honour of the nations" (Rev.21). I believe that Africa is spiritually capable of bringing its contribution of glory, to the city of God, through the elements of our religiosity and culture—healed, saved, purified and sanctified by the by the Gospel.[30]

2) Description of *homousios* using the *Ntu* concept. According to the African cosmology, there is only one Great *Muntu*. According to the Christian faith, the Great *Muntu* has a common *Ntu* with the Son and the Holy Spirit. What the African understands by 'being' and 'person' cannot be short-circuited in a task that seeks to transpose the traditional meaning of the Trinity onto the African cultural milieu. Using the African metaphysics rather than Neo-Platonism or Hegelianism to describe the standard Trinitarian formula of 'One Substance Three Persons' means that we are to reflect on the African metaphysics of God, substance and person. In the African thought, one God is not a static substance or nature described by the concept of *Ntu*; rather, the concept of One God refers to the Great *Muntu*. The African ontology knows of only one Great *Muntu*. To say that the Great *Muntu* has made himself known in three persons is to say that the Son and the Holy Spirit are perfect reflections of the Great *Muntu*. Each of these persons is a perfect reflection of the Great *Muntu* because each has a genuine *Muntu* that is not merely a tributary of the Great *Muntu*, but a genuine *Muntu* that is the Great *Muntu* himself.

3) Approach theology from the point of view of *fides quarens intellectum*. This approach allows me to address the issues of the God-man. The traditional African God language does not accept the doctrine of the Incarnation. But, as an African Christian, I have the right to use the intellectual resources of my culture to understand what the Christian

---

[30] J.S. Mbiti, "Christianity and African Culture" in *Facing the New Challenges—The Message of PACLA, 9–19 Dec 1976*. M. Cassidy and L. Verlinden, eds. (Kisumu: Evangel Publishing House, 1978), 281.

faith means by God-man. In his life on earth, the Son fully manifested the Great *Muntu*. Therefore, he must be the Great *Muntu* himself, since only God can fully manifest the Great *Muntu*.

4) It is not in our power to predict the nature of the response that these proposals are likely to generate. At the moment, these proposals are tentative, although we can hold them with integrity.

Step Four: Test and Evaluate the Solution(s)

The questions that are useful here are: Are the solutions in step three above consistent with the Christian tradition? Do they have systematic potential? Are they capable of addressing the challenges in the African context? Can I hold the solutions with personal integrity? This step assumes that we have a personal faith that we hold dear, that we understand the doctrine in question, and that we have made full advantage of the reflections of the universal church. Also important for this step is our grasp of the African concepts of God and the way the African metaphysics works.

Step Five: Revise, Restate, and Re-evaluate

This stage reminds us of the tentative nature of theology. Although I have suggested solutions to the problems of Trinitarianism in the African context, and although I can hold the proposals with integrity for the time being, I am aware that the proposals must remain tentative. This is an in-built structure within this model which ensures that we make constant adjustments to the solution(s) we propose in the light of new findings. This is possible only as we go through the five steps of the interactive model again and again.

CONCLUSION

Whereas Trinitarianism needs to take root in the African academy, an effort should be made to ensure that the believing community gets focused attention in this regard as well. The African Christian interacts with his environment and social setting in many complex ways. In all these interactions it is still true, as Placide Tempels once said, that Africans live more by "Being" than by following their own ideas.[31] Mbiti, in a way, corroborated Tempels when he said that the African is incurably religious. Religion, Mbiti explains, "permeates into all the departments of life so fully that it is not easy or possible always to isolate it."[32] The other African scholars who think in these terms are J.B. Danquah and Bolaji Idowu. Danquah argues that religion—especially the concept of God—significantly influences the moral attitude of the African.[33] Idowu indicates that Africans do not make an attempt to separate morality and religion "and it is impossible for them to do so without disastrous consequences."[34]

It is important for the Christian faith to know that the concept of God significantly influences the choices of an African. In traditional Africa, how people relate to the spirit world, to the ancestors, to the others in the community, to the animal world, and to the inanimate zone links significantly with how they understand God. The African Christian must not understand the Christian view of God only superficially. The mistake of understanding the Christian view of God superficially leads to a situation in which the African Christian does not know what to do with the African traditional past, his environment, the community, and other religions that are present. We guard against a superficial understanding of God by fully Christianizing the African concepts of God, by indigenizing the Christian understanding of God, and by encouraging our academies and churches to be involved in the gigantic task of thinking creatively and critically about the Christian view of God.

---

[31] Tempels, *Bantu Philosophy*, 23.
[32] Mbiti, *African Religions and Philosophy*, 1, 262.
[33] J.B. Danquah, *The Akan Doctrine of God* (London: Frank Cass, 1968), 2, 3, 16.
[34] B. Idowu, *Olodumare: God in Yoruba Belief* (London: Longman, 1962), 145 f.

SELECTED BIBLIOGRAPHY

Adeyemo, T. *Salvation in African Tradition*. Nairobi: Evangel Publishing House, 1979.
———. *Reflections on the State of Christianity in Africa*. Potchefstroom: Instituut vir Reformatoriese Studie, Potchefstroomse Universiteit CHO, 1995.
Anderson, A. *Moya: The Holy Spirit in and African context*. Pretoria: University of South Africa, 1991.
———. *Bazalwane: African Pentecostals in South Africa*. Pretoria: University of South Africa, 1992.
Andersson, E. *Messianic Prophet Movements in the Lower Congo*. Uppsala Studic Ethnographica Upsaliensia, 1958.
Annis, D.B. "Fostering Creativity in Philosophy" in *Metaphilosophy* vol. 29 nos. 1/2, January – April, pp. 95–106, 1998.
Albright, F.H. *New Horizons in Biblical Research*. London, 1966.
Apostel, L. *African Philosophy: Myth or Reality?* Gent: E. Story-Scientia, 1981.
Appiah, K.A. *In my Father's House: African in Philosophy of Culture*. NewYork: Oxford University Press, 1962.
Aristotle. *Metaphysics*. trans. W.D. Rose in vol. 8 of *The Works of Aristotle translated into English*, ed. J.A. Smith and W.D. Ross. England: Oxford University Press, 1912–1952.
Athenagoras of Athens. *Supplicatio*. In *Ante-Nicene Fathers: Translations of the Writings of the Fathers Down to Ad 325* Vol II. Eds. A. Roberts and J. Donaldson. Grand Rapids: Wm. B. Eerdmans, 1951.
Athanasius, Bishop of Alexandria. *De Synodis*. In *Nicene and and post-Nicene Fathers of the Christian Church*. Vol. IV. Ed. P. Schaff. Grand Rapids: Wm B. Eerdmans.
———. *Contra Arianos*. In *Nicene and and post-Nicene Fathers of the Christian Church*. Vol IV. ed. P. Schaff. Grand Rapids: Wm B. Eerdmans.
———. *Ad Serapionem de morte Arii*. In *Nicene and and post-Nicene Fathers of the Christian Church*. Vol IV. ed. P. Schaff. Grand Rapids: Wm. B. Eerdmans.
Augustine, Bishop of Hippo. *De Trinitate*. In *Basic Writings of St Augustine*. Vol II. ed. E.J. Oates. New York: Random House Publishers, 1948.
———. *Confessions*. In *Nicene and and Post-Nicene Fathers of the Christian Church*. Vol I. ed. P. Schaff. Grand Rapids: Wm. B. Eerdmans.
———. *Contra Academicos*. trans and annotated by J.J. O'Meara. New York: Newman, 1951.
Aquinas, T. *On Being and Essence*. trans. R.P. Goodwin. Indianapolis: Bobbs–Merril, 1965.
———. *Summa Theologica*. 3 Volumes. trans. by Fathers of English Dominican Province. New York: Benzinger Brothers, inc., 1947.
———. *Summa Contra Gentiles*. First published in 1956 as *On the Truth of the*

Catholic Faith. trans. A.C . Pegis, J.F. Anderson and V.J. Bourke. Notre Dame: University of Notre Dame Press, 1975.

Bahemuka, J.H. "The Hidden Christ in African Traditional Religion" in *Jesus in African Christianity: Experimentation and Diversity in African Christology.* eds. J.N.K. Mugambi and L. Magesa. Nairobi: Initiaves Ltd, pp. 1–6, 1989.

Barrett, D.B. *Kenya Churches Handbook.* Kisumu: Evangel Publishing House, 1973.

Barth, C. *God with Us: A Theological Introduction to the Old Testament.* ed. G.W. Bromiley. Grand Rapids: Wm. B. Eerdmans Publishing Company, 1991.

Barth, K. *Church Dogmatics I/1.* trans. G.T. Thompson. Edinburgh: T & T Clark, 1960.

——. *Church Dogmatics I/2.* Second edition, 1975.

——. *Church Dogmatics II/1.* trans. by Parker, Johnston, Knight and Haire. Edinburgh: T & T Clark, 1957.

——. *Church Dogmatics IV/1.*

——. *Anselm: Fides Quaerens Intellectum: Anselm's Proof of God in the Context of his Theological Scheme.* London: SCM Press.

Bartlet, J.R. "Yahweh and Quas: A Response to Martin Rose" in *JSOT* 5, pp. 29–38, 1978.

Basil "the Great" *De Spiritu Sancto.* In *Nicene and and post-Nicene Fathers of the Christian Church.* Vol VIII. ed. P. Schaff. Grand Rapids: Wm. B. Eerdmans.

BCC. *The Forgotten Trinity: The Report of the BCC Study Commission on Trinitarian Doctrine Today* vol. I. London: British Council of Churches, Interchurch House, 1989.

Beatie, J. and Middleton, J. *Spirit Mediumship and Society in Africa.* New York: Africa Publishing Corporation, 1969.

Beckwith, R. *Confessing the Faith in the Church of England.* Oxford: Latimer Studies 9, 1981.

Bediako, K. *Theology and Identity.* Oxford: Regnum Books, 1992.

——. *Christianity in Africa: The Renewal of a non- Western Religion* Edinburgh: Edinburgh University Press, 1995.

——. "The Doctrine of Christ and the Significance of Vernacular Terminology" in *International Bulletin of Missionary Research,* July, 1998, pp. 110–111, 1998.

Behrend, H. *Alice Lakwena and the Holy Spirits: War in Nothern Uganda 1985–1997.* Nairobi: EAEP, 1999.

Bell, R.H. "Narrative in African Philosophy" in *Philosophy,* 64, pp. 363–379, 1989.

Berkhof, H. *Introduction to the Study of Dogmatics.* trans. J. Vriend. Grand Rapids: William B. Eeerdmans Publishing Company, 1985.

——. *Christian Faith: An Introduction to the Study of the Faith.* trans. S. Woudstra. Grand Rapids: William B. Eerdmans Publishing Company, 1979.

Bietenhard, H. "Onoma" in *Theological Dictionary of the New Testament.* ed. G. Kittel, trans. G.W. Bromiley. Grand Rapids: Wm B. Eerdmans, 1967.

p'Bitek, O. *African Religions in Western Scholarship.* Kampala: East African Literature Bureau, 1970.

——. *Religion of the Central Luo.* Nairobi: East African Literature Bureau, 1971.

Boethius, A.M.S. *The Theological Tractates and the Consolation of Philosophy*. Revised and Translated by Stewart H.F. and Rand E.K. London: William Heinemann.

Boff, L. *Trinity and Society*. Burns & Oates, 1988.

Bondi, R. "Some Issues Relevant to a Modern Interpretation of the Language of the Nicene Creed, With Special Reference to Sexist Language" in *Union Seminary Quarterly*, vol. 40 No. 3, pp. 21–30, 1985.

Bosch, D.J. *Transforming Mission: Paradigm Shift in Theology of Mission*. Maryknoll: Orbis Books, 1991.

———. "The Problem of Evil in Africa: A Survey of African Views of Witchcraft and of the Response of the Christian Church" in *Like a Roaring Lion*. ed. P. de Villiers, pp. 38–62, 1987.

———. "God in Africa; Implications for Kerygma". *Missionalia* Vol. 1 No. 1, pp. 3–21, 1973.

Bouquet, A.C. *Man and Deity*. Cambridge: Hefter, 1933.

Braaten, C.E. *Our Naming of God: Problems and Prospects of God-Talk Today*. Minneapolis: Fortress Press, 1981.

Bray, G. *Creeds, Councils and Christ*. Leicester: Inter–Varsity Press, 1984.

———. "Explaining Christianity to Pagans: The Second Century Apologists" in the *Trinity in a Pluralistic Age: Theological Essays on Culture and Religion*. ed. K.J. Vanhoozer. Grand Rapids: William B. Eerdmans Publishing Co., pp. 9–25, 1997.

Bright, J. *The Authority of the Old Testament*. London: SCM Press, 1967.

Brown, D. *The Divine Trinity*. Duckworth, 1985.

Brown, R.T. "Creativity: What are we to Measure?" in Handbook of Creativity, ed. J.A. Glover, R.R. Ronning, and C.R. Reynolds. New York: Plenum Press, 3–32, 1989.

Brown, W.A. *Christian Theology in Outline*. Edinburgh: T & T Clark, 1907.

Brümmer, V. "The Identity of the Christian Tradition". A paper delivered at the Faculty of Theology, University of Stellenbosch, 1998.

———. "Metaphorical Thinking and Systematic Theology". A paper delivered at the Faculty of Theology, University of Stellenbosch, 1998.

Bruner, F.D. "The Son is God Inside Out: A Response to Stephen B. Bevans, SVD" in *International Bulletin of Missionary Research*, July 1998, pp. 106–109.

Brunner, E. *Revelation and Reason*. SCM Press, 1947.

Budge, E.A.W. *From Fetish to God in Ancient Egypt*. London: Oxford University Press, 1934.

Burman, T.E. *Religious Polemic and the Intellectual History of the Mozarabs, c. 1050–1200*. Leiden, 1994.

Busia, K.A. "The Ashanti of Gold Coast" in *African Worlds*. Ed. Daryll Forde. London: Oxford University Press, 1963.

Busse, T.V. & Mansfield, R.S. "Theories of Creative Process: A View and a Perspective" in *Journal of Creative Behaviour*, 14, pp. 91–103, 1980.

Butler, D.J. *Four Philosophies and their Practice in Education and Religion*. New York: Harper and Brothers Publishers, 1950.

Callaway, H. *The Religious System of the Amazulu*. Routledge and Kagan Paul, 1870.

Calvin, J. *Institutes of the Christian Religion.* trans. F.L. Battles. London: Collins. 1986.

Clement of Alexandria. *Protreptikos* (Address to the Greeks). In *Ante-Nicene Fathers: Translations of the Writings of the Fathers Down to Ad 325* Vol. II. eds. A. Roberts and J. Donaldson. Grand Rapids: Wm. B. Eerdmans, 1951.

Collins, P. "A Critical Survey of recent Wrtings in the Field of Trinitarian Theology" in *Epworth Review* vol. 24, pp. 95–99, 1997.

Congar, Y. *I Believe in the Holy Spirit vol. iii: The River of Life Flows in the East and in the West.* trans. D. Smith. London: Geoffrey Chapman, 1983.

Curtin, P.D. *The Image of Africa: British Ideas and Action, 1780–1850.* Madison: The University of Wisconsin Press, 1964.

Dacey, J.S. *Fundamentals of Creative Thinking.* Lexington: D.C. Heath, 1989.

Danielou, J. *A History of the Christian Doctrine Before the Council of Nicea, Volume I.* Trans. and ed. by Baker, J.A. London: Darton, Longmann & Todd, 1964.

———. *The Theology of Jewish Christianity.* trans. and ed. by J.A. Baker. London: Darton, Longman, and Todd, 1964.

Danquah, J.B. *The Akan Doctrine of God.* London: Frank Cass, 1968.

Davies, B. "Aquinas, God and Being". *The Monist,* vol. 80 no. 4, pp. 500–520, 1997.

Davies, W.D. *Paul and Rabbinic Judaism: Some Rabbinic Elements in Pauline Theology.* London: SPCK, 1970.

Dewey, J. *How we Think.* Boston: DC Heath, 1910.

Diagne, P. "History and Linguistics" in *General History of Africa Volume I: Methodology and Prehistory.* Ed. J. Ki-Zerbo. California: UNESCO, pp. 233–255, 1981.

Dickson, K.A. *Theology in Africa.* Maryknoll, London: Orbis Books, 1984.

———. "Towards a Theologia Africana" in *New Testament Christianity for Africa and the World.* eds. E.W. Fashole-Luke and M.E. Glasswell. London: SPCK, pp. 198–208, 1974.

Diop, C.A. *Precolonial Black Africa.* trans. H. Salemson. Trenton: Africa World Press Edition, 1987.

Dirven, P. "The Maria Legio: The Dynamics of a Break Away Church among the Luo in East Africa." PhD dissertation. Rome: Pontifica University Gregon, 1970.

Duck, R.C. *Gender and the Name of God: The Trinitarian Baptism Formula.* New York: Pilgrim Press, 1991.

Esterhuysen, P. (Ed) *African A–Z: Continental and Country Profiles.* Pretoria: African Institute of South Africa (AISA), 1998.

Evans-Pritchard, E.E. *Nuer Religion.* London: Oxford University Press, 1956.

Farmer, H.H. *Revelation and Religion: Studies in the Theological Interpretation of Religious Types.* James Nisbet and Company Ltd., 1954.

Facione, P. "Critical Thinking: A Statement of Expert Consensus for Purposes of Educational Assesment and Instruction". Research Findings and Recommendations Prepared for the American Philosophical Association, 1989.

Ferré, F. *Language, Logic, and God.* New York: Harper & Brothers, 1961.

Fichte, J.G. *Science of Knowledge* with the first and second introductions. New York: Meredith, 1970.

Fuller, C.E. "God of African Thought and Life" in *God in Contemporary Thought*. New York: Learned Publications, pp. 19–47, 1977.

Fulton, W. "Trinity" in *Encyclopedia of Religion and Ethics*. ed. J. Hastings. Edinburgh: T &T Clark, pp. 458–464, 1921.

Gehman, R.J. *African Traditional Religion in Biblical Perspective*. Kijabe: Kesho Publications, 1989.

Gilkey, L. *Naming the Whirlwind: The Renewal of God Language*. Indianapolis: Bobs–Merril, 1969.

Goldingay, J. *Approaches to Old Testament Interpretation*. Leicester: Inter–Varsity Press, 1981.

Gonzalez, J.L. *A History of Christian Thought, Volume III*. Abington: Abington Press, 1975.

Greenberg, J.H. "African Linguistic classification" in *General History of Africa Volume I: Methodology and African Prehistory*. California: UNESCO, pp. 292–308, 1981.

———. *The Languages of Africa*. The Hague: Mouton & Co, 1963.

Greene-McCreight, K. "When I Say God, I mean Father, Son and Holy Spirit: On Ecumenical Baptism Formula" in *Pro-Ecclesia* vol. VI, no. 3., pp, 1997.

Gunton, C. *The Promise of Trinitarian Theology*. Edinburgh: T & T Clark, 1991.

Gunton, C.E. *The One, the Three and the Many: God, Creation and the Culture of Modernity*. Cambridge: Cambridge University Press, 1995.

Hall, C. "Adding up Trinity" in *Christianity Today* April 28, pp. 26–28, 1997.

Harnack, A. *History of Dogma vol.* vi. ed. A.B. Bruce. London: William and Norgate's Publications, 1910.

Hastings, A. *Church and Mission in Modern Africa*. London, 1967.

Hayward, R. *Divine Name and Presence: The Memra*. Totowa: Oxford Center for Postgraduate Hebrew Studies, 1981.

Heick, O.W. *A History of Christian Thought*. Philadelphia : Fortress Press, 1966.

Hegel, G.W.F. *Phenomenology of the Spirit*. trans. A.V. Miller. Oxford: Clarendon Press, 1977.

Henle, R.J. *St. Thomas and Platonism*. The Hague: Martinus Nijhoff, 1956.

Henry, C.F.H. *God, Revelation and Authority vol. v: God who Stands and Stays Part One*. Waco: World Book Publishing House, 1982.

Hilary, Bishop of Poictiers. *De Trinitate*. In *Nicene and and post-Nicene Fathers of the Christian Church*. Vol. IX. ed. P. Schaff. Grand Rapids: Wm. B. Eerdmans.

Hinga, T.M. "An African Confession of Christ: The Christology of Legio Maria Church in Kenya" in *Exploring Afro-Christology*. ed. J.S. Pobee. Paris: Peter Lang, pp. 137–144, 1992.

———. "Inculturation and the Otherness of the Africans: Some Reflections" in *Inculturation: Otherness of Africa and Africans*. eds. P. Turkson and F. Wijsen. Kampen, KOK: pp. 10–18, 1994.

Hippolytus. *Refutation of all Heresies*. In *Ante-Nicene Fathers: Translations of theWritings of the Fathers Down to Ad 325* Vol. V. eds. A. Roberts and J. Donaldson. Grand Rapids: Wm. B. Eerdmans, 1951.

Hoernle, R.F.A. *Idealism as a Philosophica Doctrine*. London: Hodder and Stoughton Ltd, 1924.

Holter, K. "Popular and Academic contexts for Biblical Interpretation in Africa". Paper delivered at University of Stellenbosch, Department of Old and New Testaments' International Workshop, 14–15 May 1999.

Houtondji, P. "Reason and Tradition" in *Philosophy and Culture*. Eds. Oruka and Masolo. Nairobi: Bookwise, 1983.

Hume, D. *Enquiry Concerning Human Understanding*. Indianapolis: Bobs–Merril, 1955.

Idowu, B. *Olodumare: God in Yoruba Belief*. London: Longman, 1962.

———. *Towards an Indigenous Church*. London: Oxford University Press, 1965.

———. "God" in *Biblical Revelation and African Beliefs*. Eds. Dickson and Ellingworth. London: Lutterworth Press, 1969.

———. "Introduction" in *Biblical Revelation and African Beliefs*. eds. Dickson and Ellingworth. London: Lutterworth Press, 1969.

———. *African Traditional Religion—A Definition*. London: SCM Press, 1973.

Ignatius, Bishop of Antioch. *Epistle to the Magnesians*. In *Ante-Nicene Fathers: Translations of the Writings of the Fathers Down to Ad 325* Vol. I. eds. A. Roberts and J. Donaldson. Grand Rapids: Wm. B. Eerdmans, 1951.

Imbo, S.O. *An Introduction to African Philosophy*. New York: Rowman and Littlefield Publishers, 1998.

Inwood, M. "Hegel." *The Blackwell Companion to Philosophy*. eds. Bunnin and Tsui-James. Oxford: Blackwell Publishers, 1996.

Irenaeus, Bishop of Lyons. *Against Heresies*. In *Ante-Nicene Fathers: Translations of the Writings of the Fathers Down to Ad 325* Vol. I. eds. A. Roberts and J. Donaldson. Grand Rapids: Wm. B. Eerdmans, 1951.

Jacobs, J. and Zeis, J. "Form and Cognition: How to go out of Your Mind". *The Monist*, vol. 80, no. 4, pp. 539–557, 1997.

Jahn, J. *Muntu: An Outline of the New African Culture*. New York: Grove Press, 1961.

Jewett, P.K. *God, Creation, and Revelation: A Neo-Evangelical Theology*. Grand Rapids: Eerdmans, 1991.

John of Damascus. *De Fide Orthodoxa*. trans. S.D.F. Salmond. In the *Nicene and Post Nicene Fathers*. eds. P. Schaff and H. Wace. Grand Rapids: Wm. B. Eerdmans, 1955.

Johnson, A.R. *The One and the Many in the Israelite Conception of God*. Cardiff: University of Wales Press, 1961.

Johnson, E.A. *She Who is: The Mystery of God in Feminist Theological Discourse*. New York: Crossroad, 1993.

Jüngel, E. *God as the Mystery of the Universe*. trans. D.L. Guder. Grand Rapids: Eerdmans, 1983.

Kadushin, M. *Rabbinic Mind*. New York, 1972.

Kain, P.J. "Self-consciouness, the other and Hegel's dialectic of Recognition". *Philosophy and Social Criticism*, vol. 24 no. 5, pp. 105–126, 1998.

Kaiser, C.B. *The Doctrine of God*. London: Marshall Morgan and Scott, 1982.

Kelly, J.N.D. *Early Christian Doctrine*. London: Black, 1977.

Kerferd, G.B. "Aristotle". *The Encyclopedia of Philosophy*. ed. Edwards. London: Collier Macmillan Limited, 1967.

Kibicho, G.S. "The Continuity of the African Conception of God into and through Christianity: a Kikuyu case study" in *Christianity in Independent Africa*. eds. Fashole-Luke et al. Bloomington: Indiana University Press, pp. 370–388, 1978.

Kimmel, Jr. A.F. ed. *Speaking the Christian God: The Holy Trinity and the Challenge of Feminism*. Grand Rapids: Eerdmans, 1992.

Kinoti, G. *Hope for Africa*. Nairobi: AISRED, 1994.

Kinney, J.W. "The Theology of John Mbiti: His Sources, Norms and Method" in *Occassional Bulletin of Missionary Research*, April, pp. 65–67, 1979.

Kirwen, M.C. *The Missionary and the Diviner: Contending Theologies of Christian and African Religions*. Maryknoll: Orbis Books, 1987.

Ki-Zerbo, J. *General History of Africa Volume I: Methodolagy and African Prehistory*. California: UNESCO, 1981.

Klein, M.L. *Anthropomorphisms and Anthropopathisms in the Targumim of the Pentatauch with parallel citations from the Septuagint*. Jerusalem: Makor, 1982.

Korpel, M.C.A. *A Rift in the Clouds: Ugaritic and Hebrew Descriptions of the Divine*. Munster: Ugarit–Verlag, 1990.

Kraft, C.H. *Christianity in Culture*. Maryknoll: Orbis Books, 1979.

Kripke, S.A. *Naming and Necessity*. Oxford: Basil Blackwell, 1980.

Lamont, J. "Aquinas on Divine Simplicity". *The Monist*, vol. 80 no. 4, pp. 521–538, 1997.

Lang, A. *The Making of Religion*. London: Longmans, Green & Co., 1909.

Lash, N. *The Beginning and the End of Religion*. Cambridge: Cambridge University Press, 1996.

Lasker, D.J. *Jewish Philosophical Polemics Against Christianity in the Middle Ages*. New York, 1977.

Lewis, C.S. *The Problem of Pain* (font pocket edition). London: Centenary Press, 1940.

Lewry, O. "Boethian Logic in the Medieval West" in *Boethius: His Life, Thought and Influence*. Oxford: Basil Blackwell, 1981.

Lienhardt, G. *Divinity and Experience. The Religion of the Dinka*. Oxford: Clarendon Press, 1961.

Lohse, B. *A Short History of Christian Doctrine*. Philadelphia: Fortress Press, 1966.

Lonergan, B.J.F. *The Way to Nicea. Dialectical Development of Trinitarian Theology*. Philadelphia: Westminister, 1976.

Lonergan, B. *The Way to Nicea*. trans. by O'Donovan. Philadelphia: Westminster Press, 1964.

Lossky, V. *The Mystical Theology of the Eastern Church*. London, 1957.

Lowe, E.J. "Substance" in *An Encyclopedia of Philosophy*. ed. G.H.R. Parkinson. London: Routledge, pp. 255–278, 1998.

Magesa, L. *African Religion: The Moral Traditions of Abundant Life*. Maryknoll: Orbis Books, 1997.

Maluleke, T.S. "Half Century of African Christian Theology" in *Journal of Theology for Southern Africa*, 99, 4–23, 1997.

Mansfield, R.S. and Busse, T.V. *The Psychology of Creativity and Discovery*. Chicago: Nelson–Hall, 1981.

Marlan, P. "Plotinus" in *Encyclopedia of Philosophy*, vol. vi. ed. P. Edwards. London: Colier Macmillan Ltd, 1967.

Marmorstein, A. *The Old Rabbinic Doctrine of God, II, Essays in Anthropomorphism*. London, 1937.

Marsh, T. 1994. *The Triune God: A Biblical, Historical, and Theological Study*. Connecticut: Twenty-Third Publications.

Martin, M.C. "The Mai Chaza in Rhodesia" in *African Initiative in Religion*. Ed. D. Barrett. Nairobi: East African Literature Bureau, pp. 109–121, 1971.

Masolo, D.A. *African Philosophy in search of Identity*. Bloomington: Indiana University Press, 1994.

Matthews, K.A. *The New American Commentary: An Exegetical and Theological Exposition of Holy Scripture, Genesis 1–11:26, Volume 1A*. Brodman and Holman Publishers, 1996.

Matyr, J. *The First Apology* and *The Second Apology*. In *Ante-Nicene Fathers: Translations of the Writings of the Fathers Down to Ad 325* Vol. I. eds. A. Roberts and J. Donaldson. Grand Rapids: Wm. B. Eerdmans, 1951.

———. *Dialogue With Trypho, A Jew*. In *Ante-Nicene Fathers: Translations of the Writings of the Fathers Down to Ad 325* Vol. I. eds. A. Roberts and J. Donaldson. Grand Rapids: Wm. B. Eerdmans, 1951.

Maurier, H. "Do we have an African Philosophy?" in *African Philosophy: Introduction*. ed. R.A. Wright. Washington, DC: University Press of America, 1979.

Mbeki, T. "Africa's Renaissance Desperately needs your Help" in *Cape Times*, August 17, 1998.

Mbiti, J.S. *African Religions and Philosophy*. London: Heinemann, 1969.

———. *Concepts of God in Africa*. London: SPCK, 1970.

———. "Some African Concepts of Christology" in *Christ and the Younger Churches*. ed. G.F. Vicedom. London: SPCK, 1972.

———. *Introduction to African Religion*. London: Heinemann, 1975.

———. *The Prayers of African Religion*. London: SPCK, 1975.

———. "Christianity and African Culture" in *Facing the New Challenges—The Message of PACLA, 9–19 Dec 1976*. eds. M. Cassidy and L. Verlinden. Kisumu: Evangel Publishing House, 1978.

———. "On the Article of J.W. Kinney: A Comment" in *Occasional Bulletin of Missionary Research*, April, pp. 68, 1979.

———. *Bible and Theology in African Christianity*. Nairobi: Oxford University Press, 1986.

———. "Jesus in African Religion?" in *Exploring Afro-Christology*. ed. J.S. Pobee. Paris: Peter Lang, pp. 21–29, 1992.

———. "The Holy Spirit in African Independent Churches" in *Festschrift Guenter Wagner*. Faculty of Baptist Theological Seminary, Switzerland, pp. 101–111, 1994.

———. "Is the Bible in African Religion and African Religion in the Bible?" Paper Delivered at EFSA and University of Stellenbosch, department of Old and New Testaments International Workshop, 14–15 May, 1999

McFague, S. *Metaphorical Theology*. London: SCM Press, 1983.

———. *Models of God: Theology for an Ecological Nuclear Age*. London: SCM Press, 1987.

McKim, D.K. *Theological Turning Points: Major Issues in Christian Thought*. Atlanta: Knox, 1988.

McWilliams, W. "Trinitarian Doxology: Jurgen Moltmann on the Relation of Economic and Immanent Trinity" in *Perspectives in Religious Studies*, 1996.

Megilla Babylonian Talmud. Jerusalem: Makor, nd.

Migliore, D.L. *Faith Seeking Understanding*. Grand Rapids: William B. Eerdmans Publishing Company, 1991.

Moffat, R. *Missionary Labours and Scenes in South Africa*. J. Snow, 1842.

Moltmann, J. *The Crucified God*. trans. R.A. Wilson and J. Bowden. New York: Harper & Row, 1974.

———. *The Trinity and the Kingdom*. trans. M. Kohl. London: SCM Press, 1981.

———. *History and the Triune God*. trans. J. Bowden. Munich: SCM Press, 1991.

———. *The Spirit of Life: A Universal Affirmation*. Minneapolis: Fortress Press, 1993.

Moody, D. *The Word of Truth*. Grand Rapids: Eerdmans, 1981.

Morris, L. *The Gospel According to John*. Grand Rapids: Wm. B. Eerdmans Publishing Co., 1971.

Mudimbe, V.Y. *The Idea of Africa*. Bloomington and Indianapolis: Indiana University Press, 1994.

Muga, E. *African Response to Western Christian Religion*. Kampala: East African Literature Bureau, 1975.

Mugambi, J.N.K. *The African Heritage and Contemporary Christianity*. Nairobi: Longman, 1989.

Nasr, S.H. "Islamic Conception of Intellectual Life" in *Dictionary of History of Ideas II (638–652)*. ed. P.P. Wierner. New York: Charles Scribner's Sons, 1973.

Ndiokwere, N.I. *Prophecy and Revolution: The Role of Prophets in the Independent African Churches*. London: SPCK, 1981.

Needham, N. "The Filoque Clause: East or West" in *The Scottish Bulletin of Evangelical Theology*, pp. 142–162, 1997.

Newbegin, L. "The Trinity as a Public Truth" in the *Trinity in a Pluralistic Age: Theological Essays on Culture and Religion*. Ed Vanhoozer. Grand Rapids: William B. Eerdmans Publishing Co, pp. 1–8, 1997.

Newman, N.A. ed. *The Early Christian Muslim Dialogue: A Collection of Documents from the First three Islamic Centuries (632–900)*. Hatfield, 1993.

Nthamburi, Z. "Christ as seen by an African: A Christological Quest" in *Jesus in African Christianity*. ed. J.N.K. Mugambi and L. Magesa, pp. 54–59, 1989.

Nthamburi, Z. and Waruta, D. "Biblical Hermeneutics in African Instituted Churches" in *The Bible in African Christianity: Essays in Biblical Theology*. eds. H.W. Kinoti and J.M. Waliggo. Nairobi: Acton Publishers, pp. 40–57, 1997.

Nürnberger, K. "The Hidden God in Africa—Fate and Affliction." *Missionalia*. Vol. 1 No. 1 April, pp. 21–31, 1973.

Nyamiti, C. *Christ as our Ancestor: Christology from an African Perspective*. Gweru: Mambo Press, 1984.

———. "African Christologies Today" *Jesus in African Christianity*. eds. J.N.K. Mugambi and L. Magesa. Nairobi, Kenya: Initiatives Ltd., pp. 17–39, 1989.

Nyirongo, L. *Gods of Africa or the God of the Bible: The Snares of the African Traditional religion in Biblical Perspective*. Potchefstroomse Univeriteit vir Christelike Hoër Onderwys, 1997.

Obaje, Y.A. "Theocentric Christology" in *Exploring Afro-Christology*. ed. J.S. Pobee. Paris: Peter Lang, 43–53, 1992.

O'Daly, G. *The Poetry of Boethius*. London: Duckworth, 1991.

O'Donnell, J. "The Trinity as Divine Community: A Critical Reflection upon recent Theological Developments" in *Gregorinum* 69 no. 1, pp. 5–34, 1988.

Ogbonnaya, A.O. *On Communitarian Divinity*. New York: Paragon House, 1994.

Okullu, H. *Church and Politics in East Africa*. Nairobi: Uzima Press, 1974.

Olderogge, D. "Migration and Ethnic and Linguistic Differentiations" in *General History of Africa Volume I: Methodology and African Prehistory*. ed. J. Ki-Zerbo. California: UNESCO, pp. 271–286, 1981.

Oliver, R. *The Missionary Factor in East Africa*. London, 1952.

Oosthuizen, G.C. *Post Christianity in Africa*. London: C. Hurst, 1968.

Origen. *On the Gospel of John*. In *Ante-Nicene Fathers: Translations of the Writings of the Fathers Down to Ad 325* Vol. X. eds. A. Roberts and J. Donaldson. Grand Rapids: Wm. B. Eerdmans, 1951.

———. *De Prinicipiis*. In *Ante-Nicene Fathers: Translations of the Writings of the Fathers Down to Ad 325* Vol. IV. eds. A. Roberts and J. Donaldson. Grand Rapids: Wm. B. Eerdmans, 1951.

———. *Philokalia—Origen's Letter to Gregory Thaumaturgus*. In *Ante-Nicene Fathers: Translations of the Writings of the Fathers Down to Ad 325* Vol. IV. eds. A. Roberts and J. Donaldson. Grand Rapids: Wm. B. Eerdmans, 1951.

Oruka, H.O. "Traditionalism and Modernisation in Kenya—Customs, Spirits and Christianity". In *The SM Otieno Case: Death and Burial in Modern Kenya*. eds. J.B. Ojwang and J.N.K. Mugambi, 1989.

———. *Sage Philosophy: Indigenous Thinkers and Modern Debate on African Philosophy*. Leiden: E.J. Brill, 1990.

———. "Sagacity in African Philosophy" in *African Philosophy*. Ed Serequeberhan. New York: Paragon House, 1991.

Otto, R. *The Idea of the Holy*. Trans. J.W. Harvey. London: Penguin Books, 1923.

Page, J. *The Black Bishop*. London: Simpkin, 1910.

Pannenberg, W. *Systematische Theologie*. Vol. I Gottingen: Vandenhoeck and Ruprecht, 1998.

Parrinder, E.G. *Africa's Three Religions*. London: Sheldon Press, 1969.

Patch, H.R. *The Tradition of Boethius: A Study of His Importance in Medieval Culture*. New York: Oxford University Press, 1935.

Pelikan, J. *The Christian Tradition*. vol. I. Chicago: The University of Chicago Press, 1971.

Peters, T. *God as Trinity: Revelation and Temporality in Divine Life*. Louiseville: Westminister, 1993.

Placher, W.C. *Domestication of the Transcendence: How Modern Thinking about God Went Wrong*. Louiseville: Westminister John Knox Press, 1996.

Plato, *The Republic*, VI. Translated by Benjamin Jowett, 360 B.C.E., 506e.

Plato, *Timaeus*. Translated by Benjamin Jowett, 360 B.C.E, 41a.

Plotinus. *Enneads*. trans. by A.H. Armstrong. London: Heinaman, 1966–1968.

Pobee, J.S. *Toward African Theology*. Nashville: Abington, 1979.

——. *Exploring Afro-Christology* (Ed). Paris: Peter Lang, 1992.

Portalie, E. *Guide to the Thought of St Augustine*. Norwood, 1975.

Prestige, G.L. *God in Patristic Thought*. London: SPCK, 1952.

Rahner, K. *Theological Investigations* I. trans. C. Ernest. London: Darton, Longman and Todd, 1965.

——. *Theological Investigations IV*. trans. K. Smyth. London, Darton, Longman and Todd, 1966.

——. *The Trinity*. London: Herder, 1970.

——. *The Trinity*. trans. J. Doceel. New York: Seaburg, 1974.

——. *Foundations of Christian Faith: An Introduction to the Idea of Christianity*. trans. W.V. Dych. New York: Seaburg, 1978.

Rechenbach, C.W. *Swahili-English Dictionary*. Washington DC: The Catholic University of America Press, 1967.

Richardson, A. *Theological Wordbook of the Bible*. New York: McMillan, 1957.

Ritschl, D. *The Logic of Theology*. London: SCM Press, 1986.

Rose, M. "Yahweh in Israel—Quas in Edom?" in *Journal for the Study of Old Testament* 4, pp. 28–34, 1977.

Rossman, J. *The Psychology of the Inventor: A Study of the Patentee*. Washington DC: Inventors Publishing Company, 1931.

Rotenstreich, N. *From Substance to Subject: Studies in Hegel*. The Hague: Martinus Nijhoff, 1974.

Ryle, G. "Plato". *The Encyclopedia of Philosophies*. Edited by Edwards, P. London: Macmillan Company, 1967.

Sanneh, L. *West African Christianity: The Religious Impact*. London: C. Hurst, 1983.

——. *Translating the Message: Missionary Impact on Culture*. Maryknoll: Orbis Books, 1989.

Schaff, P. *A Select Library of the Nicene Fathers of the Christian Church* vol. iii. Grand Rapids: Wm. B. Eerdmans Publishing Company, 1956.

Schleiermacher, F. *The Christian Faith*. Edinburgh: T & T Clark, 1928.

Schreiter, R.J. *Constructing Local Theologies*. Maryknoll: Orbis Books, 1985.

——. *Faces of Jesus in Africa*. Maryknoll, New York: Orbis Books, 1991.

Schrenk, G. *Theological Dictionary of the New Testament* (TWNT), Vol. V. Edited by G. Kittel and translated by G.W. Bromiley, Grand Rapids: Eerdmans Publishing Company, 1935.

Scott, D.C. *Dictionary of the Nyanja Language*. ed. Heatherwick. London: Religious Tract Society, 1929.

Setiloane, G.M. "MODIMO: GOD Among the Sotho-Tswana" in *Journal of Theology for Southern Africa*, Sep 1973 No. 4, pp. 6–17, 1973.

——. *The Image of God among the Sotho-Tswana*. Rotterdam: A.A. Balkema, 1976.

——. "How the Traditional world-view persists in the Christianity of the Sotho-Tswana" in *Christianity in Independent Africa*. eds. E. Fashole-Luke et al. Bloomington: Indiana University Press, pp. 402–412, 1978.

——. "Where are we in African Theology?" in *African Theology en Route*. Ed. K. Appiah-Kubi and S. Torres. Maryknoll: Orbis Books, 1979.

——. *African Theology: An Introduction*. Johannesburg: Skotaville Publishers, 1986.

Sharon, D.W. *Communities of Resistance and Solidarity: A Feminist Theology of Liberation*. Maryknoll: Orbis Books, 1985.

Skarsaune, O. "Is Christianity Monotheistic? A Perspective on a Jewish/ Christian Debate" in *Studia Patristica* vol. 29, 340–363, 1957.

Smidt, W. *The Origin and Growth of Religion: Facts and Theories*. trans. H.J. Rose. London: Mathuen & Co Ltd, 1931.

Smith, E.W. (ed) *The Christian Mission in Africa*. London: Edinburgh Press, 1926.

——. *African Ideas of God*. London: Edinburg House Press, 1950.

Smith, W.C. *The Meaning and End of Religion*. London: SPCK, 1962.

Smith, W.R. *Lectures on the Religion of the Semites*. London: A & C Black Ltd., 1923.

Southern, R.W. *St Anselm: A Portrait in a Landscape*. Cambridge, 1990.

Steyne, P.M. *Gods of Power: A Study of Beliefs and Practices of Animists*. Houston: Touch Publications, 1989.

Sundkler, B.G.M. *Bantu Prophets in South Africa*. Oxford: Oxford University Press, 1961.

Sykes, S. *The Identity of Christianity*. London, 1984.

Taylor, J.V. *The Go-Between God: The Holy Spirit and the Christian Mission*. London: SCM Press, 1972.

Tempel, W. *Reading in St John's Gospel*. London: McMillan, 1939.

Tempels, P. *Bantu Philosophy*. ET, Paris, 1959.

Tertullian. *Adversus Iudaeus (an Answer to the Jews* trans. S. Thelwal) in *Ante-Nicene Fathers: Translations of the Writings of the Fathers Down to AD 325*. Vol. III. eds. A. Roberts and J. Donaldson. Grand Rapids: Wm B. Eerdmans, 1951.

——. *Against Praxeas* and *De Carne Christi* Trans. D. Holmes in *Ante-Nicene Fathers: Translations of the Writings of the Fathers Down to Ad 325*. Vol. III. eds. A. Roberts and J. Donaldson. Grand Rapids: Wm. B. Eerdmans, 1951.

Teugels, L. "The Backgroung of the Anti-Christian Polemics in Aggadat Bereshit" in *Journal of the Study of Judaism*, XXX, 2, pp. 178–208, 1999.

Thompson, J. *Modern Trinitarian Perspectives*. Oxford: Oxford University Press, 1994.

Tienou, T. *The Theological Task of the Church in Africa*. Achimota: Africa Christian Press, 1982.

——. "The Right to Difference: The Common Roots of African Theology and African Philosophy" in *Africa Journal of Evangelical Theology* 9.1, pp. 24–34, 1990.

——. "Which way for African Christianity: Westernisation or Indigenous Authenticity?" in *Africa Journal of Evangelical Theology* 10.2, pp. 3–12, 1991.

Tillich, P. *Systematic Theology*. Vol. I. Chicago, 1951.

Torrance, T.F. "The Christian Apprehension of God the Father" in *Speaking the Christian God*. ed. A.F. Kimel. Grand Rapids: Wm. B. Eerdmans, pp. 120–143, 1992.

——. *The Trinitarian Faith*. Edinburgh: Clark, 1988.

——. *The Trinitarian Perspectives: Toward a Doctrine Agreement.* Edinburgh: Clark, 1994.

Tracey, D. *The Anological Imagination: Christian Theology and the Culture of Pluralism.* New York: Crossroad, 1981.

Turaki, Y. *Christianity and African Gods: A Method in Theology.* Potchefstroomse Universiteit vir Christike Hoër Onderwys, 1999.

Turnbull, G.H. *The Essence of Plotinus.* New York: Oxford University Press, 1934.

Tutu, D. "Some African insights and the Old Testament" in *Journal of Theology for Southern Africa*, no. 1 Dec. 1972, pp. 16–22, 1972.

——. "Whither African Theology?" in *Christianity in Independent Africa.* ed. E. Fashole-Luke et al. Bloomington: Indiana University Press, pp. 364–369, 1978.

Ukpong, J.S. *African Theologies Now: A Profile.* Eldoret: Gaba Publications, 1984.

UNESCO. *UNESCO and its Programe III, The Race Question.* UNESCO Publication, 791, p. 9.

Urbach, E.E. *The Sages: Their Concepts and Beliefs I–II.* Jerusalem, 1975.

Van Rooy, J.A. *The Traditional World View of the Black People in Southern Africa.* Potchefstroom: PU vir CHO, 1978.

Van Ruler, A.A. *The Christian Church and the Old Testament.* ET Grand Rapids: Eerdmans, 1971.

Vriezen, T.C. "The Edomite Deity Quas" in OTS 14, 1965.

Wainwright, A.W. *The Trinity in the New Testament.* London: SPCK, 1962.

Walker, T. "Targum" in *A Dictionary of the Bible*, vol. iv. Ed. J. Hastings. Edinburgh, 1903.

Wallas, G. *The Art of Thought.* New York: Harcourt Brace, 1926.

Walls, A.F. "Towards understanding Africa's Place in Christian History" in *Religion in a Pluralistic Society: Essays Presented to Professor CG Baëta.* Leiden: E.J. Brill, pp. 180–189, 1976.

——. "Black Europeans, White Africans: Some Missionary Motives in West Africa" in *Religious Motivation: Biographical and Sociological Problems of the Church Historian.* ed. D. Baker. Cambridge: Cambridge University Press, pp. 339–348, 1978.

——. "The Anabaptists of Africa? The Challenge of the African Independent Churches" in *Occasional Bulletin of Missionary Research*, April, pp. 48–51, 1979.

——. "Old Athens and New Jerusalem: Some Signposts for Christian Scholarship in the Early History of Mission Studies" in *International Bulletin of Missionary Research*, October, 1997, pp. 146–153.

Webb, C.J. *God and Personality.* London: Allen & Unwin, 1920.

Williams, S. 'The Trinity and Other Religions' in the *Trinity in a Pluralistic Age: Theological Essays on Culture and Religion.* ed. K.J. Vanhoozer. Grand Rapids: William B. Eerdmans Publishing Co, 26–40, 1997.

Willoughby, W.C. *The Soul of the Bantu.* London: SCM, 1928.

Wiredu, K. *Philophy and an African Culture.* Cambridge: Cambridge University Press, 1980.

Wittgeinstein, L. *Culture and Value.* trans. P. Winch. Oxford: Basil Blackwell, 1980.

Wolfson, H.A. "The Muslim Attributes and the Christian Trinity" *HTR* 49, pp. 1–18, 1956.
———. *The Philosophy of the Church Fathers: Faith, Trinity, Incarnation.* London, 1970.
———. *The Philosophy of the Kalam.* London, 1976.
Yandell, K.E. "The Most Brutal and Inexcusable Error in Counting: Trinity and Consistency" in *Religious Studies*, 30, pp. 201–217, 1994.
Zinkuratire, V. "Method and Relevance in African Biblical Interpretation". Paper Delivered at the University of Stellenbosch, Department of Old and New Testaments' International Workshop, 14–15 May 1999.
Zizioulas, J.D. *Being as Communion: Studies in Personhood and the Church.* Crestwood: St Vladimir's Seminary Press, 1985.
———. "The Doctrine of the Holy Trinity: The Significance of the Cappadocian Contribution" in *Trinitarian Theology Today*. ed. C. Schwobel. Edinburgh: T & T Clark, pp. 44–60, 1995.

INDEX OF NAMES

INDEX OF SUBJECTS